Revise
AS & A2

English
Literature

Pa ... roft

Contents

Specification lists

AQA Specification A AS

Unit	Specification topic	Chapter reference
Unit 1 (LTA1)	Texts in Context	6, 8, 9, 11
	Contextual Linking	1, 2, 5
	Poetry	1, 2, 3, 8
Unit 2 (LITA2)	Creative Study	6, 9, 10

Examination analysis

Unit 1: Texts in Context

60% of AS, 30% of A-Level

Written examination. 2 hours (open book).

Section A: Contextual Linking

One compulsory question based on short unseen extract. Candidates link all of their reading in the chosen area of Literature (Victorian Literature, World War One Literature, The Struggle for Identity in Modern Literature) to a given passage.

Section B: Poetry

Choice of two questions on poetry text chosen for study. One question foregrounds one particular poem and its relation to the whole text, the other provides a view about the poems for the candidate to discuss. Candidates answer one question.

Unit 2: Creative Study

40% of AS, 20% of A-Level

Coursework assessed.

Candidates study one prose text and one drama text.

Two pieces of writing are required: one on the prose text, and the other on the drama text and then comparing it with the prose text.

The two pieces of work should total 2000–2500 words.

AQA Specification A A2

Module	Specification topic	Chapter reference
Unit 3 (LITA3)	Reading for Meaning	6, 7, 8, 9, 11
Unit 4 (LITA4)	Extended Essay and Shakespeare Study	6, 7, 8, 9

Examination analysis

Unit 3: Reading for Meaning

30% of A-Level

Written examination. 2 hours 30 minutes (closed book).

Two questions involving unprepared extracts and wider reading on the unit theme of Love Through the Ages. There will be two compulsory questions.

Question 1 requires candidates to compare two extracts of the same genre.

Question 2 asks candidates to compare two extracts (of the remaining two genres) on the theme through literature.

Unit 4: Extended Essay and Shakespeare Study

20% of A-Level

Coursework assessed.

Candidates study three texts. One must be a Shakespeare play. The other two comparison texts can be of any genre. One extended comparative essay is produced on a shared theme.

The essay should be about 3000 words in length.

AQA Specification B AS

Unit	Specification topic	Chapter reference
Unit 1 (LITB1)	Aspects of Narrative	8, 9
	Prose Texts	9
	Comparing Aspects of Narrative	3, 8, 9
Unit 2 (LITA2)	Dramatic Genres	6, 7

Examination analysis

Unit 1: Aspects of Narrative

60% of AS, 30% of A-Level

Written examination. 2 hours (open book).

Candidates study four texts (two prose texts and two poetry texts). The exam paper has two sections.

Section A: One question on each of the set prose texts. Candidates answer one question.

Section B: Candidates answer one question that involves comparing aspects of narrative across three texts that they have studied.

Unit 2: Dramatic Genres

40% of AS, 20% of A-Level

Coursework assessed.

Candidates study a minimum of two texts within the dramatic genre of Tragedy.

Two pieces of writing are required, one on a Shakespeare play (1200–1500 words) and the other on an aspect of drama with regard to at least one other play (1200–1500 words).

AQA Specification B A2

Unit	Specification topic	Chapter reference
Unit 3 (LITB3)	Texts and Genres	6, 7, 8, 9
Unit 4 (LITB4)	Further and Independent Reading	6, 7, 8, 9

Examination analysis

Unit 3: Texts and Genres

30% of A-Level

Written examination. 2 hours (closed book).

A minimum of three texts are studied, including at least one text written between 1300 and 1800.

Candidates choose one topic area for study: Elements of the Gothic or Elements of the Pastoral. Candidates answer two questions, one from Section A and one from Section B.

Unit 4: Further and Independent Reading

20% of A-Level

Coursework assessed.

A minimum of three texts are studied, including a pre-release anthology of critical material. Two pieces of work are produced: a comparative study of an aspect of two texts (1500–2000 words), and an application of an aspect of the pre-release material to a literary text (1500–2000 words).

Edexcel Specification AS

Unit	Specification topic	Chapter reference
Unit 1 (6ET01)	Explorations in Prose and Poetry	8, 9, 11
	Unseen Poetry/Prose	8, 9, 11
	Poetry	8
	Prose	9
Unit 2 (6ET02)	Explorations in Drama	6, 7, 10

Examination analysis

Unit 1: Explorations in Prose and Poetry

60% of AS, 30% of A-Level

Written examination. 2 hours 15 minutes (open book).

Candidates study one selection of poems, one core literary heritage novel and one further novel or novella from the same grouping to inform their reading and response. The exam paper has three sections.

Section A: Unseen Poetry or Unseen Prose.

Section B: Poetry. Candidates answer one question on the chosen topic area.

Section C: Prose. Candidates answer one question focusing on the core text and refer to another novel to develop their line of argument.

Unit 2: Explorations in Drama

40% of AS, 20% of A-Level

Coursework assessed.

Candidates study one play by Shakespeare, and a further play written between 1300 and 1800 – this can be another play by Shakespeare or a play by a different playwright.

Two pieces of writing are required: an explorative study and a creative critical response.

The total length for the coursework folder is 2000–2500 words maximum.

Edexcel Specification A2

Unit	Specification topic	Chapter reference
Unit 3 (6ET03)	Interpretations of Prose and Poetry	8, 9, 11
Unit 4 (6ET03)	Reflections in Literary Studies	6, 7, 8, 9, 10

Examination analysis

Unit 3: Interpretations of Prose and Poetry

60% of A2, 30% of A-Level

Written examination. 2 hours 45 minutes (open book).

A minimum of three texts are studied from a choice of six, including at least one text published after 1990, and both prose and poetry.

Section A: Unprepared Prose or Poetry.

Section B: An analytical essay referring to at least two of the texts studied.

Unit 4: Reflections in Literary Studies

40% of A2, 20% of A-Level

Coursework assessed.

Prose, poetry or drama for independent study. Free choice of texts. One text should be studied in detail and the other texts drawn on to develop knowledge or explore relevant critical reception.

The coursework will consist of either:

One extended study referring to all texts studied

OR

Two shorter studies (each must refer to more than one text)

OR

One creative response with a commentary.

Total word length: 2500–3000 words maximum.

OCR Specification AS

Unit	Specification topic	Chapter reference
Unit 1 (F661)	Poetry 1800–1945	8
	Prose 1800–1945	9
Unit 2 (F662)	Literature post-1900	6, 7, 8, 9, 10, 11

Examination analysis

Unit 1: Poetry and Prose 1800–1945

60% of AS, 30% of A-Level

Written examination. 2 hours (closed book).

Candidates study three texts (one prose text and two poetry texts). The exam paper has two sections.

Section A: Poetry 1800–1945

The focus is the study of selected poems of one poet from the period 1800–1945 chosen from the list of set poets. Candidates answer one question on one poem of the poet studied.

Section B: Prose 1800–1945

The focus is the study of a prose text from the period 1800–1945 chosen from the list of set texts. Candidates answer one question on the text they have studied.

Unit 2: Literature post-1900

40% of AS, 20% of A-Level

Coursework assessed.

Candidates are required to cover three post-1900 texts of their choice. At least one text must be work first published or performed after 1990.

A coursework folder of a maximum of 3000 words with two tasks must be produced.

Task 1: Candidates can select to do either a close, critical analysis of their chosen text or poem, or a re-creative piece with commentary.

Task 2: An essay exploring contrasts and comparisons between two texts.

OCR Specification A2

Unit	Specification topic	Chapter reference
Unit 3 (F663)	Shakespeare	7
	Drama and Poetry	6, 7, 8
Unit 4 (F664)	Texts in Time	6, 7, 8, 9, 10

Examination analysis

Unit 3: Drama and Poetry pre-1800

30% of A-Level

Written examination. 2 hours (closed book).

Section A: Shakespeare

The focus is the study of a Shakespeare play selected from the set text list. Candidates answer one play on the text they have studied.

Section B: Drama and Poetry

This section requires candidates to explore contrasts, connections and comparisons between one drama text and one poetry text they have studied from the set text lists.

Unit 4: Texts in Time

20% of A-Level

Coursework assessed.

Three texts of the candidates' own choice are studied, including one prose and one poetry text. The third text can be from any genre. Candidates are required to produce one extended essay of a maximum of 3000 words.

WJEC Specification AS

Unit	Specification topic	Chapter reference
Unit 1 (LT1)	Poetry post-1900	8
	Drama post-1990	6
Unit 2 (LT2)	Prose Study and Creative Reading	9, 10

WJEC Specification A2

Unit	Specification topic	Chapter reference
Unit 3 (LT3)	Period and Genre Study	6, 7, 8, 9
Unit 4 (LT4)	Critical Reading of Poetry	6, 7, 8, 11
	Shakespeare and Related Drama	6, 7, 8, 11

Examination analysis

Unit 1: Poetry and Drama

60% of AS, 30% of A-Level

Written examination. 2 hours 30 minutes (open book).

Section A: Poetry post-1900

Candidates are required to study in depth one text from the list of 'core' poetry texts, and to study for wider reading the designated 'partner' poetry text. Candidates answer one question based on this pair of texts.

Section B: Drama post-1990

Candidates are required to study in depth one post-1990 drama text from the set text list, and to answer one question on the chosen text.

Unit 2: Prose Study and Creative Reading

40% of AS, 20% of A-Level

Coursework assessed.

Candidates are required to submit a folder of three pieces of work, all of which require a response to wider reading of prose. In total the folder should be approximately 3000 words in length.

Section A: Candidates produce one piece of work of approximately 1500 words on two approved texts (one 'core' text and one 'partner' text).

Section B: Candidates produce two pieces of work of approximately 750 words each:

1. A creative response based on a particular genre.

2. A commentary on that response.

Examination analysis

Unit 3: Period and Genre Study

40% of A2, 20% of A-Level

Coursework assessed.

Candidates are required to produce a folder of work of approximately 3000 words. The literary focus can be selected by the candidate and must consist of an exploration of three texts, two of which must be from different periods and genres – one prose, the other poetry. These are the 'core' texts. The third 'partner' text may be drama, another poetry text or a prose text.

Unit 4: Poetry and Drama

60% of A2, 30% of A-Level

Written examination. 2 hours 30 minutes (closed book).

Section A: Critical Reading of Poetry

Candidates study one pre-1800 poetry text chosen from the set text list. One question is answered on this text, requiring detailed analysis of the text and close reference to any one of the five unseen poems or poetry extracts printed on the exam paper.

Section B: Shakespeare and Related Drama

Candidates study in depth one text from the list of 'core' Shakespeare texts, and for wider reading one of the designated 'partner' texts. One question is answered on the chosen pair of texts.

CCEA Specification AS

Unit	Specification topic	Chapter reference
Unit 1 (AS1)	The Study of Shakespeare	6, 7, 10
	The Study of a Twentieth Century Dramatist	6
Unit 2 (AS2)	The Study of Poetry Written after 1800 and The Study of Prose 1800–1945	6, 7, 8, 9, 10

CCEA Specification A2

Unit	Specification topic	Chapter reference
Unit A2 1 (A21)	The Study of Poetry from 1300–1800	6, 7, 8
	Drama	6, 7
Unit A2 2 (A22)	The Study of Prose – theme based	9

Examination analysis

Unit AS 1: *The Study of Drama*

40% of AS, 20% of A-Level

Coursework assessed.

Section A: *The Study of Shakespeare*

Candidates study one Shakespeare text from the set text list and produce one assignment of approximately 1500 words showing detailed analysis of the play.

Section B: *The Study of a Twentieth Century Dramatist*

Candidates study two plays by one of the dramatists on the list of dramatists set for study, and produce an assignment of approximately 1500 words comparing and contrasting the two texts by the individual dramatist selected. This assignment focuses on a creative, informed or original informed response.

Unit AS 2: *The Study of Poetry Written after 1800 and The Study of Prose 1800–1945*

60% of AS, 30% of A-Level

Written examination. 2 hours. Section A: open book. Section B: closed book.

Section A: *The Study of Poetry Written after 1800*

Candidates study one pair of texts selected from the list of paired texts. One question is answered on the chosen pairing, requiring the candidate to compare and contrast the pair of poets they have studied.

Section B: *The Study of Prose 1800–1945*

Candidates study one text selected from the set text list. One question is answered, which requires the candidate to show knowledge and understanding of the text and the context.

Examination analysis

Unit A2 1: *The Study of Poetry – 1300–1800 and Drama*

50% of A2, 25% of A-Level

Written examination. 2 hours (closed book).

Section A: *The Study of Poetry from 1300–1800*

Candidates study one text chosen from the set text list. One question is answered on the chosen text, which requires analysis of poetic methods such as form, structure, language and tone, as well as an awareness of contextual factors.

Section B: *Drama*

Candidates study one pairing of texts chosen from the list of paired texts. One question is answered, which requires the candidate to show sustained comparison/contrast of the plays taking into account dramatic methods and showing a knowledge of contextual factors.

Unit A2 2: *The Study of Prose – theme based*

50% of A2, 25% of A-Level

Written examination. 2 hours. Section A: closed book (resource booklet provided). Section B: closed book.

Section A: *Close analysis of an extract from a post-1990 novel*

Candidates study one post-1990 novel on a particular theme from the set text list and answer one question based on the close analysis of an extract from the chosen novel. They are expected to demonstrate detailed critical understanding of the narrative methods used by the writer.

Section B: *Comparison of two novels on the same theme as that chosen for Section A*

Candidates study two novels on the same theme as that chosen for Section A, chosen from the list of thematically linked texts. One question is answered, which demonstrates sustained comparison/contrast, understanding of narrative methods and an awareness of contextual factors.

Revision tips

The texts you have studied obviously play a key role in your final assessment for either the AS or A-Level course, and it is essential that you revise them very carefully in readiness for the exam. The key to successful revision is careful planning and being aware of how best to organise the time you have for revision.

Here are some things you can do:

- **Read, re-read, and re-read again.** By the time you are preparing for your exams you will, no doubt, have read your texts a number of times. This reading and re-reading of the texts is essential to the development of your understanding and appreciation of them.
- **Time management.** Time is a crucial factor in your revision programme. Building in time for sufficient practice on a variety of tasks is vital. To make sure that you do this, it is advisable to draw up a revision programme to cover the build-up to the final exams.
- **Past-paper and specimen paper questions.** As part of your revision programme, try to look at as many questions from past papers as you can. This will help you become very familiar with both the question formats and the kinds of question types that are set.
- **Timed essays.** The thing about exams is that you have to write within a fixed time limit. Practising writing answers in the amount of time you will have in the exam will help you enormously in preparing for the exam. The more you practise, the quicker you will get. Practising in this way will also show you how much information you can deal with in a specified time and how well you can plan your work under time constraints.
- **Essay planning.** Practice in essay planning should form another key part of your revision process. The best essays are those where students have thought about what they want to say before they actually start to write. In the exam itself you will have little time to spend on planning, but practice in the build-up to the exam will help you to develop the skills to plan quickly and effectively.

Throughout your revision period, bear in mind what you will be expected to show through your exam responses. A knowledge of your texts is essential. That you know the 'facts' about a text, the storyline, who the characters are, etc. will be taken as read. The emphasis will be much more on you showing judgement, analysis, sensitivity and perception in your responses, all clearly supported by illustration and examples from the texts.

AS/A2 English Literature course overview

A-Level English Literature courses are in two sections. Students first study the AS (Advanced Subsidiary) course. Some will then go on to study the second part of the A-Level course, called A2. There are two units at AS level and two at A2 level.

The AS and A2 courses are designed so that the level of difficulty increases from AS to A2:

- AS English Literature builds on GCSE English and English Literature.
- A2 English Literature builds on AS English Literature.

How will you be tested?

Assessment units

For AS English Literature, you will be tested by two assessment units. For the full A-Level in English Literature you will take a further two units. AS English Literature forms 50 percent of the assessment weighting for the full A-Level.

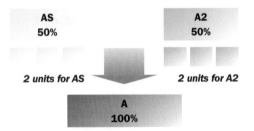

Depending on the exam board, a unit can be taken in January or June, or both. Alternatively, you may be able to study the whole course before taking any of the unit tests. There is some flexibility about when exams can be taken, and the diagram below shows some of the ways that the assessment units may be taken for AS and A-Level English Literature.

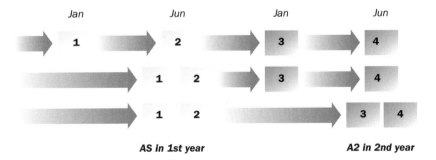

If you are disappointed with a module result, you can resit the module. The higher mark counts.

A2 and synoptic assessment

After having studied AS English Literature, you may wish to continue studying English Literature to A-Level. For this, you will need to take two further English Literature units at A2. The A2 units assess the course using a 'synoptic' approach to assessment. Synoptic assessment tests your ability to apply the knowledge, understanding and skills you have learnt throughout the course to the analysis of literary texts of various genres and periods.

Synoptic assessment takes place across the two A2 units and encourages candidates to:

● gain a detailed understanding of strategies for approaching the study of literature
● develop the ability to respond to texts critically and creatively, showing judgement and independence as readers.

Assessment objectives

Four assessment objectives are central to all of the examination boards' specifications. You will have to meet these assessment objectives in the various elements of your course.

The four assessment objectives are listed in the box below.

AO1: Articulate creative, informed and relevant responses to literary texts, using appropriate terminology and concepts, and coherent, accurate written expression.

AO2: Demonstrate detailed critical understanding in analysing the ways in which structure, form and language shape meanings in literary texts.

AO3: Explore connections and comparisons between different literary texts, informed by interpretations of other readers.

AO4: Demonstrate understanding of the significance and influence of the contexts in which literary texts are written and received.

What skills will I need?

The Advanced Subsidiary GCE and Advanced GCE in English Literature draw on the subject criteria for English Literature, which are prescribed and are compulsory. AS and A-Level English Literature should encourage you to:

- read texts in a variety of ways and respond critically and creatively
- vary strategies for reading, including for detail, overview and gist, depending on the texts being studied and purposes for reading them
- explore comparisons and contrasts between texts, establishing links and relationships
- identify and consider how attitudes and values are expressed in texts
- draw on your understanding of different interpretations in responding to and evaluating texts
- communicate fluently, accurately and effectively your knowledge, understanding and judgement of texts
- use literary critical concepts and terminology with understanding and discrimination
- make accurate reference to quotations from texts and sources
- synthesise and reflect upon your knowledge and understanding of a range of literary texts and ways of reading them
- make appropriate use of the conventions of writing in literary studies, including references to quotations and sources.

It is important that you develop your key skills throughout your AS and A2 courses. These are important skills that you need whatever you do beyond AS and A2 levels. The main key skill areas relevant to English Literature are:

- communication
- improving your own learning performance
- information and communication technology
- working with others.

Each examination board will 'signpost' where key skill developments can best take place while studying A-Level English Literature. You will have opportunities during your study of A-Level English Literature to develop your key skills.

Types of exam questions

In English Literature assessment, different types of questions and tasks are used to assess your abilities and skills. You will be assessed on a combination of exam questions and coursework tasks.

Exam questions

The kind of exam questions that you will answer in your assessment for AS and A-Level English Literature are ones that will require developed and sustained responses. Most questions will test most or all of the assessment objectives to one extent or another.

Analytical questions

Most questions on English Literature texts require some form of analysis, but some of the questions will be ones that require an analytical response to aspects of the text or texts you have studied. This will involve you examining in detail specific stylistic or dramatic techniques employed by the writer, such as the ways in which a writer presents character, or uses narrative voices, or uses imagery in the text. In this kind of question you will need to focus closely on how the writer uses language in order to create particular effects, using details from the text to support and illustrate your points and ideas.

Thematic questions

Some exam questions involve looking at two or more texts that are linked through a common theme. For example, the theme of 'Love and Relationships' might be explored through a study of *Jane Eyre* by Charlotte Brontë and *Emma* by Jane Austen. The key focus of thematic questions is the way in which particular themes are presented and developed, employing an analytical approach.

Paired text questions

Some specifications involve the study of paired texts that are linked in some way, such as through genre. For example, you might look at the ways in which dramatists present the drama of social realism by studying *A Doll's House* by Henrik Ibsen and *Look Back in Anger* by John Osborne, or at Historical Drama through a study of *Murder in the Cathedral* by T.S. Eliot and *A Man for All Seasons* by Robert Bolt.

Comparative questions

In some questions the key focus is on looking at the comparisons and contrast between two texts. Again, this kind of question needs an analytical approach, but the analysis needs to incorporate comparisons and contrast. The thing to avoid with this kind of question is writing about the texts separately – you need to adopt an integrated approach to the comparisons.

Questions on 'unseen' texts

Some examination boards set questions on texts that you have not studied in advance of the exam. This kind of question requires you to apply the skills of analysis that you have developed through your study of literature to previously unseen texts. Sometimes the questions might ask you to compare an 'unseen' text with a text or texts that you have studied, or ask you to link several unseen texts to a particular thematic area or genre. If you have developed a sound understanding of ways of reading and approaching literary texts throughout your course, you will be able to handle unseen texts confidently.

'Closed book' and 'open book' questions

Some of the questions you answer will be 'closed book' questions (you are not allowed to take the text or texts you have studied into the exam with you). This means that you are not able to refer to the text during the exam. In 'open book' exams you are allowed to take the text or texts you have studied into the exam with you. These texts must, however, be 'clean' texts, which means they must not contain any notes or marginal comments that you have written in them. 'Open book' questions sometimes ask you to look at a particular section of the text as the focus of your answer, perhaps asking you for a detailed analysis of the section and then to place it in the broader context of the text. The examinations that you take for A-Level English Literature will consist of a mixture of 'open' and 'closed' book questions.

Questions that offer you a view, proposition or quotation

None of the questions you are asked will be prescriptive, and the examiner will not have a preconceived idea of an 'ideal' answer. There will be a variety of ways in which the questions can be answered and in which views can be expressed. Questions will invite you to debate issues and encourage you to develop informed judgements on the texts and ideas that they raise. It is your ideas and judgements that the examiner is interested in reading. Where a question presents you with a quotation or proposition, you are never expected to simply accept the view it offers. You are free to accept or reject the views offered, but what matters is that you are able to support your own ideas, views and interpretations with evidence from the text – a point that applies to all the question types you might encounter.

1 Writing A-Level essays

The following topics are covered in this chapter:

- **Planning and structuring your essays**
- **Effective paragraphing**
- **Opening and closing paragraphs**
- **Accurate written expression**

1.1 Planning and structuring your essays

LEARNING SUMMARY

After studying this section, you should be able to:

- appreciate the importance of planning your essays
- understand how to structure an essay
- feel confident about producing a quick and efficient plan in a form that suits you

The importance of planning

AQA A	U 1, 2, 3, 4
AQA B	U 1, 2, 3, 4
Edexcel	U 1, 2, 3, 4
OCR	U 1, 2, 3, 4
WJEC	U 1, 2, 3, 4
CCEA	AS U1, AS U2, A2 U1, A2 U2

Assessment Objective (AO) 1 requires you to 'articulate creative, informed and relevant responses to literary texts using … coherent, accurate written expression'. This applies to every unit of every specification.

In order to achieve this objective, it is important not only that you know and understand the texts you have studied, but also that you can express your ideas about them clearly and persuasively.

If your answer (whether for a coursework task or for an exam answer) is going to be 'coherent', you probably need to spend a little time planning it. How long you spend doing this will depend on the nature of the task. For a coursework task you can take as long as you like. For an exam answer, however, you need to plan very quickly. About five minutes is enough time.

Preparing for exam questions

AQA A	U 1, 3
AQA B	U 1, 3
Edexcel	U 1, 3
OCR	U 1, 3
WJEC	U 1, 4
CCEA	AS U2, A2 U1, A2 U2

In an exam, your first task is to choose the best question for you. Make sure you read the questions carefully. It is all too easy to spot key words that remind you of a practice essay you have done or a topic you have focused on in revision and assume that you have the answer. Make sure you understand exactly what the question is asking you to do.

A good way of testing whether a question is right for you is to try answering it in one or two sentences. If you are given a choice of questions, you could try answering them all like this before deciding which one to answer.

Examples

Here are a couple of exam-style questions and examples of short answers that you could write, to give you an idea of whether it is worth choosing the question.

1. Examine the ways in which Shakespeare has presented ideas about good and bad government in *Measure for Measure*. Show how your appreciation and understanding of this element of *Measure for Measure* have been informed by your study of *The Duchess of Malfi*.

   The Duke might appear to be a good ruler because he is a good person, while Angelo is clearly shown to be corrupt, but is it this clear cut? Similarly, the Duchess and Antonio would be expected to be more honest and fair than her brothers, but they too find themselves caught up in a web of dishonesty and corruption.

2. How far, and in what ways, do you agree with the idea that *Pride and Prejudice* has more to do with money and social class than love?

   I do not agree with this statement because, while Jane Austen shows how important money and class are, she is essentially satirising society's attitudes to them and, in the end, shows that love can overcome any problems they may cause.

PROGRESS CHECK

Look up any available past papers or specimen papers for the exams you are doing. If you have not been provided with copies by your teacher, you can easily find them on your exam board's website. Find the questions on the texts you have studied and try writing brief answers on the alternatives before deciding which one you would prefer to answer.

For questions that provide you with an extract from a text to comment on (e.g. AQA A Unit 1 and WJEC Unit 4), whether from a set text or an unseen text, you might want to take a slightly different approach to your planning. You could skim read the extracts before looking at the question and then return to the text to highlight or underline key words and phrases, perhaps also making brief notes in the margins. You might prefer to read the question first or not to make notes on the text. You might then try answering the question briefly, or you might proceed straight to your plan.

Preparing for internal assessments

AQA A	U 2, 3
AQA B	U 2, 4
Edexcel	U 2, 4
OCR	U 2, 4
WJEC	U 2, 3
CCEA	AS U1

For an internally assessed unit, you might also find it useful to produce a short answer for various possible questions before deciding on a title.

Structuring your essays

AQA A	U 1, 2, 3, 4
AQA B	U 1, 2, 3, 4
Edexcel	U 1, 2, 3, 4
OCR	U 1, 2, 3, 4
WJEC	U 1, 2, 3, 4
CCEA	AS U1, AS U2, A2 U1, A2 U2

You probably already know what kind of plan works for you.

Your preferred way of planning might be:

- a spider diagram or mind map
- a bullet-pointed list of key points
- random jottings connected by arrows.

Some people might tell you that they never plan what they are going to write. It is possible that they are telling the truth, but it is more likely that what they mean is that they do not write down their plans. They probably have plans in their heads and are lucky enough to be able to retain them while they are writing. This is a rare talent, and not a method you should experiment with in an important exam.

When you have jotted down your thoughts, the next step is to number them, so that your essay follows a logical sequence.

Examples

Below are two examples of possible essay plans, answering the two questions on page 17. The first is in the form of a mind map/spider diagram, and the second is laid out as a list of bullet points.

1. Examine the ways in which Shakespeare has presented ideas about good and bad government in *Measure for Measure*. Show how your appreciation and understanding of this element of *Measure for Measure* have been informed by your study of *The Duchess of Malfi*.

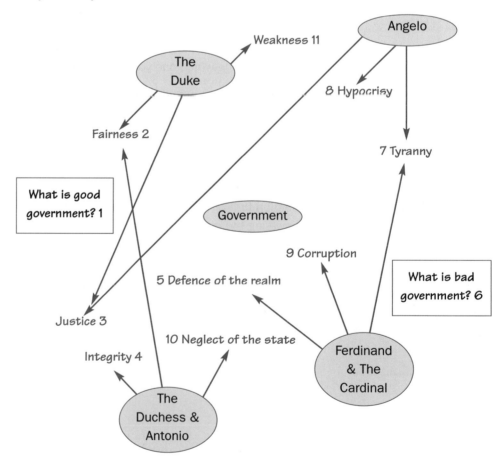

COMMENTARY

In this example, the candidate – having jotted down the names of the chief characters of both plays (all of whom are rulers) – has thought of some of the main elements of good and bad government shown in the plays, and has connected them to the characters who exemplify these qualities. The diagram clearly shows that ideas about what makes good or bad rulers are not simple in either play. The way in which the diagram has been numbered shows us that the candidate intends to deal with the qualities of a good ruler first and then with the qualities of a bad ruler. The question asks candidates to examine the ways in which good and bad government are presented in the plays. This candidate intends to introduce in turn each of the aspects of government that have been identified, and then explain how they are explored. For example, the idea of the well-governed state is introduced at the beginning of both plays. In *Measure for Measure* the Duke announces that he intends to test Angelo's qualities as a ruler, while in *The Duchess of Malfi* Antonio praises the French court, implying that Italian courts are inferior.

The candidate could have opted to deal with each of the main characters in turn, discussing the ways in which each character might be considered a good or bad ruler. However, had such a choice been made, the essay might not have compared the two plays in the way required by the question.

2. How far and in what ways do you agree with the idea that *Pride and Prejudice* has more to do with money and social class than with love?

A real plan would look a lot more rough and ready than this, and might even be illegible to anyone except the candidate. That would not matter, because it is for the candidate's – not the examiner's – benefit.

- Everybody knows how much everyone else is 'worth'. 3
- The girls need husbands because they will not inherit from their father. 1
- Everybody knows their 'place' – at least they do at first. 4
- Wickham and Lydia *do not* think about security – they are foolish. 8
- Charlotte Lucas marries for security – not the same as marrying for money. 6
- Mrs Bennett is impressed by Bingley's money. 2
- Bingley's sisters persuade him that Jane is from the wrong class. 9
- However, he overcomes his doubts. 10
- Darcy and Bingley are both rich – would it be such a happy ending if they had been poor? 14
- Collins is made fun of because of his snobbery. 7
- Lady Catherine de Burgh's wealth and position give her power – but she uses it to try to spoil things – subject of satire. 11
- Elizabeth is very impressed by Pemberley and it makes her think better of Darcy – why? 12
- Class and money are not always the same thing – Bingley's father was 'self-made'. 5
- In the end Darcy and Elizabeth's love overcomes difference of wealth and class. 14
- The author's ironic portrayal of those who are too attached to money or class shows what she thinks (mention intrusive narrator?). 13
- Money (if not class) is important, though not as important as love – it's good to have both! 15

COMMENTARY

For illustration purposes, this plan is in a bit more detail than it would be advisable to use in an examination. A real candidate, familiar with the novel, would probably use abbreviations (such as initials for the main characters) and leave out words such as 'is', 'but' and 'however'.

You can see that the candidate has written down, in a fairly random order, everything that occurred to him or her about the subject of the question. He/she has then numbered the points, so that they follow each other in a logical order, just as in the previous plan. By sticking to this plan, the candidate will ensure that the essay retains a sharp focus on the question throughout.

PROGRESS CHECK

Choose a question from a past paper or specimen paper on a text you have studied and try planning the answer using both the forms discussed in this chapter. Decide which one suits you better.

KEY POINT

A brief written plan can help to clarify your thoughts and order them in a logical sequence. This will help to make your essay coherent and focused.

1.2 Effective paragraphing

LEARNING SUMMARY	After studying this section, you should be able to:
	• better understand how to make your essays 'flow'
	• use a wider range of connecting words and phrases

The importance of paragraphs

AQA A	U 1, 2, 3, 4
AQA B	U 1, 2, 3, 4
Edexcel	U 1, 2, 3, 4
OCR	U 1, 2, 3, 4
WJEC	U 1, 2, 3, 4
CCEA	AS U1, AS U2, A2 U1, A2 U2

It is essential that you always write in paragraphs. By breaking up the text into more manageable chunks, paragraphs make your writing more accessible and pleasing to the reader. More importantly, they guide the reader through your argument as you develop a coherent and logical answer to a question.

If you have written a plan and numbered your points, you will already have a structure for your essay. You do not, however, have to use these numbers as a strict guide to paragraphing – you may need more than one paragraph for one of your points, or you may be able to cover two of the points within a single paragraph. Your plan is not a straitjacket. It is there for guidance only. You can adapt and change it as you are writing your essay.

You should begin a new paragraph every time you introduce a new idea or move on to a new subject. The best way to show that you are starting a new paragraph is to **indent**. Alternatively, you can leave a line between paragraphs, but this is more usual in typed or printed work, and should be avoided when handwriting.

Helping your work to 'flow' – examples

Essays are sometimes criticised for not 'flowing' or not being 'coherent'. However, if you have a decent plan, you should already be half way there. Your essay will make sense because you have thought about how one idea leads to another. Numbering your points will help to ensure that they are not covered in a random and confusing order in the essay itself.

The next step is to ensure that the paragraphs are linked. You can do this by including in the opening sentence (sometimes called the 'topic sentence' because it is often used to introduce a new idea) a reference back to the subject matter of the previous paragraph.

Look at this example, which is from an answer to the *Pride and Prejudice* sample question (see Example 2, page 17).

> This total disregard for social conventions by Lydia has serious consequences for her family.

COMMENTARY

It is clear from this sentence that the candidate has, in the previous paragraph, been discussing Lydia's elopement with Wickham. The topic sentence shows the reader that we are going to move on from a discussion of what their elopement tells us about the importance of class and money to a consideration of the effect their action has on other characters and the developing narrative.

The next example (from the same essay) does not refer back explicitly to the previous paragraph, but uses a connecting phrase to show the relationship between the two paragraphs.

> Elizabeth, on the other hand, is determined not to be impressed by Darcy's money and status.

COMMENTARY

It is clear from the phrase 'on the other hand' that we are moving from a discussion of one view of the importance of class and money shown in the novel to a contrasting view.

The next example is taken from an answer to the sample question on *The Duchess of Malfi* (see Example 1, page 17).

> In contrast with this apparent contempt for his duties as a prince of the Church, the Cardinal takes seriously his role as a ruler and military leader.

COMMENTARY

This sentence makes it clear that the candidate is moving from the subject of the previous paragraph (the Cardinal's contempt for his clerical duties) to discuss another aspect of his attitude to government. The student also uses a connecting phrase ('in contrast with') to 'signpost' the relationship between the two paragraphs, and to show the reader how they are connected.

Connecting paragraphs and clauses

AQA A	U 1, 2, 3, 4
AQA B	U 1, 2, 3, 4
Edexcel	U 1, 2, 3, 4
OCR	U 1, 2, 3, 4
WJEC	U 1, 2, 3, 4
CCEA	AS U1, AS U2, A2 U1, A2 U2

Connectives are words and phrases that are used to link clauses, sentences or paragraphs and show what the relationship is between them. They can act as 'signposts' – helping to guide the reader from one clause or sentence to the next, and from one paragraph to the next. They can be seen as the glue that holds your essay together.

Connectives include conjunctions and relative pronouns (e.g. 'who' and 'which'), which connect clauses within sentences to make compound and complex sentences. Adverbs that start new sentences (e.g. 'therefore' and 'however') are also connectives – do not use them to connect two parts of a sentence. You can use short adverbial phrases to link clauses, sentences or paragraphs. A connective shows the relationship of one clause, sentence or paragraph to the previous one. Make sure you are clear on what that relationship is.

The rest of this section comprises a list of some connectives that you might want to use when writing your essay answers.

Conjunctions are usually used to connect two parts of a sentence, and are placed either at the beginning of, or within, the sentence.

Examples include:

- although
- because
- and
- so
- but
- whereas.

Adverbs are used at or near the beginning of a new sentence or paragraph.

Examples include:

- however
- therefore
- nevertheless
- consequently
- alternatively
- secondly
- similarly
- equally
- thus
- moreover
- furthermore
- evidently.

Examples of **connecting phrases** are:

- in fact
- due to
- in spite of
- even so
- for example
- in conclusion
- on the one hand ... on the other hand
- in contrast to
- in the same way.

> **KEY POINT**
>
> You can make your essay 'flow' and help the reader to follow your argument by using paragraphs properly and linking them effectively.

> **PROGRESS CHECK**
>
> Re-read an essay you have written during your course, paying particular attention to paragraphing. Highlight links between paragraphs. If they are not strong enough – or simply do not exist – re-write the first sentence of each paragraph to strengthen the link.

1.3 Opening and closing paragraphs

LEARNING SUMMARY	After studying this section, you should be able to:
	• write an effective opening paragraph
	• write an effective conclusion to your essay

The first paragraph

AQA A	U 1, 2, 3, 4
AQA B	U 1, 2, 3, 4
Edexcel	U 1, 2, 3, 4
OCR	U 1, 2, 3, 4
WJEC	U 1, 2, 3, 4
CCEA	AS U1, AS U2, A2 U1, A2 U2

Keep your opening paragraphs short and to the point. Remember – the examiner already knows what the question is.

Many students have difficulty starting their essays and are uncertain about what to put in their opening paragraph. It is important that you feel confident about writing the first paragraph of an essay, because you do not want to spend valuable time worrying about it during an exam.

Essentially, a good opening paragraph tells the reader that you understand the question and gives some idea about how you are going to tackle it. You might consider what the question means – sometimes this is referred to as 'interrogating' the question. You should not simply repeat the wording of the question, nor do you need to state what you are going to do.

What not to do

Here is an example of an unhelpful and unnecessary opening paragraph, in response to this question:

> How far do you agree with the view that Emily Dickinson's poetry is obsessed with death?

> In this essay I am going to write about the poetry of Emily Dickinson. I am going to focus on the poems 'I started Early – Took my Dog', 'It was not death, for I stood up', 'I died for beauty but was scarce', 'A clock stopped' and 'A coffin is a small domain'. I will look at each poem in turn and consider whether or not Dickinson is obsessed with death.

COMMENTARY

The only good thing about this paragraph is that it gets the essay started. Perhaps the student believes that the purpose of the first paragraph is to get to the second paragraph. However, there is nothing here to engage the interest of the reader. The first sentence is pointless because the question tells the student to write about Emily Dickinson's poetry – there is no need to state the obvious. Nor is there any need to tell the examiner which poems you are going to focus on or how you are going to structure your essay. Finally, the third sentence just says that the student is going to try to answer the question.

A good first paragraph

This is a much better opening.

> It is self-evident that death is a major concern of Dickinson's poetry. The sheer number of poems in which she alludes to death and dying might suggest a morbid obsession. But is this really the case? After all, there are also many poems which have little or nothing to do with death. Furthermore, the negative

connotations of the word 'obsessed' could be seen as belittling what could be seen as the poet's duty to tackle the major concerns of humanity – and what could be of greater interest to humans than death?

COMMENTARY

Here, the student tackles the question head on. He acknowledges that it is a valid question to ask, but questions the terminology used – Dickinson does write a lot about death, but is it fair to say that she is obsessed? He also indicates that he is going to explore the question in two different ways – by considering whether death is an obsession or just one of many subjects the poet tackles, and by considering whether her apparent 'obsession' with death is something that should be applauded rather than derided. The paragraph is written in a lively style, with the rhetorical questions inviting the reader to engage and respond.

Generic questions

The example question on the previous page is about one set text. There are some exams at AS and A2, however, that include generic questions, to be answered with reference to a wide choice of texts. When answering such questions it can be useful to mention which texts you will be writing about in the opening paragraph. Here is an example of an opening response to this question:

'Gothic literature depends for its appeal on the idea that those who are morally reprehensible are both sexually attractive and deserving of sympathy.' Discuss this view in relation to at least three texts.

'Macbeth', 'Paradise Lost' and 'Wuthering Heights' are all dominated by characters who would conventionally be seen as evil – in Lucifer's case as the personification of evil. They are certainly all powerful characters, but whether that power results in sexual attractiveness is less certain. Whether we sympathise (or should sympathise) with these characters is a matter that continues to divide readers of all three texts.

COMMENTARY

This student quickly and efficiently tells the examiner which texts she is about to discuss, without resorting to clumsy phrases such as 'the three texts I have studied are …' or 'in this essay I am going to write about ….' She picks up on all the main elements of the question, casting doubt on the statement's validity as she does so. 'Morally reprehensible' becomes 'conventionally … seen as evil'; the idea of sexual attraction is linked to power and then questioned; and she picks up on the implied assumption that writers, not readers, decide which characters are sympathetic, by pointing out that different readers will have different ideas about whether a given character is sympathetic. The examiner knows that this student is going to rigorously test the validity of the given statement by trying to apply it to Macbeth, Lucifer in *Paradise Lost*, and Heathcliff in *Wuthering Heights*.

KEY POINT

An effective opening paragraph tells the examiner that you understand the question and gives some idea of how you are going to tackle it.

The final paragraph

AQA A	U 1, 2, 3, 4
AQA B	U 1, 2, 3, 4
Edexcel	U 1, 2, 3, 4
OCR	U 1, 2, 3, 4
WJEC	U 1, 2, 3, 4
CCEA	AS U1, AS U2, A2 U1, A2 U2

> Coursework moderators can be quite strict about word count, sometimes reducing marks for assignments that exceed the word limit. They may do this by ignoring anything written after the limit is reached.

Your concluding paragraph should bring together the main ideas in your essay, summarising your points and trying to give a final, personal answer to the question.

A good final paragraph

Here is an example of a concluding paragraph for the essay on gothic literature (the question is on the previous page).

All three texts are dominated by a towering, charismatic figure (either protagonist or antagonist), who not only breaks the rules of conventional morality, but questions the validity of those rules. The fact that their actions have tragic results – not only for themselves but for those around them (in Lucifer's case for the whole of mankind) – warns us of the consequences of allowing ourselves to be seduced by evil. The fact that, ultimately, the moral universe is restored is an essential element of gothic literature. However, the gothic encourages us to indulge our fascination with 'the glamour of sin', a dangerous glamour embodied in Macbeth, Heathcliff and Lucifer. At the same time, we are allowed – even encouraged – to see these figures as victims, and must emerge from a reading of the texts with a degree of sympathy for these three great tragic figures.

COMMENTARY

The student has brought together the main strands of her argument, referring back to the question and her opening remarks. Note that she mentions all three texts in the paragraph, although she does this by referring to the characters rather than the titles of the texts. This student emphasises what the three texts and characters have in common, having presumably explored their similarities and differences in the main body of the essay. She might equally have decided that they had little in common, in which case she could have used this paragraph to restate the main differences between them. As in the opening paragraph, she briefly unpicks the main concepts and assumptions present in the question – gothic literature, morality, the seductive power of evil, and the reader's sympathy. In contrast with the first paragraph, she makes her own view clear. Her consideration of the three texts has led her to conclude that she is broadly – although not entirely – in agreement with the quotation in the question.

Note that the candidate does not begin her final paragraph with 'in conclusion' or 'overall'. While there is nothing wrong with using these connectives, they can look a little clumsy and mechanical.

KEY POINT

Use your final paragraph to bring together the main strands of your argument and give a final answer to the question.

PROGRESS CHECK

Read an essay you have written during your course – whether for coursework or a practice exam – and re-write the opening and closing paragraphs.

1.4 Accurate written expression

LEARNING SUMMARY	After studying this section, you should be able to:
	• understand the importance of accuracy in written expression
	• spot common errors in spelling and be aware of how to avoid them
	• spot common errors in grammar and be aware of how to avoid them

Accuracy

AQA A	U 1, 2, 3, 4
AQA B	U 1, 2, 3, 4
Edexcel	U 1, 2, 3, 4
OCR	U 1, 2, 3, 4
WJEC	U 1, 2, 3, 4
CCEA	AS U1, AS U2, A2 U1, A2 U2

AO1 requires 'coherent, accurate written expression'. If you have structured your essay well and linked your points effectively, it should be coherent. To be accurate you need to write in correct Standard English, avoiding errors in spelling, punctuation and grammar.

The need to be accurate applies to both coursework and examination units. Examiners might be a little more forgiving than coursework moderators – making allowances for careless errors made in a stressful situation – but you cannot rely on this.

> Always try to leave a few minutes at the end of an exam for checking and correcting errors.

You should always check your work carefully for errors. You should try to leave a few minutes at the end of an examination to do this and, when you find a mistake, cross it out neatly and write your correction above it or in the margin. For coursework, you can spend as much time as you like checking for errors before you produce a final draft. You also have the advantage of being able to use a dictionary and other reference books. Do not, however, rely on your spell check. There are many errors it will not pick up.

By now you should be aware of the kind of errors you are inclined to make. Do not take the attitude that 'I'm no good at spelling' or 'I can't do punctuation'. Make a note of the things you get wrong and teach yourself to do them correctly.

In this section we will consider some of the most common problems students have with spelling, punctuation and grammar.

> **KEY POINT**
>
> Accuracy in written expression is important. If you feel you have problems in this area, it is important that you tackle them head on.

Spelling

AQA A	U 1, 2, 3, 4
AQA B	U 1, 2, 3, 4
Edexcel	U 1, 2, 3, 4
OCR	U 1, 2, 3, 4
WJEC	U 1, 2, 3, 4
CCEA	AS U1, AS U2, A2 U1, A2 U2

Some of the most common spelling errors that students make are listed below. Some may seem pretty simple, but it is amazing how many able students make them, even at A-Level. Such simple errors can give a very bad impression to the reader/examiner.

Accept/except

Accept means to receive – e.g. I accept your gift with thanks.

Except means without – e.g. All the bears except one went to bed.

Aloud/allowed

Aloud means the same as out loud – e.g. To check your punctuation, read your work aloud.

Allowed means let or permitted – e.g. Chewing is not allowed in the exam hall.

Hear/here

You hear with your ears.

Here simply means in this place.

Lay/lie

You lie down. The past tense of lie is lay – e.g. Last night I lay on my bed for a while.

In the present tense you lay a table or, if you are a hen, an egg.

There/they're/their

There means in that place – 'here' with a 't' in front – e.g. it's over there, or there is, there are, etc.

They're means they are (the apostrophe shows that the 'a' is missing), e.g. They're not our friends any more.

Their means belonging to them – e.g. They left their bags on the bus.

> You should not really be using contracted forms like 'they're' in a formal essay. Other examples in this list are 'it's', 'we're' and 'who's'.

No/know/knew/new

The silent 'k' is rare in English. It should be easy to remember the small number of words in which it is used, e.g. Did you know that Ken had knobbly knees? No, that's news to me, but I know now.

Its/it's

Its means belonging to it – e.g. The cat licked its paws.

It's is short for it is – e.g. It's a long way to Tipperary.

Lose/loose

To lose means to mislay something or not to win.

To loose is to undo or make loose. The word loose is more often seen as an adjective – e.g. Make sure you wear loose clothing.

Past/passed

Passed is a verb – e.g. I passed my driving test yesterday.

Past is a noun indicating a previous time – e.g. It's all in the past now. Past is also used in phrases such as 'he went past' or 'they are past their best'.

Practice/practise

Practice is a noun – e.g. Netball practice is cancelled.

Practise is a verb – e.g. If you practise hard you might get into the team.

One way of remembering this is to think of advi**se** (**verb**) and advi**ce** (**noun**).

Quiet/quite

Quiet means silent – e.g. I knew there was something wrong because the class was so quiet.

Quite means fairly or a bit – e.g. The essay was quite good, but could have been better.

Right/write

Right is the opposite of wrong.

Write is what you do in an exam. Someone who writes is a writer and certainly not a 'wrighter'. However, a person who writes plays is known as a 'playwright' (the derivation being from the rather archaic word 'wright' (someone who makes things), as in 'wheelwright' or 'shipwright'.

To/too/two

To means towards, or is part of the infinitive – e.g. 'to do', 'to think'.

Too means excessively – e.g. too many, too much.

Two is the number – e.g. The two bears were too tired to go to bed.

Where/we're/were/wear

Where indicates place – 'here' with a 'w' in front – e.g. Where did you say it was?

We're is short for we are – e.g. We're not sure.

Wear is used for clothes, etc. – e.g. You wear your earrings on your ears.

Whether/weather

Whether is another way of saying if – e.g. I don't know whether to go or not.

Weather refers to the sun, wind, rain, etc. – e.g. The weather was terrible.

Whose/who's

Whose means belonging to whom – e.g. Whose coat is that on the floor?

Who's is short for who is or who has – e.g. Who's that boy over there? Who's dropped that coat?

You should be aware of any other words that give you trouble. People often have difficulty remembering when to use double consonants, for example, or how to spell words that have silent letters. Make a list of words that you have spelt incorrectly in the past, look up the correct spellings and learn them.

You could also make a list of more specialised vocabulary that you might want to use in your essays. A good starting point is to test yourself on the words in the list of literary terms given in the next chapter (see pages 46–49).

> **KEY POINT**
>
> English spelling can be tricky, but it is important, and if you have any particular problems you should address them now.

> **PROGRESS CHECK**
>
> 1. Identify the correct words in the following sentences:
>   a) It is good **practice/practise** to time any essays you do at home.
>   b) Sometimes after an exam you need to **lay/lie** down in a darkened room.
>   c) We have nothing to **lose/loose** but our chains.
>   d) If you are going to improve, learn to **accept/except** criticism.
>   e) You could not say that the Brontës **were/where** typical products of **there/their** time.
>
> a) practice b) lie c) lose d) accept e) were; their.

Punctuation

The purpose of punctuation is to make clear your meaning. Essays that are poorly punctuated can be confusing, making it difficult to follow a line of argument.

Full stops

Full stops are probably the most important punctuation mark. They separate sentences, and without them writing does not make sense. The most common punctuation error is probably 'comma splicing', or the use of commas instead of full stops. This is extremely common in AS and A2 essays.

Commas

Commas mark a smaller break or pause than full stops. They must not be used to link clauses (statements that could stand alone as sentences) unless a connective is used. This is usually a conjunction ('as', 'but', 'and', 'because', 'although, 'so') or a relative pronoun ('who', 'which', 'that').

Here are some examples of when to use commas – and when not to.

I fed the dog, it was hungry.	**WRONG**
I fed the dog because it was hungry.	**RIGHT**
I fed the dog, which was hungry.	**RIGHT**

Commas are used to **separate subordinate clauses from main clauses**. Subordinate clauses give additional information, but are not necessary for the sentence to make sense.

Here are a couple of examples.

> Having eaten sixteen bananas, Amy felt very sick.
> Amy, the school's champion banana eater, had to admit defeat.

Commas are also used to:

- **mark off the items in a list** – e.g. he bought sugar, butter, half a dozen eggs and a monkey wrench
- **introduce direct speech** (before the speech marks) – e.g. 'I've had enough,' he cried, 'and I'm leaving.'
- **mark off the name of the person spoken to** – e.g. 'Don't do that, George.'

Question marks

A **question mark** comes at the end of a question. It is used in direct (or reported) speech.

'Did you see Lizzie at the party last night?' asked Daz.	**RIGHT**
Daz asked me whether I'd seen Elizabeth at the party?	**WRONG**

Apostrophes

Apostrophes seem to cause people more problems than any other punctuation mark. Some students hardly use them at all, while others litter their work with unwanted apostrophes.

The only two reasons for using them are to show:
- omission or contraction
- possession.

The apostrophe for omission is used mostly in speech or informal writing.

> They really shouldn't have eaten that.
> You'll never understand if you don't listen.
> Mark's finished his homework, but Rachel's still doing hers.

At AS and A2, you are expected to write in formal English, except possibly in the Creative Response section, so you will not often need to use the apostrophe for omission.

The apostrophe for possession is not difficult if you remember that in most cases to show ownership you add an apostrophe and an 's' to the word that indicates the 'owner'.

> The cat's tail (one cat who owns the tail)
> The child's books (one child who owns more than one book)
> A different word is used to show possession for more than one child (children's). Other examples like this are men's, women's and sheep's.
> Miss Jones's class (Miss Jones ends in 's' but she is singular)

The exception to this is when the word for the 'owner' is plural and ends in 's'. Then you simply add an apostrophe after the 's'.

> The cats' tails (more than one cat)
> The students' books (more than one student)
> The students' book (these unfortunate students are sharing one book)

Some authorities say that it is correct to use an apostrophe without an added 's' after names ending in 's' (e.g. 'Miss Jones' class' rather than 'Miss Jones's class'), while others propose complex rules about the number of syllables in the name, or whether it is a modern or ancient name. Basically, it's a matter of personal choice.

Semicolons

A **semicolon** can be used instead of a full stop if you want to show that two clauses are closely connected and you do not feel that it is appropriate to use a connective.

> Harry loves bananas; Jolene prefers coconuts.

A semicolon can also be used to separate phrases in a list.

Colons

Colons have a number of uses. The most common is to introduce a list.

> The house was surrounded by an artist's palette of flowers: sky-blue azaleas; blood-red poppies; snow-white lilies; and a riot of variegated roses.

In a literature essay, you should use a colon to introduce a quotation.

> Romeo compares Juliet to the source of light and life: 'It is the east and Juliet is the sun.'

Dashes and ellipses

Dashes (or en-rules) can be used to mark a sharp break or interruption, or they can be used instead of brackets and placed around an extra idea which has been inserted into a sentence.

An **ellipsis** (three dots) can indicate a thought that trails off, or a sense of foreboding or anticipation, or can show that something has been omitted.

KEY POINT

Good punctuation makes your meaning clear.

PROGRESS CHECK

This passage, from an essay about F. Scott Fitzgerald, has been written without punctuation or capital letters. Insert the correct punctuation and capital letters where appropriate.

his material is drawn always from the lives of the leisured classes some of his characters have earned their wealth jay gatsby and rosemary hoyt in tender is the night for example most of them however do no work whatsoever and exist only to spend money secure in their parasitical existence and unembarrassed by any questions of right or deserving

His material is drawn always from the lives of the leisured classes. Some of his characters have earned their wealth: Jay Gatsby and Rosemary Hoyt (in 'Tender is the Night') for example. Most of them, however, do no work whatsoever and exist only to spend money, secure in their parasitical existence and unembarrassed by any questions of right or deserving.

> Remember to use capital letters in titles. In an exam, put single inverted commas around the title – in typed work use *italics*.

Grammar

AQA A	**U 1, 2, 3, 4**
AQA B	**U 1, 2, 3, 4**
Edexcel	**U 1, 2, 3, 4**
OCR	**U 1, 2, 3, 4**
WJEC	**U 1, 2, 3, 4**
CCEA	**AS U1, AS U2, A2 U1, A2 U2**

> When writing about a text, remember to write in the present tense.

Grammar is defined as the study or rules of relations between words in language, or the application of such rules.

When grammar is said to be incorrect or inappropriate, it is usually because a student is writing the way he or she speaks in informal situations. This is not only a question of style – it can result in meaning becoming obscured.

Here are some of the more common grammatical errors made by students.

Done/did and seen/saw

The correct forms are:
- I did it (the simple past tense)
- I had done it (pluperfect tense)
- I have done it (the perfect tense).

Similarly, you should write:
- I saw it (simple past)
- I had seen it (pluperfect)
- I have seen it (perfect).

Could, would, should, ought to, might, may, must, can, will and shall

These words are known as modal verbs. Make sure you use them correctly.

They are **never** followed by 'of'. They should be followed by 'have':
- I could have been a contender.
- I would have passed if I had checked my work.
- I really ought to have revised more thoroughly.

This very common error probably occurs because in speech, modal verbs are usually contracted to 'could've', 'would've', etc.

Another area where candidates often make errors is by confusing words that have similar – but not identical – meanings. Below are some words that are often confused.

Less/fewer

Less tells you how much – e.g. less tea, less fat.

Fewer tells you how many – e.g. fewer students, fewer coconuts.

Imply/infer

If you imply something you are hinting at or insinuating it.

If you infer something you are taking the hint, or reading between the lines.

Uninterested/disinterested

If you are uninterested in something you are not concerned or bothered about it – e.g. Jo was totally uninterested in English.

If you are disinterested you have nothing to gain personally – e.g. I was asked to attend the meeting as a disinterested party, in order to ensure fair play.

> **KEY POINT**
>
> Like correct punctuation, correct grammar helps to make meaning clear.

> **PROGRESS CHECK**
>
> **1** Which of these sentences are correct?
>   a) After he done the murder he felt guilty.
>   b) He could not of tried any harder than he did.
>   c) Elizabeth infers from Darcy's reaction that he wants nothing further to do with her.
>   d) Heathcliff is totally disinterested in Isabella's feelings.
>   e) I made less mistakes in this exam than I did in the one in January.
>
> 1. c)

Note – As this chapter is about writing A-Level essays in general, we have not included a sample question and model answer, or practice examination questions. Please see the end of Chapter 2 (pages 50–52) for a sample answer that has been annotated in accordance with A01 and A02.

2 Writing analytically

The following topics are covered in this chapter:

- Analysing structure, form and language
- Referring to the text
- Using appropriate terminology and concepts

2.1 Analysing structure, form and language

LEARNING SUMMARY

After studying this section, you should be able to:

- understand more fully what is meant by structure and how to write about it
- understand more fully what is meant by form and how to write about it
- understand more fully what is meant by language and how to write about it

How structure, form and language fits into your A-Level course

AQA A	U 1, 2, 3, 4
AQA B	U 1, 2, 3, 4
Edexcel	U 1, 2, 3, 4
OCR	U 1, 2, 3, 4
WJEC	U 1, 2, 3, 4
CCEA	AS U1, AS U2, A2, U1, A2 U2

Assessment Objective (AO) 1 asks that you 'articulate creative, informed and relevant responses to literary texts, using appropriate terminology and concepts'. AO2 requires you to 'demonstrate detailed critical understanding in analysing the ways in which structure, form and language shape meanings in literary texts'.

To do well at both AS and A2 level you will have to:
- identify significant and relevant aspects of structure, form and language
- explore and critically analyse how these aspects shape meaning
- refer in detail to texts in support of your responses.

Aspects of form, structure and language will be discussed in greater detail in the later chapters of this book, which consider their use specifically in poetry, drama and prose. In this chapter they will be discussed in more general terms.

In every critical essay you write, you are expected to comment on these three aspects of a writer's work. How much emphasis is given to each of them depends on both the nature of the text and the wording of the question you are answering. A question could, for example, ask you to compare the use of imagery in two poems. The focus of this question – and, therefore, the answer – is clearly on the writer's use of language. However, you should still include some discussion of both form and structure.

Writing about structure

AQA A	U 1, 2, 3, 4
AQA B	U 1, 2, 3, 4
Edexcel	U 1, 2, 3, 4
OCR	U 1, 2, 3, 4
WJEC	U 1, 2, 3, 4
CCEA	AS U1, AS U2, A2 U1, A2 U2

Structure basically means a framework, or the way in which something is put together. You might find it helpful to think of the framework of a building or perhaps of a skeleton. In Chapter 1, we looked at how to go about structuring your written work. Here we will consider how you might comment on the way the writers of your texts have structured their work.

In literature, when talking about structure you could be referring to text organisation (the way in which the text is arranged), for example whether it is divided into chapters, paragraphs or, in the case of poetry, stanzas. Or you could be referring to story structure. These two aspects of structure are, of course, closely related.

Story structure

Story structure refers to how a story is developed. Regardless of the form or genre you are dealing with, most texts have a narrative or story of some kind. Most stories, however long or short, have a very similar structure.

Story structure has been described in various ways, but generally speaking it has this pattern:

1. **Exposition** (which literally means 'laying out') – during the exposition we may be introduced to the setting and the main characters. We get to know the 'world' of the play, novel or poem and what that world is like before a story really starts and things begin to change. In modern literature and films the exposition can be very brief. It tends to be longer in texts written before 1900.
2. **The inciting incident** – something happens to change things, usually for the protagonist. This is when the story really begins.
3. **Complication(s)** – we need complications or turning points to change the course of a story (if everything works out easily, there is no story). In a longer work, for example a full-length play or a novel, there are normally two or more of these.
4. **Climax** – this is when things come to a head, leading to a happy or a tragic ending. Strangely, though, this is not usually right at the end of the story.
5. **The coda** (which literally means 'tail') – this is a term used more often in music, but it is also a useful term to describe the final section of a literary work. It describes a (usually quite short) section where we can reflect on what has happened and consider how the world has changed. Quite often, the writer reminds us in some way of the beginning of the story, perhaps by having the protagonist return to the same place, or by repeating some lines from the start with slight changes. This part of the story is also referred to as the **resolution** or the **denouement**, and can give the writer an opportunity to 'tie up loose ends'.

If we were to apply this pattern to Shakespeare's *Macbeth*, we might come out with something like the following:

1. The witches are seen on the heath and we learn that Duncan's forces have been victorious over the rebels.
2. The witches tell Macbeth that he will be King of Scotland.
3. **(a)** Macbeth kills Duncan.
   (b) After the murder of Banquo, Macbeth sees the ghost.
   (c) Macbeth slaughters Macduff's family.
4. Macduff kills Macbeth.
5. Malcolm becomes King and order is restored.

If you know *Macbeth* you might disagree with some of these details. You might, for example, pick out different incidents as the turning points. Like most other things in literary criticism, it is not an exact science – just a useful way of looking at structure.

> **PROGRESS CHECK**
>
> Take one of the texts you have studied and see if it fits this pattern. If it does not, think about why this might be. Bear in mind that some texts have more than one story – the less important ones are known as sub-plots.

Text organisation

Text organisation is often closely related to story structure. In a play, the writer often puts a turning point at the end of a scene or act as a sort of mini climax. This is especially effective when there is an interval – for instance at the theatre or during a television drama – as it leaves the audience wondering what will happen next. Novelists, too, use chapters or other divisions to reflect the structure of their plot.

When you are discussing structure, it is not enough simply to say what you have spotted about it, for example 'the novel is divided into 20 chapters' or 'there are four stanzas of equal length'. You need to think about the effect of the way the story is structured and the text is organised. It can be especially useful to look at anything unusual in the structure.

You might think about whether the story is told in chronological order. Quite a few novels, for example *Wuthering Heights*, start towards the end of the story. Lockwood is intrigued by what he sees at Wuthering Heights and asks Nelly to tell him the story. How does this help to create atmosphere and intrigue the reader? Dickens, on the other hand, starts *David Copperfield* with the birth of his protagonist and we follow his adventures in chronological order. What effect does this have on the reader's reaction to David and his story?

You should carefully consider the beginning and ending of your text. Examiners quite often set questions that focus on these aspects of structure. How successful is the opening in terms of intriguing the reader? How successfully does it establish the world of the text? Does it try to shock or surprise you? Or does it lead you gently into the story?

Does the ending bring together all the strands of the plot and resolve them neatly? Or does it leave us with more questions than answers? Does it refer back to the beginning and, if so, how? How does it leave us feeling?

If there is a sub-plot, you might look at how the two stories are told. Are they told separately and brought together at the end? Is one of them told in flashback? Does one of the stories illuminate the other?

Effective comments on structure – examples

Here are some examples of effective comments on structure.

> By describing his own birth, which, as he points out, he cannot possibly remember, the eponymous hero and narrator of 'David Copperfield' sets a friendly and reassuring tone for the rest of the novel. This opening chapter seems to invite us into his world, making confidants of us and immediately endearing him to us so that we are 'on his side' from the start.

COMMENTARY

This student is commenting on the beginning of the novel, telling us how it starts and discussing the effectiveness of the opening in influencing the reader's response to the text as a whole.

Coming immediately after the Capulets' ball, this scene, which will prove a turning point in the play, changes the mood quickly. With Romeo left alone on the stage, it is quiet and dark, in contrast with the torches, music, laughter and arguments of the previous scene.

COMMENTARY

In this example, the student places the scene under discussion in the context of the play as a whole. Two aspects of structure are mentioned – the juxtaposition of two contrasting scenes and the scene's importance as a turning point in the plot.

The poem consists of six stanzas of varying lengths, each of the first five describing, in chronological order, a stage in the action from the first charge ('Forward the Light Brigade!') to the tragic return 'Back from the mouth of Hell'. Telling the story in this apparently simple way adds to the power of the poem as we share the Brigade's excitement, fear and disappointment. In the final stanza, Tennyson invites us to reflect on what happened and 'Honour the Light Brigade'.

COMMENTARY

This candidate tells us how the poet has organised his story and comments on the effect the clear and straightforward structure has on a reader.

Structure can also refer to the arrangement of the text into sentences, clauses and phrases, including how punctuation is used. In poetry it covers rhyme and metre. Here, as with the arrangement of stanzas, you should look for patterns. Are the rhyme scheme and metre regular? If so, what effect does this have? If not, what effect does the lack of a regular pattern or a departure from the usual pattern have?

Here is an example of an effective comment on this aspect of structure.

In Wordsworth's 'The Affliction of Margaret', each stanza comprises a quatrain (four lines rhyming alternately) and a rhyming triplet. The unbroken regularity of this structure could reflect the predictability of Margaret's existence, with the unusual triplet, where we might expect a rhyming couplet, possibly helping to convey her sense of hopelessness and helplessness. It is as if the stanza just goes on a little too long and remains unresolved.

COMMENTARY

This student has worked out how Wordsworth's rhyme scheme works – using the correct terms to describe it – and explains how its use helps to create a mood and convey the feelings of his persona.

KEY POINT

It is important not only to comment on the structure of the text, but also to show how the structure shapes or creates meaning.

Writing about form

AQA A	U 1, 2, 3, 4
AQA B	U 1, 2, 3, 4
Edexcel	U 1, 2, 3, 4
OCR	U 1, 2, 3, 4
WJEC	U 1, 2, 3, 4
CCEA	AS U1, AS U2, A2 U1, A2 U2

Form and structure are very closely related. In fact, a dictionary definition of form includes 'the arrangement of parts … kind, variety … method', so the section on text organisation above could just as easily come under the heading of form. Indeed, Chris Baldick in *The Concise Oxford Dictionary of Literary Terms* describes form as 'a critical term with a confusing variety of meanings'.

However, in literary criticism, form is also used to describe the kind of text that is being discussed, and is related to the concept of genre. The structure of a text and the kind of language used are to some extent dictated by – or reflect the conventions and traditions of – a particular form or genre. You will find out more about genre in relation to literary traditions and historical context in Chapter 5.

Forms of prose, poetry and drama

On a basic level, we could say that a text is in the form of prose, poetry or drama.

Forms of prose include the short story, the novel and novella, as well as non-fiction forms such as autobiography, biography, travel writing or diaries. Each of these forms has its own conventions, which a writer might choose to follow or might subvert. The same is true of the conventions of genre. In a **bildungsroman** (a novel about growing up), we would probably expect a first person narrative in chronological order. This is exactly what we get in *David Copperfield* and *Jane Eyre*. We might expect a gothic novel to use language and structure to create fear and tension, probably centred on an innocent young woman in danger. However, writers such as Angela Carter have in recent years employed the conventions of the form to subvert it. Carter and many other writers have used the traditional form of the fairy tale in a similar way.

Plays are often categorised into forms such as tragedy and comedy. The basic conventions of tragedy and comedy were established in ancient Greece and were adhered to closely by writers such as Sophocles and Euripides. Later writers such as Shakespeare and his contemporaries developed the forms in their own ways, and we now speak of Shakespearean tragedy and Shakespearean comedy (see Chapter 7). Shakespeare also blurred the lines between comedy and tragedy and writers have continued to do so. You might have heard of tragicomedy, romantic comedy, kitchen-sink drama and absurd drama, among many other genres.

In poetry, there are certain forms with fixed rules. To many poets, writing within a strict form is part of the fun and challenge of writing a poem. Poetic forms that you have probably come across include the ballad and sonnet. Both of these forms have been used by many of the great poets of the past, and continue to be used today.

Writing about form – examples

Here are two examples of how you might write about form.

> In the first quatrain of Sonnet 116, Shakespeare states his case about love, saying that love which changes easily 'is not love'. In the second, he says that, on the contrary, love is 'an ever-fixed mark', creating a strong image of hope as well as security. In the third, he makes a statement about love and time, asserting that true love is eternal. He ends with a resounding rhyming couplet that

challenges anyone to contradict him. This use of the sonnet form imposes a sense of order on his thoughts, his emotions contained by the strict form, and his argument strengthened by the sense of control it gives.

COMMENTARY

The student mentions the form by name and makes it clear that she is secure in her understanding of the form of the Shakespearean sonnet (three quatrains and a couplet). She analyses how the poet uses the form to put his case, and the effect of his adherence to the 'rules' of the form.

The following example is from an essay comparing two nineteenth-century plays – *Hedda Gabler* by Henrik Ibsen and *Miss Julie* by August Strindberg.

> This passage includes quotations from the author's preface. The mark scheme gives credit for references to 'other sources', meaning sources other than the text itself.

The suicides of Miss Julie and Hedda Gabler vividly express the differences between Strindberg and Ibsen. Strindberg called his play a 'naturalistic tragedy'. It is far from the classical ideas of tragedy: Miss Julie's death represents her total defeat and is the inevitable conclusion to the play. Strindberg says in his preface: 'I saw in it the ingredients of a tragic drama. To see an individual on whom fortune has heaped an abundance of gifts go to her ruin and destruction leaves us with a tragic feeling.' The act of suicide is not heroic, however, but 'the hara-kiri of the middle classes'. It is not the climax of a heroic drama …

COMMENTARY

Here, the student is using his understanding of the tragic genre – particularly its classical roots – as a way of analysing two plays with similar themes. He is arguing that the classical idea of tragedy implies that there is a heroism in suicide and, as there is none in Miss Julie's suicide, he wonders how far the play can be described as a tragedy.

KEY POINT

The word 'form' has many meanings in criticism. Bear in mind the sense in which it means genre, as well as the sense in which it means structure.

PROGRESS CHECK

Consider the texts you are studying. How would you describe them in terms of form and genre? Do they follow closely a particular genre's conventions, do they seek to change or subvert them in some way, or do they draw on more than one genre?

Writing about language

AQA A	**U 1, 2, 3, 4**
AQA B	**U 1, 2, 3, 4**
Edexcel	**U 1, 2, 3, 4**
OCR	**U 1, 2, 3, 4**
WJEC	**U 1, 2, 3, 4**
CCEA	**AS U1, AS U2,**
	A2 U1, A2 U2

Whatever kind of text you are writing about, you should always comment on and analyse the way the writer uses language to create meaning. You should be as precise as you can and always root your comments firmly in the text. Think about why the writer chose a particular word or group of words, considering meaning, sound and connotation.

How language is spoken

You might notice that a text is not written entirely in Standard English. This could be because it is a first person narrative and the writer wants to adopt the speech patterns appropriate to the narrator's background. It may be that different characters in a novel or play speak differently, their vocabulary telling us about the differences between them.

Vocabulary and syntax

Sometimes a text will use vocabulary and syntax that is unfamiliar or difficult. It could be simply because it was written a long time ago (such as a text by Chaucer), but it might be that the writer is using **archaic expressions** because the text is set in the past. He or she might use specialised or **technical diction** to reflect the professions or jobs of certain characters.

How words sound

You should always pay close attention to the sound of words. This is especially important in poetry, but can also be significant in prose and drama. In descriptive passages, particularly, writers may use alliteration, assonance or onomatopoeia to make their meaning clear, and to make the experience or scene described more vivid for the reader.

Imagery

Imagery is also important for conveying atmosphere or emotion. Whether you are discussing **literal imagery** – which describes a 'real' scene – or **figurative imagery** – which uses an image of one thing to tell us about another thing – you should look for patterns and themes, and consider the effect of the writer's choice of imagery. You might find techniques such as **personification**, **symbolism** or **pathetic fallacy** in the text you are studying.

Writing about language – examples

Whatever linguistic techniques are employed in your texts, remember that you do not get marks simply for spotting them and naming them. You should, of course, always use the correct terminology (see pages 46–49), but it is more important to analyse a writer's use of language and discuss its effect.

Here are some examples of how you might comment on a writer's language. The first is from an essay about Coleridge's poem *Kubla Khan*.

> The 'stately pleasure dome' is an image of beauty created in the wilderness. It is described in images of fertility and cultivated natural beauty, opposed to the powerful images of the wilderness without: the caves and the 'sunless sea'. This harsh landscape is an image of infinity – a world beyond man's conception:
>
> Through caverns measureless to man
> Down to a sunless sea. (lines 4–5)

> Against this hostile landscape is set the creation of the pleasure dome, something concrete and beautiful, a world where man can feel at home and at rest, and shut out the bewildering vastness of the exterior 'with walls and towers' (l 7). This act of 'decreeing' the pleasure dome is analogous to the poet's act of creation ...

> When you discuss the connotations of words or phrases, you are discussing their implied meanings and associations. The same word might have different connotations for different people.

> **COMMENTARY**
>
> This candidate has identified patterns in the imagery – images of fertility and barrenness – and tries to explain how these opposing images convey the poet's ideas about creation. He might also have commented on the seductive use of alliteration – the sibilance of 'sunless sea' and the gentle humming sound of the 'm' sounds in 'measureless to man'.

The next example considers D.H. Lawrence's use of sound in *Storm in the Black Forest*.

The poem moves from the heavy 'o' sounds of 'bronzey soft sky' to the short, sharp sound of the 'i' in 'liquid fire, Bright white'. So from the still, heavy sky the lightning strikes and the atmosphere changes with the change in sound.

> **COMMENTARY**
>
> This student has, very economically, explained how Lawrence uses assonance to convey the different stages of the storm.

> **KEY POINT**
>
> Good writers choose their words carefully. Their choice of language creates mood and atmosphere, as well as shaping meaning.

> **PROGRESS CHECK**
>
> Look at an essay you have written recently and highlight places where you have commented on structure, form and language. Do you think your comments are sufficiently analytical?

2.2 Referring to the text

LEARNING SUMMARY	**After studying this section, you should be able to:** ● understand the importance of referring closely to the text ● understand what is meant by paraphrasing, and when you might use it ● have confidence in how you should use quotations ● understand PEE (point, evidence, explanation) more fully

The importance of referring closely to the text

AQA A	U 1, 2, 3, 4
AQA B	U 1, 2, 3, 4
Edexcel	U 1, 2, 3, 4
OCR	U 1, 2, 3, 4
WJEC	U 1, 2, 3, 4
CCEA	AS U1, AS U2, A2 U1, A2 U2

AO1 states that your responses to texts should be 'informed and relevant'. You can convince the examiner that your views are informed and relevant by rooting them firmly in the text. Effective references to the text provide the evidence you need to persuade the examiner of the value of your arguments.

Candidates who achieve Grade A are expected to 'consistently make reference to specific texts and sources to support their responses'.

Your evidence can be in the form of a paraphrase or a direct quotation.

Paraphrasing

AQA A	U 1, 2, 3, 4
AQA B	U 1, 2, 3, 4
Edexcel	U 1, 2, 3, 4
OCR	U 1, 2, 3, 4
WJEC	U 1, 2, 3, 4
CCEA	AS U1, AS U2, A2 U1, A2 U2

Paraphrasing – putting something into your own words – is a useful skill.

In an exam, it is particularly helpful to paraphrase if you cannot remember the exact words from a text. You might not be able to look up a quotation – either because you do not have the text with you (as is the case in some, but not all, AS and A2 examinations), or because it would take too long to find a reference.

If you are writing about a longer text, such as a novel, there are times when paraphrasing might seem more appropriate than direct quotation, perhaps because you are writing about an incident and the exact wording is not important.

Here is an example from an essay on Emily Brontë's *Wuthering Heights*.

> When Catherine returns from Thrushcross Grange, there is a marked change in her attitude and behaviour – to the delight of her brother and sister-in-law, and the dismay of Heathcliff. When Hindley asks him to shake hands with Catherine, she comments on his dirty hands and seems more concerned about her new dress than her old friend's feelings. Her changed appearance and manners make him aware for the first time of the difference between them in terms of social class, gaining him sympathy from the reader.

COMMENTARY

Here, a general point is made about the change in Catherine, followed by a precise, but paraphrased, reference to the incident that encapsulates this change. Finally, the candidate gives a convincing interpretation of the significance of the incident. Quoting Brontë's account of the incident in full would have taken too long and – as the incident itself is what matters, rather than the exact words used – would have served no useful purpose.

How to set out quotations

AQA A	U 1, 2, 3, 4
AQA B	U 1, 2, 3, 4
Edexcel	U 1, 2, 3, 4
OCR	U 1, 2, 3, 4
WJEC	U 1, 2, 3, 4
CCEA	AS U1, AS U2, A2 U1, A2 U2

> During an exam, this method is usually the best to use. You are more likely to remember significant words and short phrases.

> Only put words taken directly from the text inside the inverted commas.

When the writer's choice of words is important, you should present your evidence from the text in the form of **quotations** (note that quotation – not 'quote' – is the correct term). You will probably find that you tend to quote directly from poems and plays more often than you do from prose.

The three methods you should use to set out quotations are explained below (the examples are taken from Shakespeare's *A Midsummer Night's Dream*):

1. If your quotation consists of just a few words (or even one word) and fits naturally into a sentence without spoiling the sense, put it in single inverted commas (also known as 'quotation marks'). This method is often referred to as **embedding**.

> In the opening scene, Theseus expresses both his eagerness to marry Hippolyta and the strength of his sexual desire by complaining about 'how slow/ this old moon wanes!' (lines 3–4). The reference to the moon reminds us both of Hippolyta's virginity and her prowess as a warrior, both attributes of the goddess Diana, with whom the moon is closely associated. He goes on to compare the moon to a 'step-dame or dowager' (line 5), who, while she lives, prevents a young man from inheriting wealth. This simile is both comic and rather unflattering, but vividly expresses his attitude to having to wait until he is married to fulfil his 'desires'.

2. If the quotation will not fit easily and logically into a sentence, but is fairly short (no more than one line of verse or 40 words of prose), put a colon (:) before the quotation, continue on the same line, and use inverted commas.

    Demetrius makes plain his feelings both to her and the audience: 'I love thee not, therefore pursue me not' (Act 2, Scene 1, line 188). This, his first line on entering the forest, tells us that Helena's plan has backfired, and sets the tone for the pursuits and misunderstandings that will follow.

3. If you want to use a longer quotation, leave a line and indent. You must indent the whole quotation and, when quoting verse, end the lines where they end in the original. You do not need to use inverted commas.

    Hermia's father, Egeus, is scornful of the way in which Lysander has wooed his daughter:

    > *Thou, thou, Lysander, thou hast given her rhymes*
    > *And interchang'd love-tokens with my child.*

    (Act 1, Scene 1, lines 29–30)

    The actions which he goes on to list might seem to the audience to be proof of Lysander's devotion and the strength of his feelings, rather than of deviousness. Egeus, however, is completely unaware that he is making himself appear unreasonable and unsympathetic.

> Make sure you spell and punctuate exactly as in the text.

As you can see, the method you use to set out your quotations will depend on the length of the quotation and how it fits into your sentence.

If a short quotation runs across two lines, indicate the line break with / (see example 1 above).

If you start a quotation part way into a line or sentence, or omit part of the line or sentence, show that you have done so by using an ellipsis (…), for example: 'Thou hast … interchang'd love-tokens with my child.'

Setting out quotations – example

Below is a stanza from William Blake's *The Chimney Sweeper* (from *Songs of Experience*), and two sentences from an essay about it. The sentences do not include references to the text. Re-write them, including a quotation from the poem, using each of the three methods for setting out quotations described above and on the previous page.

> *A little black thing among the snow,*
> *Crying 'weep! weep!' in notes of woe!*
> *'Where are thy father and mother? Say?'*
> *'They are both gone up to the church to pray.'*

When the speaker asks the sweep about his parents, his response is disturbing. Here, the church clearly has nothing to do with care or charity, rather seeming to accept, or even approve, the plight of the chimney sweeper.

> **COMMENTARY**
>
> Here are some possible answers:
>
> 1 When the speaker asks the sweep, 'Where are thy father and mother?', his response is disturbing. The fact that they have 'gone up to the church to pray' suggests that the church has nothing to do with care and charity, rather seeming to accept, or even approve, the plight of the chimney sweeper.
>
> 2 When the speaker asks the sweep about his parents, his response is disturbing: 'They are both gone up to the church to pray.' The church clearly has nothing to do with care or charity, rather seeming to accept, or even approve, the plight of the chimney sweeper.
>
> 3 When the speaker asks the sweep about his parents, his response is disturbing:
>
> > 'Where are thy father and mother? Say?'
> > 'They are both gone up to the church to pray.'
>
> The church here clearly has nothing to do with care and charity, rather seeming to accept, or even approve, the chimney sweeper's plight.

Line and page references for quotations

If you can, give line references for a play. This will not be possible in a 'closed book' examination, but can be helpful in coursework or an 'open book' exam. You do not need act and scene references if it is obvious which scene you are referring to (if the whole essay is about one scene, for example, or if you have just referred to the scene). It can also be helpful to give line references when quoting from a poem, especially a longer one.

For a novel, particularly in coursework, give page references. If you have not been told which edition of the novel to use, you may need to say which edition you have used in the bibliography at the end of your essay.

> **KEY POINT**
>
> It is essential that you refer closely to the text. There are several ways of doing this, and you should become familiar with them.

Understanding and developing the use of PEE

AQA A	**U 1, 2, 3, 4**
AQA B	**U 1, 2, 3, 4**
Edexcel	**U 1, 2, 3, 4**
OCR	**U 1, 2, 3, 4**
WJEC	**U 1, 2, 3, 4**
CCEA	**AS U1, AS U2, A2 U1, A2 U2**

You are probably familiar with **PEE** from your GCSE course and have a pretty good idea of how to use it.

As a reminder, PEE stands for:

- Point
- Evidence
- Explanation.

To use PEE, you make your new point, back it up with a reference to the text, and then explain (or explore) how the evidence illustrates your point. In this respect, you should be doing exactly the same thing in your AS and A2 work as you did at GCSE level, although by now your points should be more interesting and original, your evidence more appropriate, and your explanations more sophisticated.

The performance descriptors for A2 stress that good candidates should make reference to the text 'to support their responses'. AO2 is about '**analysing** the ways in which structure, form and language shape meanings'. Being analytical in this way is vital to show an understanding of how and why you are referring to the text. You are not using PEE just to show that you are familiar with the text. You are doing so to support a point you have made – to convince the reader that your point is valid – so a quotation must be carefully chosen to support your point. When you have done so, you should use it as a stimulus for further discussion and analysis, demonstrating a thorough understanding of the writer's style and techniques.

PEE – an example

Look again at the example from page 41, which we have reproduced below.

> In the opening scene, Theseus expresses both his eagerness to marry Hippolyta and the strength of his sexual desire by complaining about 'how slow/ this old moon wanes!' (lines 3–4). The reference to the moon reminds us both of Hippolyta's virginity and her prowess as a warrior, both attributes of the goddess Diana, with whom the moon is closely associated. He goes on to compare the moon to a 'step-dame or dowager' (line 5), who, while she lives, prevents a young man from inheriting wealth. This simile is both comic and rather unflattering, but vividly expresses his attitude to having to wait until he is married to fulfil his 'desires'.

COMMENTARY

This example uses two quotations. The first part can be divided into PEE as follows:

- **Point** – Theseus expresses both his eagerness to marry Hippolyta and the strength of his sexual desire.
- **Evidence** – complaining about 'how slow/ this old moon wanes!'.
- **Explanation** – the reference to the moon reminds us both of Hippolyta's virginity and her prowess as a warrior, both attributes of the goddess Diana, with whom the moon is closely associated.

The **point** introduces the idea that sexual desire and marriage are important themes of the play, introduced at this early stage through the impending marriage of Theseus and Hippolyta.

The **evidence**, in the form of a quotation, backs up the student's point that Theseus is driven by his desire, but will wait, however impatiently, for marriage.

The **explanation** focuses on Theseus's language, exploring the connotations of his imagery within the play's context.

If you look at the second part of the paragraph and try to divide it into point, evidence and explanation, you will discover that there is no 'point'. This is because the point is the same as the one made at the beginning of the paragraph. The student is reinforcing the point already made, with further evidence and more analysis.

PROGRESS CHECK

Look again at the second and third examples taken from the essay on *A Midsummer Night's Dream* (see page 42). Divide them into point, evidence and explanation, and think about how effective they are.

Example 2:
- **Point** – Demetrius makes plain his feelings, both to her and the audience.
- **Evidence** – 'I love thee not, therefore pursue me not.'
- **Explanation** – This, his first line on entering the forest, tells us that Helena's plan has backfired, and sets the tone for the pursuits and misunderstandings that will follow.

Example 3:
- **Point** – Hermia's father, Egeus, is scornful of the way in which Lysander has wooed his daughter.
- **Evidence** – 'Thou, thou, Lysander, thou hast given her rhymes And interchang'd love-tokens with my child.'
- **Explanation** – The actions which he goes on to list might seem to the audience to be proof of Lysander's devotion and the strength of his feelings, rather than of deviousness. Egeus, however, is completely unaware that he is making himself appear unreasonable and unsympathetic.

2.3 Using appropriate terminology and concepts

LEARNING SUMMARY

After studying this section, you should be able to:

- appreciate the importance of using appropriate literary terminology
- understand more fully a range of literary terms and concepts

The importance of using appropriate terminology

AQA A	U 1, 2, 3, 4
AQA B	U 1, 2, 3, 4
Edexcel	U 1, 2, 3, 4
OCR	U 1, 2, 3, 4
WJEC	U 1, 2, 3, 4
CCEA	AS U1, AS U2, A2 U1, A2 U2

The use of appropriate terminology is an important element of AO1 and applies to all units of both AS and A2. To be able to write effectively about literary texts, you need the tools to do so. One of these tools is familiarity with the specialised vocabulary critics use to discuss literature. Some of these terms describe big and quite complicated ideas, while others define precise uses of language or form. Some are used to label genres or literary traditions. Others might help you express ideas about characters or settings.

You are probably familiar with more literary terms than you realise. You will have been using some of them (like metaphor and alliteration) since you were at primary school. You will have come across others more recently, perhaps in discussions about your set texts or in your reading of critical works. When you hear a literary term for the first time, it is important to ask your teacher or lecturer what it means, or look it up yourself. Dictionary definitions do not always give you the information you need to understand specialised vocabulary – it is better to use a dictionary of literary terms. There are several of these on the market and, for anyone who is serious about studying literature, a dictionary of literary terms is a very good investment.

Remember that you do not receive credit simply for knowing literary terms. You must be able to use them appropriately and with confidence. If you are unsure about whether a term or concept is appropriate, or are confused about its meaning, do not try to use it in an examination. Your coursework options, on the other hand, provide a great opportunity for you to practise using appropriate terminology and concepts.

Using appropriate terminology – examples

Here are some passages that include examples of literary terminology. The terminology has been highlighted to help you understand how to use it properly. The extracts have all been previously used in this chapter to illustrate other skills.

> The 'stately pleasure dome' is an <u>image</u> of beauty created in the wilderness. It is described in <u>images</u> of fertility and cultivated natural beauty, opposed to the powerful <u>images</u> of the wilderness without: the caves and the 'sunless sea'. This harsh landscape is an image of infinity – a world beyond man's conception…

> The suicides of Miss Julie and Hedda Gabler vividly express the differences between Strindberg and Ibsen. Strindberg called his play a '<u>naturalistic tragedy</u>'. It is far from the classical ideas of <u>tragedy</u>: Miss Julie's death represents her total defeat and is the inevitable conclusion to the play.

> He ends with a resounding <u>rhyming couplet</u> that challenges anyone to contradict him. This use of the <u>sonnet form</u> imposes a sense of order on his thoughts, his emotions contained by the strict form, and his argument strengthened by the sense of control it gives.

COMMENTARY

In all these cases, the literary terms are used with confidence, the references showing that the students know what they mean. In the first example, the student comments on the kind of images used by the poet. The second passage introduces a concept used by the playwright and applies it to the play. The third student clearly demonstrates understanding, not only of what form a sonnet takes, but also of the effect its use can have.

Glossary of literary terms

AQA A	**U 1, 2, 3, 4**
AQA B	**U 1, 2, 3, 4**
Edexcel	**U 1, 2, 3, 4**
OCR	**U 1, 2, 3, 4**
WJEC	**U 1, 2, 3, 4**
CCEA	**AS U1, AS U2, A2 U1, A2 U2**

The following list contains some literary terms that you might find useful when writing about your texts. You should have encountered most of them before, but some may be new to you. You will also find the terms used throughout this book.

It may help you to read through this list when you are revising for an exam. You can also, of course, refer back to the list as you work your way through the book.

Alliteration: repetition of a sound at the beginning of words, e.g. 'river rushing rapidly'.

Ambiguity: the effect of a word or phrase that has more than one possible meaning (i.e. it is ambiguous).

Antagonist: someone who is opposed to the protagonist.

Anti-hero: a central character who does not have the qualities usually associated with a 'hero'.

Antithesis: direct opposite.

Aside: a line or two addressed to the audience by a character in a play.

Always bear in mind that literary criticism is not about labelling and categorising. Different people might have different ideas about whether a certain concept or term applies. For example, one critic might describe a novel as picaresque, but another would disagree. A third critic might decide that it has elements of the picaresque.

Assonance: repetition of a vowel sound within words, e.g. 'how now brown cow', in order to convey a mood or feeling.

Bildungsroman: a text, usually a novel, that describes the childhood and education of the central character.

Caesura: A pause in a line of poetry, usually shown by a punctuation mark.

Cliché: a phrase or opinion that is over-used.

Colloquial language: informal language – the sort of language used in conversation; it may include dialect words or phrases.

Connotation: a meaning that is suggested by the use of a word or phrase because of what is associated with it, e.g. red might indicate danger.

Couplet: a pair of lines in poetry.

Dialect: words or phrases particular to a region or area.

Dialogue: conversation, especially in a play.

Diction: the kind of words and phrases used, e.g. formal diction, violent diction, technical diction.

Dramatic irony: irony of situation, where the audience knows more than the character.

Elegy (*adjective* **elegiac**): a poem of mourning, originally for a friend or well-known figure. It can also be a poem that reflects on death and passing time in a melancholy mood.

Elision: running a word into others, e.g. 'fish 'n' chips'.

End-stopped: brought to an end, when a line of poetry ends at the end of a sentence or clause (as opposed to enjambment).

Enjambment: when a clause or sentence runs from one line of poetry to another, i.e. not stopping at the end of the line.

Eye rhyme (*or* **sight rhyme**): where words look as though they rhyme but do not, e.g. bear/fear.

Genre: a specific type of writing, with its own conventions, e.g. detective story, romance, science fiction.

Half rhyme: an 'imperfect' rhyme, where the consonants agree but the vowels do not, e.g. swans/stones.

Hyperbole: exaggeration.

Imagery: 'painting a picture' in words, using descriptive language, metaphors or similes.

Imperatives: commands or instructions, e.g. 'Don't do that!' or 'fry for ten minutes'.

Irony and **sarcasm**: the use of words to imply the opposite of their meaning.

Juxtaposition: putting words or phrases (often contrasting) next to each other.

Lineation: arrangement in lines that are stopped at the end (end-stopping).

Litotes: an understatement made by denying the opposite of something (a type of irony), e.g. 'no mean feat' or 'not averse to a drink'.

Metaphor: an image created by referring to something as something else, e.g. 'an **army** of nettles'.

Metre: the formal arrangement of a poem's rhythm, e.g. iambic pentameter.

Narrative: a story or an account of something.

Narrator: the person who tells a story.

- **First person narrator**: a narrator who is present in the story, using the pronoun 'I'.

- **Intrusive narrator**: a narrator who occasionally interrupts a third person narrative to make comments – usually an omniscient narrator, assumed to be the author.

- **Naïve narrator**: a narrator who does not understand what is going on.

- **Omniscient narrator**: a narrator who knows everything and can tell us about the thoughts and feelings of all the characters.

- **Unreliable narrator**: a narrator who may not be telling the truth.

Onomatopoeia: a word that sounds like what it describes, e.g. splash, clang, click.

Oxymoron: two contradictory words placed together, e.g. 'cold fire', 'bitter sweet'.

Paradox: a statement that is contradictory or seems to be nonsensical, but is true, e.g. 'to gain peace, they went to war'.

Pathetic fallacy: when the surroundings (e.g. the weather) reflect the mood of a character.

Pathos: the emotional quality of a text or part of it, causing feelings of pity, sympathy or sadness in the reader.

Persona: a 'voice' or character adopted by a writer writing in the first person.

Personification: writing about an object or animal or idea as if it were a person, giving it human qualities, e.g. 'the wind whispered', 'time will not wait for us'.

Picaresque novel: a novel that recounts the adventures of its protagonist in an episodic fashion.

Polemic: a written attack on an opinion or policy.

Protagonist: the main character.

Quatrain: a set of four lines of poetry.

Rhetorical question: a question that does not require an answer; used to make the listener think about an issue.

Rhythm: the beat of the writing, especially in poetry – fast or slow, regular or irregular.

Satire: writing that makes fun of people or society in order to criticise them.

Sibilance: the repetition of 'hissing' sounds, such as 's', 'sh' and 'zh'.

Simile: a direct comparison of one thing to another, using the words 'as', 'like' or 'than', e.g. 'as big **as** a house', '**like** an angry lion', 'faster **than** a speeding bullet'.

Soliloquy: a speech addressed to the audience by a character in a play, telling the audience what he/she really thinks.

Sonnet: a poem, usually a love poem, consisting of 14 lines.

Standard English: the conventional use of words and grammar in the English language – used in formal writing.

Stanza: a division in a poem; the equivalent of a paragraph in prose.

Structure: how a text or story is organised and arranged.

Symbol (symbolism): an object that represents an idea or feeling, e.g. a dove symbolises peace.

Tone: the overall feeling or attitude of the writing, e.g. formal, informal, sad, playful, angry, ironic.

Verse: poetry. The word is also used as an alternative to 'stanza'.

KEY POINT

Being able to use appropriate literary terminology with confidence is essential to success at AS and A-Level.

PROGRESS CHECK

1 Which literary terms would you use to describe the techniques used in the following quotations?
  a) 'Wild West Wind, thou breath of Autumn's being'
     (from *Ode to the West Wind* by Percy Bysshe Shelley).
  b) How well the skilful Gardner drew
     Of flow'r and herbes this Dial new
     (from *The Garden* by Andrew Marvell).
  c) 'Thou pure impiety and impious purity'
     (from *Much Ado About Nothing* by William Shakespeare).

1. a) Alliteration; personification.
b) Literal imagery; rhyming couplet.
c) Oxymoron.

Note – As this chapter is about writing analytically in all of your A-Level work, we have not included practice examination questions. There is a sample question and model answer on the next page in the style used for OCR Unit 3.

Sample question and model answer

1 '*Antony and Cleopatra* has more to do with politics than with love.' Evaluate the relationship between politics and love in the light of this view.

QUESTION OVERVIEW

This question is in the same style used for OCR Unit 3. The annotations to the student response refer to AO1 and AO2, which are reproduced below.

AO1: Articulate creative, informed and relevant responses to literary texts, using appropriate terminology and concepts, and coherent, accurate written expression.

AO2: Demonstrate detailed critical understanding in analysing the ways in which structure, form and language shape meanings in literary texts.

AO1: This is an effective opening paragraph, interrogating the question and introducing some of the main arguments that are to be pursued. The candidate also considers the concept of 'a history play' ('appropriate terminology and concepts').

There are many themes running through `Antony and Cleopatra' that suggest the play has a greater affinity with the `history' play than with any of the other categories that have been imposed on Shakespeare's work. The play deals with the relationship of private passions and relationships to the political world. In this it differs from `Romeo and Juliet', in which the lovers are directly opposed to the world and in which political reality works upon them with the tragic inevitability of Fate crushing insignificant mortals in its relentless progress. Antony and Cleopatra, however, do not fight against the world, but are shown in relation to it. We see how private actions shape history and how history affects, in turn, private lives. Antony and Cleopatra are history makers.

AO2: The reference to the framing of the action shows an understanding of form and structure.

In `Antony and Cleopatra', the interaction between public and private lives is seen from the point of view of the great. One of its most notable features is the constant framing of the action by the comments of observers and witnesses, or by the spreaders and hearers of reports. In this way their stature is established. They are essentially public figures - whatever they do is the stuff of public gossip, and they have no `real' private lives. The games of love and the games of politics are inextricably bound together.

In the world of power politics, personal relationships become a tool of diplomacy. Antony freely marries Octavia to cement the alliance between himself and Caesar. Family relationships are at the centre of Roman politics - a family quarrel can lead to war, just as a marriage can end a war. When Antony leaves Cleopatra for Rome, he gives as his reason the quarrels his first wife, Fulvia, has left behind, not the duty he owes to her memory as a husband:

> The business she hath broached in the state
> Cannot endure my absence
> (Act 1, Scene 2, lines 169-170)

At the same time we find respect and even affection exists between rivals. This is shown not only between Caesar and Antony, but also between them and Pompey. Politics and war are treated by these characters as a game played between great figures with its own peculiar code of honour, vividly demonstrated in Act 2, Scene 7, in the conversation between Pompey and Menas, which Pompey concludes with:

AO2: Language is analysed when the use of the word 'honour' is considered in the light of the play's setting.

> ... Thou must know
> `Tis not my profit that does lead my honour,
> Mine honour, it.
> (Act 2, Scene 7, lines 75-77)

By introducing the concept of honour, Menas reminds the audience of its importance in both personal and political dealings, perhaps causing us to question whether Antony and Cleopatra live by the same code.

Sample question and model answer (continued)

AO1: The first sentence of the paragraph picks up on the last sentence of the previous paragraph, helping to make the essay cohesive. The candidate's points are backed up by relevant and appropriate quotations, correctly laid out.

AO2: Here the candidate considers the idea of tragedy by comparing _Antony and Cleopatra_ to _Romeo and Juliet_. This shows an understanding of form. AO1: 'Tragedy' and 'tragic' are examples of the use of 'appropriate terminology and concepts'.

The paragraphs are linked by the expression 'somewhat different', clearly guiding the reader through the argument. Appropriate terminology is used – 'personae' and 'misogynistic'. AO2: These two paragraphs include detailed analysis of Shakespeare's language, considering how the connotations of words such as 'Egypt', 'whore' and 'gypsy' shape the meaning of the play and the audience's reaction.

The love of Antony and Cleopatra is not opposed to this world, but part of it. They are both politicians and Cleopatra, at least, plays the game of love together with the game of politics. Her approach from the first is political:

> She where he is, who's with him, what he does.
> I did not send you.
> (Act 1, Scene 1, lines 3-4)

This approach to love has tragic consequences when, in an attempt to regain Antony's love, she pretends death and he, believing the report, commits suicide. The woman who cannot help playing games with emotions the way she plays them with politics finally oversteps the mark. This episode recalls 'Romeo and Juliet', but is a mockery of that play's tragedy, because the tragic mistake is a result of deliberate trickery - frivolity in an inappropriate situation - not of unavoidable outside factors.

Cleopatra completes the interdependence of public and private lives by showing that she is not unwilling to use her private affairs to a public end. In her negotiations with Thyreus, she appears to be willing to give up Antony and take Caesar in his place. Antony's response is to recall how he found her 'as a morsel, cold upon/ dead Caesar's trencher' (Act 3, Scene 13, lines 116-117). In doing so, he labels her as nothing better than a whore, but this is not fair to Cleopatra. She is simply following her instinct for survival, an inborn, amoral and essentially political instinct. She is a politician as essentially as she is a woman. She is referred to as 'Egypt' and sees herself as Egypt, not as a private person. As such she can only ally herself with the powerful.

Antony's approach is somewhat different. Although he shows himself to be a master of diplomacy when dealing with Octavian and Pompey, the appearance of Cleopatra sends him mad. By following her sails he loses the battle, having already followed her misguided advice to fight by the sea. He wallows in her love and loses his political cool in the hot East. Politics and love cannot both be a part of his being, the way they are part of Cleopatra's. He does not understand her political amorality and reacts passionately to her doings in marked contrast to his cool dealings in Rome with Caesar and Octavia - in defeat he turns against her, considering himself 'beguil'd' by a 'false gypsy'. He has lost the game because he has not been able to reconcile the personae of lover and politician. Caesar complains that 'he hath given his empire/ Up to a whore' (Act 3, Scene 6, lines 55-56). The belittling and perhaps misogynistic terms they use help us to understand why they are so easily outmanoeuvred by Cleopatra. They see her womanhood as a weakness - she uses it as a weapon.

There is something impressive and magnificent about the love affairs of the powerful. True, we see the danger of giving power to people with ordinary human emotions, whose tyranny enables a whim to affect the world, but perhaps we also see more clearly the greatness of love and honour, and the dangers of jealousy and rivalry when they are magnified to this scale. Greatness or power is essential to Antony and Cleopatra. What they fear most is the indignity of defeat. Antony loves the glittering Egypt on her burnished throne, while Cleopatra loves the great Roman general. He dies not because he thinks his lover is dead, but because with defeat comes dishonour:

> ... Since Cleopatra died
> I have liv'd in such dishonour that the gods
> Detest my baseness.
> (Act 4, Scene 14, lines 55-62)

Sample question and model answer *(continued)*

Her supposed death drives him to kill himself, not because he cannot live without her, but because he does not want to be seen to `lack/ the courage of a woman´ (lines 59-60). Cleopatra, too, fears losing her greatness and her dignity more than losing Antony:

> ... Rather make
> My country's high pyramids my gibbet,
> Than hang me up in chains.
> (Act 5, Scene 2, lines 60-62)

Initially she tries to escape this fate by political means, but she sees at last that it was love that caused her and Antony's destruction. They lived as great ones and neither could go on living as anything less than great. As their love was bound up with their greatness, so they must rise above defeat with the greatness of their love intact. Their love is the love of two great politicians and, as such, tinged with the most earthly considerations, and open to the comment and censure of the world. But in death Cleopatra can at last sake of the less desirable parts of her political nature and keep only the glory of her love for Antony:

> I am fire, and air; my other elements
> I give to baser life.
> (Act 5, Scene 2, lines 288-289)

In the end, Antony and Cleopatra's love cannot survive the pressures of history and their part in it, but in this play love and politics are not necessarily opposing forces, nor is one more important than the other. Their relationship is symbiotic, but also destructive.

AO1: Throughout the essay, the candidate has maintained its cohesion and guided us through the argument by constantly referring back to the key words in the question, as well as by clearly indicating the relationship between paragraphs. The final paragraph seeks to bring the argument to a conclusion.

AO2: The candidate has not included very many direct references to form and structure, but the answer shows a confident understanding of the tragic genre. Language has been discussed in more detail, mainly in the 'E' part of PEE.

COMMENTARY

Now look at the grade descriptors for the top band of answers, taken from the mark scheme.

The AO1 grade descriptors are:
- consistently fluent and analytical writing
- confident engagement with the question in a well-structured, informed argument.

The AO2 grade descriptors are:
- consistently well informed and sophisticated understanding in analysing ways in which dramatic method, language, imagery, character construction and narrative structure generate meanings and effects.

Decide whether you think this answer deserves a top mark. If it does, why? If it does not, why not?

3 Comparing texts

The following topics are covered in this chapter:

- **Comparing texts at AS and A2**
- **Approaching the comparison**
- **Comparing poems**
- **Comparing full-length texts**
- **Types of exam questions**

3.1 Comparing texts at AS and A2

LEARNING SUMMARY

After studying this section, you should be able to:

- understand the kind of comparisons and connections you will be expected to make in each of the units you are studying
- recall the 'basics' of making comparisons

How comparing texts fits into your A-Level course

AQA A	U 1, 2, 3, 4
AQA B	U 1, 2, 3, 4
Edexcel	U 1, 2, 3, 4
OCR	U 1, 2, 3, 4
WJEC	U 1, 2, 3, 4
CCEA	AS U1, AS U2, A2 U1, A2 U2

> Intertextuality is a vital part of the study of English literature.

Individual texts are neither written nor read in isolation. Writers are influenced by the world around them, including their own reading. Readers, too, come to texts with knowledge of other texts. Therefore, making connections between texts is an important part of the study of English literature. This is often referred to as intertextuality.

AO3 requires you to 'explore connections between different literary texts, informed by the interpretations of other readers'. The second part of this requirement, 'interpretations of other readers', will be discussed in Chapter 4.

Unit requirements for comparing texts across specifications

All units of all specifications include some element of connecting and comparing texts, although the sort of texts you are asked to study and how you are asked to 'make connections' can differ widely. Possibly the most straightforward way of connecting texts is to compare two or three texts that you have studied and which are connected by theme, genre or period. You are probably used to doing this, as it is a major part of English Literature at GCSE level.

At AS level this kind of comparison is part of:
- **AQA A Unit 2** (Creative Study)
- **AQA B Unit 1** (Aspects of Narrative)
- **CCEA Unit 1** (The Study of Drama) and **Unit 2** (The Study of Poetry Written after 1800)
- **Edexcel Unit 1** (Explorations in Prose and Poetry) and **Unit 2** (Explorations in Drama).

For the following units you are required to study a 'core' and a 'partner' text, focusing on the core text but making connections and links with the partner text:
- **OCR Unit 1** (Poetry 1800–1945) and **Unit 2** (Literature Post-1900)
- **WJEC Unit 1** (Poetry and Drama 1) and **Unit 2** (Prose Study and Creative Reading).

In **AQA B Unit 1** (Texts in Context) you are asked to compare an unseen extract with texts you have studied, while in **AQA B Unit 2** (Dramatic Genres) there is no comparison as such, but you are expected to make connections to texts other than the one you have studied in depth.

At A2 level you are asked to compare two or three texts you have studied as part of:

- **AQA A Unit 4** (Extended Essay and Shakespeare Study)
- **AQA B Unit 3** (Texts and Genre) and **Unit 4** (Further and Independent Reading)
- **CCEA Unit 3** (The Study of Poetry from 1300–1800) and **Unit 4** (The Study of Prose – Theme Based)
- **Edexcel Unit 3** (Interpretations of Poetry and Prose)
- **OCR Unit 3** (Drama and Poetry Pre-1800) and **Unit 4** (Texts in Time)
- **WJEC Unit 3** (Poetry and Genre Study).

In **WJEC Unit 4** (Period or Genre Study), you are asked to compare core and partner texts, as well as comparing a text you have studied with an unseen text. **AQA Unit 3** (Reading for Meaning) requires a comparison of previously unseen extracts. **Edexcel Unit 4** (Reflections in Literary Studies) asks you to study one text in detail, drawing on other texts in your response.

Some of these units ask you to compare texts from the same period or genre (a genre in this case meaning poetry, prose or drama), or even by the same author. Other units specifically require the study of texts from different genres and/or different periods. Some have a list of set texts from which you make a choice, while others (usually coursework units) give you a fairly free choice. It is important – whether doing coursework or studying for an exam – that you are confident that the texts you have chosen fulfil the requirements of the particular unit you are doing. It is also vitally important that you know what format the questions from your specification will take. To help you, some examples of the style of question you might expect in each externally assessed unit are given at the end of this chapter, in Section 3.5 (see pages 69–74).

> **KEY POINT**
>
> Different units require you to connect texts to each other in different ways. Make sure you are familiar with the requirements of the units you are studying.

The basics of comparing texts

AQA A	U 1, 2, 3, 4
AQA B	U 1, 2, 3, 4
Edexcel	U 1, 2, 3, 4
OCR	U 1, 2, 3, 4
WJEC	U 1, 2, 3, 4
CCEA	AS U1, AS U2, A2 U1, A2 U2

Remember, when you are making connections and comparisons between texts, you need to:

- communicate clearly
- be prepared to comment on specific sections of texts and widen your comments to a consideration of whole texts
- consider thematic, generic and stylistic links and comparisons
- comment on differences as well as similarities
- discuss the ways in which form, structure and language shape meaning
- evaluate as well as analyse.

> **PROGRESS CHECK**
>
> Look up the requirements for your specification. Check that you are clear about which texts you will be comparing for the units you are studying.

3.2 Approaching the comparison

After studying this section, you should be able to:

- recognise what is involved in comparing texts
- identify the similarities and differences between your texts
- explain, analyse and evaluate these similarities and differences

What does comparison involve?

AQA A	U 1, 2, 3, 4
AQA B	U 1, 2, 3, 4
Edexcel	U 1, 2, 3, 4
OCR	U 1, 2, 3, 4
WJEC	U 1, 2, 3, 4
CCEA	AS U1, AS U2, A2 U1, A2 U2

Before you can really get to grips with comparing texts, you must read and study each of the texts carefully, looking at all the relevant features (that are discussed in this book) on the study of drama (see Chapter 6), Shakespeare (see Chapter 7), poetry (see Chapter 8) and prose (see Chapter 9). When you have developed a sound knowledge of the texts you are studying – usually two or thee texts – you will need to think carefully about the connections between them. Writing comparatively about two or three texts is inevitably a more complex process than writing about a single text. Sometimes, particularly under pressure in an exam, it may seem easier to write first about one text and then about the other, perhaps linking them in the final paragraph. However, this is not really comparative writing, and this approach rarely produces a satisfactory result, or one that will achieve a high mark.

As you are reading and studying texts, it is likely that you will note links, similarities or differences between them. However, in order to compare them fully it is useful to have some kind of framework that will help structure your thoughts and your work. Below is one suggested approach.

Identifying similarities and differences

AQA A	U 1, 2, 3, 4
AQA B	U 1, 2, 3, 4
Edexcel	U 1, 2, 3, 4
OCR	U 1, 2, 3, 4
WJEC	U 1, 2, 3, 4
CCEA	AS U1, AS U2, A2 U1, A2 U2

Here is one way in which you could approach your comparative study:

1. First, establish the major links and similarities between texts. Make sure that you are clear about similarities between them in terms of characters, themes or situations.
2. Go on to look at specific details, including:
   - themes
   - the narrative viewpoint
   - form and genre
   - structure
   - characters
   - dramatic techniques
   - settings
   - linguistic features
   - social and historical context
   - the tone of the writing
   - the writer's attitudes
   - other stylistic features.
3. When you have done this, consider the differences or contrasts between the texts using the same headings.

Explaining, analysing and evaluating the similarities and differences

Once you have broadly identified your texts' similarities and differences, you can move on to look at them a bit more closely.

Use the following prompts to help you analyse and explain the similarities and differences:

> Use appropriate connectives to establish the nature of the relationship between the texts you are comparing.

1. **Identify central contextual frameworks and structural features**, by:
   - looking at the general historical context within which each text was written
   - looking at the social structure within which each text is set
   - comparing the overall structure of each text.

2. **Describe and compare the features of each text**, by:
   - comparing the **characters** in each text – their roles, their significance within the scheme of the text, and their function in relation to other areas, such as the development of theme
   - analysing **thematic** links between the texts.

3. **Compare the ways in which language is used in each text**, e.g. through:
   - soliloquies
   - 'comic' scenes
   - diction/choice of vocabulary
   - Standard and non-Standard English/dialect
   - imagery
   - rhetorical features
   - pace
   - tone.

4. **Explore narrative or poetic or dramatic techniques, effects and meanings**, by looking at:
   - the effects created in each text
   - the techniques used to create these effects
   - the relationships between effects, themes and characters
   - the creation of 'meaning'.

5. **Use different levels of analysis**, by looking at:
   - different views of the texts
   - different interpretations of characters, themes and meanings
   - audience/reader responses.

6. **Evaluate the comparison – consider the success of each text**:
   - in terms of the various ideas and features described above
   - as a piece of narrative, poetry or drama
   - as a comment on the themes presented.

KEY POINT

Approach your comparison systematically, looking at a range of features of both texts.

PROGRESS CHECK

Now think about the pair or group of texts that you are studying. Using the methods described above, draw up a plan of how you are going to approach your comparative study of these texts. Make sure that you think about details such as the themes you are going to deal with, the characters, the use of language, etc.

3.3 Comparing poems

LEARNING SUMMARY

After studying this section, you should be able to:

- understand the types of questions about comparing poems that you will be asked in an examination
- apply strategies for comparing poems to your own work

What to expect in an examination

AQA A	U 1, 3
Edexcel	U 1
OCR	U 1
WJEC	U 1, 4
CCEA	AS U2, A2 U1

Unless you have been studying a very long poem (such as Milton's *Paradise Lost* or Wordsworth's *The Prelude*), you are unlikely to be asked to write about just one poem in an exam.

If you have studied a collection of poems (written either by a single poet or different poets), you might be asked to write about two or three specific poems from the collection. You could, however, be given a more general question, which allows you to decide which poems to discuss. In this case, it is a good idea to select three or four poems to compare and analyse in detail, perhaps referring to others briefly.

There is also a possibility that you could be asked to compare two poems that you have not previously seen, or to compare an unseen poem with poetry you have studied.

Strategies for comparing poems

AQA A	U 1, 3
Edexcel	U 1
OCR	U 1
WJEC	U 1, 4
CCEA	AS U2, A2 U1

One way of arranging your thoughts about the poems you are comparing is to complete a comparison table. Below is an example that you could use or adapt.

	Poem 1	Poem 2
Subject/theme		
Speaker/situation		
Form and structure		
Rhyme and rhythm		
Ideas/messages		
Tone/atmosphere/mood		
Imagery		
Vocabulary		
Sound effects		

How to compare poems – an example

The following poems – *Ode on a Grecian Urn* and *The Prelude* – are both from the Romantic tradition.

Read Keats's poem and the extract from *The Prelude* carefully. Then make notes and draw up a comparison table – there is a possible answer after the poems.

Ode on a Grecian Urn

Thou still unravish'd bride of quietness,
Thou foster-child of silence and slow time,
Sylvan historian, who canst thus express
A flowery tale more sweetly than our rhyme:
What leaf-fring'd legend haunts about thy shape
Of deities or mortals, or of both,
In Tempe or the dales of Arcady?
What men or gods are these? What maidens loth?
What mad pursuit? What struggle to escape?
What pipes and timbrels? What wild ecstasy?

Heard melodies are sweet, but those unheard
Are sweeter; therefore, ye soft pipes, play on;
Not to the sensual ear, but, more endear'd,
Pipe to the spirit ditties of no tone:
Fair youth, beneath the trees, thou canst not leave
Thy song, nor ever can those trees be bare;
Bold Lover, never, never canst thou kiss,
Though winning near the goal – yet, do not grieve;
She cannot fade, though thou hast not thy bliss,
For ever wilt thou love, and she be fair!

Ah, happy, happy boughs! that cannot shed
Your leaves, nor ever bid the Spring adieu;
And, happy melodist, unwearied,
For ever piping songs for ever new;
More happy love! more happy, happy love!
For ever warm and still to be enjoy'd,
For ever panting, and for ever young;
All breathing human passion far above,
That leaves a heart high-sorrowful and cloy'd,
A burning forehead, and a parching tongue.

Who are these coming to the sacrifice?
To what green altar, O mysterious priest,
Lead'st thou that heifer lowing at the skies,
And all her silken flanks with garlands drest?
What little town by river or sea shore,
Or mountain-built with peaceful citadel,
Is emptied of this folk, this pious morn?
And, little town, thy streets for evermore
Will silent be; and not a soul to tell
Why thou art desolate, can e'er return.

O Attic shape! Fair attitude! with brede
Of marble men and maidens overwrought,
With forest branches and the trodden weed;
Thou, silent form, dost tease us out of thought
As doth eternity: Cold Pastoral!
When old age shall this generation waste,
Thou shalt remain, in midst of other woe
Than ours, a friend to man, to whom thou say'st,
'Beauty is truth, truth beauty,' – that is all
ye know on earth, and all ye need to know.

The Prelude

Book 1 (1850)

And in the frosty season, when the sun
Was set, and visible for many a mile
The cottage windows blazed through twilight gloom,
I heeded not their summons: happy time
It was indeed for all of us – for me
It was a time of rapture! Clear and loud
The village clock tolled six, – I wheeled about,
Proud and exulting like an untired horse
That cares not for his home. All shod with steel,
We hissed along the polished ice in games
Confederate, imitative of the chase
And woodland pleasures, – the resounding horn,
The pack loud chiming, and the hunted hare.
So through the darkness and the cold we flew,
And not a voice was idle; with the din,
Smitten, the precipices rang aloud;
The leafless trees and every icy crag
Tinkled like iron; while far distant hills
Into the tumult sent an alien sound
Of melancholy not unnoticed, while the stars
Eastward were sparkling clear, and in the west
The orange sky of evening died away.

One possible answer is on the next page.

You will not have time to produce this sort of table in an exam, but it usually helps if you do a very brief plan before you start writing.

	Ode on a Grecian Urn	Extract from The Prelude
Subject/theme	Thoughts inspired by looking at the design on a Grecian urn.	An experience remembered from childhood.
Speaker/situation	First person. The poet describes what comes into his imagination when looking at the urn.	First person. The poet describes the experience of skating on a frozen lake.
Form and structure	Written as an ode with five ten-line stanzas.	An extract from a longer poem. No stanzas.
Rhyme and rhythm	The rhyme scheme gives a pattern and cohesion to the carefully ordered and developed thoughts. The regular rhythm (iambic pentameter) reinforces this.	The relative freedom of the verse (lack of rhyme) reflects the freedom the poet feels. The mostly regular rhythm (iambic pentameter) gives a sense of movement.
Ideas/messages	The first stanza creates an image. The second examines the 'unheard' pipes, the youth, the lover, the permanence and thus the impossibility of change in the design. The third compares the representation to nature, music and love. Stanza four examines the other figures on the urn, and the final stanza reiterates Keats's central idea that 'Beauty is truth'.	A vivid description of the scene as an almost spiritual experience. The imagery creates a strong sense of time and place and exultation.
Tone/atmosphere/mood	The poem has a meditative tone as the poet ponders on abstract ideas.	The tone is one of excitement, vitality, movement and life.
Imagery	The poem uses the imagery of the urn and the scene, which he almost brings to life.	The images reflect the natural scene (the image of the wheeling horse, the frozen hills).
Vocabulary	Words such as 'love', 'beauty', 'happy' and 'truth' suggest that he is dealing with deep and important issues.	'Rapture', 'wheeled' and 'exulting' capture the sense of movement and joy.
Sound effects	Sense of languor and almost depression created by sounds.	Assonance, alliteration and onomatopoeia add to the immediacy of the experience.

KEY POINT

These are quite basic notes. When you are comparing poems in this way, you will need to complete a much deeper analysis.

PROGRESS CHECK

Complete a comparison table for two poems that you have studied.

3.4 Comparing full-length texts

LEARNING SUMMARY	After studying this section, you should be able to:
	• compare prose texts with more confidence
	• compare drama texts with more confidence
	• compare texts from different genres with more confidence
	• compare extracts from longer texts with more confidence

Unit requirements for comparing prose texts across specifications

AQA B	U 1	WJEC	U 2
Edexcel	U 1	CCEA	A2 U2
OCR	U 2		

The kinds of texts you are most likely to be asked to compare are novels. However, you may also study non-fiction works such as biographies or collections of shorter pieces, possibly short stories.

Three of the examination boards (**CCEA**, **Edexcel** and **WJEC**) have units where candidates are required to compare two prose texts.

For both **Edexcel** and **WJEC**, you are expected to focus primarily on one (core) text and use the other (partner) text to inform and illuminate your response to the main text. It is advisable to spend roughly 75 percent of your essay discussing the core text, but make sure that you refer to the partner text throughout the essay.

For **AQA B** and **OCR**, there is an option of writing about prose texts, although in both cases you are allowed to write about texts from any genre.

Comparing prose texts

When you start to write a comparison between novels or other longer prose texts, you should follow the principles that were established earlier in this chapter (see pages 54–56). As with other texts, the first thing that you must do when comparing novels is to establish what they are about. Look for a common theme between them. Look for similarities in their styles. Once you are clear about the broad connections, you need to look for more detailed similarities and differences. It is also a good idea to identify key passages and quotations from the text that illustrate your ideas.

You could then try to draw up a table reminding you of the main similarities and differences. The one below is similar to the one we used for comparing poetry in Section 3.3 (see page 57).

	Novel 1	Novel 2
Subject		
Narrative style		
Form and structure		
Genre		
Setting		
Ideas/messages		
Tone/atmosphere/mood		
The protagonist		
The roles of men and women		
Use of language		
Social and historical context		

It is more than likely that a question – whether for coursework or an exam – will ask you to focus on a particular aspect of the texts, for example genre, narrative style or the presentation of character. Of course, if you are studying your text for an exam you will not know what the focus is. If, however, you are planning a coursework essay, you will be able to draw up your table with the question in mind. Remember, though, that just because the question foregrounds a particular aspect of the novel (e.g. its genre), it does not mean that you should ignore other aspects (e.g. narrative style or language). It just means that your discussion of these things always refers back to the main focus of the question. For more detailed guidance on studying prose, see Chapter 9.

Comparing prose texts – an example

Here is an example of a comparison table for Emily Brontë's *Wuthering Heights* and Mary Shelley's *Frankenstein*.

> If you are writing about a novel, remember to refer to it as 'the novel' rather than 'the book' or 'the story'.

	Wuthering Heights	*Frankenstein*
Subject	The story of two generations affected by the arrival of Heathcliff.	The story of a man who creates a monster.
Narrative style	Multiple first person narratives.	Multiple first person narratives.
Form and structure	Starts near the end and looks back – stories within a story – letters.	Starts near the end and looks back – stories within a story – letters.
Genre (literary tradition)	Gothic romance? Victorian novel.	Romantic – gothic.
Setting	Yorkshire – the moors, Wuthering Heights, Thrushcross Grange.	Switzerland – the Arctic – Britain.
Ideas/messages	Tragic love – social class- nature and nurture.	Playing God – nature and nurture – the role of science.
Tone/atmosphere/mood	Brooding – intense – romantic – tragic.	Adventurous – frightening – foreboding – tragic.
The protagonist	A foundling – no-one knows who he is – is he evil? Arrogant? Misunderstood? Seen mainly through others' eyes.	A scientist – ambitious – creative – arrogant? – narrates most of the novel.
The roles of men and women	Some of the women seem to have a lot of independence – some are more conventional. Some men are very strong, while others are weak.	Men are active but often wrong. Women tend to be passive.
Use of language	Language varies according to the narrator. Some dialect – intense 'poetic' language. Use of pathetic fallacy.	Uses 'scientific' language – some Romantic style descriptive passages – use of pathetic fallacy.
Social and historical context	Written in Victorian period, but set earlier – Victorian moral sense – romantic attitude to nature, etc.	Influenced by the Romantics, advances in science, Rousseau and early feminism.

This table gives you a useful overview of some of the main points of connection between the texts. A table like this can help you when you start your revision by reminding you of some of the main connections between your texts.

> **KEY POINT**
>
> A question about longer texts will probably ask you to focus on a particular aspect of the texts.

> **PROGRESS CHECK**
>
> Draw up a similar table for the prose texts you have studied. If you are planning coursework, adjust the table to focus more on the question you are answering.

Unit requirements for comparing drama texts across specifications

AQA A	**U 2**	OCR	**U 2**
AQA B	**U 2,4**	WJEC	**U 4**
Edexcel	**U 2**	CCEA	**A2 U2**

Three of the examination boards (**CCEA**, **Edexcel** and **WJEC**) have units where candidates are required to compare two plays.

For both **Edexcel** and **WJEC**, you are expected to focus primarily on one (core) text and use the other (partner) text to inform and illuminate your response to the main text. It is advisable to spend roughly 75 percent of your essay discussing the core text, but make sure that you refer to the partner text throughout the essay.

For **AQA B** and **OCR**, there is an option of writing about drama, although in both cases you are allowed to write about texts from any genre.

AQA A gives you the option of writing about one main drama text and referring to others.

Comparing drama texts

As with comparing prose texts, you should follow the principles that were established earlier in this chapter (see pages 54–56). Establish what the plays are about. Look for a common theme between them. Look for similarities in their style, form and structure. Once you are clear about the broad connections, look for more detailed similarities and differences. Make a note of any useful quotations that illustrate these differences and similarities.

Always remember that when you are writing about drama you are writing about something that was written to be performed and seen. In a sense, the texts you have in front of you are not finished products. They need to be interpreted by directors and actors. Productions may differ greatly and it is always useful to see as many productions as you can, either live or on film. Remember that different audiences – and even different members of the same audience – will react differently to the same production. For more detailed guidance on studying drama texts, see Chapter 6.

Below is a table with some starting points for comparing plays.

	Play 1	Play 2
Subject		
Genre		
Dramatic style		
Setting		
Structure		
Ideas/messages		
Tone/atmosphere		
The protagonist		
The antagonist		
Other characters		
The roles of men and women		
Use of language (dialogue)		
Use of stage directions		
Social and historical context		
Different interpretations		

When writing about drama, remember to refer to 'the audience' rather than to 'the reader'. Also, try to remember that 'the audience' is singular.

KEY POINT

A drama text is different from a prose text because it is written to be performed. Always bear this in mind when comparing two plays.

PROGRESS CHECK

Draw up a similar table for the drama text(s) you have studied. If you are planning coursework, adjust your table to reflect the focus of the question.

Requirements for comparing texts from different genres across specifications

AQA A	**U 2, 4**
AQA B	**U 1, 2, 3**
Edexcel	**U 3, 4**
OCR	**U 2, 4**
WJEC	**U 3**

Many units at AS and A-Level now either require you, or give you the option, to compare texts from different genres. Genre is used here in its broadest sense to denote poetry, prose and drama. Sometimes you are given a choice of set texts to compare and asked to choose texts from different genres. Other units, which tend to be internally assessed, give you a free choice of texts, specifying perhaps which genres or which periods you should choose them from. There must, of course, be a link between the texts, but it is usually fairly broad – a theme such as 'love and marriage' or 'war'; a literary period or tradition such as Victorian literature; or a genre (in the sense of literary form or tradition) such as gothic or pastoral.

If you are given a choice, make sure you choose wisely, taking advice from your teacher or lecturer. If you are allowed to choose the 'link' yourself, choose something that already interests you or that you have some previous knowledge of. For example, an enjoyment of modern vampire stories might lead you to explore gothic literature. For your GCSE you might have studied some poems by

First World War poets such as Wilfred Owen and want to explore writers' attitudes to war in more depth.

Once you have decided on your theme, choose your texts carefully. You may have been given a list to choose from or you may have been given certain restrictions, such as one having to be poetry and another drama, or one of the texts having to be pre-1900. Do not rush into making your choice, but read widely around the 'link' first.

Examination boards sometimes give examples of appropriate texts. Look at these, take advice from your teacher or lecturer, read critics and study guides, and discuss possible choices with your friends.

Of course, it may well be that your choice has been made for you. Practical considerations often dictate that the teacher or lecturer has to make a choice of theme and of which texts to study. If this is the case, you should still read widely around the theme.

Suppose, for example, you are planning to write a piece of coursework on the theme of war. You are studying Pat Barker's *Regeneration*, Shakespeare's *Henry V* and a selection of poems from the First World War. It would probably be useful to read the rest of Barker's war trilogy, as well as some prose that was written during the First World War, such as *All Quiet on the Western Front*. You might want to look at earlier poems on the theme of war to help you understand what was different and new about the way the First World War poets wrote about their experiences. You might want to see or read some more of Shakespeare's 'history' plays, such as *Richard III*, and perhaps later plays about war, such as *Oh What a Lovely War!*

As you are likely to be comparing texts from different historical periods, as well as from different genres, you will need to have a very firm idea of the historical, social and philosophical contexts in which your texts were written. Using the example given above, you will need to know about how attitudes towards war have changed during the 400 years that separate *Henry V* and *Regeneration*. You will find guidance about studying texts in context in Chapter 5.

> **KEY POINT**
>
> Read widely around your theme, making connections between your chosen texts and between the texts and their contexts.

Comparing texts from different genres

The fact that your texts come from different genres does not change the way you should approach comparing them. However, there are some special considerations.

To start with, when you are identifying similarities and differences, clearly you are not likely to find many similarities between the forms. Begin by thinking about the effect of the writer's choice of poetry, prose or drama. For example, poems are often more personal and intimate and, of course, shorter than other texts, although there are many exceptions. Drama, written to be performed, does not usually give us an author's or even a narrator's point of view, and is open to re-interpretation by directors and actors. Novels, on the other hand, can give writers more opportunities for commenting on the action, as well as giving detailed descriptions of both the physical world and the human mind. These differences might give you a good starting point for your comparison.

Think about the texts you are studying. Do they differ in this way because of genre? If not, why not?

You might also consider how much the writers might have been influenced by, or reacted to, each other's work. Pat Barker was obviously very influenced by the First World War poets – some of them appear as characters in her novels. Did Shakespeare's depiction of war, especially Henry's rousing speech before Agincourt, influence the poets? They certainly would have known about it. Can you see similar connections between your texts? Look for any passages or quotations that suggest connections between the texts.

Here is a suggestion for a comparison table.

> Make sure that you use the correct terminology when writing about each text, e.g. stanza when writing about poetry, and paragraph when writing about prose.

	Poetry	Prose	Drama
Subject			
Genre			
When was it written?			
Setting (time and place)			
Structure			
Ideas/messages			
Tone/atmosphere			
Narrator/voice			
The protagonist			
Other characters			
The roles of men and women			
Use of language			
Attitudes shown			
Writer's attitude			
Social and historical context			
Connections between the texts			
Critical views			

PROGRESS CHECK

Adapt the table above for your own work. What special considerations do you need to bear in mind? Add in extra rows for any aspects of the texts not included here, which you think are relevant.

Requirements for comparing extracts from longer texts across specifications

AQA A   **U 2, 4**
AQA B   **U 1, 2, 3, 4**
Edexcel **U 1, 2, 3, 4**
OCR   **U 2, 4**
WJEC   **U 2, 3, 4**
CCEA   **AS U1, AS U2**

It is not very likely that you will be asked to compare extracts from longer texts in an exam, although there are units where you may be given an extract or extracts from texts that you have never seen before, or from texts you have studied.

Nevertheless, it can be useful, especially in coursework, to look in greater depth and detail at one or two passages from your texts. A question might even ask you to focus on particular parts of the text, for example to compare the impact of the beginnings or endings of your texts.

Comparing extracts from longer texts – an example

Look at the opening pages of *The Remains of the Day* by Kazuo Ishiguro and *A Room with a View* by E.M. Forster. Compare the techniques that each writer uses to begin his novel. What differences and/or similarities do you see in these passages? How effective do you find them as openings of a novel? You should consider **style**, **language** and **content**.

Extract 1

It seems increasingly likely that I really will undertake the expedition that has been preoccupying my imagination now for some days. An expedition, I should say, which I will undertake alone, in the comfort of Mr Farraday's Ford; an expedition which, as I foresee it, will take me through much of the finest countryside of England to the West Country, and may keep me away from Darlington Hall for as much as five or six days. The idea of such a journey came about, I should point out, from a most kind suggestion put to me by Mr Farraday himself one afternoon almost a fortnight ago, when I had been dusting the portraits in the library. In fact, as I recall, I was up on the step-ladder dusting the portrait of Viscount Wetherby when my employer had entered carrying a few volumes which he presumably wished returned to the shelves. On seeing my person, he took the opportunity to inform me that he had just that moment finalized plans to return to the United States for a period of five weeks between August and September. Having made this announcement, my employer put his volumes down on a table, seated himself on the *chaise-longue*, and stretched out his legs. It was then gazing up at me, that he said:

'You realize, Stevens, I don't expect you to be locked up here in this house all the time I'm away. Why don't you take the car and drive off somewhere for a few days? You look like you could make good use of a break.'

Coming out of the blue as it did, I did not quite know how to reply to such a suggestion. I recall thanking him for his consideration, but quite probably I said nothing very definite for my employer went on:

'I'm serious, Stevens. I really think you should take a break. I'll foot the bill for the gas. You fellows, you're always locked up in these big houses helping out, how do you ever get to see around this beautiful country of yours?'

This was not the first time my employer had raised such a question; indeed, it seems to be something which genuinely troubles him. On this occasion, in fact, a reply of sorts did occur to me as I stood up there on the ladder; a reply to the effect that those of our profession, although we did not see a great deal of the country in the sense of touring the countryside and visiting picturesque sites, did actually 'see' more of England than most, placed as we were in houses where the greatest ladies and gentlemen of the land gathered. Of course, I could not have expressed this view to Mr Farraday without embarking upon what might have seemed a presumptuous speech. I thus contented myself by saying simply:

'It has been my privilege to see the best of England over the years, sir, within these very walls.'

Mr Farraday did not seem to understand this statement, for he merely went on:

'I mean it, Stevens. It's wrong that a man can't get to see around his own country. Take my advice, get out the house for a few days.'

As you might expect, I did not take Mr Farraday's suggestion at all seriously that afternoon, regarding it as just another instance of an American gentleman's unfamiliarity with what was and what was not commonly done in England. The fact that my attitude to this same suggestion underwent a change over the following days – indeed, that the notion of a trip to the West Country took an ever increasing hold on my thoughts – is no doubt substantially attributable to – and why should I hide it? – the arrival of Miss Kenton's letter, her first in almost seven years if one discounts the Christmas cards. But let me make it immediately clear what I mean by this; what I mean to say is that Miss Kenton's letter set off a certain chain of ideas to do with professional matters here at Darlington Hall, and I would underline that it was a preoccupation with these very same professional matters that led me to consider anew my employer's kindly meant suggestion.

Extract from The Remains of the Day *by Kazuo Ishiguro*

Extract 2

'The Signora had no business to do it,' said Miss Bartlett, 'no business at all. She promised us south rooms with a view close together, instead of which here are north rooms, looking into a courtyard, and a long way apart. Oh. Lucy!'

'And a Cockney, besides!' said Lucy, who had been farther saddened by the Signora's unexpected accent. 'It might be London.' She looked at the two rows of English people who were sitting at the table; at the row of white bottles of water and red bottles of wine that ran between the English people; at the portraits of the late Queen and the late Poet Laureate that hung behind the English people heavily framed; at the notice of the English church (Rev. Cuthbert Eager, M. A. Oxon.), that was the only other decoration on the wall. 'Charlotte, don't you feel, too, that we might be in London? I can hardly believe that all kinds of other things are just outside. I suppose it is one's being so tired.'

'This meat has surely been used for soup,' said Miss Bartlett, laying down her fork.

'I want so to see the Arno. The rooms the Signora promised us in her letter would have looked over the Arno. The Signora had no business to do it at all. Oh, it is a shame.'

'Any nook does for me,' Miss Bartlett continued; 'but it does seem hard that you shouldn't have a view.'

Lucy felt that she had been selfish. 'Charlotte, you mustn't spoil me: of course, you must look over the Arno, too. I meant that. The first vacant room in the front–'

'You must have it,' said Miss Bartlett, part of whose travelling expenses were paid by Lucy's mother – a piece of generosity to which she made many a tactful allusion. 'No, no. You must have it.'

'I insist on it. Your mother would never forgive me, Lucy. She would never forgive *me*.'

The ladies' voices grew animated, and – if the sad truth be owned – a little peevish. They were tired, and under the guise of unselfishness they wrangled. Some of their neighbours interchanged glances, and one of them – one of the ill-bred people whom one does meet abroad – leant forward over the table and actually intruded into their argument. He said: 'I have a view, I have a view.'

Miss Bartlett was startled. Generally at a pension people looked them over for a day or two before speaking, and often did not find out that they would 'do' till they had gone. She knew that the intruder was ill-bred, even before she glanced at him. He was an old man, of heavy build, with a fair, shaven face and large eyes. There was something childish in those eyes, though it was not the childishness of senility. What exactly it was Miss Bartlett did not stop to consider, for her glance passed on to his clothes. These did not attract her. He was probably trying to become acquainted with them before they got into the swim. So she assumed a dazed expression when he spoke to her, and then said: 'A view? Oh, a view! How delightful a view is!'

Extract from A Room with a View *by E.M. Forster*

COMMENTARY

Here are some of the **similarities** you may have noted:

1. Both passages focus on a kind of 'social etiquette'.
2. Both are concerned with a holiday of some sort.
3. Both extracts are concerned to some degree with a 'class consciousness'.
4. They are also concerned with 'Englishness'.
5. The language contains elements of formality.
6. Both writers introduce characters by name.
7. Dialogue is used to give an impression of the characters' background, both through what they say and the way they say it.
8. In both extracts there seems to be an unequal relationship between the characters (Miss Bartlett is not a servant, but is dependent on Lucy's family).
9. In both extracts a third character is introduced at the end of the passage, giving us the impression he or she will have an important role in the unfolding story.
10. Both writers use an event to create interest and make the reader want to read on to find out what will happen.

The main **differences** between the extracts are as follows:

1. The first passage is written in the first person and the second one is in the third person. The tone of the second extract is impersonal and rather ironic.
2. The first extract opens in the present tense, before taking us back. The second is entirely in the past tense.
3. The first extract is set in England and the second in Italy.
4. In the first passage the narrator is reporting events to us, whereas in the second one we see events as they happen.
5. The second passage seems to be concerned with the rather snobbish attitudes of Miss Bartlett, whereas in the first passage, the narrator – Stevens – is a butler and is aware of his place in the hierarchy. His employer does not seem to exhibit snobbish attitudes, though.

KEY POINT

When comparing longer texts, it can be helpful to compare some key passages in detail.

PROGRESS CHECK

Pick out two passages as a pair from either the novels or the plays that you are studying. They could be beginnings or endings, or two extracts that strike you as having something in common. List the similarities and differences between them.

3.5 Types of exam questions

LEARNING SUMMARY	After studying this section, you should be able to:
	• approach your exam with the confidence that you are familiar with, and understand, the style of question you will be asked

The kinds of exam questions to expect from your exam board

AQA B	**U 1, 3**
Edexcel	**U 1, 3**
OCR	**U 1, 3**
WJEC	**U 1, 4**
CCEA	**AS U2, A2 U2**

Because comparative essays are so important, and because this aspect of your course is approached in so many different ways, it is worth spending some time familiarising yourself with the kinds of question you are likely to be asked in an exam.

Below we have outlined some examples from each exam board.

AQA B

> Please read this information if you are studying the AQA B specification.

For Unit 1 (Aspects of Narrative), you are required to study four texts – two poetry and two prose – chosen from a list. In Section B of the exam, you are asked to discuss an aspect of narrative, referring to three texts. You must not use the text you have written on in Section A.

Unit 4 (Texts and Genres) has a similar approach. For this unit, you have to study a minimum of three texts chosen from a list, one of which must have been written between 1300 and 1800. There are two lists – Elements of the Gothic and Elements of the Pastoral. In Section B of the paper, the questions ask you to discuss aspects of your chosen topics by comparing at least three texts.

Here are examples of the kind of questions that might be set.

> **Unit 1 Section B**
> Write about the role of the narrator in three texts you have studied.
>
> **Unit 4 Section B**
> 'Pastoral literature is all about escaping into a world that does not and cannot exist.' Discuss this view.

Both of these questions are very broad so that they can be answered with reference to a fairly wide range of texts.

The first is not a question as such, and could be thought of as being rather vague. It would be easy to answer it simply by describing the narrators of three texts – you must be aware of the need to analyse the writers' techniques.

The second question does not tell you how many texts to use, but this will be made clear at the top of the page in your exam paper.

Neither of these questions actually uses the word 'compare'. When asked to write about more than one text, you must assume that you will have to compare the texts throughout your essay.

Please read this information if you are studying the Edexcel specification.

Edexcel

For Unit 1 (Explorations in Prose and Poetry), you study one selection of poetry on a given theme (home, land or work) and one literary heritage novel, plus a further novel or novella.

Section B of the exam asks you to compare and contrast two out of three named poems taken from the selection.

Section C asks you to focus on your 'core' prose text, referring to the other text 'in order to develop [your] line of argument'.

For Unit 3 (Interpretations of Prose and Poetry), you study three prescribed texts (chosen from a list of six), including at least one written after 1990, and including both prose and poetry. Section B of the exam asks you to compare at least two texts, one of them being a post-1990 text.

Here are some examples of the style of question that might be set.

Unit 1

Section B

'Poets often use land to explore their own identity.'

Compare and contrast at least two poems in the light of this statement.

Section C

'The men in *Wuthering Heights* are either bullies or weaklings.'

Using Chapter 14 as your starting point, explore the portrayal of men.

In your response, you should focus on *Wuthering Heights* to establish your argument and you should refer to the second text you have read to support and develop your argument.

Unit 3 Section B

'When it comes down to it, we are all only really interested in ourselves.'

Comment on and analyse the connections and comparisons between at least two texts you have studied in the light of this comment.

In your response you must ensure that at least one text is a post-1990 text. You should demonstrate what it means to be considering texts as a modern reader, in a modern context, and that other readers at other times may well have had other responses.

All three of these questions use quotations as their starting points and ask you to discuss them in the light of your reading.

The first question uses the traditional formula of 'compare and contrast', indicating that you should give equal consideration to both poems and do not need to refer to any other texts.

The second question gives you an extract as a 'starting point', giving you the opportunity to do some close analysis of this section of the text. You are reminded that your main focus is the core text, but you must refer also to a second text.

The third of these questions is very clear about what it requires you to do. Although the question might seem almost random to those who have not done the course, you will have been focusing on the theme of self and identity. The quotation gives you the focus for your discussion and you are told to look at 'connections and comparisons', indicating that these texts are to be given equal weight. The last sentence hints at the importance of considering context.

OCR

For Unit 1 (Poetry and Prose 1800–1945), you study a selection of poems by a single poet. In the exam you are given a copy of one of the poems and asked to relate it to other poems by the writer.

For Unit 3 (Drama and Poetry pre-1800), you study one drama and one poetry text and are required to compare them.

Here are some examples of the style of question that might be set.

> Please read this information if you are studying the OCR specification.

Unit 1 Section A

'Move him into the sun …'

Move him into the sun –
Gently its touch awoke him once,
At home, whispering of fields half-sown.
Always it woke him, even in France,
Until this morning, and this snow.
If anything might rouse him now
The kind old sun will know.

Think how it wakes the seeds –
Woke once the clays of a cold star.
Are limbs, so dear achieved, are sides
Full-nerved, still warm, too hard to stir?
Was it for this the clay grew tall?
O what made famous sunbeams toil
To break earth's sleep at all?

Discuss ways in which Owen presents death in war in *Futility*. In your answer, explore the effects of language, imagery and verse form, and consider how this poem relates to other poems by Owen that you have studied.

Unit 3 Section B

By comparing one drama and one poetry text you have studied, discuss ways in which writers explore the idea of damnation.

The first of these questions asks you to compare poems by the same writer, but the focus is clearly on the single poem reproduced for you. Therefore, this is not really a comparison question. You are expected to analyse the given poem in some detail and refer to others with which you think it connects. The question gives you the main points to think about. To make sure that you cover all of these, you might want to discuss each of them in turn, making sure that you refer briefly to other poems throughout the essay.

The second question gives a simple and straightforward instruction. You need to give equal weight to your two texts, comparing and contrasting them throughout the essay.

WJEC

Please read this information if you are studying the WJEC specification.

For Section A of Unit 1 (Poetry and Drama 2), you study poetry by two writers. One of these collections is referred to as the 'core' text and the other as the 'partner' text.

For Section A of Unit 4 (Poetry and Drama 2), you study a set poetry text and are asked in the exam to analyse it closely, as well as referring to an unseen extract.

For Section B, you study two plays – a play by Shakespeare as a 'core' text and a play by another writer as a 'partner' text.

Here are some examples of the style of question that might be set.

> **Unit 1**
>
> Compare the ways in which Plath and Hughes write about death.
>
> In your answer you must refer in detail to at least two poems by Plath.
>
> **Unit 4**
> **Section A**
> 'For many poets religious experience has more to do with pain than pleasure.' Discuss this view.
>
> **Section B**
> Examine the ways in which Shakespeare has presented ideas about good and bad government in *Measure for Measure*. Show how your appreciation and understanding of this element of *Measure for Measure* has been informed by your study of *The Duchess of Malfi*.

The example from Unit 1 is fairly straightforward. However, you must bear in mind that you need to devote considerably more time to the core text than to the partner text.

The first example from Unit 4 poses a general question about poetry. Whether you could answer this particular question would depend on which set text you had studied. Therefore, you must read all the questions carefully to establish which one applies to your text. You should also identify as quickly as possible the most appropriate unseen extract to use. If your text is a collection of poems, you will also need to think about which poems to focus on. Two or three will probably be enough.

The Section B question makes it clear that your main focus is the Shakespeare play. Make sure, however, that you refer to the partner text throughout the essay. You should probably spend about 25 percent of your essay discussing the partner text.

CCEA

Please read this information if you are studying the CCEA specification.

For Unit 2 Section A (The Study of Poetry Written after 1800), you study either a collection of poems by a single poet or a long poem (such as Pope's *The Rape of the Lock*). In the exam you are given one poem or an extract, which must be compared to another poem or another extract of the student's choice.

For Unit 3 Section A (The Study of Poetry 1300–1800), you study the work of two poets and have to compare them in the exam.

For Unit 4 (The study of Prose – Theme Based), you are required to compare two novels on the same theme.

Here are some examples of the style of question that might be set.

Unit 2 Section A

Dickinson and Hopkins both write about their relationship with God.

Compare and contrast two poems, one by each poet, taking account of the methods (the situation and tones of the speakers, and the form, structure and language, including imagery) which each poet uses to write about his or her relationship with God.

Unit 3 Section A

By referring to *The Flea*, printed in the accompanying resource booklet, and one other appropriately selected poem, and making use of relevant external contextual material on the nature of metaphysical poetry, examine the poetic methods which Donne uses to write about love.

N.B. Equal marks are available for your treatment of each poem.

Unit 4 Section B

'War novels tend to focus on the suffering of individuals rather than the rights and wrongs of war itself.'

Compare and contrast the two novels you have studied in this group in the light of the above opinion.

All these questions are notably clear.

In the first question you are left in no doubt about what you need to do. When you answer a question like this, take great care in your selection of the two poems you are going to discuss. Make sure that they are concerned with the theme of the question and that you know them well.

The instructions for the second question are also very clear. Again, you need to make sure that you select an appropriate poem. The question also draws attention to the fact that your understanding of context will be tested here.

The third question is also straightforward. You just need to ensure that you focus on the statement you have been given, backing up your arguments with evidence from your texts.

KEY POINT

It is important that you thoroughly understand what you are being asked to compare and how you are expected to do it.

PROGRESS CHECK

If you are taking one of these units, try to invent a similar question on your set texts and plan an appropriate answer.

Note – As Section 3.5 has covered the kinds of 'comparing text' questions you are likely to be asked in an exam, this chapter does not include practice examination questions. There is a sample question and model answer in the style of WJEC Unit 2 on the next page.

Sample question and model answer

'Our morality is the product of our upbringing.'

Basing your response on a comparison of *Wuthering Heights* (core text) and *Frankenstein* (partner text), to what extent do you agree with this view?

QUESTION OVERVIEW

This question is in the style of a coursework question from WJEC Unit 2. For this unit, you are required to write about two prose texts, one of which is designated as the 'core text' and the other as the 'partner text'.

The annotations to the student response refer to AO3, which has been reproduced below for your reference.

AO3: Explore connections and comparisons between different literary texts, informed by interpretations of other readers.

The candidate immediately applies the quotation to the core text. She then makes some general points that question the assumptions of the quotation and which apply to both novels. →

The different childhoods of the characters in Emily Brontë's `Wuthering Heights' are highly influential upon their development later in life. Each character has different views on the subject of morality, mainly focusing around Christianity. Echoes of this are also seen in Mary Shelley's `Frankenstein' as the debate over nature v. nurture is considered, in the context of Christian morality. However, it is difficult to be certain about what behaviour is `wrong' and what is `right' when morality is different for every character - characters set their own morals based upon cultural and personal values. What is `wrong' for one person may be `right' for another.

The first half of this → paragraph is concerned with the core text, focusing on its protagonist and applying the question to him. Having explored the way in which Heathcliff's upbringing influences his actions, the student makes the link to the partner text, drawing a clear and confident parallel between Heathcliff and the Monster. Note the balance between comment on the core text and comment on the partner text.

In `Wuthering Heights', the story revolves around Heathcliff, opening with Lockwood's description of him and ending with his death. For this reason, and also due to his complexities, it is of the utmost importance to analyse Heathcliff's character in depth to understand how his upbringing later affects his morality. Heathcliff's childhood is mysterious, as the most we learn is that he is an orphan from Liverpool. Nelly labels him a `gipsy' and a `vagabond', words that invoke stereotypes of a degraded character and a sense of being an outsider. This mysterious upbringing is a reflection of the character, as he often hides his emotions behind a veil of anger that he creates for himself. His only positive feeling in the novel appears as love for Catherine. I believe this destructive relationship is derived from the lack of a father figure in Heathcliff's childhood. This is closely linked to `Frankenstein', as the Monster also has no parental guidance and expresses extreme loneliness and a sense of desertion as he learns of the Bible: `I remembered Adam's supplication to his creator. But where is mine?' Thus, Heathcliff's aggressive behaviour can be linked to the Monster's violence - whilst the Monster is much more extreme in the murders of William, Henry and Elizabeth, Heathcliff is similarly violent in his treatment of Isabella and his enslavement of Cathy, and also Nelly. This suggests that a damaged upbringing will later lead to a lack of self-worth and having to prove oneself, in this case by exercising power through violence.

The Monster is completely alone in forming his character. He teaches himself through reading books that he finds, and learns to speak by following the Delacey family - much like Nelly, who appears to the reader as a well-educated servant because she took it upon herself to study and read the books in the library at Thrushcross Grange. Whilst the Monster is deprived of affection, Heathcliff is adopted into the Earnshaw family and taken on by Mr Earnshaw himself who treats him exceedingly well, even better than his own children, Catherine and Hindley. Heathcliff is regarded as an equal and is to `sleep in the same bed' as the children. Similar treatment is seen in `Frankenstein' when Elizabeth is adopted into the Frankenstein family and immediately accepted into the family, becoming very close to Victor. However, such care is

Sample question and model answer (continued)

In this paragraph the student focuses on a difference between Heathcliff and the Monster – the affection given to Heathcliff by Mr Earnshaw. This leads her to consider another similarity between the texts, as in *Frankenstein* Elizabeth is adopted by the Frankenstein family. She then contrasts the outcomes of these two adoptions. She also mentions briefly an interesting similarity between the Monster and Nelly, one of the narrators of *Wuthering Heights*.

In this paragraph the student makes links between the language used in the two novels, linking the authors' use of terms such as 'devil' and 'fallen angel' to the shared context of the novels. This leads to an explicit comparison of the protagonists' attitude to Christian morality.

Again, the context in which the novels were written is used to explore links between them, this time in terms of the idea of the 'Byronic' hero and the influence of the Romantics. The reference to a critic shows that the student's views have been 'informed by interpretations of other readers' (AO3).

short-lived for Heathcliff as, after Mr Earnshaw's death, Hindley grows resentful of his father's adoration of Heathcliff and thenceforth beats him. This leads to Heathcliff suffering a very fragmented childhood. Anger mounts in Heathcliff because, as a child, he 'would stand Hindley's blows without winking or shedding a tear'. However, when he grows he learns to defend himself and use violence as his own form of protection. It would be reasonable to assume that because Heathcliff is subjected to violence from a young age, his moral compass becomes clouded, and he may have grown to believe that it is acceptable to use violence to resolve problems.

Heathcliff is certainly the character in the novel with the least respect for morality and social norms. His actions appear to be guided by desire for revenge for not being able to marry Catherine. It is important to take into account that the novel was written in 1840, when prevailing morals were largely derived from the Bible. Arguably, along with a relative decline in the importance of religion, modern society may have witnessed a decline in morals. Therefore, Heathcliff's character and behaviour may be more accepted and sympathised with among readers today. The perception of Heathcliff from many nineteenth-century readers would probably be similar to that of Nelly, who brands him as the 'devil'. More than once Heathcliff is linked with hell, and Isabella describes him as 'not a human being', suggesting that he is other worldly and evil. Similarly, the monster in 'Frankenstein' is labelled 'the fallen angel'. Heathcliff's childhood in Liverpool may be purposely linked to his devil-like behaviour in the novel, as when Brontë wrote the novel in the 1840s cities like Liverpool were unsanitary and overcrowded places, reminiscent of William Blake's 'dark satanic mills'. In religious terms they were often referred to in terms of Hell. The Industrial Revolution is linked to the Scientific Revolution, which frames 'Frankenstein'. Social progress has its dark side and it can never be predicted when things will turn disastrous. The importance of religion is also a theme of 'Frankenstein', the novel focusing in part on the demise of Christian morality (overtaken by the new religion of science) as Frankenstein commits an act of blasphemy by creating the Monster. Frankenstein is, therefore, closely linked to Heathcliff as they both in their own way reject Christianity and conventional morality. In 'Wuthering Heights', Joseph appears to have the highest sense of Christian morality, as his comments on everything always refer back explicitly to the Bible. However, Joseph is a servant and often very unpleasant to others, somewhat contradicting his preaching of Christian morals. He is, therefore, implicitly criticised, his moral certainty being seen not only as old-fashioned but also as hypocritical.

Although Heathcliff is often viewed simply as evil, he can also be seen as a 'Byronic' hero, influenced by the Romantic movement and its reaction against eighteenth-century rationalism. He is brilliant and, at the same time, cynical and self-destructive. Like other Byronic characters, Heathcliff is haunted by his past, literally through the ghost imagery in 'Wuthering Heights'. His character may also have been influenced by the views of Rousseau, who viewed society as 'artificial and corrupt' and believed that good people are made unhappy because of their experiences. Links to this are seen in the character of the Monster in 'Frankenstein', who is initially seen as a good soul, but turns evil as he fights his abandonment and mistreatment. Like most gothic texts, 'Frankenstein' too can be seen as a product of the Romantic sensibility. Heathcliff struggles throughout his childhood and is denied marriage to the woman he loves, yet remains loyal to her, staying outside Thrushcross Grange when she is dying. There is a tremendous sense that no one truly understands the love between Catherine and Heathcliff except themselves, and the reader sympathises with Heathcliff because he never lets go of his love for Catherine, in this regard showing a high sense of morality. I believe that Heathcliff's love for Catherine is derived from a longing to be loved by someone, as he never truly

Sample question and model answer (continued)

experiences this as a child. Critic Joyce Carol Oates, agreeing with this point of view, argues that Brontë tests the reader to see how many times they can be shocked by Heathcliff's irrational and violent behaviour whilst still seeing him as the hero - this is the same theory that Heathcliff applies to Isabella. Victor Frankenstein develops a powerful and complex love for Elizabeth, as Heathcliff does for Catherine, and his love too ends in tragedy. The backgrounds of the two couples are also similar, as Elizabeth was adopted into the Frankenstein family just as Heathcliff was adopted by the Earnshaws. Such an upbringing clearly develops strong bonds between the characters and a strong moral sense based on love.

This paragraph considers the question with regard to another character in *Wuthering Heights*, Catherine. The student's view on how her early bereavement affects her sense of morality is supported by linking it to the death of Frankenstein's mother. Note that here the reference to the partner text is very brief, but still adds weight to the student's argument.

Catherine's upbringing, like Heathcliff's, is fragmented as she suffers the loss of her father at an early age. This loss results in all three children - Heathcliff, Catherine and Hindley - developing addictive habits. Heathcliff and Catherine become dependent on each other in a destructive relationship. Catherine describes Heathcliff as a `rock´, saying that her love for him will never change. Hindley becomes an alcoholic, signifying a clear lack of morals as he shows he lacks self-control. In abusing his body he defies the teaching of the Bible that the body should be treated as a `temple´. Hindley's suffering is compounded by increasing debt, which results in his having to rely on his enemy, Heathcliff. This fragmented childhood is also present in Frankenstein as Victor's mother dies of scarlet fever, giving rise to mental instability for Victor and Elizabeth. This would suggest that the loss of a parent is very damaging and might affect morals in later life. While all the children of Wuthering Heights suffer the same loss, Catherine's morality is also influenced by the materialistic values of her society. After her stay at Thrushcross Grange, she becomes superficial and materialistic, stating that it would `degrade´ her to marry Heathcliff. Instead, she marries Edgar Linton, the wealthiest man in the neighbourhood. This idolising of money shows Catherine's lack of integrity and morality as she appears to abandon her love for Heathcliff in shallow pursuit of social standing and wealth. For a while Catherine seems happy with Edgar. However, she admits that her love for him changes, but her love for Heathcliff will never change. Catherine is shown as marrying Edgar for the wrong reasons, and Heathcliff does the same - marrying Isabella out of revenge.

This short paragraph contains no references to *Frankenstein*. That does not matter as *Wuthering Heights* is the core text.

Edgar and Isabella's childhood is very different from that of the children at Wuthering Heights. They are spoiled, arousing annoyance in Heathcliff, who questions their behaviour - `... shouldn't they be happy?´ Their sheltered upbringing makes both Edgar and Isabella naïve, and they both marry foolishly. Isabella, in particular, is misled by Heathcliff. Through marrying him she abandons her family and her morality, as Edgar disowns her out of hatred for Heathcliff. The difference in behaviour between the two groups of children reflects the different upbringings at Wuthering Heights and Thrushcross Grange. At Wuthering Heights roles are much more relaxed and servants are treated as part of the family, Nelly growing up alongside the other children. However, at Thrushcross Grange it is very different, with money and status being the centre of the children's upbringing.

In the final paragraph the candidate again considers the question, commenting on the morality – or rather lack of it – of the main characters of both novels, and concluding that a reading of the novels supports the view expressed in the question.

In conclusion, the moral weakness or rejection of morality displayed by most of the characters in Wuthering Heights, but particularly by Heathcliff, suggests that it would be correct to say that morality is a product of upbringing. Similarly, in Frankenstein both Victor and the Monster, in different ways, show a lack of morality. This is associated with changes in society and particularly the decline in the influence of Christianity. During the period when these novels were produced, the gothic genre emerged out of Romanticism and remained influential. Some might argue that the popularity of gothic fiction contributed to a loss of moral certainty. On the other hand, gothic fiction can be seen as making morality clearer. Its representation of evil and wickedness forces readers to confront evil and to truly recognise what is `good´.

4 Using critics

The following topics are covered in this chapter:

- **The importance of using critics in your work**
- **Critical approaches to texts**
- **Referring to critics and writing a bibliography**

4.1 The importance of using critics in your work

LEARNING SUMMARY

After studying this section, you should be able to:

- understand what is meant by critics
- appreciate the value of using critics
- know where to find critics' views

What are critics?

AQA A	U 1, 2, 3, 4
AQA B	U 1, 2, 3, 4
Edexcel	U 1, 2, 3, 4
OCR	U 1, 2, 3, 4
WJEC	U 1, 2, 3, 4
CCEA	AS U1, AS U2, A2 U1, A2 U2

In everyday language, 'criticism' is usually used to denote a negative comment on something or someone – 'to criticise' means to comment in a negative way, and a 'critic' is someone who makes negative comments.

Literary criticism, however, is not necessarily negative. If anything, there tends to be an assumption that the text has some worth – otherwise you would not be studying it. When you 'criticise' a text, as you do every time you write an English Literature essay, you are analysing and evaluating. Your conclusions could be negative or positive, or a mixture of both. The same applies to people who write reviews of books, films, plays, and even computer games in newspapers and magazines. They too are critics. You might occasionally use the views of such a critic in your work, but you are more likely to draw on literary critics, i.e. people (usually academics working at universities) who study, teach and write about English literature.

How using critics fits into your A-Level course

AQA A	U 1, 2, 3, 4
AQA B	U 1, 2, 3, 4
Edexcel	U 1, 2, 3, 4
OCR	U 1, 2, 3, 4
WJEC	U 1, 2, 3, 4
CCEA	AS U1, AS U2, A2 U1, A2 U2

Assessment Objective (AO) 3 says that your comparisons of literary texts should be 'informed by interpretations of other readers'.

AO4 asks you to demonstrate your understanding 'of the contexts in which literary texts are given and received'.

If other people have 'informed' your views, it means that you know what their views are and understand them, that you have considered them carefully, and that you may or may not agree with them. At GCSE level, in order to obtain a high grade you had to consider alternative viewpoints. This meant acknowledging that at times texts could be interpreted in more than one way, and looking at more than one possibility before deciding which view you agreed with. At AS and A-Level, you still have to do this, but the requirements of AO3 mean that the examiners need to know that you have been informed by others' views. They can only know this if you tell them.

'Other readers' whose views you may have taken into account before reaching your own conclusions could well include other students, and will almost certainly include your teacher. However, while it is permissible to say something along the lines of 'some readers interpret this as meaning ... while others feel that ...', it is better if you say who those readers are. In order to lend weight to those views they should be people with more of a reputation in the literary world than your friends or your teacher (unless of course your teacher is a distinguished literary critic).

> Do not just repeat what your teacher has told you. The examiner is interested in what you think.

Remember, being 'informed' by someone's interpretation does not mean regurgitating his or her views as your own. If everyone in your class simply repeats what the teacher has said in class, the examiner will soon spot it and will probably not be impressed. So, if you are going to convince the examiners that your views are informed by the views of others, you need to read literary criticism.

As well as stimulating your own views, the reading of criticism will show you the range of views there are about your text, enabling you to weigh up the different views and decide which you find convincing. Observing the way that critics write about texts may also help to improve your own style. Be warned though – not all critics write in elegant and lucid prose. Some of the writing is obscure, and some downright turgid. In addition, reading a wide range of critics from different times will help you to understand 'the contexts in which literary texts are ... received', as you will begin to see how critics, like writers, can be influenced by the ideas, manners and morals of their own time. There will be more about this in Section 4.2 (see pages 79–83).

> **KEY POINT**
>
> Reading the work of critics is essential at AS and A-Level.

Where to find critical views

AQA A	U 1, 2, 3, 4
AQA B	U 1, 2, 3, 4
Edexcel	U 1, 2, 3, 4
OCR	U 1, 2, 3, 4
WJEC	U 1, 2, 3, 4
CCEA	AS U1, AS U2, A2 U1, A2 U2

You can find critical views to read and discuss in a number of places:

- **Your copy of the text** – many editions of texts which are studied at AS and A-Level include critical views. There may be a preface or foreword at the beginning of the book, or occasionally an 'afterword' at the end, in which the editor discusses the text. Editors are often distinguished academics and will give their own views on the text. They may also give some historical and biographical information (useful for AO4) and perhaps a summary of other critical views. Some editions will give extracts from other critical views in a separate section. Editions intended for study also tend to have notes, especially for older texts. Some of these notes will be explanatory, for example giving the meaning of archaic words or explaining obscure references, but others might give critical interpretations of specific parts of the text.
- **Notes given to you by your teacher** – teachers quite often do some of the work for you by collecting critical essays and extracts that they think will be useful to you, perhaps putting them together as a 'study guide' and giving them to you at the start of the unit, or maybe giving them out gradually during the course of your study. Make sure you know who wrote the extracts in your guide. Sometimes teachers include essays by former students to help you understand what is required of you. Although you can certainly use these to stimulate your own interpretation, you should not quote from them. Nor should you quote from notes that you know the teacher has written.

- **Published study guides** – study guides can be very useful and often include summaries of critical views. They might quote quite long extracts from critical essays, or just a few lines. They might also provide lists of other helpful publications.
- **Books** – do not forget that libraries contain books as well as computers! You will probably find relevant critical views in both your school or college library and in the public library. Collections of essays on single texts (such as the Casebook series) are very useful. You might find relevant material in books that discuss the whole of your writer's work or even in critical biographies. There are also more general books about particular periods, genres or literary movements, and more general guides to literature. You do not, of course, have to wade through thousands of pages to find what you want. Use the index and the contents page.
- **The Internet** – some very good critical works can be accessed through the Internet. However, always remember to use the Internet wisely. If you 'google' the name of your text or writer, you are likely to come up with quite a long list of websites and web links. If you find something that you think is relevant, look for the author's name. If it is written by a serious critic it will probably tell you something about him or her, including the name of the university or institution he or she works for. You may even be directed to the university website. If the author's name is not given, by all means read and digest the views, but be a little more wary. The same applies to views that are clearly those of other students.

> **KEY POINT**
>
> Cast your net widely in your search for critical views. Use your sources wisely.

> **PROGRESS CHECK**
>
> Visit your local library and see how many books you can find that contain references to your text.

4.2 Critical approaches to texts

LEARNING SUMMARY	**After studying this section, you should be able to:** • appreciate the value of contemporary views of the text • develop your understanding of literary theory and what it means • recognise and understand some of the main types of criticism you will come across

Contemporary views

AQA A	U 1, 2, 3, 4
AQA B	U 1, 2, 3, 4
Edexcel	U 1, 2, 3, 4
OCR	U 1, 2, 3, 4
WJEC	U 1, 2, 3, 4
CCEA	AS U1, AS U2, A2 U1, A2 U2

Reading contemporary views (the views of those who wrote at the same time as the writer of the text) can be useful in putting your text in context. These views might include prefaces or articles written by the writers themselves, or people close to them. Examples include Mary Shelley's preface to *Frankenstein*, and Charlotte Brontë's 'Biographical Notice', with which she prefaced *Wuthering Heights*. In both these cases, the articles have been so frequently reprinted that they have almost become part of the texts themselves and have had a massive influence on how readers have responded to the texts. Shelley's account of the writing of her novel complemented its concern with the creative process, adding an extra layer to an already multi-layered text. Brontë's piece did a similar job, helping to create the myth of the Brontës and enhancing the reading of their work.

Most of the texts you study will have been reviewed in newspapers or magazines when they were first published or performed. You might find these reviews in collections of criticism, in study guides, or in your edition of the text. These are often very different from modern reactions – it is important to read them, as they help us understand how the texts were received at the time, and put them in their historical, social and political context. A lot of texts that are now established as part of the 'canon' caused controversy on their first publication, either because their content was considered shocking, or because their style was so different from what contemporary critics considered 'good'.

Contemporary views – an example

As an example of how texts were viewed at the time they were written, look at the following two extracts. They are both concerned with Coleridge's *The Ancient Mariner*. The first extract is taken from a review written when the poem was first published.

In the second extract, Coleridge himself replies to a criticism made of his poem.

What do you think these views add to an understanding of the poem? Do not worry if you do not know the poem. Think in terms of the context of the writers of the extracts.

Extract 1

'The Poem of the Ancyent Marinere' with which the collection opens, has many excellencies, and many faults; the beginning and the end are striking and well conducted; but the intermediate part is too long, and has, in some places, a kind of confusion of images, which loses all effect, from not being quite intelligible. The author, who is confidently said to be Mr Coleridge, is not correctly versed in the old language, which he undertakes to employ. 'Noises of a swound' and 'broad as a weft,' are both nonsensical; but the ancient style is well imitated, while the antiquated words are so very few, that the latter might with advantage be entirely removed without any detriment to the effect of the Poem.

Anonymous Review, 1799

Extract 2: Coleridge on the moral of *The Ancient Mariner*

Mrs Barbauld once told me that she admired *The Ancient Mariner* very much, but that there were two faults in it – it was improbable, and had no moral. As for the probability, I owned that that might admit some question; but as to the want of a moral, I told her that in my own judgement the poem had too much; and that the only, or chief fault, if I might say so, was the obtrusion of the moral sentiment so openly on the reader as a principle or cause of action in a work of such pure imagination. It ought to have had no more moral than the *Arabian Nights'* tale of the merchant's sitting down to eat dates by the side of a well, and throwing the shells aside, and lo! a genie starts up, and says he *must* kill the aforesaid merchant, *because* one of the date shells had, it seems, put out the eye of the genie's son.

Table Talk, *31 May 1830*

In the first extract, it is interesting to see how one reviewer of the time responded to the poem. In the second extract, we can see Coleridge's own view on a key issue concerning the poem.

The views of a writer's contemporaries can help to put a text in context.

Find some contemporary views of one of the texts you are studying. How do these views help you to understand the context in which the text was written?

Theories and approaches

AQA A	U 1, 2, 3, 4
AQA B	U 1, 2, 3, 4
Edexcel	U 1, 2, 3, 4
OCR	U 1, 2, 3, 4
WJEC	U 1, 2, 3, 4
CCEA	AS U1, AS U2, A2 U1, A2 U2

Literary criticism is concerned with all aspects of literature, and critics take many different approaches to texts. Over the years there have been fashions in criticism, with different approaches to texts becoming popular. Some of these have remained popular, while others have fallen out of fashion. Many (though not all) of the critics you read can be identified with a particular style or 'school' of criticism. In recent years, critics have tended to be adherents of (or at least influenced by) a particular literary theory – they apply the methods of that theory to whichever text they are studying. It is useful for you to have some understanding of the main types of criticism you are likely to come across. It helps you to put a critic's views in context, and gives you the opportunity to think about which of these approaches you yourself might find useful.

Different ways of looking at texts are not mutually exclusive. Although some influential critics might have felt that theirs was the only right way of looking at a text, most critics, teachers and students are not zealous adherents of any particular school of thought. As with texts themselves, over-categorisation can be dangerous. Critics writing today do not necessarily reject the ideas and theories of their predecessors. Indeed, you will find that critics often refer to other critics in their work, perhaps in order to counter their arguments, or to lend support to their own arguments.

It is always worth reading the great critics of the nineteenth and twentieth centuries, such as A.C. Bradley, G. Wilson Knight, F.R. and Q.D. Leavis, and Frank Kermode. Not only have their interpretations of texts been influential, but they remain pertinent – and their arguments can be a lot easier to follow than those of some modern critics.

Types of criticism

AQA A	U 1, 2, 3, 4
AQA B	U 1, 2, 3, 4
Edexcel	U 1, 2, 3, 4
OCR	U 1, 2, 3, 4
WJEC	U 1, 2, 3, 4
CCEA	AS U1, AS U2, A2 U1, A2 U2

On the next two pages there are brief summaries of some of the main types of criticism you might encounter. Remember that some of these theories are complex and quite difficult to grasp.

Expressive criticism

Expressive criticism is a term sometimes used to describe criticism whose object is to discover the author's intention – what he or she is trying to say. The context of the writer's life and other writing might be especially pertinent to this approach, and its main concern would often be character and themes. This type of criticism came out of the Romantic movement – influenced by the writing of Wordsworth and others – and describes most criticism in the nineteenth and much of the twentieth century. Essentially, these critics are concerned with what writers are trying to communicate to readers ('expressing' their ideas and feelings), but that does not by any means discount the reader's response.

New criticism

New criticism tries to be more 'objective' than expressive criticism. It was fashionable from the 1930s to the 1960s and was mostly American. It concentrates on the text itself, rejecting historical and biographical context as irrelevant. The 'new' critics liked to see a text as an 'organic unity'. Influenced by critics such as I.A. Richards and William Empson, the 'new' critics reacted against the traditional separation of form and content. They favoured the close analysis of language, imagery, etc. rather than the consideration of genre and context. Their focus on 'close reading' remains influential.

Structuralism

Structuralism is also a form of 'objective' criticism, which is concerned not just with literature but with all aspects of culture. Based on linguistics (the study of language), it is concerned with underlying structures and the way in which the different elements that make up a text, or even a whole culture, relate to each other. Texts can be understood not by relating them to nature or 'real life' but to each other, seeking an underlying system. Structuralists are not interested so much in what things mean as in how they operate. Structuralism developed from French linguistic theories, influenced by Russian 'formalism'. Complex and theoretical, structuralism is one of the most difficult literary theories to get to grips with and one that not many A-Level or university students find helpful. Perhaps the best known structuralist is the French critic Roland Barthes.

Post-structuralism

Post-structuralism reacted against structuralist ideas and rejected the imposing of a theoretical system on literature. Post-structuralists also rejected the idea of fixed meanings. Their work was very influential in literary criticism of the late twentieth century. Sometimes this type of criticism is seen as a sort of 'catch-all' term for many different strands of modern literary criticism. Terms you might hear that are related to post-structuralism include **deconstruction** and **reader-response theory**.

It is now quite common to consider the way in which different readers might react to different texts, something reflected in the reference in AO4 to the way in which texts are 'received'. Reader-response theory can also be seen as a type of psychoanalytical criticism, focusing on the reader's psyche. **Psychoanalytical criticism** – influenced mainly by the work of Sigmund Freud – can also focus on the mind of the writer, linking it to expressive criticism.

Marxist criticism

Marxist criticism, in contrast to structuralism, places context at the centre of criticism. Although Marxist critics do not necessarily share all of Karl Marx's politics, they do share his view of the importance of 'class struggle'. Therefore, the social and economic conditions of the period in which the text was written are extremely important. Marxist critics are not necessarily concerned with the author's intention, more with what the text tells us about society at the time (in the light of Marxist theory), and how that society impacted on the text. Perhaps the most prominent Marxist critic of English Literature is Terry Eagleton.

Feminist criticism

Feminist criticism also focuses on political and social issues, but, as the name implies, is chiefly concerned with women. Feminist critics tend to assume that the texts being studied have emerged from a 'patriarchal' society (one dominated by men) and that women are oppressed. They are interested in how women are presented, as well as what women writers have to say. Like Marxist criticism, feminist criticism can be applied to any text, regardless of its subject matter or of its period. Although feminist criticism was hugely influenced by the work of writers such as Virginia Woolf, it really became established in the latter half of the twentieth century. A lot of female critics (and some male critics) do take a feminist approach. However, do not assume that because a critic is a woman she should automatically be described as a feminist critic.

New historicism

New historicism can be seen as a more modern version of Marxist criticism. Although not as 'political', it looks at texts within their historical contexts. It is influenced by elements of post-structuralism, Marxist criticism and literary history.

Identifying a critic's approach

Some of the critics you have read may have identified themselves – or been identified by their publishers or editors – as belonging to one of the categories above. You may be able to deduce with some certainty which approach others are taking.

> If you are confident about the name of a critic and what they have said, you can refer to, for example, 'feminist critic x' or 'the Marxist interpretation of y' in an exam. If you remember their interpretations, but are unsure of the particular critic's name, you could say something like, 'feminist critics have argued' or 'a new historicist perspective might suggest…'.

KEY POINT

Critics have taken many different approaches to looking at texts. A more general knowledge of literary theory and schools of criticism can help to put their views in context.

PROGRESS CHECK

Collect as many views as you can on one of the texts you are studying. As well as modern views, try to make sure that you find critical views from other periods of history.

4.3 Referring to critics and writing a bibliography

LEARNING SUMMARY	After studying this section, you should be able to:
	• feel confident about referring to critics in your work
	• write a bibliography

How to refer to critics with confidence

AQA A	U 1, 2, 3, 4
AQA B	U 1, 2, 3, 4
Edexcel	U 1, 2, 3, 4
OCR	U 1, 2, 3, 4
WJEC	U 1, 2, 3, 4
CCEA	AS U1, AS U2, A2 U1, A2 U2

If you want to feel confident about referring to critics in your work, the first thing you should do is keep notes of which critics you have used during your studies. Try to get into the habit of making a note of anything you read. Even if you do not feel that you will be referring directly to a source in your work, you should include it in your bibliography (see pages 86–88). You might also want to return to it when you are revising or writing up your coursework. Keep all the details you will need for a bibliography, make notes of the main points of the critic's argument, and copy down some quotations that you feel are apposite.

The importance of acknowledging sources

Many students are unsure about the difference between plagiarism and the proper use of sources. The crucial thing to remember is to acknowledge your sources – if you take an idea directly from a critic or other source you must acknowledge it in your essay. If you include a quotation from a reader or critic in your work and attribute the quotation accurately, you are using your sources properly. It is also permissible to use other readers' views to inform your own in a more general way. If you have done this – absorbing their views rather than referring directly to them – an acknowledgement in the bibliography will be fine.

However, if you use parts of another person's work without acknowledgement – using the actual words or something very close to them – you are guilty of plagiarism. As well as being morally reprehensible, plagiarism is against the law. It is also quite easy to spot, especially if you have used the Internet. Plagiarism is not normally a problem in examinations, as you are unlikely to be able to remember large chunks of someone else's work. However, it is not uncommon in coursework. Its discovery will have serious consequences for your results, and possibly the results of your whole centre.

Referring to critics in exams and coursework

In examinations it can be quite impressive if a candidate uses a few quotations from critics, or paraphrases their views, acknowledging the source. To this end, it might be useful to collect some short, memorable phrases from critics that you think might be useful. However, make sure that if you use them they are relevant to the question. If you cannot remember who said what, you could use phrases such as 'some critics have argued …' and 'it has been suggested that …' to show that you are aware of the views of others.

It is, of course, much easier to refer to critics in coursework, and a good candidate will be expected to do so. When referring to other people's views, it is important to remember that the most important view is your own. The views of others are there to support your argument or to give you something to react to. Do not overload your essay with references to critics. Choose your references carefully and use them appropriately. It can be especially useful to quote from critics who have very different – or even opposing – views on your text.

Direct quotations

If you are quoting directly, follow the guidelines set out in Chapter 2 for quoting from the text (see pages 41–43). As with quotations taken from the text, it is not really enough just to quote someone's view – you need to comment on it, using it to take your argument forward.

How to refer to critics with confidence – examples

Here are a few examples of how to refer to critics in your work.

Coleridge's attitude to symbolism is clarified to some extent by his definition of Fancy:

> The Fancy is indeed no other than a mode of Memory emancipated from the order of time and space; while it is blended with, and modified by the empirical phenomenon of the will, which we express by the word CHOICE. But equally with the ordinary memory the Fancy must receive all its materials ready made from the law of association …
>
> (Biographia Literaria c. XIII)

Coleridge's symbols are moulded by Fancy to convey the fruits of the imagination – 'the infinite I AM' – but by its very nature the Fancy imports into the poetry associations and connotations which complicate – and are sometimes foreign to – the design.

COMMENTARY

This example is taken from an essay comparing Coleridge's and Blake's use of symbols. Note that the student retains Coleridge's rather archaic use of capital letters. The source is properly acknowledged and the student goes on to comment on what the poet has said, relating it to what actually happens in his poetry. It is a good example of the use of the writer's own literary criticism.

Eleanor Prosser (1961, 83) objects strongly to the praise the play has attracted and claims the treatment is singularly inappropriate to the theme:

> … the more one laughs at the devil, instead of at something he ridicules, the weaker he seems as an adversary. In analysing comedy, we must never forget that laughter cancels fear, that man laughs from a position of superiority

This is perceptive up to a point, but in making this statement Prosser betrays a radically mistaken attitude towards the mystery cycles in particular, and Christianity, or at least Catholicism, in general.

COMMENTARY

In this essay about medieval mystery plays, the student quotes from the critic in order to disagree with her views, using them as a stimulus to confidently assert his own – opposing – views.

In his essay 'The Decline of the Novel', Edwin Muir (1965) attributes the direction the novel has taken to the disintegration of general belief in order, and the lack of common ground between author and reader. Perhaps characters can never be seen as 'wholes' because they can no longer be easily located in their environment – for the same reason novelists may find it difficult to take a particular aspect of a personality and present it as a 'character'.

COMMENTARY

This student paraphrases the critic, briefly summing up his view about the modern novel before offering an interpretation of these views and expanding on them.

Unlike the student in the previous example, who disagrees with the critic, this student seems to broadly agree with Muir.

Writing a bibliography

AQA A	**U 2, 4**
AQA B	**U 2, 4**
Edexcel	**U 2, 4**
OCR	**U 2, 4**
WJEC	**U 2, 3**
CCEA	**AS U1**

A bibliography is basically a list of books and other sources that you have used when planning and writing an essay.

It would clearly be impractical to write a bibliography at the end of an examination – you would neither have the time nor the appropriate information.

In coursework, although not compulsory, it is highly advisable to write a bibliography, for a number of reasons:

- It shows the reader that you have researched your subject.
- It provides a list of acknowledged sources, which will help to avoid any suspicion of plagiarism.
- It gives the examiner or moderator the opportunity to check your references.
- It helps make your work look professional.

How to set out your bibliography

The basic information that you need to give in each bibliographical reference is the title, the author and the date of publication. This is usually sufficient at A-Level, but it is usual for academics to give a little more detail and to present the information in a standard fashion.

There are several acceptable ways of setting out a bibliography, but the most popular now (probably because of its clarity) is the 'Author–Date System' of referencing. Basically, all of the works you have referred to are placed in a list at the end of the essay, arranged alphabetically by author. In the main text – in brackets – you give the author's name, the date of publication, and, if necessary, the page number (although if any of these details are referred to in the flow of the main text, they do not need to appear in brackets).

Here are a couple of examples:

- It has been noted that Sidebotham suffered from alcoholism and bouts of depression from an early age (Antrobus 1997).
- Jenkins (2002, 43) suggests that the imagery reflects 'a deep-seated fear and suspicion of authority'.

These are the main points to bear in mind when preparing a bibliography, or list of references:

- The list should be in alphabetical order of the authors' surnames.
- Initials can be used rather than first names.
- The date of publication should be given in brackets after the author's name.
- The place of publication and the name of the publisher should be given after the title.
- Titles of books and journals are given in italics; titles of articles are in single quotation marks.
- 'Editor' is abbreviated to 'ed'.

You should include the reference details for the text that is the subject of your essay, as there are many different editions of some texts. You can also include Internet sources.

An example of a bibliography

Below is an example of a bibliography. All of the works cited are invented.

Appleton, G.A. (1999) *Symbolism in the Works of Antonia Sidebotham*. Oxford: Geeson.

Carrot, L. (1989) 'The Rabbit and the Carnation'. *Critical Monthly*, No.223: 23–49.

Diehard, V. (1970) 'Jealousy in the Work of Antonia Sidebotham', in Houseman, W. (ed) *Women's Poetry of the 1890s*. New York: Tamara Press.

Jackson, K. (1983) *Dickinson and Rossetti and Their Worlds*. London: Dingo.

Meuller, R., translated by Carraway, S. (1921) *Symbolism and Religion*. Edinburgh: McSporran.

O'Neill, S. (2001) 'Sidebotham's Symbolism', in Makin, R. (ed) *Minor Poets of the Nineties*. London: Van Dyke.

Ronseal, U. (1998) *Selected Poems of Antonia Sidebotham*. Cambridge: Getuthrough Study Guides.

Sidebotham, A. (1899) *The Black Cat*. Inkberrow: Sidebotham Press.

Sidebotham, N. (ed) (2000) *The Complete Poems of Antonia Sidebotham*. London: Crowshank.

Websites

www.antoniaspoetry.com

www.universitybirkenhead.ac.uk

www.womenspoems.co.uk

The main point about using a system like this for your bibliography is that it is clear and consistent. Do not worry about getting it exactly right. You will not be penalised. You will, however, be credited for providing a full and interesting list of references in a clear format.

> **KEY POINT**
>
> A well set out bibliography enhances your coursework, giving evidence of careful research and a mature approach.

> **PROGRESS CHECK**
>
> Find – and make a note of – two or three short but memorable quotations from critics about each of your examination texts.

Note – As this chapter focuses on using critics, which is not directly examined, we have not included a sample question and model answer, or any practice examination questions. Have a look at the model answers in other chapters to see how students have used critics effectively.

5 Context

The following topics are covered in this chapter:

- What is context?
- The writer's biography and other works
- Historical, social and political contexts
- Genre, style and literary period
- Language

5.1 What is context?

LEARNING SUMMARY

After studying this section, you should be able to:

- understand what is meant by 'context' in terms of the exam
- understand why context is important
- understand the kinds of contexts that you might study, and see how they can help you engage with the texts you are studying

How context fits into your A-Level course

AQA A	**U 1, 2, 3, 4**
AQA B	**U 1, 2, 3, 4**
Edexcel	**U 1, 2, 3, 4**
OCR	**U 1, 2, 3, 4**
WJEC	**U 1, 2, 3, 4**
CCEA	**AS U1, AS U2, A2 U1, A2 U2**

Assessment Objective (AO) 4 requires you to 'demonstrate detailed critical understanding of the significance and influence of the contexts in which literary texts are written and received'.

We need to begin by asking what is meant by 'contexts'.

There are a range of contextual factors that influence writers' work and how we read them:

1. The context of period or era, including **significant social**, **historical**, **political** and **cultural processes**.
2. The context of the work in terms of the **writer's biography**, or his or her **environment and social surroundings**.
3. The **language** context, including relevant episodes in the use and development of literary language, colloquial language use or dialect styles, etc.
4. The different context of a work established by its **reception over time**, e.g. the recognition that works have different meanings and effects in different periods, and the awareness of different critical responses. Note the overlap here with AO3, which requires that your opinions should be 'informed by the interpretation of other readers'. This aspect was dealt with in Chapter 4.

You will already have come across the idea of 'contexts' at GCSE level, but your awareness will have been less complex than that required at AS and A2 level.

> **KEY POINT**
>
> Contextual influences can be an important factor determining the type of text a writer produces. You will need to explore and evaluate these issues as part of your A2 course.

Your understanding of context will be tested in all units. However, there are some sections where context is given slightly more marks than in others.

There are also a few sections that are not assessed at all against AO4. These are:

- OCR Unit 2 (The Re-creative Study)
- WJEC Unit 1 Section A (Poetry)
- WJEC Unit 2 Section B (Creative Reading)
- CCEA Unit 2 Section A (The Study of Poetry Written after 1800).

Why study context?

AQA A	U 1, 2, 3, 4
AQA B	U 1, 2, 3, 4
Edexcel	U 1, 2, 3, 4
OCR	U 1, 2, 3, 4
WJEC	U 1, 2, 3, 4
CCEA	AS U1, AS U2, A2 U1, A2 U2

When we study a novel, poem or play, or any other piece of writing, we usually focus primarily on the text itself. All of our efforts go into analysing the text and we spend little time looking at the historical, cultural or other influences that help to create the kind of text we are studying. However, no text has ever been produced in a vacuum. All texts are the product of a whole variety of factors that influence both the ways in which writers write and the ways in which readers read a text. Studying and learning about these background influences can provide us with information that can increase our understanding and appreciation of the text.

> **KEY POINT**
>
> Seeing a text in a wider context can enhance, or even change, the perspective that we have of it.

Why context is important – an example

Studying the contextual influences that gave rise to a text can provide information that will help us to understand and appreciate the meaning and significance of that text. The following example illustrates how even a small amount of contextual knowledge can inform, and perhaps even change, your response to a text.

Read the following poem carefully and make notes on your interpretation of it.

Here are some questions that might help:

1. Who is the narrator?
2. What state of mind does the writer appear to be in?
3. What does he have to say through his poem?

My prime of youth is but a frost of cares;
My feast of joy is but a dish of pain;
My crop of corn is but a field of tares;
And all my good is but vain hope of gain:
The day is past, and yet I saw no sun;
And now I live, and now my life is done.

My tale was heard, and yet it was not told;
My fruit is fall'n, and yet my leaves are green;
My youth is spent, and yet I am not old;
I saw the world, and yet I was not seen:
My thread is cut, and yet it is not spun;
And now I live, and now my life is done.

I sought my death, and found it in my womb;
I looked for life, and saw it was a shade;
I trod the earth, and knew it was my tomb;
And now I die, and now I was but made;
My glass is full, and now my glass is run;
And now I live, and now my life is done.

> **COMMENTARY**
>
> You will have noted that the poem seems to be about death.
>
> The narrator is a young person who is lamenting the fact that – although he still had so much life to look forward to – his life, for some reason, is at an end.

That was probably about as much as you could say after a first reading. However, a little background knowledge of the context which gave rise to the writing of this poem can improve our understanding of it considerably.

Now read the following information concerning the context within which this poem was written.

> The poem is entitled *Elegy For Himself* (an elegy is a poem that laments or mourns something and is usually sad or reflective in nature) and was written by Chidiock Tichborne (1558?–86). Both Tichborne and his father were devout Catholics. At this time, the Protestant Queen Elizabeth was on the throne and Catholics were held under much suspicion. In 1583, Tichborne was interrogated by the authorities about importing 'popish relics' when he had returned from abroad, where he had travelled without permission. In 1586 he became involved in the Babington Plot, which was a conspiracy to assassinate Queen Elizabeth and replace her with her Catholic cousin Mary (Queen of Scots). The plot was bungled, however, and the conspirators arrested. Tichborne was amongst them and he was executed on 20 September 1586. He is said to have written this poem while imprisoned in the Tower of London, the night before his execution.

Having read the background to this poem, make a list of the ways in which this information has informed, or even changed, your response to the poem.

> **COMMENTARY**
>
> Here are some ways the contextual information might have informed your response:
> 1. On a **historical** level, this poem is clearly the product of an Elizabethan writer, with all the political aspects which that period involves.
> 2. On an **analytical** level, the knowledge that Tichborne was shortly to be executed helps you make sense of phrases like 'dish of pain', 'now my life is done', 'My youth is spent, and yet I am not old'.
> 3. On an **emotional** level, this knowledge adds an intensity to the poem. You can imagine this young man – in his cell the night before his execution – writing this poem. You can imagine his feelings and his grief at the thought of the life that he would not live.

> **KEY POINT**
>
> Even a small amount of contextual information can have a significant impact on your perception of a text.

Contexts to consider

AQA A	U 1, 2, 3, 4
AQA B	U 1, 2, 3, 4
Edexcel	U 1, 2, 3, 4
OCR	U 1, 2, 3, 4
WJEC	U 1, 2, 3, 4
CCEA	AS U1, AS U2, A2 U1, A2 U2

When studying literature at AS and A-Level, you are expected to learn to recognise and comment on aspects of context that are relevant to the text you are studying. At GCSE level, you simply had to show an awareness of these aspects, but at A2 level you are expected to show a deeper understanding of their significance. So it is important to recognise what kinds of things you need to consider in order to place a text that you are studying 'in context'.

Our suggestions include:
- the **biography** of the writer
- the **other works** the writer has produced
- the **historical period** in which the text was written
- the **place** in which the text was written
- the **genre** chosen or **literary style** of the period
- the ways in which **language** was used at the time the text was written
- how our reading of the text can be influenced by the way **other readers** – both at the time the text was written and since – have interpreted or received the text.

In the following section we will look at these areas in more detail, using some practical examples.

> **PROGRESS CHECK**
>
> Using the above bullet points as a guide, briefly (about one sentence per bullet point) summarise what you know about the context of one of your chosen texts.

5.2 The writer's biography and other works

LEARNING SUMMARY	**After studying this section, you should be able to:** - understand the value of learning about a writer's biography, and see how this knowledge can help you understand the texts you are studying - recognise any common themes, philosophies, ideas explored, etc. in a writer's work

The writer's life

AQA A	U 1, 2, 3, 4
AQA B	U 1, 2, 3, 4
Edexcel	U 1, 2, 3, 4
OCR	U 1, 2, 3, 4
WJEC	U 1, 2, 3, 4
CCEA	AS U1, AS U2, A2 U1, A2 U2

Finding out about a writer's life can be both interesting and enjoyable, but more than this, it can shed valuable light on the text you are studying. In fact, it can be difficult to make sense of some writing unless you know something about the writer's life and views.

Some critics believe that a text should stand alone, independent of any biographical details about the author. Others insist that we should learn as much as we can about writers, in order to understand their work as fully as possible. In many ways both these views are valid, and to a large extent how valuable biographical knowledge is depends on the work itself.

The writer's life – an example

The following poem by William Wordsworth stands alone as a poem, but some biographical knowledge of the author can help us towards a fuller understanding of the text.

Read the following poem through carefully.

Elegaic Stanzas, Suggested by a Picture of Peele Castle in a Storm, Painted by Sir George Beaumont

I was thy Neighbour once, thou rugged Pile!
Four summer weeks I dwelt in sight of thee:
I saw thee every day; and all the while
Thy Form was sleeping on a glassy sea.

So pure the sky, so quiet was the air!
So like, so very like, was day to day!
Whene'er I look'd, thy Image still was there;
It trembled, but it never pass'd away.

How perfect was the calm! it seem'd no sleep;
No mood, which season takes away, or brings:
I could have fancied that the mighty Deep
Was even the gentlest of all gentle Things

Ah! THEN, if mine had been the Painter's hand,
To express what then I saw; and add the gleam,
The light that never was, on sea or land,
The consecration, and the Poet's dream;

I would have planted thee, thou hoary Pile!
Amid a world how different from this!
Beside a sea that could not cease to smile;
On tranquil land, beneath a sky of bliss;

Thou shouldst have seem'd a treasure-house, a mine
Of peaceful years; a chronicle of heaven;—
Of all the sunbeams that did ever shine
The very sweetest had to thee been given

A Picture had it been of lasting case,
Elysian quiet, without toil or strife;
No motion but the moving tide, a breeze,
Or merely silent Nature's breathing life

Such, in the fond delusion of my heart,
Such Picture would I at that time have made:
And seen the soul of truth in every part;
A faith, a trust, that could not be betray'd.

So once it would have been,—'tis so no more;
I have submitted to a new control:
A power is gone, which nothing can restore;
A deep distress hath humaniz'd my Soul.

Not for a moment could I now behold
A smiling sea and he what I have been.
The feeling of my loss will ne'er be old.
This, which I know, I speak with mind serene.

Then, Beaumont, Friend! who would have been
    the Friend
If he had lived, of Him whom I deplore,
This Work of thine I blame not, but commend;
This sea is anger, and that dismal shore.

Oh 'tis a passionate Work!—yet wise and well:
Well chosen is the spirit that is here;
That Hulk which labours in the deadly swell,
This rueful sky, this pageantry of fear!

And this huge Castle, standing here sublime,
I love to see the look with which it braves,
Cased in the unfeeling armour of old time,
The light'ning, the fierce wind, and trampling waves.

Farewell, farewell the Heart that lives alone,
Hous'd in a dream, at distance from the Kind!
Such happiness, wherever it be known,
Is to be pitied; for 'tis surely blind.

But welcome fortitude, and patient chear,
And frequent sights of what is to be born!
Such sights, or worse, as are before me here. —
Not without hope we suffer and we mourn.

William Wordsworth

COMMENTARY

The subject matter of the poem is Sir George Beaumont's painting depicting Peele Castle in a storm. In the first half of the poem (lines 1–32), Wordsworth tells us that he once visited the castle in calm weather. Had he been a painter at that time he would not have produced a painting like Beaumont's, but he would have painted the sea in a tranquil and calm mood.

He now sees that these youthful ideas were deluded. In the second part of the poem he feels that he is no longer a dreaming poet and he sees that the depiction of the castle in a storm represents reality – Beaumont's picture represents a true image of human life. He rejects his former views and recognises the realities of life. He adopts a stoical view and resolves to endure in patience the harshness of life.

Now read the following biographical details.

> The change of view reflected in this poem reflects a more fundamental change of view in Wordsworth's philosophy. He had been greatly affected by the death of his brother, John. John was captain of the merchant ship, *Earl of Abergavenny*, and was drowned when the ship was wrecked in Weymouth Bay in a storm on 5 February, 1805. Peele Castle is near Barrow-in-Furness in Cumbria and Wordsworth had stayed near there in a period of calm summer weather in 1794. In 1806, he visited Sir George Beaumont and saw his painting of the castle. The poem depicts the shift in Wordsworth's attitude to life, by comparing his original impressions of the castle with his response 12 years later to Beaumont's painting.

KEY POINT

Knowledge of a writer's life and the circumstances in which a text was written can help your understanding and appreciation of a text.

PROGRESS CHECK

Now look at the texts you are studying and on which you will need to evaluate contextual influences. Find out as much as you can about the life of the writer of each text.

Other works by the same writer

AQA A	U 1, 2, 3, 4
AQA B	U 1, 2, 3, 4
Edexcel	U 1, 2, 3, 4
OCR	U 1, 2, 3, 4
WJEC	U 1, 2, 3, 4
CCEA	AS U1, AS U2, A2 U1, A2 U2

It can be important to know not only about the lives of the writers that you are studying, but also about the other works that they have written. If you know something about the other works of the writer, and, better still, if you have read any of them, you will be in a better position to draw conclusions about the text you are studying. For example, you will be able to determine whether or not the text is typical of the work of that writer. You might also be able to tell whether authors have particular themes that they explore through their books. For example, if you are studying D.H. Lawrence's *The Rainbow*, you will find that a knowledge of some of his other writing, such as *Sons and Lovers* and *Women in Love*, will help you to see how he explores similar themes across several texts. You will also be able to see where the particular text you are studying stands in the context of the writer's other works.

Works by the same writer – an example

One of the areas that Lawrence felt passionate about was education and how, very often, it failed those it was meant to educate. (He was a teacher himself for a while and so had first-hand experience.) Many of his writings contain elements to do with the theme of education.

The following two pieces are examples of these. The first is taken from his novel *The Rainbow*, where Ursula Brangwen has recently taken up a teaching post. The second is a poem written by Lawrence.

Read the two pieces through very carefully, and consider the following questions:
1. What view of education do these two pieces express?
2. How are these views conveyed to the reader?
3. What similarities and/or differences do you see between the extracts?

Ursula felt her heart faint inside her. Why must she grasp all this, why must she force learning on fifty-five reluctant children, having all the time an ugly, rude jealousy behind her, ready to throw her to the mercy of the herd of children, who would like to rend her as a weaker representative of authority. A great dread of her task possessed her. She saw Mr Brunt, Miss Harby, Miss Schofield, all the schoolteachers, drudging unwillingly at the graceless task of compelling many children into one disciplined, mechanical set, reducing the whole set to an automatic state of obedience and attention, and then of commanding their acceptance of various pieces of knowledge. The first great task was to reduce sixty children to one state of mind, or being. This state must be produced automatically, through the will of the teacher, and the will of the whole school authority, imposed upon the will of the children. The point was that the headmaster and the teachers should have one will in authority, which should bring the will of the children into accord. But the headmaster was narrow and exclusive. The will of the teachers could not agree with his, their separate wills refused to be so subordinated. So there was a state of anarchy, leaving the final judgement to the children themselves, which authority should exist.

So there existed a set of separate wills, each straining itself to the utmost to exert its own authority. Children will never naturally acquiesce to sitting in a class and submitting to knowledge. They must be compelled by a stronger, wiser will against which will they must always strive to revolt. So that the first great effort of every teacher of a large class must be to bring the will of the children into accordance with his own will. And this he can only do by an abnegation of his personal self, and an application of a system of laws, for the purpose of achieving a certain calculable result, the imparting of certain knowledge. Whereas Ursula thought she was going to become the first wise teacher by making the whole business personal, and using no compulsion. She believed entirely in her own personality.

So that she was in a very deep mess. In the first place she was offering to a class a relationship which only one or two of the children were sensitive enough to appreciate, so that the mass were left outsiders, therefore against her. Secondly, she was placing herself in passive antagonism to the one fixed authority of Mr Harby, so that the scholars could more safely harry her. She did not know, but her instinct gradually warned her. She was tortured by the voice of Mr Brunt. On it went, jarring, harsh, full of hate, but so monotonous, it nearly drove her mad: always the same set, harsh monotony. The man was become a mechanism working on and on and on. But the personal man was in subdued friction all the time. It was horrible – all hate! Must she be like this? She could feel the ghastly necessity. She must become the same – put away the personal self, become an instrument, an abstraction, working upon a certain material, the class, to achieve a set purpose of making them know so much each day. And she could not submit. Yet gradually she felt the invincible iron closing upon her. The sun was being blocked out. Often when she went out at playtime and saw a luminous blue sky with changing clouds, it seemed just a fantasy, like a piece of painted scenery. Her heart was so black and tangled in the teaching, her personal self was shut in prison, abolished, she was subjugate to a bad, destructive will. How then could the sky be shining? There was no sky, there was no luminous atmosphere of out-of-doors. Only the inside of the school was real – hard, concrete, real and vicious.

Extract from Chapter 13 of The Rainbow *by D.H. Lawrence*

Last Lesson of the Afternoon by D.H. Lawrence

When will the bell ring, and end this weariness?
How long have they tugged the leash, and strained apart,
My pack of unruly hounds! I cannot start
Them again on a quarry of knowledge they hate to hunt,
I can haul them and urge them no more.

No longer now can I endure the brunt
Of the books that lie out on the desks; a full threescore
Of several insults of blotted pages, and scrawl
Of slovenly work that they have offered me.
I am sick, and what on earth is the good of it all?
What good to them or me, I cannot see!

So, shall I take
My last dear fuel of life to heap on my soul
And kindle my will to a flame that shall consume
Their dross of indifference; and take the toll
Of their insults in punishment? – I will not! –

I will not waste my soul and my strength for this.
What do I care for all that they do amiss!
What is the point of this teaching of mine, and of this
Learning of theirs? It all goes down the same abyss.

What does it matter to me if they can write
A description of a dog, or if they can't?
What is the point? To us both, it is all my aunt!
And yet I'm supposed to care, with all my might.

I do not, and will not; they won't and they don't; and that's all!
I shall keep my strength for myself; they can keep theirs as well.
Why should we beat our heads against the wall
Of each other? I shall sit and wait for the bell.

COMMENTARY

Here are some points that you might have noted:

1. Both extracts express a strong dissatisfaction with the system as it exists. Ursula finds the idea of producing mass uniformity amongst her pupils undesirable. She also senses the negativity of the children to the ideas of restriction and enforced learning. Lawrence's poem expresses much the same view, except that there is more a sense of someone who has tried and failed, and given up the struggle. It has become a case of self-preservation for the poet.

2. Both extracts use a good deal of imagery to convey ideas. Much of the imagery relates to personal development (or lack of it) and the 'inner self'.

3. In the extract from *The Rainbow*, there is the sense that Ursula finds the whole process unsatisfactory and disappointing – quite different from what she had expected. However, she is still involved with her pupils – she is still part of the struggle. In the poem there is very much the feeling of a teacher who has given up. He has resigned himself to the fact that he cannot win this struggle and so has withdrawn from it out of a sense of self-preservation.

5.3 Historical, social and political contexts

LEARNING SUMMARY	After studying this section, you should be able to: • recognise the significance of historical context • understand the significance of social and political context • understand what is meant by cultural context

Historical context

AQA A	U 1, 2, 3, 4
AQA B	U 1, 2, 3, 4
Edexcel	U 1, 2, 3, 4
OCR	U 1, 2, 3, 4
WJEC	U 1, 2, 3, 4
CCEA	AS U1, AS U2, A2 U1, A2 U2

Some knowledge of the historical background of a text, and of the social and political climate of the time, can help you to make sense of some aspects of the writing. Different times, places and cultures have their own style and conventions, and even variations in language. While social, political and historical context are closely linked, it can be useful to consider historical context on its own because – while even contemporary texts have social and political contexts – the notion of historical context is usually associated with the study of texts that were written a long time ago. We often find older texts difficult to understand because their language and references seem obscure to us in a way that they would not have been for their first readers and audiences.

Example – *Dr Faustus*

The extract on the next page is taken from the beginning of the play *Dr Faustus* by Christopher Marlowe, which was written in the latter part of the sixteenth century. To help you understand some of the language used by Faustus and the references he uses, the extract has been marked up with numbers from **1–12**. The explanations are listed at the end of the extract.

Read the extract through carefully and consider these questions:
1. What is Faustus doing in this extract?
2. What difficulties have you encountered in establishing meaning?

Dr Faustus, Act I, Scene i

Faustus in his study

FAUSTUS Settle thy studies, Faustus, and begin
To sound the depth of that thou wilt profess;
Having commenc'd, be a divine in show,
Yet level at the end of every art,
And live and die in Aristotle's[1] works.
Sweet Analytics, 'tis thou hast ravish'd me!
Bene disserere est finis logices.[2]
Is to dispute well logic's chiefest end?
Affords this art no greater miracle?
Then read no more, thou hast attain'd that end;
A greater subject fitteth Faustus' wit.
Bid on kai me[3] on farewell, Galen come,
Seeing *ubi desinit philosophus, ibi incipit medicus.*[4]
Be a physician, Faustus, heap up gold,
And be eterniz'd for some wondrous cure.
Summum bonum medicinae sanitas,[5]
The end of physic is our body's health.
Why, Faustus, hast thou not attain'd that end?
Is not thy common talk sound aphorisms?
Are not thy bills hung up as monuments,
Whereby whole cities have escap'd the plague
And thousand desperate maladies been cur'd?
Yet art thou still but Faustus, and a man.
Couldst thou make men to live eternally
Or being dead raise them to life again,
Then this profession were to be esteem'd.
Physic, farewell! Where is Justinian?[6]
Si una eademque res legatur duobus, alter rem,
    alter valorem rei, etc.[7]
A petty case of paltry legacies!
Exhereditare filium non potest pater, nisi—[8]
Such is the subject of the Institute
And universal body of the law.
This study fits a mercenary drudge
Who aims at nothing but external trash,
Too servile and illiberal for me.
When all is done, divinity is best.
Jerome's[9] Bible, Faustus, view it well.
Stipendium peccati mors est.[10] Ha! *Stipendium,*
    etc. The reward
of sin is death: that's hard. *Si peccasse negamus,*
    fallimur, et
nulla est in nobis veritas.[11] If we say that we have
    no sin, we
deceive ourselves, and there's no truth in us. Why,
    then,
belike we must sin, and so consequently die.
Ay, we must die an everlasting death.
What doctrine call you this? *che sara, sara:*
What will be, shall be! Divinity, adieu!
These metaphysics of magicians
And necromantic books are heavenly;
Lines, circles, letters, and characters:
Ay, these are those that Faustus most desires.
O, what a world of profit and delight,
Of power, of honour, of omnipotence,
Is promis'd to the studious artisan!
All things that move between the quiet poles
Shall be at my command: emperors and kings
Are but obey'd in their several provinces,
Nor can they raise the wind or rend the clouds;
But his dominion that exceeds in this
Stretcheth as far as doth the mind of man:
A sound magician is a demi-god;
Here tire, my brains, to get a deity.[12]

Explanations

1. Ancient Greek philosopher.
2. 'To argue well is the goal of logic.'
3. 'Being and not being' – a traditional subject for philosophical debate.
4. 'Where philosophy ends the physician begins.'
5. 'The ultimate goal of medicine is health.'
6. Roman emperor who codified Roman law – used as a text book by law students.
7. 'If one and the same thing is left to two people, one should receive the thing; the other should receive the value of the thing.'
8. 'A father may not disinherit his son unless ....'
9. Fourth century AD monk and scholar.
10. 'The payment for sin is death.'
11. 'We deceive ourselves if we say we do not sin, and there is no truth in us.'
12. To become a god.

COMMENTARY

1 Faustus is listing the great authors he has read, all of whom now seem useless to him.

2 There are probably a number of things that you found difficult here:
- The actual language used by Faustus is different from modern-day English, and therefore the meaning is not always clear.
- Many of the references Faustus uses, such as to necromantic books, Jerome's Bible, etc. need explanation in order to fully understand what is meant.
- The frequent use of Latin phrases also tends to obscure meaning.

The significance of historical context

The main point in this example is that the historical period in which the text was written is very different from our own time. In order to fully understand all the references and language, a certain amount of research needs to be done. Having established the meaning of words and looked up references that we do not understand, we find it easier to interpret and analyse the text.

However, we also need a deeper understanding of the context. We need to appreciate how people lived in the period, what they may have believed in, and what attitudes they had that were different from those that are usual now. For example, most of you will be aware that many more people were religious at the time *Dr Faustus* was written, as well as often believing in magic and astrology. In this context, the play would have had a very different effect from the one it has on most modern audiences. An understanding of the important and influential ideas that were current at the time your text was written is important, whether that involves knowing about King James VI's attitude to witches when you study *Macbeth*, or understanding the philosophy of Jean-Jacques Rousseau when studying Mary Shelley's *Frankenstein*. This is sometimes referred to as **philosophical context**.

Another aspect of historical context is the way in which the events of the time in which the text was written or is set affect the people and events of the text. Jane Austen's novel *Persuasion*, for example, is set just after the end of the Napoleonic wars. The consequences of the end of the war impact on the characters in the novel, just as they impacted on the people of Britain. It is also interesting to consider what use authors have made of what was already history to them. Modern historians may have a very different view of the Wars of the Roses from that given in Shakespeare's history plays.

KEY POINT

An understanding of the historical context in which a text was written can add a lot to our understanding and appreciation.

PROGRESS CHECK

Make sure you know when each of your texts were written and when they are set. Do some research to find out about the main historical events and influential thinkers.

Social and political context

AQA A	U 1, 2, 3, 4
AQA B	U 1, 2, 3, 4
Edexcel	U 1, 2, 3, 4
OCR	U 1, 2, 3, 4
WJEC	U 1, 2, 3, 4
CCEA	AS U1, AS U2, A2 U1, A2 U2

Works written in more recent times may be written in language similar to our own, and we may feel that they are more accessible. However, they often show people leading lives that are very different from our own, and deal with political ideas with which we are not familiar.

Example – *Hard Times*

Charles Dickens, for example, often used his novels as a vehicle for social criticism, as a way of showing the literate middle classes what life was like for the poor. For him, it was a way of campaigning for political change through the medium of entertainment.

The following extract is taken from his novel, *Hard Times*. Read it through carefully. Dickens seems to be making a social comment here. What point do you think he is making?

Coketown, to which Messrs Bounderby and Gradgrind now walked, was a triumph of fact; it had no greater taint of fancy in it than Mrs Gradgrind herself. Let us strike the key-note, Coketown, before pursuing our tune.

It was a town of red brick, or of brick that would have been red if the smoke and ashes had allowed it; but, as matters stood it was a town of unnatural red and black like the painted face of a savage. It was a town of machinery and tall chimneys, out of which interminable serpents of smoke trailed themselves for ever and ever, and never got uncoiled. It had a black canal in it, and a river that ran purple with ill-smelling dye, and vast piles of buildings full of windows where there was a rattling and a trembling all day long, and where the piston of the steam-engine worked monotonously up and down, like the head of an elephant in a state of melancholy madness. It contained several large streets all very like one another, and many small streets still more like one another, inhabited by people equally like one another, who all went in and out at the same hours, with the same sound upon the pavements, to do the same work, and to whom every day was the same as yesterday and tomorrow, and every year the counterpart of the last and the next.

These attributes of Coketown were in the main inseparable from the work by which it was sustained; against them were to be set off, comforts of life which found their way all over the world, and elegancies of life which made, we will not ask how much of the fine lady, who could scarcely bear to hear the place mentioned. The rest of its features were voluntary, and they were these.

You saw nothing in Coketown but what was severely workful. If the members of a religious persuasion built a chapel there – as the members of eighteen religious persuasions had done – they made it a pious warehouse of red brick, with sometimes (but this only in highly ornamented examples) a bell in a bird-cage on the top of it. The solitary exception was the New Church; a stuccoed edifice with a square steeple over the door, terminating in four short pinnacles like florid wooden legs. All the public inscriptions in the town were painted alike, in severe characters of black and white. The jail might have been the infirmary, the infirmary might have been the jail, the town-hall might have been either, or both, or anything else, for everything that appeared to the contrary in the graces of their construction. Fact, fact, fact, everywhere in the immaterial. The M'Choakumchild school was all fact, and the school of design was all fact, and the relations between the lying-in hospital and the cemetery, and what you couldn't state in figures, or show to be purchaseable in the cheapest market and saleable in the dearest, was not, and never should be, world without end, Amen.

Extract from Hard Times *by Charles Dickens*

Dickens seems to be saying that Coketown is a place that is driven by the industrial processes that sustain it. It lacks feeling and imagination and this has been carried into every aspect of the place. The children learn 'FACTS' and the name of the teacher, Mr M'Choakumchild, sums up the effect that he has on the children he teaches. Dickens's point is that industrialisation has produced a society that is lacking in human warmth and feeling.

The significance of social and political context

Social context refers to the way of life shown in a text, whether it is the life of the poor in *Hard Times*, or the life of the upper middle class characters of Jane Austen's novels. It is also concerned with ideas about society, for example about social class. In this way it is closely linked to political context. If we are studying a text that is written, or set, in the past, both social and political context can be seen as part of historical context. We have probably heard about the Industrial Revolution through our study of history. We also know something about the effect this had on the way many people lived, and the way radicals and campaigners reacted politically to what was sometimes known as 'the condition of the poor'. We probably also have some knowledge of the Napoleonic Wars. The effect of these wars on the landowners and middle classes, as well as on those who served in the navy, is shown in Jane Austen's *Persuasion*. Unlike Dickens, Austen is not usually thought of as a political writer, but an understanding of the politics and social conditions of her time can be just as useful.

KEY POINT

Historical, political and social context are very closely connected.

PROGRESS CHECK

Find any notes you have about the social and political context of the texts you are studying. Think about how the social and political context relates to the text itself.

Cultural context

AQA A	U 1, 2, 3, 4
AQA B	U 1, 2, 3, 4
Edexcel	U 1, 2, 3, 4
OCR	U 1, 2, 3, 4
WJEC	U 1, 2, 3, 4
CCEA	AS U1, AS U2, A2 U1, A2 U2

'Place' is another important element to consider when studying a text. Many modern writers who write in English can trace their roots to other countries. Some of this is what we call 'post-colonial' writing – writing by people who were born or grew up in countries that were former colonies, such as the West Indies, India, several African states, Canada, Australia and New Zealand. Very often, such writers set their work within a particular cultural context, which can have a significant bearing on their work. Examples of writers with this kind of background that you might study are Wole Soyinka, Peter Carey and Derek Walcott. You might also study work by American writers, such as Alice Walker or J.D. Salinger, or even texts that were originally written in other languages.

In all of these cases you should consider the culture of the place where the text is set. Culture means the way of life associated with a particular nation, region or ethnic group. Culture is usually associated with the arts, religion, rituals and traditions. In literature, characters' cultural backgrounds often have an important impact on their sense of identity, as well as their attitude to the world around them.

> **KEY POINT**
>
> Writers writing in English come from many different cultures. An understanding of cultural context will enhance your appreciation of their work.

> **PROGRESS CHECK**
>
> Consider the cultural context of the texts you are studying. If any of them are set in a place that you do not know anything about, find out about its culture.

5.4 Genre, style and literary period

LEARNING SUMMARY	After studying this section, you should be able to: • understand the importance of genre, style and literary period • recognise the features in the texts you are studying

Why do genre and literary style matter?

AQA A	U 1, 2, 3, 4
AQA B	U 1, 2, 3, 4
Edexcel	U 1, 2, 3, 4
OCR	U 1, 2, 3, 4
WJEC	U 1, 2, 3, 4
CCEA	AS U1, AS U2, A2 U1, A2 U2

As well as belonging to a historical period, texts often belong to a 'literary' period. The literary period a text belongs to will often influence the style of the writing, and even the genre. Texts written in the same historical period are likely to have some similarities (although this is not always the case). You will often find a text referred to by the period it was written in, for example a 'Victorian novel' or a 'Restoration comedy'. In these kinds of texts, we would expect to find certain stylistic features that were typical of writers of that time, as well as ideas and attitudes that were current in the period.

> The first letters of literary 'movements' are given a capital letter. So, for instance, you would write '**R**omantic' if you were talking about the writing of, say, Keats, but 'romantic' if you were talking about feelings of love.

Other writers might be referred to as part of a literary 'movement', a group of writers who knew each other and/or were influenced by each other's work. Examples of these movements include the Augustans, the Romantics and the Modernists. You might also come across groupings of writers or texts according to their subject matter or style, regardless of whether they were writing at the same time, for example 'war poets', 'gothic novels' and 'pastoral poetry'. We refer to both of these categories when we talk about 'genre'.

Bear in mind that these terms are quite flexible. It can be a matter of opinion whether a certain writer is 'gothic' or whether a novel is a 'thriller'. You might also detect elements of more than one genre in a given text. Many critics, for example, have noted a gothic element in the novels of the Brontë sisters, though few would go so far as to describe them as 'gothic novels', while Daphne du Maurier's *Rebecca* has been described as having elements of both 'modern gothic' and the detective story.

Recognising the typical features of a genre

AQA A   U 1, 2, 3, 4
AQA B   U 1, 2, 3, 4
Edexcel U 1, 2, 3, 4
OCR   U 1, 2, 3, 4
WJEC   U 1, 2, 3, 4
CCEA   AS U1, AS U2,
         A2 U1, A2 U2

To help you understand the way in which such categories can be useful in putting texts in context, we will look more closely at the Romantics.

The Romantics

A number of 'Romantic' poets appear across specifications. Normally, the word 'romantic' brings to mind images of romantic love or 'romance'. However, when we refer to the 'Romantic Poets', we mean something rather different. The Romantic Period refers to a specific period of time – roughly between the years of 1780 and 1830. A number of writers were part of the Romantic Movement and were connected by the ideas and philosophies they shared. Not all writers of this period were 'Romantic' writers in this sense, though. For example, Jane Austen wrote her novels during this period and they are not 'Romantic' in terms of the principles of the Romantic Movement, although you might detect the growing influence of the Romantics in *Persuasion*, whose protagonist is a reader of Byron and Scott.

'Romanticism' refers to a new set of ideas – of a philosophy which presented a new way of looking at the world, life, and Man's place within the Universe. These ideas spread throughout Europe during the latter part of the eighteenth century and remained influential throughout much of the nineteenth century. The Romantics were interested in the freedom of the individual, emotions, nature and the soul. Inspired initially by the French Revolution, they were also interested in ideas about equality and freedom. The ideas of the Romantics influenced music and painting, as well as literature. Ultimately, these new ways of thinking encapsulated most aspects of life, including politics, religion and science. The Romantics were also reacting against the style and philosophy of the 'Augustans' – eighteenth-century poets such as Pope and Dryden – whose work was very formal and who, like many of the philosophers of the time, valued reason above emotion. The Romantics are often thought of as 'nature poets'. However, they were also interested in the lives of ordinary people, a concern reflected in their rejection of 'classical' forms of poetry, in favour of traditional and popular forms, such as the ballad.

In order to fully understand Romantic writing, it is important that you learn as much as possible about the historical background and events of the time, because it was a time of great upheaval, revolution and war. Much of the writing of the time was influenced by these events.

In terms of English Literature, the most important writers of this period were:
- William Blake (1757–1827)
- William Wordsworth (1770–1850)
- Samuel Taylor Coleridge (1772–1834)
- Lord Byron (1788–1824)
- Percy Bysshe Shelley (1792–1822)
- John Keats (1795–1821).

Some critics do not include Blake in the Romantic movement, but he certainly influenced the later poets. The Scottish poet Robert Burns is often considered a Romantic. The poet and novelist, Sir Walter Scott, and the novelist, Mary Shelley, the author of *Frankenstein*, are also often included as Romantic writers, although you will also see Mary Shelley's work described as 'gothic', usually thought of as a rather sensational and more popular version of Romanticism.

Much Romantic poetry is either:

- **lyrical** – poetry that tends to be reflective, perhaps capturing a particular moment or experience, and which then goes on to ponder its deeper meaning or significance, **or**
- **narrative** – poetry that tells a story and often encapsulates the ideas and philosophies of the Romantics, e.g. Coleridge's *The Ancient Mariner*.

Here are two stanzas from *Fidelity* by William Wordsworth.

A barking sound the Shepherd hears,
A cry as of dog or fox
He halts – and searches with his eyes
Among the scattered rocks:

And now at distance can discern
A stirring in a brake or fen;
And instantly a dog is seen,
Glancing through the covert green.

What would you say is typically Romantic about these stanzas?

COMMENTARY

Here are some of the points you may have noted:

1. They are concerned with man's relationship with nature.
2. They are about a working man – a shepherd.
3. They are telling a story.
4. The form of this poem could be described as a variation on the traditional ballad form. Normally a ballad is arranged in quatrains. In each one the first and third lines have four stresses, and the second and fourth have three – each quatrain rhymes ABAB. Wordsworth varies this form.
5. If you look up the poem and read the rest of it, you will see that it features descriptions of wild nature, which is dangerous as well as beautiful, and that its theme is the dog's fidelity to his dead master – not rational, but emotional.

KEY POINT

Genre, style and literary period can exert an important influence on writing, and a knowledge of them can help you understand the text.

PROGRESS CHECK

Can the texts you are studying be placed in a particular historical period? Do they reflect in any way what was happening at the time that they were written? Does the period have any bearing on the genre or style of the texts?

5.5 Language

LEARNING SUMMARY	**After studying this section, you should be able to:** ● understand the relationship between context and language ● see how the context can influence the language used in a text

The relationship between context and language

AQA A	**U 1, 2, 3, 4**
AQA B	**U 1, 2, 3, 4**
Edexcel	**U 1, 2, 3, 4**
OCR	**U 1, 2, 3, 4**
WJEC	**U 1, 2, 3, 4**
CCEA	**AS U1, AS U2, A2 U1, A2 U2**

Language is not a static thing. It is constantly changing and evolving, and the older the text the more the language is likely to have changed. For example, we can see major differences between the Middle English of Chaucer and our modern English. The language of Shakespeare is also different, but less so than Chaucer's. Even in fairly recent texts there may be elements of vocabulary and usage that are unfamiliar to us.

Example – *Paradise Lost*

The following extract is taken from a very long 'epic' poem called *Paradise Lost*, written by John Milton in the seventeenth century. This is from Book One and is the opening of the poem. Read it through carefully and make a note of anything you find difficult to understand.

> Of Man's First Disobedience and the Fruit
> Of that Forbidden Tree, whose mortal taste
> Brought Death into the World; and all our woe,
> With loss of *Eden*, till one greater Man
> Restore us, and regain the blissful Seat,
> Sing Heav'nly Muse, that on the secret top
> Of *Oreb*, or of *Sinai*, didst inspire
> That Shepherd, who first taught the chosen Seed,
> In the Beginning how the Heav'ns and Earth
> Rose out of *Chaos*: or if *Sion* Hill
> Delight thee more, and *Siloa's* Brook that flow'd
> Fast by the Oracle of God; I thence
> Invoke thy aid to my adventurous Song,
> That with no middle flight intends to soar
> Above th'*Aonian* Mount, while it pursues
> Things unattempted yet in Prose or Rime
> And chiefly Thou O Spirit, that dost prefer
> Before all Temples th'upright heart and pure,
> Instruct me, for Thou know'st, Thou from the first
> Wast present, and with mighty wings outspred
> Dove-like satst brooding on the vast Abyss
> And mad'st it pregnant: What in me is dark
> Illumin, what is low raise and support;
> That to the highth of this great Argument
> I may assert Eternal Providence
> And justifie the wayes of God to men.

Extract from Paradise Lost *by John Milton*

You might have found parts of the extract difficult to understand because:
- there are some archaic spellings that might have caused confusion
- there are some obscure metaphorical references
- some of the names are strange and do not mean anything to us
- the word order might have seemed a little odd in places.

How context can influence the language used in a text

AQA A	U 1, 2, 3, 4
AQA B	U 1, 2, 3, 4
Edexcel	U 1, 2, 3, 4
OCR	U 1, 2, 3, 4
WJEC	U 1, 2, 3, 4
CCEA	AS U1, AS U2, A2 U1, A2 U2

Obviously, one of the problems in reading and understanding poetry that was written hundreds of years ago is that the language we use today is not quite the same as the language that was used then. Words may have changed in meaning, hold different connotations, or may simply have become outmoded.

The second problem is that the references or allusions used would have been understood and have held some significance to a reader in the poet's own age, but often mean little to us today. Good editions usually contain notes and glossaries to help you understand these more obscure references and so appreciate the text more fully. Make sure you use them to the full. Milton uses many references and allusions to classical literature and to the Bible in his work. His readers in the seventeenth century would have possessed this kind of background and would understand immediately the biblical references and classical allusions. For them, the references would serve to illuminate and illustrate the work, as Milton intended. Most of us, as twenty first-century readers, do not have this kind of background, and the references can initially act as barriers to meaning, rather than assisting our understanding.

Here are some things you can do to help you understand this kind of text more fully:
- Read the piece several times and adopt a systematic approach.
- Use the parts of the poetry that you understand as clues to help you understand more difficult sections.
- Highlight particularly difficult words, phrases, lines, images, etc.
- Look up words that you do not understand in a good dictionary.
- Refer to the notes or glossary in the text book.
- Do some background reading about the writer and their period.

These suggestions apply to any kind of text, not just poetry.

There are lots of things you can do to become more familiar with texts written in other periods, and in a language or style that is different from modern English.

Cultural context – 'place'

Language can also change according to the place in which the text is set. For example, some writers use dialect forms to give a sense of place. D.H. Lawrence uses a dialect form to try to capture the Nottinghamshire dialect, and Emily Brontë does the same for the Yorkshire dialect in *Wuthering Heights*. Using language in this way helps to provide another kind of 'context' for the text.

Here is an example from *Wuthering Heights* of how Emily Brontë used the Yorkshire dialect. Why do you think she used this dialect form for the character of Joseph?

On that bleak hill-top the earth was hard with a black frost, and the air made me shiver through every limb. Being unable to remove the chain, I jumped over, and, running up the flagged causeway bordered with straggling gooseberry bushes, knocked vainly for admittance, till my knuckles tingled, and the dogs howled.

'Wretched inmates!' I ejaculated mentally, 'you deserve perpetual isolation from your species for your churlish inhospitably. At least, I would not keep my doors barred in the day-time. I don't care – I will get in!' So resolved, I grasped the latch and shook it vehemently. Vinegar-faced Joseph projected his head from a round window of the barn.

'Whet are ye for?' he shouted, 'T' maister 's dahn i' t' fowld. Goa rahnd by th' end ut' laith, if yah went tuh spake tull him.'

'Is there nobody inside to open the door?' I hallooed, responsively.

'They's nobbut t missis: and shoo'll nut oppen 't an ye mak yer flaysome dins till neeght.'

'Why? cannot you tell her who I am, eh, Joseph?'

'Nor-ne me! Aw'll hae noa hend wi't,' muttered the head, vanishing.

The snow began to drive thickly. I seized the handle to essay another trial: when a young man without coat, and shouldering a pitchfork, appeared in the yard behind. He hailed me to follow him, and, after marching through a wash-house, and a paved area containing a coal-shed, pump, and pigeon-cote, we at length arrived in the huge, warm, cheerful apartment, where I was formerly received.

Extract from Wuthering Heights *by Emily Brontë*

COMMENTARY

Here is a possible answer:
1. Brontë used this dialect form to add realism to Joseph's character. This manner of speech is clearly in context with the kind of character Brontë was portraying and the effect that she wanted to achieve.
2. This dialect form differentiates Joseph's speech from other characters such as Lockwood. Brontë also gives Heathcliff his own way of speaking.

KEY POINT

Writers' use of language is often related to the philosophical, social and cultural contexts in which they wrote.

PROGRESS CHECK

Look at the ways in which language is used in the texts that you are studying.

Sample question and model answer

To what extent would you agree with the view that the work of John Donne represents a change in the nature of English poetry?

QUESTION OVERVIEW

This question is in the style of a question from AQA B Unit 3.

Although a real answer would be assessed using all four AOs, this essay has been annotated with reference to AO4 only, which has been reproduced below for your reference.

AO4: Demonstrates understanding of the significance and influence of the contexts in which literary texts are written and received.

The candidate refers to the time when Donne wrote ('the last years of the sixteenth century') and confidently discusses the accepted conventions of Elizabethan love poetry in terms of tradition and style. →

During the last years of the sixteenth century, literature began to emerge in a rather different light - a more critical, dramatic and complex light - which provided a whole new power of expression. Much of the poetry up to the end of the sixteenth century conformed very much to a convention - the convention of courtly love. The main aim of the Elizabethan poems was not to relate individually, but to conform to the convention. This convention of courtly love consisted of prescribed styles and semi-dramatic stylised behaviour, but within the convention the writer could produce his own variations. The transition from `artificiality to realism' can be very clearly illustrated through a comparison of the poems of John Donne with some of the other, more traditional, Elizabethan poets.

The reference to Donne's 'contemporaries' places the discussion firmly in the context of what was happening in poetry at the time, acknowledging that Donne's work still adheres to the conventions of the time to some extent. →

However, even Donne, although he rejected the sentimentality and blatant unreality of this tradition, did not reject it entirely. He still wrote of the experiences of love in a semi-detached way, but he widened immensely its range of moods and expressions, giving it a sense of reality, and therefore life and meaning. His work has none of the smooth, superficial coating of poetic sweetness that his contemporaries had. The true subject of Donne's love poetry goes much deeper than simply the experiences he had of love, to the subject of love itself - and all situations concerned with love - its moods and attitudes, its experiences and experiments. His poems are concerned with complexities and incongruities, and therefore expressiveness rather than beauty is the aim. The beauty of Donne's poems comes rather as a by-product, from the result of successful expression. Poems that have no convention to which they must adhere are able to make full use of language that gives total expression, and it is this language that Donne utilises to the full.

The marked difference in the two styles - the old style and the new - can perhaps best be seen by a comparison of a Donne poem with one written in a more traditional style, for example a poem by Thomas Campion. He was celebrated equally as a poet and composer and therefore he insisted on a union of words and music. His poem that begins `There is a garden in her face' is written in the typical, traditional, Elizabethan style.

The artificiality becomes immediately apparent at the opening of the poem:

> There is a garden in her face
> Where roses and white lilies blow

The metaphor that the poet uses here to liken the lady's face to a garden is very artificial, and perhaps even a little absurd. What the poet has tried to do is to use the image of the garden, and the roses and the lilies, to convey the feeling of freshness and beauty that he sees in her face.

Sample question and model answer (continued)

Although artificial and strained, the image is successful in so far as it conveys a feeling of pleasantness, the roses and lilies relating perhaps to the lady's complexion.

The image of the garden is taken up in the next two lines:

> A heavenly paradise is that place,
> herein all pleasant fruits do flow

This raises the image still further - speaking of the garden, and indirectly the lady's face, as a `heavenly paradise'. However, there is a feeling that this image has been pushed too far, and it is too removed from the actual reality of the lady's face to be fully effective.

The image is carried on in the next line, taking a different turn - in the garden:

> There cherries grow which none may buy
> Till `Cherry-ripe' themselves do cry.

This refers to the lips of the lady and is broadened in the next stanza:

> Those cherries fairly do enclose
> Of Orient pearl a double row,
> Which when her lovely laughter shows
> They look like rosebuds filled with snow

The introduction of a comparison with another poet, Campion, is an effective way of putting Donne's work in context in order to demonstrate that, in the context of his time, his poetry could be seen as revolutionary. The student shows a fairly sophisticated understanding of the 'artificiality' of much Elizabethan love poetry, focusing on the fashion for elaborate metaphors. →

Like the image in the first stanza, this image is a `pretty' one and it conjures up pictures of beauty and sweetness. However, it lacks the depth of realism, and the poem continues in this vein.

A point that should be borne in mind about a poem like this is that they were often written to be set to music and sung at court. Because of this, the poets had to work within certain bounds, and their object was to produce something pleasant and pleasing to the ear, rather than something that had depth and meaning. The ideas in this poem, though, seem to be forced. It lacks depth and meaning and is, therefore, very superficial and artificial. When we compare this to a poem by John Donne, the difference between artificiality and realism becomes very marked.

For example, here is the first stanza from `The Canonisation':

> For God's sake hold your tongue, and let me love,
> Or chide my palsie, or my gout,
> My five gray haires, or ruin'd fortune flout,
> With wealth your state, your minde with Arts improve,
> Take you a course, get you a place,
> Observe his honour, or his grace,
> Or the Kings reall, or his stamped face
> Contemplate, what you will, approve,
> So you will let me love.

The candidate shows his knowledge of the period by his reference to setting poems to music and to 'court'. The fact that the song might have been sung at court indicates the kind of society the poet moved in, or hoped to move in. It is implied that the need to entertain the court was detrimental to the quality of poetry. The student's discussion of Donne's 'realism' puts the poet in the context of his age by drawing attention to his use of words like 'gout' and 'palsie' as examples of his engagement with real life. →

In this first stanza, it can be seen that there is a vast difference between this and the poem previously examined. The poem opens with a colloquial outburst which immediately creates an atmosphere that is essentially dramatic. Instead of speaking of `gardens', `roses', `lilies' and `heavenly paradise', Donne's stress lies on words such as `palsie' and `gout'. Donne also uses a form of short phrases, but within a rather more complex structure. These short phrases add to the rather dramatic atmosphere created - they add urgency, almost a rush to express his feelings. Here the aim is not to attain sweetness, grace or melody either for its own sake or to

Sample question and model answer (continued)

accommodate the musician, but instead to achieve a realistic expressiveness, the like of which had never appeared before in lyric poetry.

In the second stanza, Donne goes on to reinforce his argument - to be allowed to love without interference:

> Alas, alas, who's injured by my love?
> What merchant ship have my sighs drown'd
> Who saies my teares have overflowed his ground?
> When did my colds a forward spring remove?
> When did the heats which my veines fill
> Adde one man to the plaguie Bill?
> Soldiers finde warres, and Lawyers find out still
> Litigious men which quarrels move,
> Though she and I do love

Again, the student focuses on Donne's interest in the less 'courtly' side of Elizabethan life. The penultimate sentence, bringing us back to the question, establishes the poet firmly as a man of his time, but in the vanguard of change.

Here, Donne's arguments are sound, down to earth and realistic. He uses logical reasoning to support his arguments. He does not use artificial images and he avoids the ornamental convention, instead using references to wars, quarrels and the plague. From this example, then, it can be seen that Donne achieves an intensity of feeling and emotion that Campion never reaches. Donne's style achieves a truth to emotion and conveys a feeling of genuine, serious thought. The ideas and ideals embodied in the poetry of John Donne show clearly the change that was taking place in literature at the end of the sixteenth century and beginning of the seventeenth century. It typifies the changes in thought and fundamental attitudes to poetry that were the basis of the change from artificiality to realism.

SUMMATIVE COMMENT

This question has AO4 as its dominant AO, clearly asking candidates to focus on a poet's relationship to the context in which he wrote. This student has maintained focus on the question and the AO, showing perceptive understanding of the literary conventions of the time, and alluding to social and historical context in a natural and relevant fashion.

Practice examination questions

AS

AQA B Unit 1

Samuel Taylor Coleridge: *The Rime of the Ancient Mariner*

A) How does Coleridge tell the story in Part IV of *The Rime of the Ancient Mariner*?

B) How far do you agree with the view that *The Rime of the Ancient Mariner* is both nightmarish and revelatory?

Edexcel Unit 1

Jane Austen: *Pride and Prejudice*

'To Austen's women wealth and social status are far more important than love.' How far and in what ways do you agree with this statement?

WJEC Unit 1

Arthur Miller: *Broken Glass*

Re-read Scene five. Explore the ways in which Miller presents Sylvia in this extract and elsewhere in the play.

CCEA Unit 2

Elizabeth Gaskell: *North and South*

'*North and South* is as much about the oppression of women as it is about the oppression of the working class.'

With reference to appropriately selected parts of the novel and relevant external contextual influences on the novel, give your response to the above statement.

Practice examination questions (continued)

A2

AQA Unit 3

Read the two poems (A and B) carefully. They were written at different times by different writers. Bringing to your answer, where appropriate, your wider reading in the poetry of love, compare the ways in which the two poets have used poetic form, structure and language to express their thoughts and ideas.

A) *To Celia* by Ben Jonson (1572–1637)

Come my Celia, let us prove,
While we may, the sports of love;
Time will not be ours, forever:
He, at length, our good will sever.
Spend not then his guifts in vaine.
Sunnes, that set, may rise againe:
But if at once we lose this light,
'Tis with us, perpetuall night.
Why should we deferre out joyes?
Fame, and rumor are but toyes.
Cannot we delude the eyes
Of a few poor household spyes?
Or his easier eares beguile,
So removed by our wile?
'Tis no sinne, loves fruit to steale,
But the sweet theft to reveale:
To be taken, to be seene,
These have crimes accounted beene.

B) *Remember* by Christina Rossetti (1830–1894)

Remember me when I am gone away,
Gone far away into the silent land;
When you can no more hold me by the hand,
Nor I half turn to go yet turning stay.
Remember me when no more day by day
You tell me of our future that you planned:
Only remember me; you understand
It will be late to counsel then or pray.
Yet if you should forget me for a while
And afterwards remember, do not grieve:
For if the darkness and corruption leave
A vestige of the thoughts that I once had,
Better by far you should forget and smile
Than that you should remember and be sad.

AQA B Unit 3

Elements of the Gothic

John Webster: *The White Devil*

'The world of John Webster is not only a world full of violence and corruption, but is also a world which lacks a moral compass.'

Do you agree with this view?

Edexcel Unit 3

Shakespeare: *Twelfth Night*

'*Twelfth Night* does not have a happy ending.' Evaluate this view of the play.

6 Studying drama

The following topics are covered in this chapter:

- The nature of drama texts
- Plot and structure
- Opening scenes
- Creating characters
- Endings
- Themes and issues
- Text and context

6.1 The nature of drama texts

LEARNING SUMMARY

After studying this section, you should be able to:

- appreciate how a drama text differs from other kinds of text
- understand – and have ideas about – how to study a drama text
- appreciate the difference between reading the text and seeing it performed

How drama fits into your A-Level course

AQA A	U 1, 2, 3, 4
AQA B	U 2, 3
Edexcel	U 2, 4
OCR	U 2, 3, 4
WJEC	U 1, 3, 4
CCEA	AS U1, A2 U1

As part of your A-Level course you will study at least two drama texts. One of these must be a play by Shakespeare (see Chapter 7). The other drama text or texts that you will study could be drawn from any time period, ranging from modern texts to ones that might have been written before 1800.

The exam boards' specifications are structured in different ways. This means that the texts that you will study at AS and at A2 level, and the method by which you will be assessed on particular texts – either through coursework or exam – will depend on the particular specification that you are studying.

How to approach a drama text

AQA A	U 1, 2, 3, 4
AQA B	U 2, 3
Edexcel	U 2, 4
OCR	U 2, 3, 4
WJEC	U 1, 3, 4
CCEA	AS U1, A2 U1

If you look up the word 'drama' in a dictionary, you will find a definition that says something like this.

> 1. A play for acting on the stage or for broadcasting.
> 2. The art of writing and presenting plays.

Such definitions point to one of the main differences between a drama text and the other texts that you will study. The drama text is primarily written to be 'seen' rather than read. This is an important point to bear in mind when you are writing about a play for your coursework or in an exam answer, because students often write about plays as if they were novels rather than a piece of drama. In many ways a play can only be fully appreciated when seen as a **performance**. The elements that create the drama are much more than simply words on a page – the whole effect can only be truly created through the play being acted out on the stage in front of an **audience**, who share the experience of watching the play and responding to it.

So, when studying a play, it will really help if you are able to see a live performance of it at the theatre. Unfortunately, this is not always possible and so – when studying the play in the classroom – it is vital that you always bear in mind the performance element of the text. You should recognise that studying a play is very different from studying a novel, and that you will need to employ different techniques in approaching it. Watching a performance of the play on DVD, or even listening to an audio recording of it, will help you get a sense of the play in performance. You should also try to visualise the action in your mind as you are reading the play.

> **KEY POINT**
>
> Remember, plays are meant to be seen as a shared experience and not read in isolation.

Work with others to dramatise scenes from the text. Talk to them about staging implications. Imagine you are a theatre director – plan carefully how you would stage a production of the play, the kind of actors you would cast, how you would bring your own interpretation out live on stage, etc. Use diagrams, drawings and models to work out sets, stage layout, and props for selected scenes.

Here are some things you can do to help you approach your drama text:
- Read the play in a group, each taking a different part.
- Act out scenes of the play with other people.
- Take note of the **stage directions** – these will help you to visualise what is happening.
- Try to see a live performance of the play.
- Try to see a DVD performance.
- Listen to an audio recording of the play.
- Recognise that each performance of the play presents just one interpretation – a play can be interpreted in lots of different ways. Every production of a play is different in some way, whether it takes place in the theatre or on film.

> **PROGRESS CHECK**
>
> Identify three ways that you can try to see a play that you are studying as a performance.
>
> Internet research; obtain information from local and national theatres to see if any of the plays you are studying are being performed, either now or in the future; check DVD availability – some libraries have a DVD section.

6.2 Plot and structure

> **LEARNING SUMMARY**
>
> After studying this section, you should be able to:
> - understand the relationship between plot and structure in a drama
> - identify some key elements in the structure of the play you are studying

The plot

AQA A   U 1, 2, 3, 4
AQA B   U 2, 3
Edexcel U 2, 4
OCR   U 2, 3, 4
WJEC   U 1, 3, 4
CCEA   AS U1, A2 U1

All plays have some kind of storyline or **plot**. The plot is of central importance to most plays, although there are some plays – particularly some modern drama – where the plot is stripped away to a bare minimum, and the fact that nothing happens is the very point of the play. For example, some of Samuel Beckett's plays, such as *Waiting for Godot*, work in this way.

At its simplest the plot is the story of the play – what actually happens. Having said that, there is much more to plot than simple 'storyline'. In most plays, the plot is a highly developed and crafted fundamental aspect of the play.

Creating an effective plot

The whole notion of plot, and the way that it develops, is bound up with the way that the play is put together – the way in which it is structured. The creation of an order or pattern needs careful planning, and the dramatist needs to consider a number of factors.

Generally speaking, an effective plot should:
- maintain the interest of the audience from beginning to end
- move the action on from one episode to the next
- arouse the interest of the audience in **character** and **situation**
- create high points, climaxes or moments of crisis at intervals
- build up **dramatic tension**, and create expectation and surprise.

Key elements in the structure of a play

AQA A	**U 1, 2, 3, 4**
AQA B	**U 2, 3**
Edexcel	**U 2, 4**
OCR	**U 2, 3, 4**
WJEC	**U 1, 3, 4**
CCEA	**AS U1, A2 U1**

Although every play is different, very often the **structure** of a play follows a similar pattern, which consists of a number of elements or stages:

1. **Exposition**: this opens the play and often introduces the main characters and provides background information.
2. **Dramatic incitement**: the incident that provides the starting point for the main action of the play.
3. **Complication**: this usually forms the main action of the play, in which the characters respond to the dramatic incitement and other developments that stem from it.
4. **Crisis**: the climax of the play.
5. **Resolution**: this is the final section of the play, where things are worked out and some kind of conclusion is arrived at.

Applying structural elements to a play

Here is how this structure applies to the eighteenth-century play, *The Rivals*, by Richard Sheridan.

Sheridan's play, because of the complexities and confusions of the plot, may seem to have no structure at all on first reading (or viewing). However, a closer study of it reveals that it is very carefully structured indeed:

1. **Exposition**: the opening scene is a classic example of an exposition. Two servants, Fag and Thomas, through their conversation, provide the audience with all the information that they need to follow the action. We are introduced to the stories of the two pairs of lovers (Jack and Lydia and Faulkland and Julia), whose fortunes run parallel to each other throughout the play and reach their resolution in the final scene.
2. **Dramatic incitement**: we are made aware of this through the exposition, where we are told that Jack Absolute is wooing the beautiful Lydia Languish by pretending to be a character called Ensign Beverley.
3. **Complication**: there are many complications and twists to the plot. Jack's father, Sir Anthony, arranges for his son to marry a young woman (who happens to be Lydia), Lydia's aunt forbids her to see Ensign Beverley (although she would be happy if she knew he was, in fact, Sir Anthony's son), and many more complications develop.
4. **Crisis**: the main crisis comes when Lydia finds out who her beloved Ensign Beverley really is – thus shattering her notions of a romantic elopement – and she refuses to have any more to do with him.
5. **Resolution**: the final scene brings the reconciliation of Jack and Lydia. Other strands of the plot that created problems and complications for most of the other characters are also resolved.

Sub-plots

> Look at the play you are studying and see if you can identify any sub-plots that run alongside the main plot, but are separate to it.

In addition to the main plot involving Lydia and Jack, Sheridan makes use of various **sub-plots** (the most obvious being the action involving Julia and Faulkland, another pair of lovers for whom the course of love does not run smoothly). Sub-plots are secondary plots, sometimes separate from the main action but often linked to it in some way. Sub-plots tend to echo themes explored by the main plot, or shed more light on them. They contribute to the interest of the play, but do not detract from the main plot.

Pace

The **pace** of the action is also integral to the idea of plot and structure. Varying the pace at which the plot unfolds is another factor in maintaining the interest of the audience. Variations in the lengths of scenes, and in **mood**, **setting** and action, can all influence a play's dramatic effectiveness.

> **PROGRESS CHECK**
>
> Look carefully at the play you are studying and see how closely it follows this kind of structure. Make a plan of the structure of your play.

6.3 Opening scenes

LEARNING SUMMARY

After studying this section you should be able to:

- understand the importance of the opening scene
- understand some of the ways in which plays can open
- appreciate the impact on the audience of the opening scene
- apply these ideas to the play you are studying

The importance of the opening scene

AQA A	U 1, 2, 3, 4
AQA B	U 2, 3
Edexcel	U 2, 4
OCR	U 2, 3, 4
WJEC	U 1, 3, 4
CCEA	AS U1, A2 U1

The **opening scene** of a play is very important – a successful play must engage the audience's attention right from the start. Dramatists can do this in a variety of ways, depending on the effects they wish to create.

When looking at the opening scene of a play, there are two key questions that you should think about:

1. What **effect(s)** does the writer want this scene to have on the audience?
2. What **purpose** does the scene serve to the play as a whole?

Here are some possible answers:

- The dramatist might want to create a certain mood, or present a particular background to the plot.
- The opening scene is meant to create a certain impact on the audience, perhaps to shock them, or keep them gripped, perhaps through the creation of tension.
- The opening scene provides the audience with a good deal of background information about what is going on, the characters, etc.
- Characters are introduced, and situations and relationships established.
- The opening scene can arouse the audience's curiosity and make them want to know more, therefore sustaining interest in the play.

Plays open in many different ways, but every opening scene reflects the dramatist's purpose, and achieves the particular effects desired.

Example – *Doctor Faustus*

The following extract is from the opening of *Doctor Faustus* by Christopher Marlowe. Marlowe begins his play with a **Prologue**, using a **Chorus**. This was a way of beginning plays that dates back to Greek drama, but it was also sometimes used in the sixteenth century when Marlowe wrote *Doctor Faustus*.

Read the extract through carefully. What purpose do you think the Chorus serves?

Enter CHORUS.

CHORUS: Not marching now in fields of
    Trasimene,
Where Mars did mate the Carthaginians;
Nor sporting in the dalliance of love,
In courts of kings where state is overturned;
Nor in the pomp of proud audacious deeds,
Intends our Muse to vaunt her heavenly verse:
Only this, gentlemen,—we must perform
The form of Faustus' fortunes, good or bad:
To patient judgements we appeal our plaud,
And speak for Faustus in his infancy.
Now is he born, his parents base of stock,
In Germany, within a town called Rhode:
Of riper years, to Wittenberg he went,
Whereas his kinsmen chiefly brought him up.
So soon he profits in divinity,
The fruitful plot of scholarism graced,
That shortly he was graced with doctor's name,
Excelling all whose sweet delight disputes
In heavenly matters of theology;
Till swoll'n with cunning, of a self-conceit,
His waxen wings did mount above his reach,
And, melting, heavens conspired his overthrow;
For, falling to a devilish exercise,
And glutted now with learning's golden gifts,
He surfeits upon cursed necromancy;
Nothing so sweet as magic is to him,
Which he prefers before his chiefest bliss:
And this the man that in his study sits.

                   [Exit.]

Extract from the opening of Doctor Faustus
by Christopher Marlowe

COMMENTARY

Here are some points that you may have noted:

1. The Chorus introduces the play using highly rhetorical language, which – in the theatre – adds to the sense of pageant and spectacle. It reminds the audience that they are about to see a play, and that the action has a symbolic element to it. Note the classical references, which the audience of the time would appreciate and expect.

2. In terms of the content of the speech, the Chorus tells us of Faustus' lowly background. It sets the scene, with details of his rise as a scholar and his downfall, brought about by his self-conceit.

Now the play itself begins. How does Marlowe begin the play, and what do you learn from this opening?

Dr Faustus, **ACT 1, Scene 1**

Enter FAUSTUS in his study.

FAUSTUS: Settle thy studies, Faustus, and begin
To sound the depth of that thou wilt profess:
Having commenced, be a divine in show,
Yet level at the end of every art,
And live and die in Aristotle's works.
Sweet Analytics, 'tis thou hast ravished me!
[*He read*] '*Bene disserere est finis logices.*'
Is, to dispute well, logic's chiefest end?
Affords this art no greater miracle?
Then read no more; thou hast attained that end:
A greater subject fitteth Faustus' wit:
Bid On *kai me* on farewell. Galen come,
Seeing, *Ubi desinit philosophus*, *ibi incipit medicus*,
Be a physician, Faustus; heap up gold,
And be eternized for some wondrous cure:
[*He reads*] '*Summum bonum medicinae sanitas*':
The end of physic is our body's health.
Why Faustus, hast thou not attained that end?
Is not thy common talk sound aphorisms?
Are not thy bills hung up as monuments,
Whereby whole cities have escaped the plague,
And thousand desperate maladies been eased?
Yet art thou still but Faustus, and a man.
Couldst thou make men to live eternally,
Or, being dead, raise them to life again,
Then this profession were to be esteemed.
Physic, farewell! Where is Justinian?

Extract from Act 1, Scene 1 of Doctor Faustus *by Christopher Marlowe*

COMMENTARY

The play itself opens with a soliloquy from Faustus. (The extract shown above is just the first part of it.) Notice how Marlowe uses the setting of Faustus' study to reinforce to the audience that he is a scholar. The opening of this soliloquy reveals Faustus as a character who has a thirst for learning and a questioning mind. Marlowe's use of the Latin that Faustus reads aloud furthers this first impression of his character.

Example – *Translations*

Now look at the extract on the next page. It is from the opening of *Translations* by Brian Friel – a play written in 1980.

Read it through carefully, making a note of:
- your impression of the characters
- the information conveyed to the audience/reader, and the techniques used to put it across
- the kind of atmosphere created.

Translations, **Act One**

The hedge-school is held in a disused barn or hay-shed or byre. Along the back wall are the remains of five or six stalls – wooden posts and chains – where cows were once milked and bedded. A double door left, large enough to allow a cart to enter. A window right. A wooden stairway without a banister leads to the upstairs living-quarters (off) of the schoolmaster and his son. Around the room are broken and forgotten implements: a cart-wheel, some lobster-pots, farming tools, a battle of hay, a churn, etc. There are also the stools and bench-seats which the pupils use and a table and chair for the master. At the door a pail of water and a soiled towel. The room is comfortless and dusty and functional – there is no trace of a woman's hand.

When the play opens, MANUS *is teaching* SARAH *to speak. He kneels beside her. She is sitting on a low stool, her head down, very tense, clutching a slate on her knees. He is coaxing her gently and firmly and – as with everything he does – with a kind of zeal.*

MANUS *is in his late twenties/early thirties; the master's older son. He is pale-faced, lightly built, intense, and works as an unpaid assistant – a monitor – to his father. His clothes are shabby; and when he moves we see that he is lame.* SARAH's *speech defect is so bad that all her life she has been considered locally to be dumb and she has accepted this: when she wishes to communicate, she grunts and makes unintelligible nasal sounds. She has a waiflike appearance and could be any age from seventeen to thirty-five.*

JIMMY JACK CASSIE:– *known as the Infant Prodigy – sits by himself, contentedly reading Homer in Greek and smiling to himself. He is a bachelor in his sixties, lives alone, and comes to these evening classes partly for the company and partly for the intellectual stimulation. He is fluent in Latin and Greek but is in no way pedantic – to him it is perfectly normal to speak these tongues. He never washes. His clothes – heavy top coat, hat, mittens, which he wears now – are filthy and he lives in them summer and winter, day and night. He now reads in a quiet voice and smiles in profound satisfaction. For* JIMMY *the world of the gods and the ancient myths is as real and as immediate as everyday life in the townland of Baile Beag.*

MANUS *holds* SARAH's *hand in his and he articulates slowly and distinctly into her face.*

MANUS: We're doing very well. And we're going to try it once more – just once more. Now – relax and breathe in … deep … and out … in … and out …

(SARAH *shakes her head vigorously and stubbornly.*)

MANUS: Come on, Sarah. This is our secret.

(*Again vigorous and stubborn shaking of* SARAH's *head.*)

MANUS: Nobody's listening. Nobody hears you.

JIMMY: *Ton d'emeibet epeita thea glaukopis Athene …*

MANUS: Get your tongue and your lips working. 'My name—' Come on. One more try. 'My name is—'. Good girl.

SARAH: My …

MANUS: Great. 'My name—'

SARAH: My … my …

continued

MANUS: Raise your head. Shout it out. Nobody's listening.

JIMMY: *... alla hekelos estai en Atreidao domois...*

MANUS: Jimmy, please! Once more—just once more— 'My name—' Good girl. Come on now. Head up. Mouth open.

SARAH: My ...

MANUS: Good.

SARAH: My ...

MANUS: Great.

SARAH: My name ...

MANUS: Yes?

SARAH: My name is ...

MANUS: Yes?

(SARAH *pauses. Then in a rush.*)

SARAH: My name is Sarah.

MANUS: Marvellous! Bloody marvellous!

(MANUS *hugs SARAH. She smiles in shy, embarrassed pleasure*)

Did you hear that, Jimmy? – 'My name is Sarah' – Clear as a bell.

Extract from Act One of Translations *by Brian Friel*

COMMENTARY

Here are some points that you might have noted about this opening:

1. Friel gives a very detailed description of the school. This description is all given through the stage directions, although in performance you would actually see these rather than read them in the text.

2. Apart from the physical description, we are given insights into the character of Manus. For example, he has a kind of 'zeal' for everything he does. Again, if you were watching a performance, you would form this impression from how the character comes across on the stage, through the actor's presentation.

3. There are a number of points that could not be converted directly into action on the stage, but they do help the actor or director understand the effects the dramatist wants to convey to the audience.

4. See how Friel builds up the tension in this opening section, and how we get a sense of the relationship between Manus and Sarah, and his determination and dedication to make her speak.

Now consider the following questions:

1. What general impression do you get of the characters in this extract?
2. How do you get this impression?
3. Why do you think Friel included such detailed stage directions?
4. Could all these directions be conveyed on the stage?

continued

The answers are as follows:
1. They are ordinary villagers interested in teaching and learning.
2. Mainly through the stage directions.
3. To give potential actors, and those reading the play, details of how he visualised the play.
4. Not all of them immediately. Some would need to be developed through the action of the play.

PROGRESS CHECK

Look carefully at the opening section of the drama text that you are studying, and answer the following questions:
- What is the effect of this opening scene on the audience?
- What do you think the dramatist wanted to achieve by beginning the play in this way?
- What techniques have been used?
- What is the purpose of any stage directions?

Specific answers cannot be given for this, as it depends on the individual drama text you are studying. Make sure that you have considered all the aspects of the scene.

6.4 Creating characters

LEARNING SUMMARY	**After studying this section, you should be able to:** - recognise the ways in which dramatists present characters to the audience - identify the techniques used to reveal characters - apply these ideas to the play you are studying

How dramatists present characters to the audience

AQA A	**U 1, 2, 3, 4**
AQA B	**U 2, 3**
Edexcel	**U 2, 4**
OCR	**U 2, 3, 4**
WJEC	**U 1, 3, 4**
CCEA	**AS U1, A2 U1**

A dramatist can use a range of ways to present various aspects of the characters in a play.

Here are some of the techniques:
- Explicit **stage directions** can be used, so the dramatist can define explicitly how the characters in the play should be interpreted.
- The appearance of the characters, the clothes they wear and how they appear physically contribute to the impressions we form.
- How the characters speak can reveal important aspects of their characters.
- What characters say about each other can be important.
- What the characters say and do can show a good deal about them.

> When writing about how a character is presented, look at the range of evidence that you can draw on from the text to help formulate your ideas.

The techniques in action

AQA A	**U 1, 2, 3, 4**
AQA B	**U 2, 3**
Edexcel	**U 2, 4**
OCR	**U 2, 3, 4**
WJEC	**U 1, 3, 4**
CCEA	**AS U1, A2 U1**

The Duchess of Malfi

Now look at the extract on the following three pages, which is taken from *The Duchess of Malfi* by John Webster. The Duchess – whose 'crime' was to re-marry after the death of her first husband – has been imprisoned by her wicked brothers, and she believes that her second husband is dead. Cariola is her faithful lady-in-waiting and Bosola is a treacherous servant to her brothers.

As you read, think about the Duchess' attitude to death, and how Webster shows this to the audience. How does he show that Cariola's attitude to death is different to the Duchess'?

The Duchess of Malfi, Act IV, Scene ii

DUCHESS:	Farewell Cariola:
	In my last will I have not much to give;
	A many hungry guests have fed upon me,
	Thine will be a poor reversion.
CARIOLA:	I will die with her.
DUCHESS:	I pray thee, look thou giv'st my little boy
	Some syrup for his cold, and let the girl
	Say her prayers, ere she sleep.

[Executioners force CARIOLA off.]

	Now what you please—
	What death?
BOSOLA:	Strangling: here are your executioners.
DUCHESS:	I forgive them; The apoplexy, catarrh, or cough o'th' lungs
	Would do as much as they do.
BOSOLA:	Doth not death fright you?
DUCHESS:	Who would be afraid on't?
	Knowing to meet such excellent company
	In th' other world.
BOSOLA:	Yet, methinks,
	The manner of your death should much afflict you,
	This cord should terrify you?
DUCHESS:	Not a whit:
	What would it pleasure me to have my throat cut
	With diamonds? or to be smothered
	With cassia? or to be shot to death with pearls?
	I know death hath ten thousand several doors
	For men to take their exits; and 'tis found
	They go on such strange geometrical hinges,
	You may open them both ways – any way, for heaven-sake,
	So I were out of your whispering – tell my brothers
	That I perceive death, now I am well awake,
	Best gift is they can give, or I can take.
	I would fain put off my last woman's fault,
	I'd not be tedious to you.
EXECUTIONER:	We are ready.
DUCHESS:	Dispose my breath how please you, but my body
	Bestow upon my women, will you?
EXECUTIONER:	Yes.

continued

DUCHESS: Pull, and pull strongly, for your able strength
Must pull down heaven upon me —
Yet stay; heaven-gates are not so highly arch'd
As princes' palaces, they that enter there
Must go upon their knees. [Kneels] Come violent death,
Serve for mandragora to make me sleep!
Go tell my brothers, when I am laid out,
They then may feed in quiet.

[They strangle her]

BOSOLA: Where's the waiting woman?
Fetch her: some other strangle the children.

[Executioners fetch CARIOLA, and one goes to strangle the children.]

Look you, there sleeps your mistress.

CARIOLA: O, you are damn'd
Perpetually for this – my turn is next,
Is't not so order'd?

BOSOLA: Yes, and I am glad
You are so well prepar'd for't.

CARIOLA: You are deceiv'd sir,
I am not prepar'd for't, I will not die;
I will first come to my answer, and know
How I have offended.

BOSOLA: Come, despatch her —
You kept her counsel, now you shall keep ours.

CARIOLA: I will not die, I must not, I am contracted
To a young gentleman.

EXECUTIONER: Here's your wedding ring.

CARIOLA: Let me but speak with the duke: I'll discover
Treason to his person.

BOSOLA: Delays —throttle her.

EXECUTIONER: She bites, and scratches —

CARIOLA: If you kill me now
I am damn'd: I have not been at confession
This two years —

BOSOLA: When?

CARIOLA: I am quick with child.

BOSOLA: Why then,
Your credit's sav'd —

[The Executioners strangle Cariola.]

bear her into th' next room;
Let this lie still.

[Exeunt Executioners with the body of Cariola.]

Extract from Act IV, Scene ii of The Duchess of Malfi *by John Webster*

123

Now answer the following questions:

1 In this extract, what do you learn about the Duchess' character by her words and behaviour towards the other characters?
2 What is further shown about her by her references to her children and her brothers?
3 What is her attitude towards death, and how does this contrast with Cariola's?
4 How does Webster create a sense of dignity in the Duchess' character?
5 What is your impression of the character of Bosola, and how does Webster create this impression?

Here are the answers:

1 She is brave and defiant.
2 She is forgiving.
3 Bosola is surprised she is not afraid. Cariola fights against her killers and is afraid.
4 Through the elevated and dignified language she uses.
5 He shows no mercy or feeling for his victims. He calmly oversees the murder of the Duchess and the children, and is clearly unmoved by Cariola's pleas that she should be spared because she is pregnant.

KEY POINT

In the drama text that you are studying, look at how characters act, what they say, and what others say about them and to them, to help form your ideas of how characters are presented.

A Streetcar Named Desire

Now look at the extract on the next page, which is from *A Streetcar Named Desire* by Tennessee Williams. Blanche has gone to stay with her sister, Stella. Stella's husband, Stanley, arrives home and discusses plans for a poker night with his friends, Steve (Eunice's husband) and Mitch.

Read the extract through carefully. Note, in particular, the way that Williams presents Stanley – the way he speaks and behaves, and his attitude towards Blanche.

A Streetcar Named Desire, Scene 1

STEVE: Playing poker tomorrow night?

STANLEY: Yeah – at Mitch's.

MITCH: Not at my place. My mother's still sick. *(He starts off)*

STANLEY: *(calling after him)* All right, we'll play at my place … but you bring the beer.

EUNICE: *(hollering down from above)* Break it up down there! I made the spaghetti dish and ate it myself.

STEVE: *(going upstairs)* I told you and phoned you we was playing. *(To the men.)* Jax beer!

EUNICE: You never phoned me once.

STEVE: I told you at breakfast – and phoned you at lunch …

EUNICE: Well, never mind about that. You just get yourself home here once in a while.

STEVE: You want it in the papers?

More laughter and shouts of parting come from the men. STANLEY throws the screen door of the kitchen open and comes in. He is of medium height, about five feet eight or nine, and strongly, compactly built. Animal joy in his being is implicit in all his movements and attitudes. Since earliest manhood the centre of his life has been pleasure with women, the giving and taking of it, not with weak indulgence, dependency, but with the power and pride of a richly feathered male bird among hens. Branching out from this complete and satisfying centre are all the auxiliary channels of his life, such as his heartiness with men, his appreciation of rough humour, his love of good drink and food and games, his car, his radio, everything that is his, that bears his emblem of the gaudy seed-bearer. He sizes women up at a glance, with sexual classifications, crude images flashing into his mind and determining the way he smiles at them.

BLANCHE: *(drawing involuntarily back from his stare)* You must be Stanley. I'm Blanche.

STANLEY: Stella's sister?

BLANCHE: Yes.

STANLEY: H'lo, Where's the little woman?

BLANCHE: In the bathroom.

STANLEY: Oh. Didn't know you were coming in town.

BLANCHE: I – uh –

STANLEY: Where you from, Blanche?

BLANCHE: Why, I – live in Laurel.

(He has crossed to the closet and removed the whisky bottle.)

STANLEY: In Laurel, huh? Oh, yeah. Yeah, in Laurel, that's right. Not in my territory. Liquor goes fast in hot weather. *(He holds the bottle to the light to observe its depletion.)*

BLANCHE: No, I – rarely touch it.

STANLEY: Some people rarely touch it but it touches them often.

BLANCHE: *(faintly)* Ha-ha.

STANLEY: My clothes are stickin' to me. Do you mind if I make myself comfortable? *(He starts to remove his shirt.)*

COMMENTARY

The stage directions are there to give an actor or director a clear understanding of how the dramatist sees the characters he has created, and they give you a good impression of how Stanley should appear on the stage. Note the emphasis placed on him being physically strong – 'strongly, compactly built' – and the way he is linked with the image of an animal, both in his movements and attitudes. Note the comparison of him having the 'power and pride of a richly feathered male bird among hens'. Williams stresses that a sense of 'manhood' is a very important element in the presentation of the character of Stanley, and that 'pleasure with women' and his sexuality is at the centre of his life – 'he sizes up women at a glance, with sexual classifications, crude images flashing into his mind and determining the way he smiles at them'. He is also very much a 'man's man' – enjoying the company of men, drinking, gambling, playing games – a man with a great appetite for life. On stage, the audience would form this kind of impression of the character through the way the actor presents visual effects, such as body language and facial expressions, and the ways in which lines are delivered.

The **dialogue** and the ways in which Blanche and Stanley respond to each other – the **character interaction** – reveal a good deal about the characters:

● Blanche introduces herself to Stanley, but note the short stage direction – 'drawing back involuntarily from his stare' – which suggests that Blanche finds his stare intimidating, or that she senses something slightly threatening in the strong male sexuality he projects.

● Stanley's reference to his wife Stella (Blanche's sister) as 'the little woman' again reinforces the sense of the 'macho' male image – the dominant character in the marriage.

● Stanley's reference to the whisky bottle and how much it has been depleted shows that he has quickly assessed Blanche and knows that she has been drinking it (earlier, the audience saw that she was used to strong drink). He also knows, as does the audience, that her claim to 'rarely touch it' is not true. His comment – 'Some people rarely touch it but it touches them often' – makes this clear.

● The removal of his shirt again suggests the 'macho' image, but Stanley also uses this as another kind of provocative act, designed to test Blanche's response.

Here are some questions about the extract:

1 What impression do you form of the character of Stanley?
2 How have you formed that impression?
3 How much have the stage directions contributed towards your impression?

The answers are as follows:

1 He is a 'macho' male chauvinist type of character.
2 The stage directions, and the way he speaks about his wife and to Blanche.
3 They create a vivid and detailed impression, and capture the essential sense of the character.

Comparing the two examples

You will have noticed some marked differences between the two extracts. In the extract from *The Duchess of Malfi*, there are very few stage directions, except those that simply describe what actions are meant to be taking place. The impression you form of the Duchess (and the other characters) is very much created by the things that she says and does on stage. In other words, Webster is creating and presenting his characters through the language of the play.

Although this is partly true of the extract from *A Streetcar Named Desire* – we do learn things about Stanley from the way he acts and the things that he says – Williams has supplemented this with a detailed description through the stage directions. These directions give much more than surface detail – they give an insight into the inner man. Phrases like 'animal joy in his being' and 'the power and pride of a richly feathered male bird among hens' reveal much about the kind of man Stanley is. Obviously, these directions are read in the text, but on stage they would be translated into visual effects.

Writing about characters

AQA A	**U 1, 2, 3, 4**
AQA B	**U 2, 3**
Edexcel	**U 2, 4**
OCR	**U 2, 3, 4**
WJEC	**U 1, 3, 4**
CCEA	**AS U1, A2 U1**

One key point to remember when writing about characters is that you are not writing about 'real' people, and so you should avoid describing them as if they were real. They do not have lives of their own, and so the 'what if they had done that instead of the other?' type of approach is pointless. They act as they do and are what they are because that is the way that the dramatist created them. The question to ask is 'Why did the dramatist create and present them in that way?' Dramatists can use various techniques to present the characters they create. Gather all the details you can from the text, but remember that characters are the creations of the dramatist.

> **KEY POINT**
>
> Gather information about character from as many sources as you can. Look at all aspects of the drama, and the effects created.

> **PROGRESS CHECK**
>
> Now look at the play you are studying and make notes on the methods used by the dramatist to create and present the characters.

6.5 Endings

	After studying this section, you should be able to:
LEARNING SUMMARY	● understand the ways that plays can end
	● identify techniques that dramatists can use to end their plays
	● apply these ideas to the play you are studying

The importance of an ending

AQA A	**U 1, 2, 3, 4**
AQA B	**U 2, 3**
Edexcel	**U 2, 4**
OCR	**U 2, 3, 4**
WJEC	**U 1, 3, 4**
CCEA	**AS U1, A2 U1**

Just as the opening of the play is an important element in a drama, the way in which a play ends can be important too, as shown in the following two extracts.

Example – *Doctor Faustus*

Read the following extract, which is the ending of *Doctor Faustus* by Christopher Marlowe.

***Doctor Faustus*, Scene xix**

FAUSTUS: Ah, Faustus,
Now hast thou but one bare hour to live,
And then thou must be damned perpetually.
Stand still, you ever-moving spheres of heaven,
That time may cease, and midnight never come!
Fair nature's eye, rise, rise again, and make
Perpetual day; or let this hour be but
A year, a month, a week, a natural day,
That Faustus may repent and save his soul.
O lente, lente currite noctis equi!
The stars move still; time runs; the clock will strike;
The devil will come, and Faustus must be damned!
O, I'll leap up to my God! Who pulls me down?
See, see where Christ's blood streams in the firmament!
One drop would save my soul, half a drop. Ah, my
Christ!
Rend not my heart for naming of my Christ!
Yet will I call on him. O, spare me, Lucifer!
Where is it now? 'Tis gone: and see where God
Stretcheth out his arm and bends his ireful brows!
Mountains and hills, come, come, and fall on me,
And hide me from the heavy wrath of God!
No, no!
Then will I headlong run into the earth.
Earth, gape! O, no, it will not harbour me.
You stars that reigned at my nativity,
Whose influence hath allotted death and hell,
Now draw up Faustus like a foggy mist
Into the entrails of yon labouring cloud,
That, when you vomit forth into the air,

continued

My limbs may issue from your smoky mouths,
So that my soul may but ascend to heaven.

The watch strikes

Ah, half the hour is pass'd:
'Twill all be pass'd anon.
O God,
If thou wilt not have mercy on my soul,
Yet for Christ's sake, whose blood hath ransomed me,
Impose some end to my incessant pain.
Let Faustus live in hell a thousand years,
A hundred thousand, and at last be saved.
O, no end is limited to damned souls.
Why wert thou not a creature wanting soul?
Or why is this immortal that thou hast?
Ah, Pythagoras' *metempsychosis*, were that true,
This soul should fly from me and I be changed
Unto some brutish beast.
All beasts are happy, for, when they die,
Their souls are soon dissolved in elements;
But mine must live still to be plagued in hell.
Cursed be the parents that engendered me!
No, Faustus, curse thyself. Curse Lucifer,
That hath deprived thee of the joys of heaven.

The clock striketh twelve

O, it strikes, it strikes! Now, body, turn to air,
Or Lucifer will bear thee quick to hell!

Thunder and lightning

O soul, be changed into little water drops,
And fall into the ocean, ne'er be found!

Enter Devils

My God, my God! Look not so fierce on me!
Adders and serpents, let me breathe awhile!
Ugly hell, gape not! Come not, Lucifer;
I'll burn my books! Ah, Mephostophilis!

[The Devils] exeunt with him

Epilogue

Enter Chorus

CHORUS: Cut is the branch that might have grown full straight,
And burned is Apollo's laurel bough
That sometime grew within this learned man.
Faustus is gone: regard his hellish fall,
Whose fiendful fortune may exhort the wise
Only to wonder at unlawful things,
Whose deepness doth entice such forward wits
To practise more than heavenly power permits.

[Exit]

> **COMMENTARY**
>
> In this closing section of the play, Faustus, who has sold his soul to the Devil, has now reached the last hour of his life before the devils come to claim his soul. The climax approaches as the devils pull and tear at him. He feels a devil tearing at his heart because he has spoken the name of Christ. He becomes almost insane with desperation, as he wants to turn to air or water to hide from the devils before his life is finally torn away. After the tension and excitement of the climax, the calm dignity of the Chorus sums up Faustus' end. They comment on the tragedy of his death as a lost opportunity for virtue and learning. Their comments end by inviting the audience to learn from Faustus' example and not attempt to transgress divine law.
>
> In his final soliloquy, Faustus goes through changing moods – from the hopeless foolishness of trying to order the stars to obey him, to the cold, hard realisation that he has no one to blame but himself for his damnation. It is worth comparing the tone and mood of this soliloquy with that of the opening soliloquy of the play (see page 118), where Faustus sets out what he aspires to do.
>
> How does Marlowe create tension in this final scene of the play?
>
> You may have noted the following:
> 1. Faustus' increasing desperation is reflected in his language as midnight draws near.
> 2. A sense of time is created through the stage directions.
> 3. There is thunder and lightning as the clock strikes twelve.
> 4. There is an image of the devils pulling at Faustus' heart, because he has called the name of Christ.

Example – *The Rivals*

Now look at the second example of an ending, which is taken from *The Rivals* by Richard Sheridan.

The Rivals, **Act V, Scene iii**

SIR LUCIUS: With your leave, Ma'am, I must put in a word here – I believe I could interpret the young lady's silence. Now mark—

LYDIA: What is it you mean, Sir?

SIR LUCIUS: Come, come, Delia, we must be serious now – this is no time for trifling.

LYDIA: 'Tis true, Sir; and your reproof bids me offer this gentleman my hand, and solicit the return of his affections.

ABSOLUTE: Oh! my little angel, say you so? – Sir Lucius, I perceive there must be some mistake here with regard to the affront which you affirm I have given you – I can only say, that it could not have been intentional. And as you must be convinced, that I should not fear to support a real injury you shall now see that I am not ashamed to atone for an inadvertency – I ask your pardon. But for this lady, while honoured with her approbation, I will support my claim against any man whatever.

SIR ANTHONY: Well said, Jack, and I'll stand by you, my boy.

ACRES: Mind, I give up all my claim – I make no pretensions to anything in the world – and if I can't get a wife, without fighting for her, by my valour! I'll live a bachelor. *continued*

SIR LUCIUS: Captain, give me your hand – an affront handsomely acknowledged becomes an obligation – and as for the lady – if she chooses to deny her own handwriting here – *Taking out letters*

MRS MALAPROP: Oh, he will dissolve my mystery! Sir Lucius, perhaps there's some mistake – perhaps, I can illuminate –

SIR LUCIUS: Pray, old gentlewoman, don't interfere, where you have no business. Miss Languish, are you my Delia or not?

LYDIA: Indeed, Sir Lucius, I am not.

LYDIA and ABSOLUTE walk aside

MRS MALAPROP: Sir Lucius O'Trigger – ungrateful as you are – I own the soft impeachment – pardon my blushes, I am Delia.

SIR LUCIUS: You Delia – pho! pho! be easy.

MRS MALAPROP: Why, thou barbarous Vandyke – those letters are mine. When you are more sensible of my benignity – perhaps I may be brought to encourage your addresses.

SIR LUCIUS: Mrs Malaprop, I am extremely sensible of your condescension; and whether you or Lucy have put this trick upon me, I am equally beholden to you. And to show you I'm not ungrateful, Captain Absolute! Since you have taken that lady from me, I'll give you my Delia into the bargain.

ABSOLUTE: I am much obliged to you, Sir Lucius; but here's our friend, Fighting Bob, unprovided for.

SIR LUCIUS: Hah! little Valour – here, will you make your fortune?

ACRES: Odds wrinkles! No. But give me your hand, Sir Lucius, forget and forgive; but if ever I give you a chance of pickling me again, say Bob Acres is a dunce, that's all.

SIR ANTHONY: Come, Mrs Malaprop, don't be cast down – you are in your bloom yet.

MRS MALAPROP: O Sir Anthony! – men are all barbarians—

All retire but JULIA and FAULKLAND

JULIA: He seems dejected and unhappy – not sullen – there was some foundation, however, for the tale he told me – O woman! how true should be your judgment, when your resolution is so weak.

FAULKLAND: Julia! – how can I sue for what I so little deserve? I dare not presume – yet hope is the child of penitence.

JULIA: Oh! Faulkland, you have not been more faulty in your unkind treatment of me, than I am now in wanting inclination to resent it. As my heart honestly bids me place my weakness to the account of love, I should be ungenerous not to admit the same plea for yours.

FAULKLAND: Now I shall be blest indeed!

SIR ANTHONY comes forward

SIR ANTHONY: What's going on here? So you have been quarrelling too, I warrant. Come, Julia, I never interfered before; but let me have a hand in the matter at last. All the faults I have ever seen in my friend Faulkland, seemed to proceed from what he calls the *delicacy* and *warmth* of his affection for you – there, marry him directly, Julia, you'll find he'll mend surprisingly!

continued

The rest come forward

SIR LUCIUS:	Come now, I hope there is no dissatisfied person, but what is content; for as I have been disappointed myself, it will be very hard if I have not the satisfaction of seeing other people succeed better——
ACRES:	You are right, Sir Lucius. So, Jack, I wish you joy – Mr Faulkland the same. Ladies, come now, to show you I'm neither vexed nor angry, odds tabors and pipes! I'll order the fiddles in half an hour, to the New Rooms – and I insist on your all meeting me there.
SIR ANTHONY:	Gad! Sir, I like your spirit; and at night we single lads will drink a health to the young couples, and a husband to Mrs Malaprop.
FAULKLAND:	Our partners are stolen from us. Jack – I hope to be congratulated by each other – yours for having checked in time the errors of an ill-directed imagination, which might have betrayed an innocent heart; and mine, for having, by her gentleness and candour, reformed the unhappy temper of one, who by it made wretched whom he loved most, and tortured the heart he ought to have adored.
ABSOLUTE:	Well, Faulkland, we have both tasted the bitters, as well as the sweets, of love – with this difference only, that you always prepared the bitter cup for yourself, while I——
LYDIA:	Was always obliged to me for it, hey! Mr Modesty?– But come, no more of that – our happiness is now as unallayed as general.
JULIA:	Then let us study to preserve it so: and while hope pictures to us a flattering scene of future bliss, let us deny its pencil those colours which are too bright tobe lasting. When hearts deserving happiness would unite their fortunes, virtue would crown them with an unfading garland of modest, hurtless flowers; but ill-judging passion will force the gaudier rose into the wreath, whose thorn offends them, when its leaves are dropped!

> **COMMENTARY**
>
> *The Rivals* has a quite different ending. The whole drama has been based around the love affairs of two young couples. Throughout the play there has been much mistaken identity and pretending, which has led to various confusions. The ending of the play is a time for sorting out the confusions and unravelling the complicated threads of the plot that have developed. The play ends on a high note, with everything being happily resolved for everyone (perhaps with the exception of Mrs Malaprop), hopefully leaving the audience in a similar happy mood.

The techniques used to end plays

AQA A	**U 1, 2, 3, 4**
AQA B	**U 2, 3**
Edexcel	**U 2, 4**
OCR	**U 2, 3, 4**
WJEC	**U 1, 3, 4**
CCEA	**AS U1, A2 U1**

You may find it useful to think about the **dramatic techniques** that Marlowe and Sheridan use to draw their dramas to an end:

- *Doctor Faustus* ends with a dramatic climax, which comes at the end of a passage of mounting tension as the hour approaches when Lucifer will claim Faustus's soul. In the final lines he is dragged away by devils, which creates a shock effect on the audience. The lines of the Chorus that conclude the drama bring the tension down, but also serve to remind the audience what they have seen in the fall of Faustus, and that they should learn from it.

When studying a play, ask yourself how the dramatist draws the play to a conclusion, and how effective you find the final scene as an ending to the play.

- In *The Rivals*, Sheridan also brings his drama to a climax with the revelation of the true identities of several characters. This climax, though, is followed by the resolution of all the confusions, disputes and arguments that have been developed throughout the play – so the play ends on a happy note, with everything reconciled.

KEY POINT

Different endings serve different purposes – plays end in different ways depending on the effect the dramatist wants to achieve. The ending of a play is a very important element in the structure of the whole drama.

PROGRESS CHECK

Now look carefully at the play that you are studying and answer the following questions.

1 What is the effect created by the final scene?
2 What impact do you think that the dramatist wanted to achieve by ending the play in this way?
3 What techniques have been used?
4 What is the purpose of any stage direction?

6.6 Themes and issues

LEARNING SUMMARY

After studying this section, you should be able to:
- identify ways in which dramatists present themes in their plays
- recognise the themes in the play that you are studying

How dramatists present themes in their plays

AQA A   **U 1, 2, 3, 4**
AQA B   **U 2, 3**
Edexcel **U 2, 4**
OCR   **U 2, 3, 4**
WJEC   **U 1, 3, 4**
CCEA   **AS U1, A2 U1**

One of the main purposes of a play is to entertain the **audience**. However, very often a play has another purpose too – that of making us think. By reading and watching plays, we can learn a great deal about human relationships and the kind of problems, dilemmas and conflicts that human beings may encounter in their lives.

Very often a dramatist creates his or her play around an idea – or set of ideas – that will be explored through the development of the drama. These ideas are the **themes** of a play.

The audience can be made aware of themes in a number of ways:
- The dramatist can use a character to express certain ideas or views.
- The action of the play can involve the development of the theme(s).
- The setting might be important and contribute to thematic development.
- Stage directions can reveal attitudes or ideas.
- The dramatist may use **symbolism** and **imagery**.

Plays can have the power to provoke deep thought and personal reactions from members of the audience or readers.

KEY POINT

Dramatists can develop their themes through a variety of techniques. When studying your play, be alert to how various techniques can be used to develop themes and explore ideas.

Example – *The Doll's House*

Ibsen's *The Doll's House* explores a number of themes or ideas, but one of the central ones is the sacrifices made by women in a male-dominated society. The play created much controversy when it first appeared in 1879 for the way in which it challenged the traditional roles of men and women in nineteenth-century marriage.

In the play, after an incident that has shattered her confidence in her husband, Torvald Helmer – and after years of playing the dutiful wife and mother – Nora realises that she must re-assess her life. She sees that she must leave her husband.

Look at the following passage from the point in the play when Nora confronts her husband. Make a note of the ideas that Ibsen explores through the dialogue of the play.

NORA: We have been married now eight years. Does it not occur to you that this is the first time we two, you and I, husband and wife, have had a serious conversation?

HELMER: What do you mean by serious?

NORA: In all these eight years—longer than that—from the very beginning of our acquaintance, we have never exchanged a word on any serious subject.

HELMER: Was it likely that I would be continually and forever telling you about worries that you could not help me to bear?

NORA: I am not speaking about business matters. I say that we have never sat down in earnest together to try and get at the bottom of anything.

HELMER: But, dearest Nora, would it have been any good to you?

NORA: That is just it; you have never understood me. I have been greatly wronged, Torvald—first by papa and then by you.

HELMER: What! By us two—by us two, who have loved you better than anyone else in the world?

NORA: *(shaking her head)* You have never loved me. You have only thought it pleasant to be in love with me.

HELMER: Nora, what do I hear you saying?

NORA: It is perfectly true, Torvald. When I was at home with papa, he told me his opinion about everything, and so I had the same opinions; and if I differed from him I concealed the fact, because he would not have liked it. He called me his doll-child, and he played with me just as I used to play with my dolls. And when I came to live with you—

HELMER: What sort of an expression is that to use about our marriage?

NORA: *(undisturbed)* I mean that I was simply transferred from papa's hands into yours. You arranged everything according to your own taste, and so I got the same tastes as your else I pretended to, I am really not quite sure which—I think sometimes the one and sometimes the other. When I look back on it, it seems to me as if I had been living here like a poor woman—just from hand to mouth. I have existed merely to perform tricks for you, Torvald. But you would have it so. You and papa have committed a great sin against me. It is your fault that I have made nothing of my life.

HELMER: How unreasonable and how ungrateful you are, Nora! Have you not been happy here?

NORA: No, I have never been happy. I thought I was, but it has never really been so.

HELMER: Not—not happy!

NORA: No, only merry. And you have always been so kind to me. But our home has been nothing but a playroom. I have been your doll-wife, just as at home I was papa's doll-child; and here the

continued

children have been my dolls. I thought it great fun when you played with me, just as they thought it great fun when I played with them. That is what our marriage has been, Torvald.

HELMER: There is some truth in what you say—exaggerated and strained as your view of it is. But for the future it shall be different. Playtime shall be over, and lesson-time shall begin.

NORA: Whose lessons? Mine, or the children's?

HELMER: Both yours and the children's, my darling Nora.

NORA: Alas, Torvald, you are not the man to educate me into being a proper wife for you.

HELMER: And you can say that!

NORA: And I—how am I fitted to bring up the children?

HELMER: Nora!

NORA: Didn't you say so yourself a little while ago—that you dare not trust me to bring them up?

HELMER: In a moment of anger! Why do you pay any heed to that?

NORA: Indeed, you were perfectly right. I am not fit for the task. There is another task I must undertake first. I must try and educate myself—you are not the man to help me in that. I must do that for myself. And that is why I am going to leave you now.

HELMER: *(springing up)* What do you say?

NORA: I must stand quite alone, if I am to understand myself and everything about me. It is for that reason that I cannot remain with you any longer.

COMMENTARY

Here are some ideas that you might have noted:

1. Torvald does not regard his wife as capable of involvement in 'serious' matters. As Nora points out to him, 'We have been married ... eight years ... this is the first time we two, you and I, husband and wife, have had a serious conversation'.

2. Nora feels that both Torvald and her father have treated her like a play thing – 'He called me his doll-child and he played with me just as I used to play with my dolls'. Marriage simply meant that she was passed on from her father to her husband. Note how the image of 'dolls' is used here as a symbol for the way in which Nora has been regarded by both her father and husband.

3. Nora's whole life has been governed by Torvald and everything has been done to his taste – Nora feels that she has existed simply to 'perform tricks' for him.

4. Nora blames Torvald and her father for preventing her from making something of her life – 'I have been your doll-wife, just as at home I was papa's doll-child'.

5. Nora knows now that she must leave her husband if she is really to understand herself and be able to live her own life.

You will have noticed from this extract that Ibsen uses a repeated image that reflects Nora's perception of how she sees her own life and existence – that of the 'doll-wife'. This image is a symbol for a key theme of the play, which is reflected in the play's title – *The Doll's House*.

Example – *Murmuring Judges*

In his play, *Murmuring Judges*, David Hare examines different aspects of the criminal justice system, focusing on three elements – the police, the courts and the prisons. Through the play he explores a number of themes, including the position of women in the police force and the legal profession, conditions in prisons, and the disparity between the privileged classes and those at the bottom of the social spectrum. He also explores the issue of corruption of different kinds.

In this extract, a young woman police officer, identified as a 'high-flyer', confronts her friend and colleague, Barry, a detective constable, about his illegal methods of achieving arrests.

Think about the ways in which Hare presents this episode, and reveals to the audience both Sandra's and Barry's attitude towards policing.

SANDRA: What are you saying? That we're all beyond criticism?

BARRY: No. No, I'm not saying that. I'm saying, you stand there, Sandra, you tell stories about how we're all getting touchy. Touchy? Really? You're touchy? When people say everything's your fault? I can't think why. Surely you can take twenty-four-hours round-the-clock criticism and learn not to react? *(He stops, suddenly quietening to make his point.)* Well, actually you can. By dissembling. That's how you do it. By being secret. By doing things your way. *(He smiles.)* Yes, a copper is allowed something. It's all he's got. You're allowed a few private moments with criminals. You're allowed a way of doing things which is actually your own.

(SANDRA's gaze does not waver. She is quiet when she speaks, not accusing.)

SANDRA: You mean you're bent?

(There is a silence. BARRY is so angry at the question that his reply comes out as politeness, ice cold.)

BARRY: I'm sorry?

SANDRA: You mean those men are innocent?

(Again he pauses, to repress his anger.)

BARRY: No. How can they be? We found the goods.

SANDRA: If they're guilty, then why are you so defensive?

BARRY: The obvious reason. I don't think I've done anything wrong. *(He looks at her a moment.)* I went in there, all right. I knew this gang of old. I thought, right, this is it. This is what you wait for. So … yes … I came out with my bag.

SANDRA: Bag?

BARRY: I did my trick. It always works.

SANDRA: What sort of trick?

(There is a pause. He is quite still.)

BARRY: I carry dynamite. I carry sticks of dynamite. Semtex, actually. I keep it at home. It works pretty well. It's always worked well for me. People never quite know. Once they see it, they stop thinking clearly. Especially if they're from over the sea …

(SANDRA is still now.)

SANDRA: I saw them.

BARRY: That's right. Yes, you did.

SANDRA: At your place. In the fridge. I didn't think. In a packet. You told me it was wax for the kid.

continued

BARRY: *(Smiles)* It may be wax. Or it may not be. Excuse me, Sandra, but that's the whole point. *(He is suddenly insistent.)* It's about acting, it's about credibility, Sandra, it's about going nuts. They have to believe that you are a complete bloody fruitcake. *(He is nodding.)* You've never seen it but I've got a good act.

SANDRA: Yes, I'm sure.

BARRY: You have to convince them. I said, you're both going down for six years. well, you'll get another five, now this has been found on the premises. How do you like that? You got it. Unless...

SANDRA: Unless? Unless what?

BARRY: *(Shakes his head)* Unless what do you think? Christ almighty, what is our trade? What is our living? You're a policeman. What is your oxygen? You need information. (He turns suddenly acting it out.) 'Give me information, you shits ...'

SANDRA: And they did?

(He laughs with excitement.)

BARRY: Oh yes. So three weeks later in the City of London when some Mick bullion robbers – Kilmartin? Remember? Yes, you read about it – on the front page – when Kilmartin and his gang turned up at the bank, thanks to that little package I showed Travis and Fielding, the Flying Squad was waiting! Bang! Double bubble! Two lots of villains. Both gangs very nasty, very nasty people. No Sweat. *(He nods, pleased with this.)* And, what's more, I'm up for the Commisioner's medal.

(But before he has even said this, SANDRA has moved away across the room.)

COMMENTARY

Here are some of the ideas you may have had:

1. Sandra – although clearly not enjoying finding out the truth from Barry – is determined to press him for answers. Notice her attitude as described in the stage directions – 'SANDRA's gaze does not waver. She is quiet when she speaks, not accusing'.

2. Sandra is direct – 'You mean you're bent?' She believes that Barry's attitude that 'a copper is allowed something' (in other words, the police have to bend the rules in order to catch the criminals) is wrong. He does not agree and is angered by her accusation, although he keeps control – 'Barry is so angry at the question that his reply comes out as politeness, ice cold'.

3. As well as the stage directions showing how the actors would behave on stage, they also provide visual movements, for instance through the direction, 'But before he has even said this, Sandra has moved away slowly across the room'. This physical distancing of Sandra from Barry is symbolic of her moral and ideological distancing from him.

PROGRESS CHECK

Make a note of the key themes and ideas that the dramatist explores in the text you are studying, and the techniques used to present them.

6.7 Text and context

After studying this section, you should be able to:

- appreciate the importance of context in which a play was written
- make use of relevant contextual information when studying your play

The importance of context

AQA A   U 1, 2, 3, 4
AQA B   U 2, 3
Edexcel U 2, 4
OCR   U 2, 3, 4
WJEC   U 1, 3, 4
CCEA   AS U1, A2 U1

It is important that you understand exactly what **context** is and why it is important in terms of the texts that you are studying (see Chapter 5), as it is one of the assessment objectives that you will be tested on.

Assessment Objective 4 (AO4) requires you to 'demonstrate understanding of the significance and influence of the contexts in which literary texts are written and received'.

Contextual influences

As you will have seen earlier, **contextual influences** cover a range of aspects that can influence the ways in which a text was written, and the ways in which it is received by an audience.

Contextual influences can include aspects such as:
- the historical period the play was written in
- the kind of society the dramatist lived in
- the political climate prevalent at the time
- the cultural influences the writer was subject to
- the way the language of the play reflects a particular time or place
- how the play has been influenced by the events of the dramatist's life
- how our reading of the text might be influenced by our own contextual factors, ideas and beliefs.

As an example, to fully understand Marlowe's *Doctor Faustus*, we need to appreciate that it was written towards the end of the sixteenth century, and that it is the product of the kind of drama that preceded it and which has links with it, and the beliefs and ideas that were current in sixteenth-century Britain. It is also important to understand that different audiences at different times would respond differently to the play and hold different views on it.

Using relevant contextual information and ideas

Part of your study of literature, both at AS and A2 level, will involve you being familiar with the contexts within which the play or plays you are studying were written. This means that you will need to be familiar with the **historical period**, events and also the ideas, beliefs and other influences that have helped to shape the dramatist's work and creation of characters, exploration of themes, and use of language.

Do not write about the dramatist's life – the play is at the centre of your study. Biography can help you understand it more fully, but a critical analysis of the literature should be your key focus.

A starting point is to read about the life of the dramatist you are studying, the kind of society he or she lived in, and the kind of ideas and beliefs he/she held. This will help you form an idea of the background against which the work you are studying was written. It is important to remember, though – particularly when thinking about the biography of a dramatist – that although this information can help you to understand the play and its ideas, the text should always be at the centre of your study. Your response – whether in the form of an exam answer or piece of coursework – should focus on the play itself, and you should avoid being side-tracked into writing about the dramatist's life.

Knowledge of the historical context is very important in fully understanding the literature you are studying. Different times use language in different ways (sometimes even common words can have a different meaning from the meaning that we place on them), and you need to be aware of these **language variations**. Different times also have different beliefs and ideas, conventions, manners, attitudes and styles to our own time, and it is important that you appreciate these in order to gain a full understanding of the text.

> **KEY POINT**
>
> You need to be aware of all the contextual factors relevant to the play you are studying, in order to gain a full appreciation of it.

> **PROGRESS CHECK**
>
> Think about the play that you are studying and make notes on any contextual factors that you think are important in reaching a full and detailed understanding of it.

Sample question and model answer

Re-read Act 1, Scene 5 of *Murmuring Judges*. Discuss Hare's presentation of Sandra in the extract and the play as a whole.

QUESTION OVERVIEW

This question is in the style of a question from WJEC Unit 1.

> **This is a clear introduction, showing focus on the question. There is a good use of stage directions as a source of information about the character. The student shows an awareness of Hare's method of having her address the audience directly.**

We are first introduced to Sandra Bingham in Act 1, Scene 5, where she is described in the stage directions as a `WPC, in her mid-twenties with neat, dyed-blonde short hair. She is quite small and tidy´, and the overall impression we form is of a smart, business-like young police officer. At the opening of the scene Hare uses her to address the audience directly through a monologue. She begins, like several of the police officers, by giving us an insight into the frustrating nature of her job, which involves chasing up trivial crimes and arresting people for `petty thieving, deception, stealing car radios, selling stolen credit card in pubs´.

> **This reveals Sandra's attitude towards the job.**
>
> **This makes the reader aware of her clear view of police work – it also shows her sense of humour.**

To compound the frustrations of the job, Sandra describes how officers chasing up such trivial crimes are overloaded with paperwork to such an extent that it interferes with their ability to do their job effectively. She sums up her view with the wry comment - `Policing's largely the fine art of getting through biros. And keeping yourself ready for the interesting bits.´ The initial impression that is given of her character is of an intelligent young officer who is dedicated to her job, but who is also aware of the problems and frustrations created by the systems that the police have to work to. The comments that the sergeant, Lester, makes about her being a `high-flyer´ and being in `the fast lane´ suggests that her superior officers have already noted her intelligence and ability, and that she is being fast-tracked for career progression.

> **This is a good summary of the initial impression of her character.**

Later in the same scene, we see Sandra's astuteness emerging when she questions Barry about the arrest of the criminals. The stage directions describing her responses to his answers - `Sandra frowns´, and `She turns away, disbelieving´ show that there are serious doubts forming in her mind, and it is clear that she suspects that Barry is not being entirely straight with her. She voices her thought that she wasn't sure that Gerard was guilty, but this is immediately dismissed by Barry. We also see her sensitivity emerging here when she disagrees with Barry's suggestion that Gerard being `kind of Irish as well´ made him more suspicious. She corrects him - `He wasn't Irish, he's British´ - a point that she reinforces again a little later. At this stage in the play, Hare seems to be presenting a character who wants things to be fair, but who also has some compassion - a point reinforced by her comments suggesting that she feels sorry for Gerard - `He's just a lad,´ and `He's got a very young family.´

> **These are perceptive points, with good supporting evidence linked to presentational techniques used by Hare.**
>
> **This is another perceptive point focused on presentation, with good supporting evidence.**

What also emerges here is the developing conflict between her attitudes towards policing and those of Barry. This develops further as Sandra begins to realise that the key question is - `Why did the accused men pretend not to know Barry?´ Later in the play, Sandra finds her answer to this question and it's an answer that places Barry firmly at the centre of a case of police corruption. This puts Sandra in a serious quandary. Her natural sense of justice and fair play means that she is unhappy about turning a blind eye, and it is clear that she does not think that Barry's method of obtaining arrests are right. We learned earlier that Sandra had grown up in a police family and her father had given her the sense that police work was exciting as well as demanding, but she had developed a strong sense of right and wrong. In the end she confronts Barry with her suspicions, but he does not respond well. He sees her as being concerned with the theory of policing and with gaining

> **This sums up the fundamental difference between her attitude and Barry's. It is a cohesive point relating to later in the play.**
>
> **This is a good point, showing awareness of character, with sound background evidence from the text.**

Sample question and model answer (continued)

This shows awareness of Sandra's direct and strong character – she is prepared to stand up for her principles.

She is also aware of the practical legal implications of Barry's actions.

This is a clear expression of her inner struggle posed by the dilemma she is faced with.

Good use of the stage direction to show her awareness of the sacrifice she is making.

promotion, as opposed to his pragmatic rule bending in order to achieve results. As he puts it – `You're allowed a few moments with criminals. You're allowed a way of doing things which is actually your own.´ Sandra's response to this, though, is blunt and to the point – `You mean you're bent?´ However, she does not just disagree with Barry's methods because of her principles. She has a very practical reason for objecting to them too – convicting the men on dubious evidence means an `unsafe conviction´. As she tells him – `...they've gone down the crappy way´ and `...at some point someone will notice.´

At the end of the play, Sandra struggles with her dilemma and comes to terms with the fact that the man who she is having a relationship with – and who she admired so much – is `bent´. Hare does not spell out to the audience what she decides to do about it, but the closing lines of the play have a strong suggestion that she is doing what she thinks is morally right. Significantly, as the stage direction says, `she stands alone´ as she asks to see the Chief Superintendent.

SUMMATIVE COMMENT

This is an effectively structured and individual response to the text and question. The student has a confident grasp of the presentation of Sandra, with sound analysis of Hare's use of techniques, such as the use of stage directions and monologue, and the ways in which the conflict with Barry reveals aspects of her character. There is a clear sense of overview and confident handling of implicit meaning. The writing is fluent, with clear and accurate written expression.

Practice examination questions

AS

WJEC Unit 1

Diane Samuels: *Kindertransport*

Re-read the final section of the play. Explore the ways in which Samuels presents Eva's past shaping her future in the extract and elsewhere in the play.

A2

AQA B Unit 3

Christopher Marlowe: *Doctor Faustus*

Discuss Marlowe's presentation of Mephistophilis and his role in bringing about Faustus' damnation.

John Webster: *The White Devil*

Explore the ways in which Webster presents corruption in society in *The White Devil*.

OCR Unit 3

By comparing one drama text and poetry text you have studied, explore the ways in which writers present human failings.

'Love and death are at the heart of much great literature.' By comparing one drama text and one poetry text you have studied, explore the ways in which you find this comment relevant.

CCEA Unit 3

Historical drama

Eliot: *Murder in the Cathedral*
Bolt: *A Man for All Seasons*

Bolt presents a stronger sense of the conflict between human and divine power in his play than Eliot does in his.

By **comparing and contrasting** appropriately selected parts of the two plays, show how far you would agree with the view expressed above. Your **argument** should include relevant comments on each writer's **dramatic methods** and **relevant external contextual material** on the historical background to these plays.

Drama and social realism

Ibsen: *The Doll's House*
Osborne: *Look Back in Anger*

Osborne presents a more effective portrayal of an individual disillusioned with society in his play than Ibsen does in his.

By **comparing and contrasting** appropriately selected parts of the two plays, show how far you would agree with the view expressed above. Your **argument** should include relevant comments on each writer's **dramatic methods** and **relevant external contextual material** on society in the 1950s and in the 1890s.

7 Approaching Shakespeare

The following topics are covered in this chapter:

- Shakespeare's plays
- Opening scenes
- Presenting characters
- Soliloquies and asides
- Shakespeare's themes and ideas
- Shakespeare's language

7.1 Shakespeare's plays

LEARNING SUMMARY

After studying this section, you should be able to:

- appreciate how plays were performed in the Elizabethan theatre
- understand the different genres of Shakespeare's plays
- understand the features of different kinds of Shakespeare's plays

Elizabethan theatres

AQA A	**U 4**
AQA B	**U 2, 3**
Edexcel	**U 2**
OCR	**U 3**
WJEC	**U 4**
CCEA	**AS U1, A2 U1**

In Shakespeare's time, theatres were very different from what we are used to today, and the way plays were performed was different too. It is worth bearing this in mind when you are studying your text.

Here are some of the key differences:

- Plays in Elizabethan theatres were performed during the day – usually in the afternoon – because there was no artificial lighting in theatres. This also meant that there were no lighting effects, although sometimes music and songs were used to create a particular atmosphere. Most of the effects, though, were created through the language of the play and the imaginations of the audience.
- The actors used few props and costumes, and there was no scenery as we know it. A door was perhaps suggested by a curtain, and only key props – such as something to represent a throne or a bed – would be used.
- There were no female actors and so the female roles were played by young boys.
- The theatre was a much rowdier place than it is now. Many members of the audience watched the play standing in a crowd in front of the stage, and they often drank beer and ate during the performance. If they did not like the play they would shout and jeer and throw things at the stage.

Genres of Shakespeare's plays

AQA A	**U 4**
AQA B	**U 2, 3**
Edexcel	**U 2**
OCR	**U 3**
WJEC	**U 4**
CCEA	**AS U1, A2 U1**

There are several ways in which the plays of Shakespeare can be categorised, but a useful and simple method is to divide them into tragedies, comedies and histories.

The main texts set for study at AS and A2 level are as follows.

Tragedies	Comedies	Histories
Hamlet	The Taming of the Shrew	Richard II
Macbeth	Love's Labour's Lost	Henry IV (Part 1)
Othello	A Midsummer Night's Dream	Henry IV (Part 2)
King Lear	Much Ado About Nothing	Henry V
Romeo and Juliet	The Merchant of Venice	Richard III
Julius Caesar	Twelfth Night	
Antony and Cleopatra	As You Like It	
Coriolanus	The Tempest	
Titus Andronicus	The Winter's Tale	
	Measure for Measure	

Each of these **genres** of play have certain features in common, and it is useful to recognise these features and see how they apply to the play or plays you are studying.

The tragedies

The tragedies contain the four plays that are regarded as the **'great' tragedies** – *Hamlet*, *King Lear*, *Othello* and *Macbeth* – and these plays are very often set for study at A-Level.

At the centre of each of these plays is the character after whom the play is named – the **eponymous hero** as he is sometimes called – and the action focuses very much on this character. Each of these plays end with the death of the main character, although during the course of the action several other (sometimes innocent) characters die too. It has often been noted that the downfall of the central character in these plays is due to some kind of weakness or flaw in the character themselves, often referred to as 'the fatal flaw', and so, in a way, he or she brings about his/her own downfall. Disorder is a key element in the action of the plays, but at the end of each of them order is re-established.

As well as these four 'great' tragedies, the earlier tragedy, *Romeo and Juliet*, and the plays which are sometimes also known as the 'Roman plays' – *Julius Caesar*, *Antony and Cleopatra*, *Coriolanus* and *Titus Andronicus* – are included in this group. These plays follow a similar pattern to the other tragedies.

In general, Shakespeare's tragedies have many of the key features we associate with the concept of dramatic tragedy in general:

1. At the beginning of the play, **an event** occurs, or has already occurred, that **creates disruption** to normal life or the natural order.
2. **Chaos or disorder** ensues that not only affects the life of the central character, but draws into the action many of the other characters too.
3. This results in **conflict** (either psychological, physical or both), creating tension and heightened emotion as the normal social restraints disintegrate.
4. A **climax** is reached, which results in the death of the main character and several other characters.
5. **Order and peace are restored**, often pointing the way to a new beginning.

The comedies

Our modern understanding of the term 'comedy' usually suggests something fairly amusing that makes us laugh. However, although many of Shakespeare's comedies do contain amusing elements, the term 'comedy' applied to the plays of Shakespeare simply means a play that has a happy ending. Although the action of the play up to this happy ending may be light-hearted and funny, this is not always the case. Some aspects of the plot might contain darker, more serious elements.

Shakespeare's comedies vary a great deal, both in style and the mood created. Comedies such as *The Taming of the Shrew, Love's Labour's Lost, A Midsummer Night's Dream, Much Ado About Nothing, As You Like It* and *Twelfth Night* are often called **romantic comedies**, as love plays a key part in the plot.

These comedies tend to follow a similar structure:
1. **Characters fall in love** or are **already in love** at the opening of the play.
2. **Various confusions**, misunderstandings or unfortunate events threaten the happiness of the lovers.
3. The **problems are overcome** and resolved.
4. The **play ends happily**, with the various lovers united.

Although most of Shakespeare's more light-hearted comedies follow roughly this pattern, some of them do not. In some plays – such as *Much Ado About Nothing*, for example – there are parts of the play where the action is closer to tragedy than comedy. This serious edge is clearly shown in *The Merchant of Venice* too. Although the play ends happily for everyone except Shylock, much of the play deals with darker issues such as racial hatred (although an Elizabethan audience would have viewed these issues differently from us). The scene where Shylock prepares to take his pound of flesh from Antonio, for example, is serious and full of **dramatic tension**, and at the end Shylock is almost a tragic figure. In fact, some have described this play as a **tragicomedy**. The difference between a play like this and a tragedy is in the way the action is resolved, and that in the end the play ends 'happily'. Some plays are 'dark' to such an extent that they form a small sub-group that has been called **problem comedies**.

The problem comedies group is generally seen as consisting of three plays – *Measure for Measure, Troilus and Cressida*, and *All's Well That Ends Well* (although some people include *The Merchant of Venice* and *The Winter's Tale* in this group too). In many ways these plays fall somewhere between tragedy and comedy. They avoid becoming tragic because they end 'happily', at least in so far as no one dies at the end of the play. They are also known as the **problem plays** or **dark comedies**. The tone of these plays is **dark** and **ambiguous**, the characters are often flawed, and the play moves between sections of dark, psychological complexity and something more conventionally 'comic'. They explore unsettling and uncomfortable issues and ideas, often involving the darker side of human nature, and are more likely to disturb than amuse. Disorder and confusion is at the centre of these plays too, but unlike the other comedies that operate in make-believe, fantasy worlds, the world of the problem play is much bleaker and coldly realistic.

There are a small group of other plays that do not fit the normal 'comedy' style – *Cymbeline, The Winter's Tale* and *The Tempest*. These plays mix comic and tragic elements, and combine romance and realism in a style that is different from the other plays. Although each of these plays ends 'happily', the endings lack the complete sense of harmony that is typical of other comedies. The plays are called the **romances** (or '**last plays**', as they were the last plays Shakespeare wrote). Again, the idea of disorder is important, but unlike the problem comedies – which have a more bleak and realistic setting – these plays make more use of **fantasy** elements and **magic** to explore their central ideas.

Certain key ideas can be seen emerging in each of the romances or 'last plays':

1. The play is focused on a **noble family and a king**.
2. An **evil or misguided deed** is done.
3. This causes **great suffering** to characters and they endure years of separation.
4. Through the suffering, **something new and positive begins to emerge**.
5. In the end, this **new element transforms the old evil**.
6. An **act of forgiveness** resolves the problems, and **reconciliation** takes place.

The histories

The main **history** plays that you are likely to encounter when studying English at AS or A-Level are *Richard II*, *Henry IV (Part 1)*, *Henry IV (Part 2)*, *Henry V* and *Richard III*, all of which focus on a specific period of English history. In his history plays, Shakespeare takes real historical characters and events and creates his dramas from them. However, the ways in which he adapts historical facts to suit his dramatic purpose, develop his characters and explore themes and ideas makes real dramas, rather than a simple re-telling of an historical event.

Although, in many respects, each of Shakespeare's histories is very different, they do have certain features in common.

The histories usually:

- focus on famous historical figures at significant points in their lives
- raise questions to do with order and the stability of the state
- portray rebels who create problems
- have heroes who have weaknesses or human failings
- examine the ideal of kingship and how the characters fall short of the ideal
- explore the nature of social disorder and its consequences.

> **KEY POINT**
>
> Be aware of the kind of play that you are studying and what its key features are.

The structure of Shakespeare's plays

AQA A **U 4** AQA B **U 2, 3** Edexcel **U 2** OCR **U 3** WJEC **U 4** CCEA **AS U1, A2 U1**	In Chapter 6, we looked at some of the key features of dramatic works in general. Much of what you looked at in that chapter is applicable to Shakespeare's plays too.

For example, Shakespeare's plays follow the general structural pattern that we looked at on page 115.

EXPOSITION ⟶ DRAMATIC INCITEMENT ⟶ COMPLICATION ⟶ CRISIS ⟶ RESOLUTION

Shakespeare's plays also make use of **sub-plots** or secondary plots which, although separate from the main action, link with it in some way.

Approaching your text

When approaching your study of a Shakespeare text you should make use of all the knowledge you already have about the nature of drama generally. This can help you understand the plot of your Shakespeare text, particularly in the early stages of your study.

It will also help if you have some understanding of the general structure of the kind of Shakespeare play you are studying – this is outlined in the following sections of this chapter. This knowledge can provide you with a framework for your analysis of the play as a whole. One of the problems that students frequently encounter is that they focus so closely on detailed scene summaries that they lose sight of the fact that the play is an integrated whole. Being able to see a Shakespeare play in terms of its overall framework can help you to appreciate the pattern of the text, and this will help you to move on to your more detailed study of action, character and theme.

> **PROGRESS CHECK**
>
> Look at the kind of play you are studying and what its key features are. Make a plan of the overall structure of your play.

7.2 Opening scenes

LEARNING SUMMARY	**After studying this section, you should be able to:**
	• understand the importance of the opening of a play
	• appreciate some ways in which Shakespeare opened his plays
	• analyse the effects created by the opening of Shakespeare's plays

The importance of the opening scene

AQA A   **U 4**
AQA B   **U 2, 3**
Edexcel **U 2**
OCR   **U 3**
WJEC   **U 4**
CCEA   **AS U1, A2 U1**

> When writing about the opening of a play, make sure that you look at what purpose the opening serves, and what effects are created.

The **opening scene** of any play is vital, because it is here that the dramatist must engage the audience's attention and interest them right from the start. Dramatists can do this in a variety of ways depending on the effects they wish to create, and on the purpose they want the opening to serve.

As we saw in Chapter 6, when looking at the opening scene of a play, these are the two key questions that you should think about:

1. What **effect(s)** does the dramatist want this scene to have on the audience?
2. What **purpose** does the scene serve to the play as a whole?

Shakespeare uses a variety of ways to begin his plays, which include:
- creating a certain mood
- presenting particular background information about the plot
- creating a certain impact on the audience, perhaps by a shock effect, or by the creation of a particularly tense scene
- providing the audience with a good deal of background information about the plot, what is going on, or what has happened prior to the play starting, etc.
- introducing characters, and establishing situations and relationships
- arousing the audience's curiosity and making them want to know more, thereby sustaining their interest.

Example – *Hamlet*

Look at the following extract from the start of *Hamlet* – it has just struck midnight and the guard is being changed at the castle of Elsinore.

As you read, think about the effects created by this opening.

Scene I, *Elsinore.*

Enter BARNARDO *and* FRANCISCO, *two sentinels*

BARNARDO : Who's there?

FRANCISCO: Nay, answer me: stand, and unfold yourself.

BARNARDO: Long live the king!

FRANCISCO: Barnardo?

BARNARDO: He.

FRANCISCO: You come most carefully upon your hour.

BARNARDO: 'Tis now struck twelve. Get thee to bed, Francisco.

FRANCISCO For this relief much thanks: 'tis bitter cold,
And I am sick at heart.

BARNARDO: Have you had quiet guard?

FRANCISCO: Not a mouse stirring.

BARNARDO: Well, good night.
If you do meet Horatio and Marcellus,
The rivals of my watch, bid them make haste.

Enter HORATIO *and* MARCELLUS

FRANCISCO: I think I hear them.—Stand, ho, who is there?

Enter HORATIO *and* MARCELLUS

HORATIO: Friends to this ground.

MARCELLUS: And liegemen to the Dane.

FRANCISCO: Give you good-night.

MARCELLUS: O, farewell, honest soldier;
Who hath relieved you?

FRANCISCO: Bernardo has my place.
Give you good-night.

[Exit]

MARCELLUS: Holla, Bernardo!

BARNARDO: Say,
What, is Horatio there?   *continued*

HORATIO: A piece of him.

BARNARDO: Welcome, Horatio, welcome good Marcellus.

MARCELLUS: What, has this thing appeared again tonight?

BARNARDO: I have seen nothing.

MARCELLUS: Horatio says 'tis but our fantasy,
And will not let belief take hold of him
Touching this dreaded sight, twice seen of us:
Therefore I have entreated him along
With us to watch the minutes of this night;
That if again this apparition come,
He may approve our eyes and speak to it.

HORATIO: Tush, tush, 'twill not appear.

BARNARDO: Sit down awhile,
And let us once again assail your ears,
That are so fortified against our story,
What we two nights have seen.

HORATIO: Well, sit we down,
And let us hear Bernardo speak of this.

BARNARDO: Last night of all,
When yond same star that's westward from the pole
Had made his course t'illume that part of heaven
Where now it burns, Marcellus and myself,
The bell then beating one –

Enter GHOST

MARCELLUS: Peace, break thee off. Look where it comes again!

BARNARDO: In the same figure, like the king that's dead.

MARCELLUS: Thou art a scholar, speak to it Horatio.

BARNARDO: Looks 'a not like the King? Mark it Horatio.

HORATIO: Most like. It harrows me with fear and wonder.

COMMENTARY

Here are some points that you may have noted:

1. The opening challenge – 'Who's there?' – creates a sense of **tension**. The sentries on guard duty are clearly on edge, and this tension immediately captures the interest of the audience.

2. A sense of the darkness of the scene is created through the language and the acting. This is shown by the guards shouting to one another as they cannot see clearly in the dark, and the reference to the clock striking twelve (remember, Shakespeare's plays were performed in daylight).

continued

> ③ There is a sense of trepidation and fear about what is to happen next – for example, Barnardo's anxious query about whether Francisco has had a 'quiet guard', and his request to Francisco that if he sees Horatio and Marcellus, to ask them to hurry to meet him.
>
> ④ With the arrival of Horatio and Marcellus, another element of anxiety is added, as Marcellus asks, '... has this thing appeared again tonight?', and it is revealed that they are waiting to see if 'this apparition' will come again.
>
> ⑤ Tension mounts further still with the shock effect as the ghost appears, and with Barnardo's comment that it looks 'like the king that's dead' (Hamlet's father).

The extract you have looked at ends here, but in the play further tension is built up in this scene as Horatio attempts to speak to the ghost. Shakespeare also uses the scene to give the audience some background information about the state of Denmark being on a war footing, and that there is the possibility of invasion by Norway. At the end of the scene Shakespeare reduces the tension as dawn begins to break and the darkness is dispelled, and Horatio says he will find Hamlet and tell him what they have seen.

You can see how an audience is likely to be gripped with an opening such as this, which contains tension, mystery and the appearance of a ghost.

> **KEY POINT**
>
> Look for a variety of ways in which effects are created when examining the impact of an opening scene.

Example – *Twelfth Night*

The following opening from *Twelfth Night* presents a complete contrast to the effects created in the opening of *Hamlet*. The opening scene is quite short, and the passage here is the complete scene.

Read it through carefully. What do you think Shakespeare's purpose is in this opening scene, and what effects does he achieve?

ACT I. SCENE I. An Apartment in the DUKE'S Palace.

[Enter DUKE, CURIO, Lords; Musicians attending.]

DUKE: If music be the food of love, play on,
Give me excess of it; that, surfeiting,
The appetite may sicken and so die.—
That strain again;—it had a dying fall;
O, it came o'er my ear like the sweet south,
That breathes upon a bank of violets,
Stealing and giving odour.—Enough; no more;
'Tis not so sweet now as it was before.
O spirit of love, how quick and fresh art thou!
That, notwithstanding thy capacity
Receiveth as the sea, nought enters there,
Of what validity and pitch soever,

continued

But falls into abatement and low price
Even in a minute! so full of shapes is fancy,
That it alone is high-fantastical.

CURIO: Will you go hunt, my lord?

DUKE: What, Curio?

CURIO: The hart.

DUKE: Why, so I do, the noblest that I have:
O, when mine eyes did see Olivia first,
Methought she purged the air of pestilence;
That instant was I turned into a hart;
And my desires, like fell and cruel hounds,
E'er since pursue me.—How now! what news from her?

[Enter VALENTINE.]

VALENTINE: So please my lord, I might not be admitted,
But from her handmaid do return this answer:
The element itself, till seven years' heat,
Shall not behold her face at ample view;
But like a cloistress she will veiled walk,
And water once a-day her chamber round
With eye-offending brine: all this to season
A brother's dead love, which she would keep fresh
And lasting in her sad remembrance.

DUKE: O, she that hath a heart of that fine frame
To pay this debt of love but to a brother,
How will she love when the rich golden shaft
Hath killed the flock of all affections else
That live in her; when liver, brain, and heart,
These sovereign thrones, are all supplied and filled,—
Her sweet perfections,—with one self king!—
Away before me to sweet beds of flowers:
Love-thoughts lie rich when canopied with bowers.

[Exeunt.]

COMMENTARY

This scene is a complete contrast to the opening of *Hamlet* in a number of ways. Instead of the very tense action taking place in the darkness of night, the opening of *Twelfth Night* creates a very relaxed and light mood as Duke Orsino listens to music, which, at first, fills him with thoughts of love and passion. He is clearly in love, but he becomes tired of the music and ponders on the idea of love and how it consumes those who are in love themselves. It is then revealed that the Duke is in love with Olivia, and that he feels like a hunted animal pursued by his love for her. We learn a little more about why he feels this way when Valentine enters with a message from Olivia revealing that as she is in mourning for her brother's death, she will not see anyone for seven years. Far from being

continued

discouraged from this, though, he feels reassured that she is a woman who loves deeply. When her love and passions are focused on him, he says he will be like a 'king'.

This opening, then, serves several purposes:

1. It establishes a relaxed atmosphere and mood, and introduces the idea of 'love' and 'being in love', which is a central theme of the play. It also hints at the pain as well as the pleasure that love can cause.
2. It provides information for the audience so they know what is going on – that Orsino is in love with Olivia, and that his love is not returned.
3. It introduces two of the play's central characters – Orsino and Olivia – and we learn something about them (even though we do not actually see Olivia).

Example – *Othello*

Now look carefully at the following extract, which is the opening from *Othello*. What effect is created, what information is conveyed to the audience, and what techniques does Shakespeare use to put it across?

Act 1, Scene 1

Enter RODERIGO *and* IAGO

RODERIGO: Tush, never tell me! I take it much unkindly
That thou, Iago, who hast had my purse
As if the strings were thine, shouldst know of this.

IAGO: 'Sblood, but you will not hear me!
If ever I did dream of such a matter, Abhor me.

RODERIGO: Thou told'st me thou didst hold him in thy hate.

IAGO: Despise me, if I do not. Three great ones of the city,
In personal suit to make me his Lieutenant,
Off-capped to him: and by the faith of man,
I know my price, I am worth no worse a place.
But he, as loving his own pride and purposes,
Evades them with a bombast circumstance
Horribly stuffed with epithets of war,
And in conclusion
Non-suits my mediators. For 'Certes,' says he,
'I have already chose my officer.'
And what was he?
Forsooth, a great arithmetician,
One Michael Cassio, a Florentine –
A fellow almost damned in a fair wife –
That never set a squadron in the field,
Nor the division of a battle knows
More than a spinster – unless the bookish theoric,
Wherein the toged consuls can propose

continued

As masterly as he. Mere prattle without practice
Is all his soldiership. But he, sir, had th'election:
And I, of whom his eyes had seen the proof
At Rhodes, at Cyprus, and on other grounds
Christian and heathen, must be leed and calmed
By debitor and creditor; this counter-caster,
He in good time must his Lieutenant be,
And I – God bless the mark! – his Moorship's Ancient.

RODERIGO: By heaven, I rather would have been his hangman.

IAGO: Why, there's no remedy. 'Tis the curse of service:
Preferment goes by letter and affection,
And not by old gradation, where each second
Stood heir to th' first. Now sir, be judge yourself
Whether I in any just term am affined
To love the Moor.

RODERIGO: I would not follow him then.

IAGO: O, Sir, content you:
I follow him to serve my turn upon him.
We cannot all be masters, nor all masters
Cannot be truly followed. You shall mark
Many a duteous and knee-crooking knave
That, doting on his own obsequious bondage,
Wears out his time, much like his master's ass,
For naught but provender, and when he's old –
cashiered!
Whip me such honest knaves. Others there are
Who, trimmed in forms and visages of duty,
Keep yet their hearts attending on themselves,
And, throwing but shows of service on their lords,
Do well thrive by them; and when they have lined
their coats,
Do themselves homage: these fellows have some soul,
And such a one do I profess myself.
For, sir,
It is as sure as you are Roderigo,
Were I the Moor, I would not be Iago:
In following him, I follow but myself.
Heaven is my judge, not I for love and duty,
But seeming so for my peculiar end:
For when my outward action doth demonstrate
The native act and figure of my heart
In compliment extern, 'tis not long after,
But I will wear my heart upon my sleeve
For daws to peck at – I am not what I am.

> **COMMENTARY**
>
> The play opens in the middle of an interchange between Roderigo and Iago, so the audience only gradually forms an understanding of who the characters are and what is happening – this serves to arouse their curiosity and interest. What is immediately established is that Roderigo has a grievance against Iago, whom he has trusted with his personal finances. We also learn that Iago has a grievance himself. His grievance is against Othello (not named by Iago, but referred to as 'his Moorship' or 'the Moor'), who has promoted Michael Cassio to be his lieutenant rather than giving the job to Iago. Iago also reveals that he will continue to serve Othello until he finds a way of taking revenge on him.

> **KEY POINT**
>
> Shakespeare's plays open in different ways depending on what purpose Shakespeare wants the play to serve, and what effects he wants to create.

7.3 Presenting characters

LEARNING SUMMARY

After studying this section, you should be able to:

- recognise how Shakespeare presents characters
- identify how characters are revealed and developed

Techniques for revealing and developing characters

AQA A	**U 4**
AQA B	**U 2, 3**
Edexcel	**U 2**
OCR	**U 3**
WJEC	**U 4**
CCEA	**AS U1, A2 U1**

The ways in which dramatists create and present their **characters** is a key aspect of any play. An essential part of the study of your Shakespeare text(s) will be to examine the characters and the ways in which Shakespeare presents and uses them to create **dramatic effects** in the play.

Shakespeare uses several techniques to create, reveal and develop characters, including:

- what characters say about themselves and others
- what other characters say about them
- the language characters use
- how characters act, and how characters' words match their actions
- how characters are viewed by other characters.

Example – how Shakespeare presents *King Lear*

Characters in plays usually have distinctive **voices**, which the dramatist creates in order to shape the kind of response he or she wants from the audience. Often in Shakespeare's plays, characters change in some way during the course of the play, and these changes are reflected in their language.

In *King Lear*, the character of Lear goes through various changes in response to the various events that befall him.

Below are four extracts from *King Lear*. Read them carefully. Then examine how Shakespeare presents Lear in each of the four extracts, focusing on:

- the **use of language** (look out for particular features of language, e.g. key words or phrases, whether imagery is used, and, if so, at the effects created by it)
- the **rhythm** and **syntax** of the speech (whether it flows smoothly, or is disjointed, and at any effects created by it)
- the way the language reflects Lear's **mood** and state of mind
- the **dramatic effect** created.

> When looking at the dramatic effects created in the play you are studying, make sure that you include details of language use to illustrate and support your ideas.

In Extract A, from the opening scene of the play, Lear announces that he has divided his kingdom into three and intends to give one part to each of his three daughters: Goneril, Regan and Cordelia. He is doing this so that he can live out his remaining days without the worries of running the state. In order to decide who has what portions of the country, he wants to decide which of his daughters loves him the most.

Extract A

Sennet. Enter one bearing a coronet, KING LEAR, CORNWALL, ALBANY, GONERIL, REGAN, CORDELIA, *and Attendants*

LEAR: Attend the Lords of France and Burgundy, Gloucester.

GLOUCESTER: I shall, my Liege.

LEAR: Meantime, we shall express our darker purpose.
Give me the map there. Know that we have divided
In three our kingdom; and 'tis our fast intent
To shake all cares and business from our age,
Conferring them on younger strengths, while we
Unburthened crawl toward death. Our son of Cornwall,
And you, our no less loving son of Albany,
We have this hour a constant will to publish
Our daughters' several dowers, that future strife
May be prevented now. The Princes, France and Burgundy,
Great rivals in our youngest daughter's love,
Long in our court have made their amorous sojourn,
And here are to be answered. Tell me my daughters,
(Since now we will divest us both of rule,
 Interest of territory, cares of state)
Which of you shall we say doth love us most?
That we our largest bounty may extend
Where nature doth with merit challenge. Goneril,
Our eldest-born, speak first.

(Act 1, Scene 1, lines 33–53)

In Extract B, on the next page, Lear has banished his youngest daughter Cordelia for refusing to say how much she loves him, and has divided his kingdom between his other two daughters, Goneril and Regan. Lear carries out his plan to live with each of them alternately, but his daughters are not very keen on this idea. Here, Goneril and Regan band together against him and want him to get rid of the company of knights that he brings with him when he stays with them. They want to isolate him so they can control him.

Extract B

GONERIL: Hear me, my Lord.
What need you five-and-twenty, ten, or five,
To follow in a house where twice so many
Have a command to tend you?

REGAN: What need one?

LEAR: O! reason not the need; our basest beggars
Are in the poorest thing superfluous:
Allow not nature more than nature needs,
Man's life is cheap as beast's. Thou art a lady;
If only to go warm were gorgeous,
Why, nature needs not what thou gorgeous wear'st,
Which scarcely keeps thee warm. But, for true need, —
You heavens, give me that patience, patience I need! —
You see me here, you Gods, a poor old man,
As full of grief as age; wretched in both!
If it be you that stirs these daughters' hearts
Against their father, fool me not so much
To bear it tamely; touch me with noble anger,
And let not women's weapons, water-drops,
Stain my man's cheeks! No, you unnatural hags,
I will have such revenges on you both
That all the world shall — I will do such things,
What they are, yet I know not, but they shall be
The terrors of the earth. You think I'll weep;
No, I'll not weep:
I have full cause of weeping, *[Storm heard at a distance]* but this heart
Shall break into a hundred thousand flaws
Or ere I'll weep. O Fool! I shall go mad.

(Act 2, Scene 4, lines 259–285)

In Extract C, Lear has left Regan's castle in a rage, accompanied only by his Fool. Regan and her husband Cornwall have closed their doors against him, and Lear and the Fool wander the heath in a wild storm.

Extract C

Another part of the heath. Storm still.

[Enter LEAR and FOOL]

LEAR: Blow, winds, and crack your cheeks! rage! blow!
You cataracts and hurricanoes, spout
Till you have drenched our steeples, drowned the cocks!
You sulphurous and thought-executing fires,

continued

Vaunt-couriers to oak-cleaving thunderbolts,
Singe my white head! And thou, all-shaking thunder,
Smite flat the thick rotundity o' the world!
Crack nature's moulds, all germains spill at once,
That make ingrateful man!

FOOL: O nuncle, court holy-water in a dry house is better
Than this rain-water out o' door. Good nuncle, in, and
ask thy daughters' blessing: here's a night pities neither
wise man nor fool.

LEAR: Rumble thy bellyful! Spit, fire! spout, rain!
Nor rain, wind, thunder, fire, are my daughters:
I tax not you, you elements, with unkindness;
I never gave you kingdom, called you children,
You owe me no subscription: then let fall
Your horrible pleasure: here I stand, your slave,
A poor, infirm, weak, and despised old man:
But yet I call you servile ministers,
That have with two pernicious daughters joined
Your high engendered battles 'gainst a head
So old and white as this. O! O! 'tis foul!

(Act 3, Scene 2, lines 1–24)

In Extract D, from the end of the play, Cordelia has returned to help her father against his enemies, including Goneril and Regan, who have raised an army against him and defeated him. Lear and Cordelia have been captured, and are being led away to prison.

Extract D

CORDELIA: We are not the first
Who, with best meaning, have incurred the worst.
For thee, oppressed King, I am cast down;
Myself could else out-frown false Fortune's frown.
Shall we not see these daughters and these sisters?

LEAR: No, no, no no! Come, let's away to prison;
We two alone will sing like birds i'th'cage:
When thou dost ask me blessing, I'll kneel down,
And ask of thee forgiveness: so we'll live,
And pray, and sing, and tell old tales, and laugh
At gilded butterflies, and hear poor rogues
Talk of court news; and we'll talk with them too,
Who loses and who wins; who's in, who's out;
And take upon's the mystery of things,
As if we were God's spies: and we'll wear out,
In a walled prison, packs and sects of great ones
That ebb and flow by th'moon.

(Act 5, Scene 3, lines 3–19)

COMMENTARY

Below are some ideas you might have noted.

- In **Extract A**, Lear speaks with the confidence of a king in complete control. He acts imperiously, savouring his own performance as the patriarch. His entry comes with all the entourage and pomp that reflects his power, ready to begin his abdication ritual. Lear's use of the royal plural emphasises his regal status. He introduces the motives behind assembling the court together – to announce his abdication of power, and his intention to 'retire' from his public function. Also Lear claims there is a 'darker purpose' – his plan to arrange a marriage for Cordelia. This speech marks the beginning of Lear's identity as king being stripped. He uses phrases like 'conferring them on younger strengths' and 'divest us' to describe his giving away of power.

- In **Extract B**, as Goneril and Regan seek to force him to dismiss all his supporters, Lear resists and argues that man is superior to animals, because his needs are much greater than the basic needs that animals have. Throughout the play, Lear makes reference to nature and animals, but the references are much more pointed when he is in a rage. Lear asks for patience, but immediately he moves to anger and revenge. Note how this is reflected in the increasing use of exclamations, broken and interrupted syntax, and shorter phrases. He becomes more irrational and his language more extreme as he swears he will be revenged on them:

    > I will have such revenges on you both
    > That all the world shall – I will do such things,
    > What they are, yet I know not, but they shall be
    > The terrors of the earth.

    Symbolically, a storm is heard approaching in the distance as Lear's words mark the onset of the madness that will soon overtake him as he breaks down.

- In **Extract C**, Lear and the Fool rage against the storm as they wander aimlessly on the heath. Lear's language reflects the breakdown of his mind and reason. Note the frequent exclamations, the short phrases and single words as he urges the storm to destroy the earth – 'Blow, winds, and crack your cheeks! rage! blow!'. He calls for a second Flood, and his language is full of the imagery of destruction – 'sulphurous and thought-executing fires', 'oak-cleaving thunderbolts'. He feels that the heavens have joined forces with his 'two pernicious daughters' in punishing him.

- In **Extract D**, Lear's sanity is restored when he is reunited with Cordelia, completing his recovery and his redemption. He recognises the important things in life and his mind has been healed through Cordelia's love. In this, Lear's final speech to Cordelia, he hastens to reassure her, and his tone is that of a father comforting a distraught and frightened child:

    > We two alone will sing like birds i'th'cage

    and

    > ... so we'll live,
    > And pray, and sing, and tell old tales, and laugh
    > At gilded butterflies, and hear poor rogues
    > Talk of court news ...

continued

Lear has come to learn to appreciate what he had not recognised earlier in the play – the value of his loyal daughter's love, and how precious the time they have together is. Although in prison he will be happy being with Cordelia, he is insulating himself from reality. He is presented as a broken and pathetic figure, but his renunciation of power is complete.

Key characters can rarely be seen in clear-cut, black and white terms. As part of your preparation for the examination, make notes on each of the characters in the play(s) you are studying. Make sure that you consider all possible interpretations of each character. Assess the role or function that they perform in the play, and look in detail at the key speeches each character makes, and the scenes in which he or she appears. Remember to use evidence from the play to support your view of the character.

PROGRESS CHECK

Choose one of the central characters from the Shakespeare play(s) that you are studying. Imagine that you are an actor who has been asked to play the part in a forthcoming production. Collect evidence from the play to support your view of the character, and the way that you intend to play him or her on stage.

Your evidence should consist of:
- what the character says about himself or herself, and about others
- what others say about the character
- what the character does when speaking
- what the character does when silent
- how the character's words match his or her actual deeds or underlying motives
- how the character is viewed by those around him or her.

7.4 Soliloquies and asides

LEARNING SUMMARY	**After studying this section, you should be able to:**
	- understand the purpose and importance of soliloquies in a play
	- understand the purpose and importance of asides in a play
	- identify the use and function of soliloquies and asides in the play you are studying

What are soliloquies and asides?

AQA A	**U 4**
AQA B	**U 2, 3**
Edexcel	**U 2**
OCR	**U 3**
WJEC	**U 4**
CCEA	**AS U1, A2 U1**

In most of his plays, Shakespeare makes full use of the dramatic devices of **soliloquies** and **asides** as a means of developing aspects of character.

A **soliloquy** is an extended speech directed at the audience rather than other characters, and very often the character delivers the speech when he or she is alone on the stage. Through their soliloquy, characters explore their inner thoughts or feelings, plans, future intentions or motivations, and so allow the audience to see what is in their thoughts.

An **aside**, on the other hand, is a comment (usually short) spoken by a character during a passage of dialogue, which is meant to be heard by the audience, but not the other character or characters. In an aside, characters can comment on what is being said in the dialogue, or express their thoughts and feelings towards another character or situation to the audience.

Soliloquies

AQA A	**U 4**
AQA B	**U 2, 3**
Edexcel	**U 2**
OCR	**U 3**
WJEC	**U 4**
CCEA	**AS U1, A2 U1**

Soliloquies, then, are used extensively to convey both information and the inner thoughts and feelings of a character to the audience.

Example – *Hamlet*

In *Hamlet*, it is possible to trace the development of Hamlet's shifting emotions through the sequence of soliloquies he delivers at various points in the action.

In his first soliloquy, delivered early in the play, he reveals his feelings about the death of his father, the old King, and the hasty marriage of his mother to his father's brother.

Read the soliloquy through carefully. What do you think is the purpose of the soliloquy at this point in the play, and what do you learn from it?

> **HAMLET:** O, that this too too solid flesh would melt
> Thaw and resolve itself into a dew!
> Or that the Everlasting had not fixed
> His canon 'gainst self-slaughter! O God! God!
> How weary, stale, flat and unprofitable,
> Seem to me all the uses of this world!
> Fie on't! ah fie, 'tis an unweeded garden,
> That grows to seed; things rank and gross in nature
> Possess it merely. That it should come to this!
> But two months dead: nay, not so much, not two:
> So excellent a king; that was, to this,
> Hyperion to a satyr; so loving to my mother
> That he might not beteem the winds of heaven
> Visit her face too roughly. Heaven and earth,
> Must I remember? Why, she would hang on him,
> As if increase of appetite had grown
> By what it fed on: and yet, within a month—
> Let me not think on't—frailty, thy name is woman.
> A little month, or ere those shoes were old
> With which she followed my poor father's body,
> Like Niobe, all tears:—why she, even she—
> O, God, a beast, that wants discourse of reason,
> Would have mourned longer—married with my uncle,
> My father's brother, but no more like my father
> Than I to Hercules: within a month—
> Ere yet the salt of most unrighteous tears
> Had left the flushing in her galled eyes,
> She married. O, most wicked speed, to post
> With such dexterity to incestuous sheets.
> It is not nor it cannot come to good:
> But break, my heart; for I must hold my tongue.
>
> *(Act 1, Scene 2, lines 129–159)*

COMMENTARY

Here are some ideas:

1. Shakespeare uses this soliloquy primarily to establish Hamlet's mood and reaction to his father's death and his mother's marriage to his uncle. We see immediately that Hamlet's mood, when he is alone, is very low. He wishes that he could cease to exist, and even considers suicide had God '… not fixed / His canon 'gainst self-slaughter!' He is clearly deep in grief and in his depressed state can see nothing of any worth in the world, likening it to '… an unweeded garden / That grows to seed; things rank and gross in nature / Possess it merely'.

2. His thoughts then turn to his dead father and his re-married mother, his mind dwelling on the haste with which she re-married after his father's death – 'But two months dead: nay, not so much, not two'. Notice how this period becomes shorter and shorter the more it eats away at him – '… and yet, within a month –' and then, 'A little month, or ere those shoes were old / With which she followed my poor father's body', and finally, 'within a month'. He feels that 'a beast … Would have mourned longer'. He also compares his uncle unfavourably to his dead father, who was 'So excellent a king; that was, to this / Hyperion to a satyr'.

3. Towards the end of his soliloquy, he dwells on how his mother was so eager to go to his uncle's bed (which he sees as incest), and that no good can come of it. Hurt and miserable as he is, though, he knows he can do nothing about it, and he must keep his feelings to himself.

This soliloquy, then, provides the audience with a graphic insight into Hamlet's state of mind and the pain that he feels. It provides the background to his mother's relationship with his uncle. It also creates the idea that, as Hamlet says, the relationship 'cannot come to good'. The audience is left with a sense of expectation as they wait to see how events will develop.

Example – *Henry IV (Part 1)*

Now have a look at this example from *Henry IV (Part 1)*. The Prince has been a disappointment to his father, King Henry, and spends most of his time drinking and carousing with a group of dubious characters.

In this soliloquy, again from early in the play, the Prince reveals a different side to his character when he is left alone.

When you have read the soliloquy, answer the following questions:

1. What is the Prince saying here?
2. What does he reveal to the audience?
3. Why do you think Shakespeare has placed this soliloquy at such an early point in the play?

PRINCE: I know you all, and will awhile uphold
The unyok'd humour of your idleness.
Yet herein will I imitate the sun,
Who doth permit the base contagious clouds
To smother up his beauty from the world,
That, when he please again to be himself,
Being wanted he may be more wonder'd at
By breaking through the foul and ugly mists
Of vapours that did seem to strangle him.
If all the year were playing holidays,
To sport would be as tedious as to work;
But when they seldom come, they wish'd-for come,
And nothing pleaseth but rare accidents:
So, when this loose behaviour I throw off,
And pay the debt I never promised,
By how much better than my word I am,
By so much shall I falsify men's hopes;
And, like bright metal on a sullen ground,
My reformation, glittering o'er my fault,
Shall show more goodly, and attract more eyes
Than that which hath no foil to set it off.
I'll so offend to make offence a skill,
Redeeming time when men think least I will. *(Exit)*

(Act 1, Scene 2, lines 188–210)

COMMENTARY

Here are the answers:

1. The Prince opens the soliloquy as if addressing the companions he has just been spending time with, telling them that he knows what they arc like and that, for the moment, he will play along with them and 'will awhile uphold / The unyok'd humour of your idleness'.

2. He reveals, though, that this will be just an act – that he will play the part of the idle waster and then, at the appropriate moment, throw off this 'loose behaviour'. His reformation, being so unexpected, will have all the more impact, and will show him in a good light 'like bright metal on a sullen ground'.

3. Giving the audience this information early in the play allows them to see the Prince's behaviour in a different light. They are in on the secret that his behaviour is temporary, and that adds to the humour of how he interacts with his companions. Also, it sets up a sense of anticipation for when he reveals himself in his true colours.

Example – *Othello*

In *Othello*, Iago lets the audience in on a rather different plan. The opening lines of this soliloquy refer to Roderigo (see page 152) – we learn that Iago regards him as a fool, and uses his money as if it were his own.

Read the soliloquy carefully. What do you think the main purpose of this soliloquy is?

> **IAGO**: Thus do I ever make my fool my purse:
> For I mine own gained knowledge should profane
> If I would time expend with such a snipe
> But for my sport and profit. I hate the Moor,
> And it is thought abroad that 'twixt my sheets
> He's done my office. I know not if't be true
> But I, for mere suspicion in that kind,
> Will do as if for surety. He holds me well:
> The better shall my purpose work on him.
> Cassio's a proper man: let me see now;
> To get his place and to plume up my will
> In double knavery. How? How? Let's see.
> After some time, to abuse Othello's ear
> That he is too familiar with his wife;
> He hath a person and a smooth dispose
> To be suspected, framed to make women false.
> The Moor is of a free and open nature,
> That thinks men honest that but seem to be so,
> And will as tenderly be led by th'nose
> As asses are.
> I have't. It is engendered. Hell and night
> Must bring this monstrous birth to the world's light. *(Exit)*
>
> *(Act 1, Scene 3, lines 381–402)*

COMMENTARY

Shakespeare uses this soliloquy to reveal to the audience Iago's plan for taking his revenge on Othello. The effect is as if we are actually watching Iago formulate his plan as he is speaking – 'How? How? Let's see'. His plan is to make Othello think that Cassio has been too 'familiar' with his wife. We can sense his satisfaction as this plan begins to take shape in his mind – 'I have't. It is engendered'.

Asides

AQA A	**U 4**
AQA B	**U 2, 3**
Edexcel	**U 2**
OCR	**U 3**
WJEC	**U 4**
CCEA	**AS U1, A2 U1**

Shakespeare uses both short and longer asides in his plays. As we touched on earlier, asides can reveal to the audience what is going on in the mind of the speaker as dialogue or action is taking place.

Example – *Othello*

In the following long aside from *Othello* (reproduced on the next page), Iago reveals his thoughts to the audience as he watches his enemy, Cassio, take the hand of Othello's wife, Desdemona.

IAGO: *[Aside]* He takes her by the palm: ay, well said, whisper: with as little a web as this will I
ensnare as great a fly as Cassio. Ay, smile upon her, do; I will
gyve thee in thine own courtship. You say true; 'tis so, indeed: if such tricks as these strip
you out of your lieutenantry, it had been better you had not
kissed your three fingers so oft, which now again you are most apt to play the sir in. Very
good; well kissed, an excellent courtesy. 'Tis so, indeed. Yet
again your fingers to your lips? Would they were clyster-pipes for your sake!

(Act 2, Scene 1, lines 164–174)

From Iago's soliloquy that we looked at earlier, we can see that Cassio is
playing completely into Iago's hands, even though we know that Cassio's
actions are innocent.

In this extract from a little later in the play, Iago manipulates the conversation
with Cassio as Othello listens in unobserved. Othello believes that Cassio is
talking about Desdemona (Othello's wife), but he is actually talking about a
prostitute whom he knows and who is in love with him. Iago is deliberately setting
Cassio up by leading the conversation to convince Othello that Cassio and
Desdemona are in love and having an affair.

OTHELLO: *(Aside)* Look, how he laughs already!

IAGO: I never knew a woman love man so.

CASSIO: Alas, poor rogue! I think i'faith she loves me.

OTHELLO: *(Aside)* Now he denies it faintly, and laughs it out.

IAGO: Do you hear, Cassio?

OTHELLO: *(Aside)* Now he importunes him to tell it o'er.
Go to, said, well said!

IAGO: She gives it out that you shall marry her.
Do you intend it?

CASSIO: Ha, ha, ha!

OTHELLO: *(Aside)* Do you triumph, Roman? Do you triumph?

CASSIO: I marry her! What! A customer! Prithee bear some charity to my wit: do not think it
so unwholesome. Ha, ha, ha!

OTHELLO: *(Aside)* So, so, so, so: they laugh that win.

(Act 4, Scene 1, lines 110–122)

Here, Othello's repeated asides give the audience an insight into his jealousy and
torment as he believes Cassio's words and laughter are about Desdemona.
Dramatic tension is built up through the cumulative effect of the asides.

> **PROGRESS CHECK**
>
> Look at the play(s) you are studying and identify the points where
> soliloquies or asides are used. Make notes on the purpose and effects
> created by each example you identify.

7.5 Shakespeare's themes and ideas

LEARNING SUMMARY	After studying this section, you should be able to:
	• appreciate the range of themes that Shakespeare explores through his plays
	• understand the nature of these themes
	• identify the key themes in the play(s) you are studying

The themes that Shakespeare explores

AQA A	U 4
AQA B	U 2, 3
Edexcel	U 2
OCR	U 3
WJEC	U 4
CCEA	AS U1, A2 U1

Every Shakespeare play, as well as providing entertainment for the audience, explores certain themes, ideas or issues that are at the centre of the play's design. These themes give a shape and pattern to the play, which endow it with a significance that is beyond the plot or storyline it presents.

The themes are developed through the events, characters and language of the play. Often, Shakespeare uses recurring images to reinforce these themes (see, for example, pages 171–172).

One of the reasons that Shakespeare's plays continue to be relevant for twenty-first century audiences is that they deal with universal themes that are of fundamental importance in our lives. They are to do with human existence and experiences that are just as relevant to us today as they were to people in Elizabethan England – things like love, hate, envy, jealousy, death, revenge, guilt, corruption and ambition.

Some themes seem to have particularly interested Shakespeare, and can be seen in one form or another in most of his plays. These themes are:
- **conflict**
- **appearance and reality**
- **order and disorder**
- **love**.

We will look at each of these themes in turn.

Conflict

Conflict, of one type or another, is the starting point for many plays, not just those by Shakespeare, and conflicts can take many forms. For example, in *King Lear* the conflict between Lear and Goneril and Regan is an important part of the play. In *Richard II* the conflict between Bolingbroke and Richard is of central importance. In comedies such as *Twelfth Night*, the conflict is of a different kind, and begins with Olivia's rejection of Orsino's suit, and Viola shipwrecked on the coast of Illyria.

Appearance and reality

In many of Shakespeare's plays, there is a discrepancy between how things seem to be and how they actually are.

In *Othello*, for example, everyone thinks Iago is 'honest', when in fact he is completely the opposite. In *Twelfth Night*, Viola disguises herself as a boy. In

Hamlet, the apparently popular and effective King Claudius, is, in reality, guilty of the murder of his brother, the former King, (Hamlet's father), and of the seduction of his brother's wife. *Measure for Measure* is very concerned with 'seeming' – the whole plot of the play is based on the idea of the Duke leaving his apparently incorruptible deputy, Angelo, in charge of the state, to see 'If power change purpose, what our seemers be'.

Order and disorder

In one way or another, in many of Shakespeare's plays there is some kind of breakdown in order, and some form of confusion or uncertainty ensues. In plays such as *Henry IV (Part 1)*, *Richard II* and *Julius Caesar*, the breakdown affects the order of the whole country or state, and results in turmoil or war.

The causes of the disruption vary from play to play, but they tend to include strong emotions such as jealousy, love, hate and ambition. In the tragedies, order is normally re-established after the death of the central characters, and often characters undergo some kind of change during the course of the play before order is re-established.

Love

Love of one kind or another is a key feature of many plays.

As we saw earlier in this chapter, *Twelfth Night* begins with the words 'If music be the food of love, play on'. The play goes on to present a world of romantic love, but in plays such as *A Midsummer Night's Dream* and *Much Ado About Nothing* the lovers have to endure many trials and setbacks before final happiness is achieved. The path of love is never a smooth one. In *Othello*, we see a quite different portrayal of love, as Othello's love for Desdemona is corrupted into jealousy and hate by the scheming Iago.

How themes are developed

AQA A	**U 4**
AQA B	**U 2, 3**
Edexcel	**U 2**
OCR	**U 3**
WJEC	**U 4**
CCEA	**AS U1, A2 U1**

Shakespeare develops **themes**, and makes his audience aware of them in a number of ways:

- **He uses characters to express certain ideas or views** – often an individual character who experiences some personal difficulties or inner turmoil, perhaps moral or spiritual, that causes some mental conflict. For example, Hamlet struggles to come to terms with events around the death of his father; Othello struggles with his deep feelings of love for Desdemona and his rising jealousy, prompted by Iago's lies and insinuations.
- **He uses the action of the play** – often the family, society or the country is affected by turmoil or disorder of some kind. For example, Rome is at war with Egypt in *Antony and Cleopatra*; rebellion and battles between armies are a consequence in *Henry IV (Part 1)*; Frederick's usurpation of his brother in *As You Like It* has various repercussions.
- **He uses setting and imagery** – nature or the universe may be disordered, or supernatural events may be involved. For example, there is storm imagery in *King Lear*; the appearance of the ghost in *Hamlet*; the importance of Prospero's magic in *The Tempest*.

Example – *Measure for Measure*

Shakespeare's plays can have the power to provoke deep thought and personal reactions from the audience.

In *Measure for Measure*, for example, the theme of 'morality' is explored in all kinds of ways. One aspect of this involves one of the characters, Isabella, being faced with a dilemma. The play is set in Vienna and the Duke has mysteriously left, leaving his deputy, Angelo, in charge. Morality in the city has become very lax over the years and Angelo has decided to enforce stringent laws to clean it up. Claudio, Isabella's brother, has been arrested and sentenced to death for getting his fiancée, Juliet, pregnant. Isabella, who is about to enter a nunnery, has been to Angelo to plead for her brother's life. In the following extract, she visits her brother in prison to tell him what has happened.

Read the extract through carefully and then answer the following questions:

1. On what condition is Angelo prepared to free Claudio?
2. How has Isabella responded to Angelo's offer? What is your view on her decision?
3. Who do you feel the most sympathy for in this extract – Isabella or Claudio?
4. How do you respond to Claudio's behaviour?
5. What moral issues do you think Shakespeare is raising here?

CLAUDIO: Now, sister, what's the comfort?

ISABELLA: Why,
As all comforts are; most good, most good indeed.
Lord Angelo, having affairs to heaven,
Intends you for his swift ambassador,
Where you shall be an everlasting leiger:
Therefore your best appointment make with speed;
To-morrow you set on.

CLAUDIO: Is there no remedy?

ISABELLA: None, but such remedy as, to save a head,
To cleave a heart in twain.

CLAUDIO: But is there any?

ISABELLA: Yes, brother, you may live:
There is a devilish mercy in the judge,
If you'll implore it, that will free your life,
But fetter you till death.

CLAUDIO: Perpetual durance?

ISABELLA: Ay, just; perpetual durance, a restraint,
Though all the world's vastidity you had,
To a determined scope.

CLAUDIO: But in what nature?

ISABELLA: In such a one as, you consenting to't,
Would bark your honour from that trunk you bear,
And leave you naked.

continued

CLAUDIO: Let me know the point.

ISABELLA: O, I do fear thee, Claudio; and I quake,
Lest thou a feverous life shouldst entertain,
And six or seven winters more respect
Than a perpetual honour. Dar'st thou die?
The sense of death is most in apprehension;
And the poor beetle, that we tread upon,
In corporal sufferance finds a pang as great
As when a giant dies.

CLAUDIO: Why give you me this shame?
Think you I can a resolution fetch
From flowery tenderness? If I must die,
I will encounter darkness as a bride,
And hug it in mine arms.

ISABELLA: There spake my brother; there my father's grave
Did utter forth a voice. Yes, thou must die:
Thou art too noble to conserve a life
In base appliances. This outward-sainted deputy,
Whose settled visage and deliberate word
Nips youth i' th' head and follies doth enew
As falcon doth the fowl, is yet a devil
His filth within being cast, he would appear
A pond as deep as hell.

CLAUDIO: The precise Angelo!

ISABELLA: O, 'tis the cunning livery of hell,
The damned'st body to invest and cover
In precise guards! Dost thou think, Claudio?
If I would yield him my virginity,
Thou mightst be freed.

CLAUDIO: O heavens! it cannot be.

ISABELLA: Yes, he would give't thee, from this rank offence,
So to offend him still. This night's the time
That I should do what I abhor to name,
Or else thou diest to-morrow.

CLAUDIO: Thou shalt not do't.

ISABELLA: O, were it but my life,
I'd throw it down for your deliverance
As frankly as a pin.

CLAUDIO: Thanks, dear Isabel.

ISABELLA: Be ready, Claudio, for your death tomorrow.

CLAUDIO: Yes. Has he affections in him,
That thus can make him bite the law by the nose,
When he would force it? Sure, it is no sin,
Or of the deadly seven, it is the least.

continued

ISABELLA: Which is the least?

CLAUDIO: If it were damnable, he being so wise,
Why would he for the momentary trick
Be perdurably fined? O Isabel!

ISABELLA: What says my brother?

CLAUDIO: Death is a fearful thing.

ISABELLA: And shamed life a hateful.

CLAUDIO: Ay, but to die, and go we know not where;
To lie in cold obstruction and to rot;
This sensible warm motion to become
A kneaded clod; and the delighted spirit
To bathe in fiery floods, or to reside
In thrilling region of thick-ribbed ice;
To be imprisoned in the viewless winds,
And blown with restless violence round about
The pendent world; or to be worse than worst
Of those that lawless and incertain thought
Imagine howling: 'tis too horrible!
The weariest and most loathed worldly life
That age, ache, penury and imprisonment
Can lay on nature is a paradise
To what we fear of death.

ISABELLA: Alas, alas!

CLAUDIO: Sweet sister, let me live:
What sin you do to save a brother's life,
Nature dispenses with the deed so far
That it becomes a virtue.

ISABELLA: O you beast!
O faithless coward! O dishonest wretch!
Wilt thou be made a man out of my vice?
Is't not a kind of incest, to take life
From thine own sister's shame? What should I think?
Heaven shield my mother play'd my father fair!
For such a warped slip of wilderness
Ne'er issued from his blood. Take my defiance!
Die, perish! Might but my bending down
Reprieve thee from thy fate, it should proceed:
I'll pray a thousand prayers for thy death,
No word to save thee.

CLAUDIO: Nay, hear me, Isabel.

ISABELLA: O, fie, fie, fie!
Thy sin's not accidental, but a trade.
Mercy to thee would prove itself a bawd:
'Tis best thou diest quickly.

(Act 3, Scene 1, lines 53–149)

COMMENTARY

Here are the answers:

1. On condition that she sleeps with him – 'If I would yield him my virginity / Thou mightst be freed'.
2. She has rejected it.
3. There is no correct answer – you must decide.
4. Again, you must decide for yourself.
5. The question of Isabella's attitude to her chastity, Angelo's corruption, and Claudio's attitude towards his sister's predicament.

Remember, Shakespeare presents this scene so that it creates maximum impact on the audience in terms of dramatic tension and effect.

Here is how Shakespeare achieves this:

- The audience already knows what Angelo has proposed to her, but Isabella does not tell her brother immediately what has happened, or what the situation is. This serves to heighten the dramatic tension as the audience waits for Isabella to tell him, wondering how he is going to react.
- Isabella has earlier convinced herself that Claudio would be willing to die for her, but she cannot be sure how he will respond – she knows how she would like him to react but is not entirely confident that he will respond in that way.
- Claudio's initial response is what Isabella has hoped for – he claims that he does not want his sister to sacrifice herself for him.
- The fact that he begins to waver and change his mind sets up conflict between him and Isabella. This further heightens the dramatic tension, culminating in her harsh response to him.

PROGRESS CHECK

Think about the play(s) you are studying and make a list of the key themes that Shakespeare explores. Make notes on each theme and how they are presented through the action of the play.

7.6 Shakespeare's language

LEARNING SUMMARY	After studying this section, you should be able to: - understand the importance of imagery in Shakespeare's plays - understand Shakespeare's use of verse and prose

Shakespeare's imagery

AQA A	**U 4**
AQA B	**U 2, 3**
Edexcel	**U 2**
OCR	**U 3**
WJEC	**U 4**
CCEA	**AS U1, A2 U1**

The use of **imagery** is very important to the overall effects created in Shakespeare's plays. Imagery is a very important aspect of the way in which Shakespeare uses language to create heightened effects and vivid ideas in the audience's imagination.

Imagery plays a key part in every Shakespeare play, and is often very closely linked to its central themes. In this section, we will look at some of the imagery used in *Othello* and *The Tempest*.

Example – *Othello*

In *Othello*, one of the themes of the play is the conflict between good and evil, and there are recurring images that use the idea of opposites (for instance, black and white, night and day, angel and devil, heaven and hell) to constantly keep this antithesis in the audience's mind.

This use of imagery is illustrated in the following extract, from the closing scene of the play, where Othello has murdered Desdemona. Desdemona's maid, Emilia (who is also Iago's wife) has arrived and realised that Othello is to blame for her death.

> **EMILIA:** O, the more angel she,
> And you the blacker devil!
>
> **OTHELLO:** She turn'd to folly, and she was a whore.
>
> **EMILIA:** Thou dost belie her, and thou art a devil.
>
> **OTHELLO:** She was false as water.
>
> **EMILIA:** Thou art rash as fire, to say
> That she was false: O, she was heavenly true!
>
> **OTHELLO:** Cassio did top her. Ask thy husband else.
> O, I were damned beneath all depth in hell,
> But that I did proceed upon just grounds
> To this extremity. Thy husband knew it all.
>
> *(Act 5, Scene 2, lines 131–140)*

Example – *The Tempest*

In *The Tempest,* the sea provides a central image – related to both the theme and the action.

The play is set on an island (and so is surrounded by the sea), and the play opens with a tempest at sea which wrecks Ferdinand's ship on Prospero's island.

More than that though, the image of the sea represents a universal and supernatural force, sometimes linked to Prospero's magic. This is seen, for example, in his soliloquy (reproduced on the next page), where he speaks of his power over nature and the elements.

PROSPERO: Ye elves of hills, brooks, standing lakes and groves,
And ye that on the sands with printless foot
Do chase the ebbing Neptune and do fly him
When he comes back; you demi-puppets that
By moonshine do the green sour ringlets make,
Whereof the ewe not bites, and you whose pastime
Is to make midnight mushrooms, that rejoice
To hear the solemn curfew; by whose aid,
Weak masters though ye be, I have bedimm'd
The noontide sun, call'd forth the mutinous winds,
And 'twixt the green sea and the azured vault
Set roaring war: to the dread rattling thunder
Have I given fire and rifted Jove's stout oak
With his own bolt; the strong-based promontory
Have I given fire and rifted Jove's stout oak
With his own bolt; the strong-based promontory
Have I made shake and by the spurs pluck'd up
The pine and cedar: graves at my command
Have waked their sleepers, oped, and let 'em forth
By my so potent art.

(Act 5, Scene 1, lines 33–50)

Sometimes the sea seems to represent a mysterious force for change and transformation. This is illustrated, for example, through the image of the 'sea-change' described in Ariel's song.

Full fathom five thy father lies
Of his bones are coral made,
Those are pearls that were his eyes;
Nothing of him that doth fade
But doth suffer a sea-change
Into something rich and strange.
Sea-nymphs hourly ring his knell:

(Act 1, Scene 2, lines 395–401)

PROGRESS CHECK

1. Look at the play(s) you are studying and make a list of the different kinds of imagery that Shakespeare uses.
2. Are there any links between the kind of imagery the play contains and the themes of the play?
3. Pick two examples of imagery and analyse the ways in which Shakespeare uses language to achieve his effects.

Shakespeare's use of verse and prose

AQA A	**U 4**
AQA B	**U 2, 3**
Edexcel	**U 2**
OCR	**U 3**
WJEC	**U 4**
CCEA	**AS U1, A2 U1**

One of the features of Shakespeare's drama is the way that he uses language in different ways to suit his purpose, depending on the particular mood, occasion and character.

Much of Shakespeare's work is written in **blank verse**, i.e. unrhymed verse, each line consisting of ten syllables – an unstressed syllable followed by a stressed syllable. This type of verse closely resembles the rhythm of normal speech. This makes it an ideal and flexible form that he adapts to suit many purposes – from presenting scenes of intense passion to scenes of light comedy or bawdy bantering. Often Shakespeare alters this form towards the end of a scene and ends the scene with rhyming couplets. This creates a sense of closure to draw a scene to an end.

Although blank verse is used much of the time, Shakespeare also makes substantial use of **prose**. So why does Shakespeare switch between verse and prose in his plays?

A common answer to this question is that the noble or important characters use poetry – in keeping with their elevated natures and the substance of their dialogue – while the 'low' or comic characters use the more plebeian prose. Another answer is that Shakespeare uses prose for sub-plots, or to indicate madness, or a highly emotional state in a character. To some extent all of these reasons have some truth in them, and it is easy to find examples to support these ideas, but it is also easy to find examples to disprove them. All of these explanations are true some of the time, but the real reason is not so clear-cut.

Example – *Hamlet*

Hamlet begins with the guards, Francisco and Barnardo – who are minor characters and 'ordinary' soldiers – speaking in verse (see pages 148–149). The use of verse here helps to create a solemn and serious tone, in keeping with the serious nature of the scene.

Later in *Hamlet*, Ophelia speaks in verse at some points, but when she loses her sanity she speaks in prose. However, she also speaks in prose at other points in the play where she is perfectly sane.

Hamlet himself speaks both prose and verse, depending on the situation and who he is speaking to.

The importance of context

To understand the real reason why Shakespeare uses verse in some parts of a play and prose in others, you need to look at the context of the particular part of the play in question. The decision whether to use verse or prose is determined by the **dramatic effect** that Shakespeare wants to create at that point in the play.

> **KEY POINT**
>
> Always look at the context in which language is being used, to determine why Shakespeare uses language in a particular way at a certain point in the play.

> **PROGRESS CHECK**
>
> Look at the play(s) that you are studying and find the points at which Shakespeare switches from verse to prose and prose to verse. Look carefully at the context of each point, and make a note of the reason why you think the change takes place in each case.

Sample question and model answer

1. At different points in the play Lodovico refers to Othello as a 'noble Moor' and a 'damned slave'.

Evaluate Shakespeare's presentation of Othello in the light of these comments.

QUESTION OVERVIEW

This question is in the style of a question from OCR Unit 3.

> *A good focus on the question from the start, and the student gives his view and direction of response.* →

Although these two descriptions seem at odds with each other, in a sense both are equally true of the presentation of the character of Othello in the play. The reason for this is that there are really two Othellos in the play - the one we see in the earlier part of the play (the 'noble Moor' deeply in love with Desdemona), and the one that he changes into after Iago has set to work on him.

> *The student begins a more detailed examination of the presentation of Othello through the language of the play. The initial focus is on the 'noble' Othello.* →

When Othello first appears in Act 1, Scene 2, he is presented as a calm and commanding character, who is confident in his own abilities and the importance of his services to the state. He receives the warning from Iago that Brabantio is approaching with his followers, and he is determined to part him from Desdemona calmly. When the angry Brabantio arrives with his followers, Othello handles the situation with dignity and authority.

Othello's noble character seems immediately evident. His language is both poetic and commanding and shows a good sense of restraint:

> *This is a well selected quotation to illustrate and support the point.* →

> Keep up your bright swords, for the dew will rust them.
> Good signor, you shall more command with years
> Than with your weapons.

A little later, when Othello appears before the Duke and senators, we again see his dignified and respectful attitude and his calm responses to Brabantio's charges. Othello's speech to the senators explaining how he and Desdemona fell in love reveals him as an articulate and confident speaker. His language is vivid and poetic, and he talks of his experiences in battle:

> *Another relevant example selected emphasising Othello's noble nature, and good supporting evidence.* →

> Of hair-breadth scapes i' the imminent deadly breach,
> Of being taken by the insolent foe,
> And sold to slavery.

> *This is a sound comment, showing sensitivity to Othello's language and effects.* →

Othello also shows great sensitivity in his description of Desdemona's reactions to his words, and how she is captivated by his stories and shows affection towards him.

Othello's noble and poetic speech is seen again when he arrives in Cyprus and is reunited with Desdemona. His language contains richness when he describes Desdemona as 'my soul's joy!' We soon see his commanding nature again when he is disturbed by the commotion stirred up by Iago provoking the quarrel between Cassio and Montano on the evening of Othello's marriage celebrations. Having retired with Desdemona, Othello is angry at being disturbed and acts decisively. He threatens that:

> He that stirs next to carve for his own rage
> Holds his soul light; he dies upon his motion.

Sample question and model answer (continued)

This is a further example of Othello's 'noble' language, but also introduces suggestions of another side to his character that we have not seen yet – a dangerous side to his temperament. These are good supporting illustrations.

There is a focus on the change that begins to come about in Othello, and how his noble character is becoming corrupted by Iago's insinuations. This is another good illustration.

We begin to see another side to Othello here - his dangerous temper and the fact that when he becomes angry his judgment becomes affected:

> Now by heaven,
> My blood begins my safer guides to rule.

During Act 3, Scene 3, we see the character of Othello begin to change as Iago's insinuations begin to work on his mind. Iago has sown seeds of jealousy and they now begin to take hold and grow, helped along by Iago's clever and subtle manipulation. The change in Othello's attitude towards Desdemona is reflected in his language. The poetic imagery so often used by the Othello of the earlier scenes is replaced with a cruder, darker imagery, spurred on by Iago's suggestions of animalistic, sexual desire. Now the `noble Moor' begins to be replaced by a character eaten up with jealousy. His language reflects, increasingly, his desire for revenge:

> Arise, black vengeance, from the hollow hell.
> Yield up, o love, thy crown and hearted throne
> To tyrannous hate.

There is a focus on Shakespeare's use of imagery to reflect the change that has come about in Othello – sexual and violent language.

Othello's language also begins to take on the crude, animalistic sexual imagery that we see in Iago's language when he speaks of his life being like a `cistern for foul toads / To knot and gender in'. Ominously, his language takes on an edge of extreme violence. For instance, when he is speaking to Iago about Desdemona, he says `I will chop her into messes'.

At the end of the play we see, to some extent, a return to the Othello of earlier in the play. When he realises what he has done in murdering Desdemona, and he sees Iago for what he really is, we see a return of his old sense of dignity and command. He has killed Desdemona out of what he thought was a sense of duty and honour and justice. Now, having realised the huge mistake he has made, he kills himself out of the same sense of honour and justice. He regains something of the old warrior, Othello, and takes charge of events once more. His language assumes something of the old poetry, as he speaks of:

> ... one that loved not wisely, but too well;
> Of one, not easily jealous but being wrought
> Perplexed in the extreme.

There are sound comments on the return of the 'old Othello' at the end of the play – a hint of the old nobility evident in the language use. This is another good illustration and the student returns to the focus of the question in the final comment.

He compares himself to the `base Indian' who `threw a pearl away / Richer than all his tribe before'. Playing the role of the warrior to the end, he stabs himself.

Ultimately, the character of Othello embodies elements both of the `noble Moor' and the `damned slave'.

SUMMATIVE COMMENT

This is a well-focused argument. The student has clearly developed ideas, and focused on the question. There is a good understanding of the presentation of Othello, and this is a well-structured and informed response. There are clearly developed comments on the use of language, supported with appropriate and well-chosen evidence. The writing is fluent. The response could be improved further by more detailed analysis of the effects of language and context, and alternative interpretations of the character of Othello.

Practice examination questions

AQA B Unit 3

1 Explore Shakespeare's dramatic use of the relationship between Macbeth and Lady Macbeth.

2 Discuss the ways in which Shakespeare uses the pastoral tradition in *As You Like It*.

OCR Unit 3

1 Iago has been described as a 'motiveless malignity'.
Evaluate Shakespeare's presentation of Othello in the light of this comment.

2 Hal's rejection of Falstaff represents his rejection of humanity.
Evaluate Shakespeare's presentation of Prince Hal in *Henry IV (Part 1)* in the light of this comment.

WJEC Unit 4

1 Examine Shakespeare's presentation of revenge in *Hamlet*. Show how far your appreciation and understanding of this aspect of *Hamlet* have been informed by your study of *The Revenger's Tragedy* and critical reading of both plays.

2 Discuss how Shakespeare explores ideas about the status of women in *Measure for Measure*. Show how your appreciation and understanding of this aspect of *Measure for Measure* has been informed by your study of *The Duchess of Malfi* and critical readings of both plays.

CCEA Unit A2 1

Tragedy

Shakespeare: *King Lear*

Heaney: *Burial at Thebes* (Sophocles' *Antigone* translated by Seamus Heaney)

The tragedy of both plays lies in a willingness to ignore the truth.

By **comparing and contrasting** appropriately selected parts of the two plays, show how far you would agree with the view expressed above.

Studying poetry

The following topics are covered in this chapter:

- The nature of poetry
- Structure, form and language

8.1 The nature of poetry

LEARNING SUMMARY

After studying this section, you should be able to:

- understand what examiners require from a response to poetry
- appreciate what is meant by poetry
- approach the study of poetry with greater confidence

What examiners are looking for

AQA A	**U 1, 3, 4**
AQA B	**U 3, 4**
Edexcel	**U 1, 3, 4**
OCR	**U 1, 2, 3, 4**
WJEC	**U 1, 3, 4**
CCEA	**AS U2, A2 U1**

Poetry is covered in many different ways in your course, ranging from the study of a single long poem to considering a poem or groups of poems in conjunction with prose and drama texts. Your understanding of poetry may be assessed internally or externally.

Whatever the approach or the style of question, examiners will be looking for evidence of:

- a logically organised answer, using **appropriate** and **clear language**, written as accurately as possible, and using the **appropriate terminology** correctly [Assessment Objective (AO)1]
- an awareness of the ways in which poetry works – that is, how it differs from other genres [AO2]
- an awareness of how poems are written, not just what they are about – the key words are **structure**, **form** and **language** [AO2]
- an independent view of poetry, supported by textual evidence and informed by other interpretations [AO3]
- an understanding of the poet's opinions and attitudes, even when they are not specifically stated [AO4]
- an understanding of the ways that **contexts** influenced the poet in writing the poem, as it influences you in reading it [AO4].

> **KEY POINT**
>
> Make sure you know what your examiners expect from you in your study of poetry for examination or internal assessment.

What is poetry?

AQA A	**U 1, 3, 4**
AQA B	**U 3, 4**
Edexcel	**U 1, 3, 4**
OCR	**U 1, 2, 3, 4**
WJEC	**U 1, 3, 4**
CCEA	**AS U2, A2 U1**

The study of poetry is a central element in all AS and A2 level English Literature courses, and it presents particular challenges that are rather different from those posed by either drama or prose. The question of what exactly poetry is – what makes it different from prose – is a question that many have asked.

Here are some attempts at defining poetry:

- 'Prose = words in their best order; poetry = the best words in the best order' (Samuel Taylor Coleridge).
- 'Poetry is the spontaneous overflow of powerful feelings: it takes its origin from emotion recollected in tranquillity' (William Wordsworth).
- 'It is much easier to say what it is not. We all know what light is but it is not easy to tell what it is' (Samuel Johnson).

Certainly, poetry can take many forms, and poets can employ a wide range of different techniques and styles when writing their poetry.

Although most poetry is written to be read by others, it can also be a very private and personal medium that can evoke very individual responses from the reader. This means, of course, that your response to a poem may not be the same as someone else's response. On the other hand, this does not mean that you can say just what you want about a poem. As with the other forms of literature that you study, your views need to be supported by close reference to the text itself.

In terms of its features, a poem might:

- rhyme
- be organised in stanzas
- be organised in lines
- have a regular rhythm
- start each line with a capital letter
- contain imagery.

Note the word 'might' – a poem does not necessarily have any of these features, which illustrates that poetry can be extremely varied in nature. It is best to look very closely and carefully at what poets have written, and the ways they have chosen to shape and present their ideas and feelings.

> **PROGRESS CHECK**
>
> Write down as many different kinds of poems as you can think of. Think about the ways in which they are written, as well as their content.
>
> Here is a possible answer:
> 1. Narrative poems (poems that tell stories).
> 2. Poems that express emotions such as love, e.g. sonnets.
> 3. Poems that explore philosophical ideas.
> 4. Poems that express spiritual or religious ideas.
> 5. Poems that are humorous.
> 6. Poems that deliberately use language in a way that does not make conventional sense, e.g. nonsense verse.

Poems then, can serve many purposes. They can:

- amuse
- describe
- entertain
- express emotions
- narrate
- inform
- express grief or sadness
- celebrate
- commemorate
- disturb
- influence others
- reflect.

The main thing to recognise is that every poem is an individual piece of work. When reading a poem for the first time, it is important to try to establish three key pieces of information about it.

> The first time you refer to a poet in an essay you should refer to him/her by both names, e.g. Christina Rossetti or William Shakespeare. After that, always use the surname only, or refer to 'the poet'. **Never** refer to the poet by his/her first name.

To do this, you need to ask yourself the following questions:

1. **What** is the poet saying in this poem?
2. **Why** has the poem been written – what might be the poet's purpose?
3. **How** does the poet use language to express his or her views and achieve the desired effects?

Of course, a poem may have more than one purpose – the main thing is to be able to identify what the poet wants to achieve by writing the poem. In order to express their ideas through poetry, poets make various choices with regard to vocabulary, style, form, the use of imagery and other poetic features. A close examination of these features can provide useful clues as to what the poet's creative purposes are.

> **KEY POINT**
>
> Poetry can come in many different forms and can have a wide range of purposes.

Approaching poetry

AQA A	**U 1, 3, 4**
AQA B	**U 3, 4**
Edexcel	**U 1, 3, 4**
OCR	**U 1, 2, 3, 4**
WJEC	**U 1, 3, 4**
CCEA	**AS U2, A2 U1**

Different kinds of poetry sometimes require different approaches.

Some poems are short and contain relatively straightforward ideas that are easy to understand. On the other hand, you need to work really hard at some poems in order to develop your understanding of them.

There are a number of reasons why some poems might seem difficult to understand:

1. It could be because a poem was written a long time ago when a different form of language was used. For example, in order to understand the poetry of Chaucer you need first to understand the Middle English in which he wrote his works. A poet like Milton uses references to mythology, the classical world or the Bible that you might need to research in order to appreciate fully what his poetry is saying.
2. It might be because the ideas are complex, the ways the poet expresses ideas are obscure, or the content, style or structure of the poem is difficult. In this case, you need to work hard to tease meaning from the poem. This is often the case with a poet like T.S. Eliot, for example. There may be words, phrases and lines that are never fully understood. That might be just as the poet wanted it.
3. The poem may appear uncomplicated and use simple vocabulary, but the ideas that it contains are deceptively complex. Much of the work of Philip Larkin is like this.

It is no good looking for a 'secret formula' that you can apply to any poem. Words and images that might be used in poems hold meanings, feelings and connotations that might provoke different responses in different people, but this does not mean that 'anything goes' and that you can say exactly what you want about a poem. At A-Level, the personal response is important, but it is a personal response that should be informed by literary judgement and close analysis of the text.

Here are some ideas to help with your understanding of poetry:

- Read as much poetry as you can, and become familiar with different types and styles.
- Think about the ideas in the poems that you read.
- Think about the way in which language is used in the poems that you read.
- Read poems aloud – sometimes this can help you to understand them more. Reading Chaucer aloud, for example, can help a good deal with your understanding of meaning.
- Ask questions – whenever you come across a new poem, ask yourself questions about it (you may find the three key questions listed at the top of page 179 helpful).
- Read around the work of an individual poet to help you understand his or her work more fully.
- Find out as much biographical detail about the poet as you can – this can sometimes throw light on the poetry.
- Understand the historical, social and political context within which the poet produced their work – for example, knowing something about the history of the troubles in Northern Ireland can help you understand some of the poems of Seamus Heaney.

> If you do refer to social/historical context in an essay, refer to it at appropriate points throughout the essay. Do not use your opening paragraph to describe the context in which the poem was written.

PROGRESS CHECK

Use the bullet points above as a checklist to see how fully you have explored the poetry you are studying.

8.2 Structure, form and language

LEARNING SUMMARY	**After studying this section, you should be able to:** - understand what examiners mean when they ask you to analyse structure, form and language - understand what is meant by 'content' and 'voice' in poetry - understand and appreciate how poets use structure and form - understand and appreciate how poets create tone and mood - appreciate and analyse poets' use of imagery and sound - appreciate and analyse how poets use rhyme and rhythm

What examiners mean when they ask you to analyse structure, form and language

AQA A	**U 1, 3, 4**
AQA B	**U 3, 4**
Edexcel	**U 1, 3, 4**
OCR	**U 1, 2, 3, 4**
WJEC	**U 1, 3, 4**
CCEA	**AS U2, A2 U1**

AO2 asks you to 'demonstrate detailed critical understanding in analysing the ways in which form, structure and language shape meanings in literary texts'.

The words 'structure, form and language' seem straightforward, but they do cause difficulty in their interpretation and application. However, if you look closely at this AO, you can see that there are clues to help you understand what is meant.

The word 'shape' indicates that there is a crafting happening when writers write – that conscious decisions are made. 'Meanings' tells you that the meanings are not just those intended by the writer, but those given by individual readers in response to the writers' choices of form, structure and language. The word 'analysing' is important – you will need to write about how a poem works, not just identify and describe its features, or explain its content.

The importance of understanding how poems work

In order to fully understand a poem and the ways in which it achieves its effects, you have to understand the various elements that help to make it up. In most poems, several key elements combine to create the overall effect of the poem. Among these elements are content, voice, structure and form, tone and mood, imagery and sounds, rhyme and rhythm. We will now look at each of these elements in more detail.

> **KEY POINT**
>
> The effect achieved by a poem is the result of a number of related features working together to produce the complete text.

Content and voice

AQA A	**U 1, 3, 4**
AQA B	**U 3, 4**
Edexcel	**U 1, 3, 4**
OCR	**U 1, 2, 3, 4**
WJEC	**U 1, 3, 4**
CCEA	**AS U2, A2 U1**

Content

Basically, the **content** of a poem is what it is all about – the ideas, themes and storyline that it contains.

When you read a poem, it is useful to begin by establishing a general outline of what it is saying. This is sometimes referred to as the 'surface meaning' of the poem. Having an idea of this will give you a framework on which to build the more detailed and complex ideas that will form as your analysis of the poem develops.

Voice

When considering the content of a poem, it is also important to identify the **poetic voice** of the poem – in other words, to decide who the 'speaker' of the poem is.

In many cases the poetic voice may well be the poet's, but it may be that the words of the poem are 'spoken' through a character that the poet has created, or a narrator figure other than the poet. This happens almost all the time in *The Canterbury Tales*, where usually a particular character is telling the tale. Chaucer (the writer) often then interrupts his character (his fictitious narrator) to address the reader. This can often happen in poems that are not so narrative-based too. Identifying the speaker also helps to determine a number of other aspects of the poem, such as tone, mood, and the overall intention behind the poem. The poetic voice could be the poet's genuine voice expressing a heartfelt emotion, or it could be the voice of a narrator or persona expressing a view or feeling that the poet may or may not share.

Content and voice – examples

Read the following poem, which was written by the twentieth-century poet Philip Larkin.

Naturally the Foundation Will Pay Your Expenses

Hurrying to catch my Comet
One dark November day,
Which soon would snatch me from it
To the sunshine of Bombay,
I pondered pages Berkeley
Not three weeks since had heard,
Perceiving Chatto darkly
Through the mirror of the third.

Crowds, colourless and careworn,
Had made my taxi late,
Yet not till I was airborne
Did I recall the date –
That day when Queen and Minister
And Band of Guards and all
Still act their solemn-sinister
Wreath-rubbish in Whitehall.

It used to make me throw up,
These mawkish nursery games:
O when will England grow up?
– But I outsoar the Thames,
And dwindle off down Auster
To greet Professor Lal
(He once met Morgan Forster),
My contact and my pal.

Philip Larkin

PROGRESS CHECK

Look at the poem again.
1. Write a brief outline of what the poem is about.
2. Who is the speaker?
3. What obstacles to understanding did you encounter when looking at
   the poem?

1. The poem describes a lecturer who is flying out to India to give a lecture.
2. You might have had some difficulty establishing the 'poetic voice', as this could be the poet himself speaking, or it could be a character he has created.
3. Some of the words and expressions were unfamiliar, e.g. 'Chatto' and 'Auster'.

It is usually possible to respond to and appreciate a poem without knowing what every single word means. However, being aware of what the references mean will probably help to enrich your understanding of the poem. When you are studying a poem, you will probably have the opportunity to look up obscure references and to discuss them with your teacher and other students. If you see a poem for the first time in an exam, you might be given a few notes of explanation.

Here are some explanations of words and phrases that might have puzzled you in *Naturally the Foundation Will Pay Your Expenses*:

- 'Berkeley' refers to the University of California – the narrator looks through the pages of his lecture, which he had given at that university less than three weeks before.
- 'Chatto' – this refers to the publisher, Chatto and Windus, who he thinks might publish the book he will write, based on his lectures.
- 'The third' – this is a radio station, now Radio Three. The narrator thinks he might be invited to give his lecture on radio.
- 'Wreath-rubbish in Whitehall' – this refers to the Remembrance Day parade.
- 'Mawkish' – this means sentimental in a feeble, sickly kind of way.
- 'Auster' – a poetic name for the south wind.

The poetic voice may be a little more difficult to establish, but if you know anything at all about the poet Philip Larkin, you will know he was a very private man who hated travelling abroad. It is not likely, therefore, that the jet-setting, ambitious lecturer of the poem is Larkin himself. The voice, therefore, must be that of a character or 'persona' that he has adopted.

This raises a series of other questions:

1. What is the poet's attitude towards the poem's narrator?
2. What does he think about his views (on the Remembrance Day Parade, for example)?
3. Does Larkin use the narrator to make a point of his own?
4. Is Larkin's own 'voice' discernible behind the narrator's voice – is he mocking the 'character', for example?
5. Does the tone of the poem help you with any of these questions? (See pages 191–193 for more information on tone.)

> **KEY POINT**
>
> Background reading and research can help you establish the meaning of some poems.

Now read the poem on the next page, by Alfred, Lord Tennyson, and establish its surface meaning.

Once you have looked at the poem carefully, try and answer the following questions:

- What kind of voice is created here?
- What use is made of the classical background?
- What attitude does the speaker adopt?
- What comments can you make on the language and images?

Ulysses

It little profits that an idle king,
By this still hearth, among these barren crags,
Matched with an aged wife, I mete and dole
Unequal laws unto a savage race,
That hoard, and sleep and feed, and know not me.
I cannot rest from travel: I will drink
Life to the lees: all times I have enjoyed
Greatly, have suffered greatly, both with those
That loved me, and alone; on shore, and when
Thro' scudding drifts the rainy Hyades
Vext the dim sea. I am become a name;
For always roaming with a hungry heart
Much have I seen and known, cities of men
And manners, climates, councils, governments,
Myself not least, but honoured of them, all;
And drunk delight of battle with my peers,
Far on the ringing plains of windy Troy.
I am a part of all that I have met;
Yet all experience is an arch wherethro'
Gleams that untravelled world, whose margin fades
For ever and for ever when I move.
How dull it is to pause, to make an end,
To rust unburnished, not to shine in use!
As tho' to breathe were life. Life plied on life
Were all too little, and of one to me
Little remains, but every hour is saved
From that eternal silence something more,
A bringer of new things; and vile it were
For some three suns to store and hoard myself,
And this grey spirit yearning in desire
To follow knowledge, like a sinking star
Beyond the utmost bound of human thought.

Alfred, Lord Tennyson

COMMENTARY

Ulysses (Greek name Odysseus) was absent from his home, Ithaca, for 20 years, at Troy, and then journeyed home (his 'Odyssey'). He longed to return home to his wife and son, but Tennyson presents us with a Ulysses who feels unfulfilled and yearns for further adventure. He thought he would be content when he returned home, but he finds himself dissatisfied and still yearning for further adventure:

> ... I will drink
> Life to the lees:

He longs to be useful still: 'To rust unburnished, not to shine in use!' Both these images present the reader with a picture of a desire to live, and live with some purpose. He wants to drink his wine right to the dregs, to experience everything, to leave nothing. He fears the consequences of a

continued

dull life, which leads to 'rust' – as when a tool or a weapon is not used, but merely abandoned. Although he is old, he still wants more:

> And this grey spirit yearning in desire
> To follow knowledge, like a sinking star
> Beyond the utmost bound of human thought.

He sees no need to settle for the life he is now living – adventure and experience are still within his spirit.

Tennyson is making use of a story – assumed to be familiar to his readers – to comment on old age, perhaps in a more universal way. We can link this poem to the situation of anyone used to an active and fulfilled life, who does not want to settle for less. The rhythm of the poem, with its steady iambic pentameter, lends weight to the feelings and thoughts in it. Overall, it has the feeling of a thoughtful but impassioned speech given by a great, but elderly, leader and adventurer.

KEY POINT

Before you do anything else, you need to establish what is happening in a poem, and who the speaker is.

PROGRESS CHECK

Look at a poetry text that you have been studying and choose one of the poems – or an extract if you are studying a long poem. Examine the poem to establish the surface meaning and the poetic voice.

Structure and form

AQA A	**U 1, 3, 4**
AQA B	**U 3, 4**
Edexcel	**U 1, 3, 4**
OCR	**U 1, 2, 3, 4**
WJEC	**U 1, 3, 4**
CCEA	**AS U2, A2 U1**

Structure and **form** are another two important elements in poems that can contribute to the overall effect of a poem. As discussed in Chapter 2, both words have more than one meaning when used in literary criticism.

Structure normally refers to the way that the various ideas or emotions in a poem are arranged to form a coherent shape that satisfies the poet's purpose. Sometimes it can mean the metrical pattern of the poem and the arrangement of stanzas and so on, but it can also mean the order of ideas, etc.

Form normally refers to the way in which the poem is actually written down on the page – the arrangement of the stanzas, the length and shape of the lines – but can also refer to a particular kind of poem, e.g. a sonnet, ballad or narrative poem.

You can see that it is difficult to give precise definitions of form and structure, and almost impossible to separate them. Therefore, it is best to consider them together.

Structure and form – an example

As a general starting point in a consideration of structure and form, here is one arrangement of a poem written by Edward Thomas during the First World War.

No one so Much as You

No one so much as you loves this my clay,
Or would lament as you its dying day.
You know me through and through though I have not told,
And though with what you know you are not bold.

None ever was so fair as I thought you:
Not a word can I bear spoken against you.
All that I ever did for you seemed coarse
Compared with what I hid nor put in force.

Scarce my eyes dare meet you lest they should prove
I but respond to you and do not love.
We look and understand, we cannot speak
Except in trifles and words the most weak.

I at most accept your love, regretting
That is all: I have kept a helpless fretting
That I could not return all that you gave
And could not ever burn with the love you have,

Till sometimes it did seem better it were
Never to see you more than linger here
With only gratitude instead of love –
A pine in solitude cradling a dove.

COMMENTARY

Let's think about what the poet is saying here. He is writing about a one-sided relationship, and feels what? Guilt? Sorrow? Resignation? Pity? His language reflects his feelings, though the words chosen are simple – even spare (think about the effects of choice of language). One or two words stand out – like the final image and perhaps the word 'burn' – because they form a contrast to the simplicity and directness of the rest of the language.

What about the form and structure of the poem? Each stanza deals with an aspect of the relationship. The last two stanzas are linked together grammatically because they form one sentence – otherwise, each stanza is self-contained. There are rhyming couplets that link lines, ideas and feelings together. This gives the feeling perhaps of containing the pain that the poet is writing about.

This discussion attempts to link together the content of the poem with its form and structure. However, the poem we have just examined is not the poem that Thomas wrote. The words are the same, and in the same order, but he set them out differently.

Have a look now at the layout that Edward Thomas actually used when he was writing this poem. How is this different from the poem you looked at before? Think about the way it works when it is 'shaped' like this.

No one so Much as You

No one so much as you
Loves this my clay,
Or would lament as you
Its dying day.

You know me through and through
Though I have not told,
And though with what you know
You are not bold.

None ever was so fair
As I thought you:
Not a word can I bear
Spoken against you.

All that I ever did
For you seemed coarse
Compared with what I hid
Nor put in force –

Scarce my eyes dare meet you
Lest they should prove
I but respond to you
And do not love.

We look and understand
We cannot speak
Except in trifles and
Words the most weak.

I at the most accept
Your love, regretting
That is all: I have kept
A helpless fretting

That I could not return
All that you gave
And could not ever burn
With the love you have,

Till sometimes it did seem
Better it were
Never to see you more
Than linger here

With only gratitude
Instead of love –
A pine in solitude
Cradling a dove.

Edward Thomas

This version of the poem seems emotionally less contained and controlled. The rhyming couplets have gone, and now every other line rhymes. This makes the poem more jagged – less unified. Because the word 'burn' is placed at the end of a line, we notice it more. (This shows the interlinking of word choice and form and structure.)

The splitting of the last line means that we see more of a separation between 'pine' and 'dove'. The poem now seems more of a series of individual statements, as if the poet is working out his feelings, or is unwilling to admit them to himself. The pain of the poem is emphasised, rather than any resignation. In the third stanza, the separation of the first two lines stresses that he 'thought' she was fair – the short lines emphasise the fact that this was in the past, and is no longer true. In the fifth stanza there is a gap between 'respond' and 'love', since they are on separate lines. This reinforces the gap between the feelings of the poet and the woman to whom he is addressing the poem.

This is not a comprehensive discussion, but it should point you in the direction of analysing and evaluating the effects of the form of this poem. You must avoid using words such as 'flowing' when you talk about form and structure. You have to be precise, and link the lines, words, feelings and ideas.

The way a poem is laid out – its arrangement into lines and stanzas – can make a big difference to its impact on the reader.

Poetic forms – with a focus on the sonnet form

The term 'form' is also used to refer to specific types of poems.

The forms you might be familiar with include:

- limerick
- haiku
- sonnet
- ode
- elegy
- blank verse
- free verse
- rhyming (heroic) couplets
- ballad.

Look up – and make a note of – the meaning of each of the above forms of poetry. You will find that some of the terms refer to a poem's subject matter (e.g. an elegy is a poem of mourning), and others, e.g. haiku, to its structure.

The **sonnet form** is particularly popular in English poetry, and poets have written using this form for centuries. You may be studying a poet who wrote many sonnets – Shakespeare or Keats, for example. Some of the best-known poems in this language are written in this form. Basically, a sonnet is a poem consisting of 14 lines, with a very structured rhyme scheme and a very definite rhythm pattern, usually iambic pentameter. It is traditionally a love poem, but the form has been used in many other ways.

The two main kinds of sonnet are:

1. **the Petrarchan/Italian sonnet** (named after the medieval Italian writer, Petrarch)
2. **the Shakespearean/English sonnet**.

The difference between the two kinds of sonnet lies mainly in their structure.

Here is the structure of the Italian sonnet.

> Eight lines, known as the **octave**

> Six lines, known as the **sestet**

The rhyme scheme in this kind of sonnet can vary, but generally the pattern is 'ABBAABBA CDECDE', or 'ABBAABBA CDCDCD'. In terms of structure, the octave sets out the theme or key idea of the poem, and the sestet provides a response to it.

Here is the pattern for the English sonnet.

> Four lines of verse, known as a **quatrain**

> **quatrain**

> **quatrain**

> **rhyming couplet**

The rhyme scheme of this kind of sonnet generally follows the pattern 'ABAB CDCD EFEF GG'. The theme or idea is developed through the quatrains, and the concluding comment is provided through the final rhyming couplet.

Read the following two sonnets and then answer these questions:
1. Which of the poems is an English sonnet and which is an Italian sonnet?
2. Why do you think each poet chose to write in sonnet form? What does the form add to the poem?

On First Looking into Chapman's Homer

Much have I travell'd in the realms of gold,
And many goodly states and kingdoms seen;
Round many western islands have I been
Which bards in fealty to Apollo hold.
Oft of one wide expanse had I been told
That deep-brow'd Homer ruled as his demesne;
Yet did I never breathe its pure serene
Till I heard Chapman speak out loud and bold:
Then felt I like some watcher of the skies
When a new planet swims into his ken;
Or like stout Cortez when with eagle eyes
He star'd at the Pacific – and all his men
Look'd at each other with a wild surmise –
Silent, upon a peak in Darien.

John Keats

Prayer

Some days, although we cannot pray, a prayer
utters itself. So, a woman will lift
her head from the sieve of her hands and stare
at the minims sung by a tree, a sudden gift.
Some nights, although we are faithless, the truth
enters our hearts, that small familiar pain;
then a man will stand stock-still, hearing his youth
in the distant Latin chanting of a train
Pray for us now. Grade I piano scales
console the lodger looking out across
a Midlands town. Then dusk, and someone calls
a child's name as though they named their loss.
Darkness outside. Inside, the radio's prayer –
Rockall. Malin. Dogger. Finisterre.

Carol Ann Duffy

COMMENTARY

Here are the points you may have noted:

1. The poem by Keats is an Italian or Petrarchan sonnet. The poem by Duffy is an English or Shakespearean sonnet.

2. **John Keats** wrote his sonnet in the Italian form. It is divided into two sections – the first group of eight lines (the octave), and the concluding group of six lines (the sestet). The poem concerns Keats' first experiences of looking at Chapman's translation of Homer's epic poems, *The Iliad* and *The Odyssey*. The octave reveals Keats' previous reading of classical poetry, expressed as a journey through 'realms of gold'. The whole experience is described in ornate, 'poetic' language, expressing lofty ideas of beauty. In the sestet, Keats changes direction to describe the impact of reading Chapman's Homer for the first time. He describes this experience through two images – sighting a new planet, and discovering a new ocean. These last six lines use a simpler vocabulary and everyday language.

   Prayer is a sonnet written by the modern poet **Carol Ann Duffy**, and she adopts the Shakespearean sonnet form. The poem consists of three quatrains, each with an ABAB rhyme scheme, through which she builds up and develops her ideas to bring them to a conclusion in the rhyming couplet at the end. This rhyming couplet not only provides an unexpected ending to the poem, but it gives the last line a feeling of finality.

KEY POINT

It is important to look at the structure and form of a poem, as these elements can play an important part in shaping the poem's overall effect.

Tone and mood

AQA A	**U 1, 3, 4**
AQA B	**U 3, 4**
Edexcel	**U 1, 3, 4**
OCR	**U 1, 2, 3, 4**
WJEC	**U 1, 3, 4**
CCEA	**AS U2, A2 U1**

The tone and mood that a poem creates can have a significant effect on the overall impact of the poem on the reader. As we have seen, a poem contains a 'voice', and like any voice it can project a certain tone that gives the listener (or reader) certain messages. Obviously, there are many different kinds of tone. The tone might be angry or reflective, melancholy or joyful, bitter or ironic. Just as the tone of voice in which someone speaks tells us a great deal about the way he or she feels, so the tone of the 'poetic voice' tells us a great deal about how the poet or the narrator of the poem feels. The mood of a poem is not quite the same thing as the tone, although the two are very closely linked. When we refer to the mood of a poem, we are really talking about the atmosphere that the poet creates in the poem.

One way to try to establish the mood of a poem is to read it aloud. You can experiment with various readings, seeing which one you think best fits the particular poem. (Don't try this in an exam, of course.) The more practice you get at reading poems aloud, and the more you are able to hear others read them, the better you will be at 'hearing' poems in your mind when you read them to yourself.

There are various ways in which tone and mood can be created, for example through:

- the loudness or softness of the voice speaking the poem
- the rhythm that is created
- the poet's choice of words
- the emphasis placed on particular words or phrases
- the breaks and pauses that the poet places in the poem.

Read the following three poems carefully. You could try reading them aloud.

What kind of tone do you think is appropriate to each, and what kind of mood does each poem create?

Ah! Sun-flower

Ah, Sun-flower! Weary of time,
Who countest the steps of the Sun,
Seeking after that sweet golden clime
Where the traveller's journey is done.

Where the Youth pined away with desire,
And the pale Virgin shrouded in snow,
Arise from their graves and aspire
Where my Sun-flower wishes to go.

William Blake

Adlestrop

Yes. I remember Adlestrop –
The name, because one afternoon
Of heat the express-train drew up there
Unwontedly. It was late June.

The steam hissed. Someone cleared his throat.
No one left and no one came
On the bare platform. What I saw
Was Adlestrop – only the name.

And willows, willow-herb, and grass,
And meadowsweet, and haycocks dry,
No whit less still and lonely fair
Than the high cloudlets in the sky.

And for that minute a blackbird sang
Close by, and round him, mistier,
Farther and farther, all the birds
Of Oxfordshire and Gloucestershire.

Edward Thomas

Engineers' Corner

Why isn't there an Engineers' Corner in Westminster Abbey? In Britain we've always made more fuss of a ballad than a blueprint ... How many schoolchildren dream of becoming great engineers?

Advertisement placed in The Times by the Engineering Council

We make more fuss of ballads than of blueprints –
That's why so many poets end up rich,
While engineers scrape by in cheerless garrets.
Who needs a bridge or dam? Who needs a ditch?

Whereas the person who can write a sonnet
Has got it made. It's always been the way,
For everybody knows that we need poems
And everybody reads them every day.

Yes, life is hard if you choose engineering –
You're sure to need another job as well;
You'll have to plan your projects in the evenings
Instead of going out. It must be hell.

While well-heeled poets ride around in Daimlers,
You'll burn the midnight oil to earn a crust,
With no hope of a statue in the Abbey,
With no hope, even, of a modest bust.

No wonder small boys dream of writing couplets
And spurn the bike, the lorry and the train.
There's far too much encouragement for poets –
That's why this country's going down the drain.

Wendy Cope

COMMENTARY

You may have noted the following tone and mood for each of the poems:
1. Sadness and regret.
2. Nostalgic but happy.
3. Humorous and light-hearted.

In the short poem by Blake, the first stanza traces the daily movement of the sunflower as it follows the sun. Blake imagines that it does so out of a yearning for another, kinder world. The second stanza concerns two young lovers who yearned for a better world too, but who died. The mood then is sad and melancholy, and an atmosphere of regret, yearning and disappointment permeates the poem.

In *Adlestrop*, Thomas describes how his train stopped at a deserted country station one summer's day. The poem conveys the poet's response to the total scene through his memory. It is a memory that brings him happiness rather than sadness, though. Thomas succeeds in conveying the atmosphere of quietness, of the peacefulness of the natural scene and the steam train at the platform. A sense of nostalgia surrounds the experience.

continued

The tone of Wendy Cope's poem is light. She is writing with her tongue firmly in her cheek (although there is an underlying serious point about the poem if we choose to take it), and the rhyme scheme, rhythm and her choice of vocabulary and Images combine to create a humorous poem, light in tone.

KEY POINT

Tone and mood can be created in a variety of ways. Always be sensitive to the tone and mood when reading a poem.

PROGRESS CHECK

Look at the poetry texts you are studying. Pick three poems (or use parts of the poem if you are studying a single long poem) and think about the tone and atmosphere the poet creates in them. Look at how a sense of a particular tone or atmosphere is created.

Imagery and sounds

AQA A	**U 1, 3, 4**
AQA B	**U 3, 4**
Edexcel	**U 1, 3, 4**
OCR	**U 1, 2, 3, 4**
WJEC	**U 1, 3, 4**
CCEA	**AS U2, A2 U1**

Very often, the effect a poem has on a reader will not simply consist of a response to what the poet has to say, but will draw on the reader's own intellectual and emotional experience. Imagery can be of central importance in creating this response within the reader.

An image, quite simply, is words used in such a way as to create a picture in the mind of the reader, so that ideas, feelings, description and so on are conveyed more clearly or vividly. Images can work in several ways in the mind of the reader. On a simple level, an image can be used literally to describe something. For example, in Wordsworth's *Daffodils*, the lines 'I saw a crowd / A host of golden daffodils, / Beside the lake, beneath the trees, / Fluttering and dancing in the breeze' create a literal image in our minds of the scene that Wordsworth wishes to describe. However, even here, in this apparently simple description, Wordsworth is using language metaphorically by describing the daffodils as 'dancing'.

Often images are non-literal or figurative – the thing being described is compared to something else with which it has something in common, to make the description more vivid to the reader. You will no doubt already be familiar with images – such as similes and metaphors – that work in this way.

KEY POINT

Imagery can make an important contribution to the overall effect of a poem.

How many examples of figurative language can you think of? You might have thought of some of these:
- A **simile** is easy to spot because it makes a comparison quite clear, often by using the words 'as' or 'like'.
- A **metaphor** is like a simile in that it too creates a comparison. However, it is less direct than a simile in that it does not use 'as' or 'like' to create a comparison. The comparison is implied.

- **Personification** occurs when poets attribute an inanimate object or abstract idea with human qualities or actions.
- **Aural imagery** – some kinds of images rely not upon the pictures that they create in the mind of the reader, but on the effect that they have on the ear, or a combination of both.

Aural imagery

Aural imagery is a general term for the ways in which poets create images through sounds.

Here are some of the techniques that poets use to achieve aural imagery:

- **Alliteration** involves the repetition of the same consonant sound, usually at the beginning of each word, over several words together. Larkin uses this technique in *Naturally the Foundation Will Pay Your Expenses* (see page 182), for example. It can be seen in phrases such as 'I pondered pages ...', 'Crowds, colourless and careworn ...', 'Still act their solemn-sinister ...', and much of its impact lies in the effect that the repetition of the sounds creates on the reader's ear, as well as the mind's eye.
- **Assonance** involves the repetition of a vowel sound to achieve a particular kind of effect.
- **Onomatopoeia** refers to words that by their sound reflect their meaning. On a simple level, words like 'bang' or 'thud' actually sound like the noises they describe.

> There is little value in simply identifying these features – you will gain no marks at all, for example, for saying something like, 'the poet uses a good deal of alliteration in this poem'. Identifying imagery, and the techniques whereby it is created, is only of any value if you describe the possible **effects** that this use of language has on the poem and the reader.

> **PROGRESS CHECK**
>
> Look at the poems you are studying. Make a note of any uses of imagery that strike you as particularly effective, and try to describe why they have any impact on you.

Rhyme and rhythm

AQA A   U 1, 3, 4
AQA B   U 3, 4
Edexcel U 1, 3, 4
OCR   U 1, 2, 3, 4
WJEC   U 1, 3, 4
CCEA   AS U2, A2 U1

Rhyme

You have already looked at sonnets and their rhyming patterns in some detail, and the idea of rhyme in poetry is one that you are likely to be familiar with. In fact, the association between rhyme and poetry is so strong that some people still try to insist that poetry isn't 'proper' poetry unless it rhymes. Although that isn't true, of course, rhyme can play an important part in contributing to the overall effect of a poem. The pattern of rhyme within a poem is called the **rhyme scheme**, and is easy to work out.

For example, look at John Donne's poem, *The Flea*.

The Flea	
Mark but this flea, and mark in this,	A
How little that which thou deny'st me is;	A
Me it sucked first, and now sucks thee,	B
And in this flea, our two bloods mingled be;	B
Confess it, this cannot be said	C
A sin, or shame, or loss of maidenhead,	C
Yet this enjoys before it woo,	D

continued

And pampered swells with one blood made of two, D
And this, alas, is more than we would do.   D

Oh stay, three lives in one flea spare,
Where we almost, nay more than married are.
This flea is you and I, and this
Our marriage bed, and marriage temple is;
Though parents grudge, and you, we're met,
And cloistered in these living walls of jet.
Though use make you apt to kill me,
Let not to this, self murder added be,
And sacrilege, three sins in killing three.

Cruel and sudden, hast thou since
Purpled thy nail, in blood of innocence?
In what could this flea guilty be,
Except in that drop which it sucked from thee?
Yet thou triumph'st, and say'st that thou
Find'st not thyself, nor me the weaker now;
'Tis true, then learn how false, fears be;
Just so much honour, when thou yield'st to me,
Will waste, as this flea's death took life from thee.

John Donne

You will notice in this poem that the first line – which we have labelled 'A' – rhymes with the second line, so we have called this one 'A' too. Line three – which we have labelled 'B' – rhymes with the fourth line, which we have also called 'B'. The fifth line – which we have called C – rhymes with the sixth line, and then the last three lines of the first stanza all rhyme together, so we have called them all D. The rhyme scheme of this poem, therefore, is 'AABBCCDDD'. You will find that this pattern is repeated in the remaining two stanzas of the poem.

Of course, simply identifying a rhyme scheme is a pretty meaningless activity in itself. The important question comes after the rhyme scheme has been identified – what effect does the rhyme scheme have on the poem overall?

Now look at *The Flea* again. Write down any ideas you have on the effect that the rhyme scheme has. (It is worth reading the poem aloud to get the full impact of the rhyme scheme.)

> **COMMENTARY**
>
> Here are some ideas that you might have noted:
> 1. Each stanza is written in rhyming couplets, ending with a triple rhyme. This gives a sense of unity and completeness to each stanza. Each stanza works through a complete thought and then is rounded off.
> 2. The way the rhyme scheme builds stanza by stanza as Donne gathers his argument seems to add a sense of movement and momentum to the poem. He is, of course, trying to persuade his lady to sleep with him.
> 3. The rhyme scheme also seems to give the poem a sense of something complete in its own right – his argument has been brought to an end, his case proven, and there is no more to be said.

Sometimes a poet may use **internal rhyme** – rhymes that occur within the line itself.

Here is an example from *The Ancient Mariner* by Coleridge.

> The fair breeze blew, the white foam flew,
> The furrow followed free;
> We were the first that ever burst
> Into that silent sea.

The rhyming of 'blew' and 'flew' combines with the effect of the alliteration to add emphasis to the sense of speed and movement of the ship.

On occasions, a rhyme can seem to be incomplete or inaccurate. It may be that the vowels in the words are not pronounced in the same way – for example, love/move or trough/plough. These kinds of rhymes are called eye rhymes or sight rhymes. Sometimes poets make the consonant or vowel different to create a half-rhyme. These are sometimes called slant rhymes or para-rhymes. Wilfred Owen was particularly fond of using this kind of rhyme.

KEY POINT

A rhyme scheme can be an important element in creating a poem's effect on the reader or listener.

PROGRESS CHECK

Rhyme can have many effects in a poem. List as many as you can.

Here are some possible answers:
1. Rhyme can **emphasise** and **draw attention** to certain words.
2. Rhyme can add a **musical quality** to a poem.
3. Rhyme can create a deliberately **discordant effect**.
4. Rhyme can **draw a poem's ideas together**.
5. Rhyme can create an **incantational or ritualistic effect**.
6. Devices such as rhyming couplets can add a **sense of finality**.

Rhythm

Rhythm can also play an important part in the effect poems achieve. Nursery rhymes – which are probably the first kinds of poetry that you encountered – have very strong rhythms. It is the presence of these strong rhythm patterns that gives the rhymes such a strong appeal to children. However, rhythms do not only appeal to children, and a sense of rhythm can exert a powerful effect on any poem. A strong rhythm can help to create mood in a poem, and therefore influence its whole tone and atmosphere, and its feeling of movement and life.

Several factors can influence the rhythm of a poem:
- **Syllable stress** – language possesses natural rhythms which we use every time we speak and pronounce words. Poets often make use of these natural stresses and in-built rhythm patterns to help contribute to the overall rhythmic effect.
- **Emphatic stress** – poets often deliberately place the emphasis on a particular word, or part of the word, in order to achieve a particular effect.
- **Phrasing and punctuation** – the rhythm of poetry, along with other kinds of writing, can be influenced by other factors such as word order, length of phrases, or the choice of punctuation marks, line and stanza breaks, and use of repetition.

If you recognise the metre of a poem, e.g. iambic pentameter, use the correct terminology. If you are unsure, discuss rhythm in more general terms, e.g. 'a strong insistent rhythm'.

Metre is the pattern of stressed and unstressed syllables in a line of poetry, and as such is very closely linked to the idea of rhythm. By analysing the metre, an activity known as 'scansion', the reader can see how the poet is using the stress patterns within the language to help convey the meaning of the poem. Variations in the pattern could mark changes in mood or tone, or signify a change of direction in the movement of the poem.

> **KEY POINT**
>
> Rhythm can add an important dimension to a poem. Always look for the effects that it can create in a poem.

Rhyme and rhythm – examples

Look at the poem, *Daffodils*, by William Wordsworth. Try to describe the effects created by both the rhyme and the rhythm of the poem.

Daffodils

I wandered lonely as a cloud	A
That floats on high o'er vales and hills,	B
When all at once I saw a crowd,	A
A host, of golden daffodils;	B
Beside the lake, beneath the trees,	C
Fluttering and dancing in the breeze.	C

Continuous as the stars that shine
And twinkle on the Milky Way,
They stretched in never-ending line
Along the margin of a bay:
Ten thousand saw I at a glance,
Tossing their heads in sprightly dance.

The waves beside them danced, but they
Out-did the sparkling waves in glee:
A poet could not but be gay,
In such a jocund company:
I gazed – and gazed – but little thought
What wealth the show to me had brought:

For oft, when on my couch I lie
In vacant or in pensive mood,
They flash upon that inward eye
Which is the bliss of solitude;
And then my heart with pleasure fills,
And dances with the daffodils.

William Wordsworth

COMMENTARY

The regular lines (eight syllables per line consisting of four iambic feet) give an almost incantatory quality to the poem, and impose a pattern on the lines and the experience described. The whole poem is carefully regular – four stanzas, with regular line length – but it is perhaps the rhyme scheme that creates the greatest effect on the words. The 'ABABCC' scheme gives each stanza a sense of completeness in itself, as each stanza contains its own focal point, given unity through the rhyme.

The overall effect is to produce a sense of balance and harmony, reflecting the harmonious quality of nature and the comforting effect of the experience.

When we discuss rhyme and rhythm, we are looking at **patterns** and **sounds**. In order to consolidate what you have learned, let's examine another poem.

What Soft – Cherubic Creatures …

What Soft – Cherubic Creatures –
These gentlewomen are –
One would as soon assault a Plush –
Or violate a Star –

Such Dimity Convictions –
A Horror so refined
Of freckled Human Nature –
Of Deity – ashamed –

It's such a common – Glory –
A Fisherman's – Degree –
Redemption – Brittle Lady –
Be so – ashamed of Thee –

Emily Dickinson

COMMENTARY

If we apply to this poem some of the techniques discussed above, we can analyse the effects of the poem. Remember, we are trying to think about how the poet's choices shape meaning, not just what we think the meaning is.

There are three stanzas of four lines each, and all of the lines are a similar length. At first, the poem seems neat, regular and self contained. The rhyme scheme is basically 'ABCB', but can 'refined' and 'ashamed' truly be said to rhyme? The incompleteness of the rhyme underlines the incongruity of the word 'ashamed' in this context. The tone of the first stanza is one of gentle mockery, but to suggest that the fastidiousness of these women could extend to being ashamed of God introduces a harsher, more serious tone.

continued

The metre is basically iambic trimeter, with three stressed syllables per line, suggesting something simple, playful, even child-like – perhaps a nursery rhyme. However, Dickinson varies the metre from time to time. Notice the use of 'masculine' and 'feminine' endings. The first and third lines of the second and third stanzas have an extra unstressed syllable at the end (a feminine ending), causing the line to fade away, perhaps reflecting the listlessness of the ladies. These lines could be described as truncated tetrameter, there being a sense that the final stressed syllable has been cut off. This does not happen in the third line of the first stanza, which completes the tetrameter with 'plush', the stress on this word adding to its absurdity. The juxtaposition of the language of violence, even rape ('assault' and 'violate'), with the domestic imagery of the textiles 'dimity' and 'plush' (it is almost as if they have sewn their own identities), creates a tension that is both comic and shocking.

Dickinson's characteristic use of dashes (the only punctuation) causes the reader to pause either at the end of a line or in the middle of a line, and to thereby place greater emphasis on certain words. The number of dashes increases towards the end of the poem, making it jerky and a little awkward to read. Redemption is not lady-like or soft, but muscular and democratic. The ladies themselves are brittle – easily broken – and a cause of shame. There is a sense in the final stanza that the poet is hammering home her point, attacking the gentlewomen with the reality of Jesus' disciples, who were fishermen. Dickinson has moved from gentle mockery to violent assault.

PROGRESS CHECK

Choose any of the poems that you are studying and write a short description showing the effect of rhyme and rhythm on your chosen poem.

Sample question and model answer

Read the following two poems carefully. Compare the ways in which Clare and Kipling use their poetry to search for answers.

QUESTION OVERVIEW

The focus of this question is a poem by John Clare and a poem by Rudyard Kipling – the question asks candidates to compare the ways in which the poets use their poetry to search for answers. It is an open-ended question, which requires candidates to reflect on what 'answers' might be, and to consider the nature of poetry itself.

I Am! Yet What I Am None Cares or Knows

I am: yet what I am none cares or knows,
My friends forsake me like a memory lost;
I am the self-consumer of my woes,
They rise and vanish in oblivious host,
Like shades in love and death's oblivion lost;
And yet I am! and live with shadows tost

Into the nothingness of scorn and noise,
Into the living sea of waking dreams,
Where there is neither sense of life nor joys,
But the vast shipwreck of my life's esteems;
And e'en the dearest—that I loved the best—
Are strange—nay, rather stranger than the rest.

I long for scenes where man has never trod;
A place where woman never smil'd or wept;
There to abide with my creator, God,
And sleep as I In childhood sweetly slept:
Untroubling and untroubled where I lie;
The grass below—above the vaulted sky.

John Clare

Sample question and model answer (continued)

The Way Through the Woods

They shut the road through the woods
Seventy years ago.
Weather and rain have undone it again,
And now you would never know
There was once a road through the woods
Before they planted the trees.
It is underneath the coppice and heath,
And the thin anemones.
Only the keeper sees
That, where the ring-dove broods,
And the badgers roll at ease,
There was once a road through the woods.

Yet, if you enter the woods
Of a summer evening late,
When the night-air cools on the trout-ringed pools
Where the otter whistles his mate,
(They fear not men in the woods,
Because they see so few.)
You will hear the beat of a horse's feet,
And the swish of a skirt in the dew,
Steadily cantering through
The misty solitudes,
As though they perfectly knew
The old lost road through the woods.
But there is no road through the woods.

Rudyard Kipling

AO1: Different methods are used to support the points the candidate is making – longer quotations, one-word quotations and some paraphrasing – all of which are acceptable.
AO2: The language is analysed closely.
AO3: The candidate immediately establishes a point of view about → the two poems, making specific and supported connections between them.

Below are some extracts from a good answer by an AS candidate – she compares the two poems effectively, while referring to the contexts in which they were written. The essay extracts have been annotated with reference to all four AOs.

'I Am!' by John Clare was written when he felt abandoned, isolated and disengaged from the world. For the first two stanzas, Clare presents a world filled with fear and chaos. This ends in a climax of despair:

> And e'en the dearest–that I loved the best–
> Are strange–nay, rather stranger than the rest.

There is a pun on 'stranger', as he feels he does not know his friends or cannot engage with them.

This sense of the hostility of the environment is repeated in Kipling's poem. He repeatedly refers to an anonymous and malevolent 'they' - shutting the road, planting trees. Here Nature is not positive. Nature thrives - 'the ring-dove broods' and 'the badgers roll at ease' - but the first two stanzas create an atmosphere of a hostile place where people are not meant to go. The faceless 'keeper' is part of the scenery, but the reader is not...

Sample question and model answer (continued)

AO1: Some of the candidate's written expression is not as clear as it could be – the last sentence is difficult to understand.
AO3: The linking of the texts continues, this time via contrast.
AO4: The poet's context is used in the interpretation, and there is careful reference to the text.

AO1/AO3: The candidate continues to compare the poems, linking the paragraphs with 'in contrast' and reflecting on the idea in the question.
AO2: Structure is referred to, as the candidate indicates how the poet uses the final stanza.

AO1: The discussion is still grounded in the actual poems, and the candidate is not too speculative.
AO3: The comparison continues, and extends to the different contexts of the two poets.
AO4: Again, reference is made to context, although in a rather superficial way.

AO1/AO3: The candidate points out what is similar and what is different in the poems quite succinctly, bringing the argument to a conclusion in an effective closing paragraph.

The third stanza of Clare's poem presents a sharply contrasting view of nature, a virginal forest 'where man has never trod'...he wants to be 'untroubling and untroubled' where he lies, as he feels trapped and far from God in the asylum he lives in. Clare is obviously offering an answer, but does not expect people to accept it. The poet realises even as he writes that this is an answer which is doomed never to be reached...

In contrast, Kipling does offer some hope at the start of his final stanza. He speaks of 'summer evening late' and the 'trout-ringed pools'. However, the tranquillity and gentleness are because 'they see so few' [people]...

Both of these poets question the nature of life – however, they do resolve the poems in a way. They both assert that there is no real solution – Clare less certainly, but he does not suggest any solution to 'the living sea of waking dreams' except for the fact that he does not want to be part of it. He is a troubled, even broken man, describing the 'vast shipwreck of my life's esteems'. He simply wants to abandon all of this and live in untroubled harmony with nature.

Kipling leaves us in no doubt that the world is beyond redemption – this is shown in the overall bleak tone of the poem and in the final line. Both of these men suffered greatly – Clare in a primitive and probably horrific asylum, after a life as one of the rural poor in the earlier nineteenth century, and Kipling lost his son in World War 1...

Common to both of these poems is the sense of being forsaken or disengaged from the world and other people. This is shown through the anonymity of Kipling's characters; Clare states it clearly.

SUMMATIVE COMMENT

These are extracts from an essay, and not a full and developed answer. However, you get a sense of how the candidate keeps making connections between the poems – without compromising on detailed comments on the actual poems – and keeps a focus on the central idea in the question. It is not a perfect answer, but it is a confident and perceptive commentary on the two poems, and the connections and differences between them.

Practice examination questions

AS

AQA A Unit 1

Thomas Hardy: *Selected Poems*

Hardy's poetry has been described as having more to do with the supernatural than the natural world. To what extent do you agree with this view?

In your answer you should **either** refer to **two** or **three** poems in detail **or** range more widely through the whole selection.

OCR Unit 1

William Wordsworth

'Oh! pleasant, pleasant were the days ....' Discuss the ways in which childhood is made significant by Wordsworth.

In your answer, explore the effects of language, imagery and verse form, and consider how this poem relates to other poems by Wordsworth that you have studied.

> ### To A Butterfly
>
> Stay near me – do not take thy flight!
> A little longer stay in sight!
> Much converse do I find in thee,
> Historian of my infancy!
> Float near me; do not yet depart!
> Dead times revibe in thee:
> Thou bring'st, gay creature as thou art!
> A solemn image to my heart,
> My father's family!
>
> Oh! pleasant, pleasant were the days,
> The time, when in our childish plays,
> My sister Emmeline and I
> Together chased the butterfly!
> A very hunter did I rush
> Upon the prey; – with leaps and springs
> I followed on from brake to bush;
> But she, God love her! Feared to brush
> The dust from off its wings.

WJEC U1

Plath and Hughes

Compare the ways in which Plath and Hughes use imagery to explore relationships. In your answer refer in detail to at least two of Plath's poems.

Practice examination questions (continued)

A2

AQA A Unit 3

For an example of a question in the style of this unit, please see Chapter 3, page 74.

AQA B Unit 3

Elements of the Pastoral

William Blake: *Songs of Innocence and Experience*

'In *Songs of Innocence and Experience* the state of innocence is neither attractive nor desirable.'

With reference to appropriate poems, discuss the validity of this view.

CCEA Unit 3

By referring closely to *The Flea* and one other appropriately selected poem, and making use of relevant external contextual material on the nature of metaphysical poetry, examine the poetic methods which Donne uses to write about sexual desire.

N.B. Equal marks are available for your treatment of each poem.

9 Studying prose

The following topics are covered in this chapter:

- Studying a novel
- Approaching your text
- Opening pages
- Narrative viewpoint
- Characters and their development
- Setting and atmosphere
- Studying short stories
- Studying non-fiction
- Preparing yourself for the exam

9.1 Studying a novel

LEARNING SUMMARY

After studying this section, you should be able to:

- understand ways of thinking about a novel
- understand some different aspects of studying a novel
- have some idea of the features to look for in the text you are studying

How prose fits into your A-Level course

AQA A	**U 2, 3, 4**
AQA B	**U 1, 3, 4**
Edexcel	**U 1, 3, 4**
OCR	**U 1, 2, 4**
WJEC	**U 1, 3**
CCEA	**AS U2, A2 U2**

The first thing to note is that novels – like other forms of writing – come in many forms, and you need to adapt your approach to suit the kind of text you are looking at. For example, you might be studying a pre-1900 work by someone like Dickens or Hardy, where, for the most part, the writers portray life-like characters in realistic settings. On the other hand, you might be studying a twentieth-century novel that does not follow realistic conventions of plot or character.

Ways of thinking about a novel

One thing that you can do to help yourself undertake and make sense of your novel is to develop **strategies** for approaching them, and identify the most important things to pay attention to.

There are two main ways of looking at a novel:

1. You can look at the '**content**' of the book – the world that the novel describes and creates – almost as if it were a real world. You may find that you can enter into this world and see the characters and events as real, and that you develop feelings about them, such as liking them, or pity, or hatred. Looking at your novel from this position, you are likely to discuss the characters as if they were real people, able to choose their actions and words for themselves.
2. The second way that you can look at your novel is to see it as a '**text**' – as a creation of the author. The characters are not real people, but they are creations of the author, designed to perform specific functions in the text. The author uses them and manipulates them to create particular effects, and they only exist through the words on the page.

The first of these ways of viewing a novel may be how you approach a novel when reading purely for pleasure, or when you start to study a novel for the first time. As your study increases in depth, however, you will move much more towards the second method. This requires a much more detached and analytical approach, which examiners look for at A-Level. This analytical viewpoint is essential to achieve a high mark.

There are two main levels of narrative:
1. The basic storyline – the events that occur and things that happen, often developed in chronological order. This is the **plot** of the novel.
2. The techniques or devices used by the writer for telling the story and creating characters and effects. These are **stylistic** or **narrative techniques**.

> **KEY POINT**
>
> Remember – you always need to know how the text is written as well as what it says.

The main features of a novel – and what you need to know about them

When studying your novel there are a number of aspects that you need to know well.

In one way or another, most of the exam questions you encounter will be linked to one or other of the following:
- An **overview** – you need a clear understanding of the plot and how it is structured.
- **Narrative viewpoint** – who tells the story? This then leads to the question 'Why?' – why has the writer chosen to use this viewpoint?
- **Character** – you need a sound understanding of the ways in which writers create and present their characters, and the functions they perform in the text.
- **Language and style** – you need to be aware of the language choices the writer makes, and the stylistic techniques he/she uses to create effects.
- The **setting** of the novel – you need to be aware of the kind of setting the novel has, and the ways in which the writer uses language to create a sense of setting and atmosphere.
- The **context** in which the novel was written – you need to be fully aware of the historical, social and political context, or the personal context of the writer, and the ways in which these factors influenced the shaping of the novel.
- The **kind of novelist** that you are studying – knowing something about the writer and his or her life might help you develop your understanding of the text. Do not fall into the trap of writing about a writer's biography, though. Your main focus is always the text, not the life of the writer.

> **KEY POINT**
>
> You need to examine the novel you are studying analytically, as a 'text' created by the writer.

> **PROGRESS CHECK**
>
> Think about these features in relation to a novel you are studying. Make brief notes on each point.

9.2 Approaching your text

LEARNING SUMMARY

After studying this section, you should be able to:

- approach the study of your novel effectively
- recognise the range of genres that novels can cover

Planning your approach

AQA A   **U 2, 3, 4**
AQA B   **U 1, 3, 4**
Edexcel **U 1, 3, 4**
OCR   **U 1, 2, 4**
WJEC   **U 1, 3**
CCEA   **AS U2, A2 U2**

Novels – especially the kind set for A-Level study – are usually substantial texts, and it is important that you get to know the text you are studying very well.

You need to know:

- **what happens**
- **who the characters are** (and how to spell their names correctly)
- the **themes** and **ideas** that are dealt with
- the **stylistic and narrative techniques** that the writer employs, and why.

You also need to be able to find a particular detail that you might want to refer to in an exam quickly and easily.

How to get to know your novel

Here are some ways to help you become familiar with your novel:

- **Read the novel through quickly** from beginning to end before you begin to study it. This will give you an overview of what it is about, and help you to see the details of plot, structure and character.
- **Do some research on the novel**. Find out about the author and the historical and social context in which he/she wrote. Knowing something about the historical and social attitudes, conventions and circumstances of the time can help with your understanding of the text.
- **Keep a notebook or file** for your work on each text. Keep separate sections on the different aspects of your study, such as character, setting, themes, narrative viewpoint, etc.
- **Annotate your text**. If you are studying the text for a closed book exam it can be useful to annotate your text using marginal notes, or underlining or sidelining important sections. If you are studying for an open book exam, you must not annotate your texts, as they need to be clean of all annotations and notes when you take them into the exam. Students sometimes find it useful to have one working copy, which they annotate for study purposes, and a clean copy to take into the exam.

KEY POINT

Plan in detail how you are going to approach the study of your novel.

Different kinds – or genres – of novel

AQA A   **U 2, 3, 4**
AQA B   **U 1, 3, 4**
Edexcel **U 1, 3, 4**
OCR   **U 1, 2, 4**
WJEC   **U 1, 3**
CCEA   **AS U2, A2 U2**

Novels come in all kinds of different forms or **genres**, and vary tremendously in style, theme and content. Some are relatively short, with few characters and quite simple plots, while others are very complex, with many characters and layers to the plot. Novels can also vary a great deal in terms of the subject matter they deal with, and how they deal with it.

Here are some different genres of novels:

- **'Social' novels** deal with themes to do with social issues, and usually have a message to convey to the reader. Much of the writing of Charles Dickens and D.H. Lawrence, for example, contains social comment in one form or another.
- **Picaresque novels** follow a central character on a journey, during which various adventures or incidents take place. *Moll Flanders* by Daniel Defoe is an example of this kind of novel.
- **Historical novels**, such as Kazuo Ishiguro's *Remains of the Day* and Graham Swift's *Waterland*, deal with events set in the past.
- **Fictional biography** and **autobiography** focuses on the life and developments of one particular character. In this kind of novel some of the events or experiences are often based on experiences of the author, for example Dickens' *David Copperfield*.
- **Humorous novels** – many novels contain elements of humour. For example, the novels of Evelyn Waugh and much of Jane Austen's writing could be said to be humorous.
- **Tragedies** – some novels deal with tragic themes, such as Emily Brontë's *Wuthering Heights*, and Thomas Hardy's *Tess of the D'Urbervilles*.
- **Futuristic novels** are set in a future time, such as Orwell's *Nineteen Eighty-Four* and Huxley's *Brave New World*. Very often in this kind of novel the writer uses the futuristic setting or theme to make some social comment on the society of the day.

KEY POINT

There are many different kinds of novel. Be aware of the kind of novel you are studying.

PROGRESS CHECK

Think about a novel you are studying and decide what kind of novel you think it is. Remember, though, that often novels do not fit snugly into one category. Think also about the purpose that the writer of your novel had in writing the text.

9.3 Opening pages

LEARNING SUMMARY	After studying this section, you should be able to:
	- understand the importance of the opening of a novel
	- identify some of the important features of the opening of a novel
	- apply these ideas to the text(s) you are studying

The importance of the opening of a novel

AQA A	U 2, 3, 4
AQA B	U 1, 3, 4
Edexcel	U 1, 3, 4
OCR	U 1, 2, 4
WJEC	U 1, 3
CCEA	AS U2, A2 U2

The opening pages of a novel are particularly important – often the first few pages tell the reader a good deal about the novel itself. In the opening pages, the writer tries to capture the reader's attention so that he/she wants to read on. The writer will probably also introduce some key characters, themes or situations.

Identifying important features in openings – examples

We are going to look at two openings in detail. The first is from a ghost story by Susan Hill; the second is the opening from *Hard Times* by Charles Dickens.

What effects does Hill create in the opening to her novel? Pick out some specific features that catch your attention.

It was nine-thirty on Christmas Eve. As I crossed the long entrance hall of Monk's Piece on my way from the dining room, where we had just enjoyed the first of the happy, festive meals, towards the drawing room and the fire around which my family were now assembled, I paused and then, as I often do in the course of an evening, went to the front door, opened it and stepped outside.

I have always liked to take a breath of the evening, to smell the air, whether it is sweetly scented and balmy with the flowers of midsummer, pungent with the bonfires and leaf-mould of autumn, or crackling cold from frost and snow. I like to look about me at the sky above my head, whether there are moon and stars or utter blackness, and into the darkness ahead of me; I like to listen for the cries of nocturnal creatures and the moaning rise and fall of the wind, or the pattering of rain in the orchard trees, I enjoy the rush of air towards me up the hill from the flat pastures of the river valley.

Tonight, I smelled at once, and with a lightening heart, that there had been a change in the weather. All the previous week, we had had rain, thin, chilling rain and a mist that lay low about the house and over the countryside. From the windows, the view stretched no farther than a yard or two down the garden. It was wretched weather, never seeming to come fully light, and raw, too. There had been no pleasure in walking, the visibility was too poor for any shooting and the dogs were permanently morose and muddy. Inside the house, the lamps were lit throughout the day and the walls of larder, outhouse and cellar oozed damp and smelled sour, the fires sputtered and smoked, burning dismally low.

My spirits have for many years now been excessively affected by the ways of the weather, and I confess that, had it not been for the air of cheerfulness and bustle that prevailed in the rest of the house, I should have been quite cast down in gloom and lethargy, unable to enjoy the flavour of life as I should like and irritated by my own susceptibility. But Esmé is merely stung by inclement weather into a spirited defiance, and so the preparations for our Christmas holiday had this year been more than usually extensive and vigorous.

I took a step or two out from under the shadow of the house so that I could see around me in the moonlight. Monk's Piece stands at the summit of land that rises gently up for some four hundred feet from where the little River Nee traces its winding way in a north to south direction across this fertile, and sheltered, part of the country. Below us are pastures, interspersed with small clumps of mixed, broad leaf woodland. But at our backs for several square miles it is a quite different area of rough scrub and heathland, a patch of wildness in the midst of well-farmed country. We are but two miles from a good-sized village, seven from the principal market town, yet there is an air of remoteness and isolation which makes us feel ourselves to be much further from civilization.

Extract from The Woman in Black *by Susan Hill*

Here are some ideas you might have noted:

1. This is the opening of a ghost story, and 'Christmas Eve' gives a specific location in time. Also, it sets up the traditional connection between Christmas and a ghost story.
2. Hill uses contrast a lot in this opening, for example the contrasts in the weather, between a sense of civilization and isolation, between warmth and cold, and gloom and cheerfulness. It is worth thinking about the effects these create.
3. Note the image of cold, rain, mist and generally dismal weather, and the use of detail such as 'oozed damp' and 'smelled sour'.
4. The narrator reveals something of his own susceptibility to melancholy.
5. Note how Hill creates a sense of isolation.

Now look at the opening of *Hard Times* by Charles Dickens, where the speaker emphasises to the schoolmaster and another adult how boys and girls should be taught nothing but facts.

What overall impression does this opening create? How does Dickens create his effects here?

'Now, what I want is Facts. Teach these boys and girls nothing but Facts. Facts alone are wanted in life. Plant nothing else, and root out everything else. You can only form the minds of reasoning animals upon Facts; nothing else will ever be of any service to them. This is the principle on which I bring up my own children, and this is the principle on which I bring up these children. Stick to Facts, sir!'

The scene was a plain, bare, monotonous vault of a schoolroom, and the speaker's square forefinger emphasized his observations by underscoring every sentence with a line on the schoolmaster's sleeve. The emphasis was helped by the speaker's square wall of a forehead, which had his eyebrows for its base, while his eyes found commodious cellarage in two dark caves, overshadowed by the wall. The emphasis was helped by the speaker's mouth, which was wide, thin, and hard set. The emphasis was helped by the speaker's voice, which was inflexible, dry, and dictatorial. The emphasis was helped by the speaker's hair, which bristled on the skirts of his bald head, a plantation of firs to keep the wind from its shining surface, all covered with knobs, like the crust of a plum pie, as if the head had scarcely warehouse-room for the hard facts stored inside. The speaker's obstinate carriage, square coat, square legs, square shoulders – nay, his very neckcloth, trained to take him by the throat with an unaccommodating grasp, like a stubborn fact, as it was – all helped the emphasis. 'In this life, we want nothing but Facts, sir; nothing but Facts!' The speaker, and the schoolmaster, and the third grown person present, all backed a little, and swept with their eyes the inclined plane of little vessels then and there arranged in order, ready to have imperial gallons of facts poured into them until they were full to the brim.

Extract from Hard Times *by Charles Dickens*

Here are some ideas you might have noted:

1. The emphasis is placed on 'Facts'. Note how the word is repeated five times in the opening paragraph. This emphasis on facts suggests a lack of importance given to the idea of the imagination. In other words, children should only be exposed to hard facts – imaginative ideas are discouraged.

2. Notice the bareness of the schoolroom. Its monotony is emphasised, and this is reflected in the description of the speaker – even his finger is 'square' and his forehead a 'square wall'. In the extended metaphor used to describe him, everything suggests rigidity and inflexibility. His mouth is 'wide, thin, and hard set', perhaps suggesting the views that his mouth expresses are equally 'hard set'.

3. Even the speaker's voice is described as 'inflexible, dry, and dictatorial', and his head gives the impression of scarcely having 'warehouse-room for the hard facts stored inside'.

4. Everything about the speaker gives the impression of squareness, and he regards children as 'little vessels', waiting to have facts poured into them 'until they were full to the brim'.

How to tackle the opening of a text you are studying

When thinking about the opening of a novel, ask yourself the following questions:

- What **situation** is being presented?
- What kind of **atmosphere** is created?
- Are things **explained** to you, or are you **plunged into the middle** of the story?
- What do you notice about the writer's **style**? (Take note of the vocabulary, imagery, sentence structure, etc. used.)
- How does the writer **arouse your interest** and make you want to read on?

PROGRESS CHECK

Look at a novel you are studying and read the opening section through very carefully.

Make notes on:
- what you learn from these opening pages
- how the writer creates effects
- how effective you find the opening, and why.

9.4 Narrative viewpoint

LEARNING SUMMARY	**After studying this section, you should be able to:** ● understand the importance of narrative viewpoint ● identify different types of narrative viewpoint ● appreciate the effect viewpoint can have on a narrative

Different types of narrative viewpoint

AQA A	**U 2, 3, 4**
AQA B	**U 1, 3, 4**
Edexcel	**U 1, 3, 4**
OCR	**U 1, 2, 4**
WJEC	**U 1, 3**
CCEA	**AS U2, A2 U2**

In the previous two extracts, Susan Hill was writing in the first person, while Charles Dickens had chosen to write his narrative in the third person. Both forms of narrative have their advantages and disadvantages, and each hold various possibilities for the writer.

Have another look at these two extracts and note down what effect is created by each **narrative viewpoint**.

Here are some ideas you might have considered about each type of viewpoint.

First person narrative

In a **first person narrative**:
● the author takes on the role of a character
● the story is told from the 'inside'
● the narrator appears to address you directly
● the illusion that the story is 'real' is heightened
● the viewpoint is more limited because we can only 'see' things through the narrator's eyes
● we do not know what is going on inside other people's heads.

Third person narrative

In a **third person narrative**:
● the narrator becomes almost 'god-like' in that he/she sees and hears everything – a kind of 'fly on the wall' approach (sometimes called the omniscient or 'all-knowing' narrator)
● the narrator can tell us of events that happen in different places at different times
● we are told how different characters feel, and what they are thinking
● the narrator is more detached and can make comments on the characters, perhaps mocking them or making positive or negative judgements on them.

Multiple narration

Sometimes a writer may choose to make the narrator of the story quite clearly a character in that story. The writer might even choose to have more than one narrator. This is called **multiple narration**. Emily Brontë uses this technique in *Wuthering Heights*.

The effects that viewpoint can have on a narrative – examples

AQA A	**U 2, 3, 4**
AQA B	**U 1, 3, 4**
Edexcel	**U 1, 3, 4**
OCR	**U 1, 2, 4**
WJEC	**U 1, 3**
CCEA	**AS U2, A2 U2**

Now we are going to look at three extracts, to see the effects that viewpoint can have on a narrative.

Once you have read the extracts carefully, think about the following points:

- Decide on the narrative viewpoint of each piece.
- What effects does each narrative viewpoint have on the narrative?
- What do you learn about the narrator(s) in each extract?
- How is information conveyed to you?

There are some notes in response to these questions at the end of the extracts.

The first extract is from *Tess of the D'Urbervilles* by Thomas Hardy. As you read, be aware of how much of the description is given through the dialogue and narration. Note how we see into characters' minds.

It was eleven o'clock before the family were all in bed, and two o'clock next morning was the latest hour for starting with the beehives if they were to be delivered to the retailers in Casterbridge before the Saturday market began, the way thither lying by bad roads over a distance of between twenty and thirty miles, and the horse and waggon being of the slowest. At half-past one Mrs Durbeyfield came into the large bedroom where Tess and all her little brothers and sisters slept.

'The poor man can't go,' she said to her eldest daughter, whose great eyes had opened the moment her mother's hand touched the door.

Tess sat up in bed, lost in a vague interspace between a dream and this information.

'But somebody must go,' she replied. 'It is late for the hives already. Swarming will soon be over for the year; and if we put off taking 'em till next week's market the call for 'em will be past, and they'll be thrown on our hands.'

Mrs Durbeyfield looked unequal to the emergency. 'Some young feller, perhaps, would go? One of them who were so much after dancing with 'ee yesterday,' she presently suggested.

'O no – I wouldn't have it for the world!' declared Tess proudly. 'And letting everybody know the reason – such a thing to be ashamed of! I think I could go if Abraham could go with me to keep me company.'

Her mother at length agreed to this arrangement. Little Abraham was aroused from his deep sleep in a corner of the same apartment, and made to put on his clothes while still mentally in the other world. Meanwhile Tess had hastily dressed herself; and the twain, lighting a lantern, went out to the stable. The rickety little waggon was already laden, and the girl led out the horse Prince, only a degree less rickety than the vehicle.

The poor creature looked wonderingly round at the night, at the lantern, at their two figures, as if he could not believe that at that hour, when every living thing was intended to be in shelter and at rest, he was called upon to go out and labour. They put a stock of candle-ends into the lantern, hung the latter to the off-side of the load, and directed the horse onward, walking at his shoulder at first during the uphill parts of the way, in order not to overload an animal of so little vigour. To cheer themselves as well as they could, they made an artificial morning with the lantern, some bread and butter, and their own conversation, the real morning being far from come. Abraham, as he more fully awoke (for he had moved in a sort of trance so far), began to talk of the strange shapes assumed by the various dark objects against the sky; of this tree that looked like a raging tiger springing from a lair; of that which resembled a giant's head.

Extract from Tess of the D'Urbervilles *by Thomas Hardy*

In the second extract, taken from *The Remains of the Day* by Kazuo Ishiguro, note how the narrator explains what is on his mind. Look carefully at the description. Think about the impression this creates of the man.

Tonight, I find myself here in a guest house in the city of Salisbury. The first day of my trip is now completed, and all in all, I must say I am quite satisfied. This expedition began this morning almost an hour later than I had planned, despite my having completed my packing and loaded the Ford with all necessary items well before eight o'clock. What with Mrs Clements and the girls also gone for the week, I suppose I was very conscious of the fact that once I departed, Darlington Hall would stand empty for probably the first time this century – perhaps for the first time since the day it was built. It was an odd feeling and perhaps accounts for why I delayed my departure so long, wandering around the house many times over, checking one last time that all was in order.

It is hard to explain my feelings once I did finally set off. For the first twenty minutes or so of motoring, I cannot say I was seized by any excitement or anticipation at all. This was due, no doubt, to the fact that though I motored further and further from the house, I continued to find myself in surroundings with which I had at least a passing acquaintance. Now I had always supposed I had travelled very little, restricted as I am by my responsibilities in the house, but of course, over time, one does make various excursions for one professional reason or another, and it would seem I have become much more acquainted with those neighbouring districts than I had realized. For as I say, as I motored on in the sunshine towards the Berkshire border, I continued to be surprised by the familiarity of the country around me. But then eventually the surroundings grew unrecognizable and I knew I had gone beyond all previous boundaries. I have heard people describe the moment, when setting sail in a ship, when one finally loses sight of the land. I imagine the experience of unease mixed with exhilaration often described in connection with this moment is very similar to what I felt in the Ford as the surroundings grew strange around me. This occurred just after I took a turning and found myself on a road curving around the edge of a hill. I could sense the steep drop to my left, though I could not see it due to the trees and thick foliage that lined the roadside. The feeling swept over me that I had truly left Darlington Hall behind, and I must confess I did feel a slight sense of alarm – a sense aggravated by the feeling that I was perhaps not on the correct road at all, but speeding off in totally the wrong direction into a wilderness. It was only the feeling of a moment, but it caused me to slow down. And even when I had assured myself I was on the right road, I felt compelled to stop the car a moment to take stock, as it were.

Extract from The Remains of the Day *by Kazuo Ishiguro*

In the final extract – from *Wuthering Heights* by Emily Brontë – Mr Lockwood speaks the opening words. He is renting a property near Wuthering Heights and he has recently been to pay a neighbourly call on Heathcliff. He begins by narrating the story, and then asks Nelly Dean to tell him about Heathcliff and the others at Wuthering Heights. Nelly Dean takes over the narration of the story in the last paragraph of the extract.

'I see the house at Wuthering Heights has "Earnshaw" carved over the front door. Are they an old family?'

'Very old, sir; and Hareton is the last of them, as our Miss Cathy is of us – I mean, of the Lintons. Have you been to Wuthering Heights? I beg pardon for asking: but I should like to hear how she is.'

'Mrs. Heathcliff? she looked very well, and very handsome; yet, I think, not very happy.'

'Oh dear, I don't wonder! And how did you like the master?'

'A rough fellow, rather, Mrs. Dean. Is not that his character?'

'Rough as a saw-edge, and hard as whinstone. The less you meddle with him the better.'

'He must have had some ups and downs in life to make him such a churl. Do you know anything of his history?'

'It's a cuckoo's, sir – I know all about it: except where he was born, and who were his parents, and how he got his money, at first. And Hareton has been cast out like an unfledged dunnock! The unfortunate lad is the only one in all this parish that does not guess how he has been cheated.'

'Well, Mrs, Dean, it will be a charitable deed to tell me something of my neighbours: I feel I shall not rest, if I go to bed; so be good enough to sit and chat an hour.'

'Oh, certainly, sir! I'll just fetch a little sewing, and then I'll sit as long as you please. But you've caught cold: I saw you shivering, and you must have some gruel to drive it out.'

The worthy woman bustled off, and I crouched nearer the fire; my head felt hot, and the rest of me chill: moreover I was excited, almost to a pitch of foolishness, through my nerves and brain. This caused me to feel, not uncomfortable, but rather fearful (as I am still) of serious effects from the incidents of to-day and yesterday. She returned presently, bringing a smoking basin and a basket of work; and, having placed the former on the hob, drew in her seat, evidently pleased to find me so companionable.

Before I came to live here, she commenced – waiting no further invitation to her story – I was almost always at Wuthering Heights; because my mother had nursed Mr. Hindley Earnshaw, that was Hareton's father, and I got used to playing with the children: I ran errands too, and helped to make hay, and hung about the farm ready for anything that anybody would set me to. One fine summer morning – it was the beginning of harvest, I remember – Mr. Earnshaw, the old master, came downstairs, dressed for a journey; and after he had told Joseph what was to be done during the day, he turned to Hindley, and Cathy, and me – for I sat eating my porridge with them – and he said, speaking to his son, 'Now, my bonny man, I'm going to Liverpool to-day, what shall I bring you? You may choose what you like: only let it be little, for I shall walk there and back: sixty miles each way, that is a long spell!' Hindley named a fiddle, and then he asked Miss Cathy; she was hardly six years old, but she could ride any horse in the stable, and she chose a whip. He did not forget me: for he had a kind heart though he was rather severe sometimes.
He promised to bring me a pocketful of apples and pears, and then
he kissed his children good-bye and set off.

Extract from Wuthering Heights *by Emily Brontë*

Here are some points that you have may have noted in response to the questions you were asked to think about:

1. The first extract, from *Tess of the D'Urbervilles*, is written in the third person. The 'omniscient' narrator can tell us that when Tess sat up in bed she was 'lost in a vague interspace between a dream and this information'. The narrator is also able to tell us what goes through the horse's mind when he is woken. This narrative perspective gives us a detailed view of what is happening, and the information is conveyed to us through a combination of dialogue and narrative description.

2. The second extract, from *The Remains of the Day*, is written in the first person, which gives a more intimate feel to the narrative. It seems as if the character is speaking to us directly. It is made even more intimate because the character is telling us what is on his mind. Because the narrative is in the first person, all the information we have is given by the character himself. We can gather that he worked at Darlington Hall and that he had been responsible for the running of it (he is, in fact, the butler), but he has now left to go on a trip. The hall is left completely empty and he feels a sense of unease about this. The fact that he has travelled so little is a sign of his commitment to his job. The tone is very restrained and almost formal, as you might expect from a butler used to the formality of mannered society.

3. The third extract, from *Wuthering Heights*, presents a more complex narrative. Although the narrative is told in the first person by Lockwood, much of the story is as it was told to him by Nelly Dean, and these parts are told in the first person too. In the extract Lockwood begins the narrative, but this is taken over later by Nelly Dean. If you are studying this novel, you will know that there are other narrators at different points. One of the effects of this multiple-narrator approach is to allow us to see things from different perspectives – each narrator brings their own perspective to the story. It also allows Brontë to unfold the elements of the plot in a natural way, as well as providing a variety of narrative voice. In the extract it is clear that Lockwood has had a bad experience at Wuthering Heights and knows nothing of the history of the family. Nelly, on the other hand, is an old family retainer who has a wealth of knowledge about Wuthering Heights that she is only too willing to share with him. The majority of this information is conveyed to us through the dialogue between the two of them, before she begins her narrative in the final paragraph of the extract.

KEY POINT

The narrative viewpoint from which a novel is written has an important effect on the way that the story is told.

PROGRESS CHECK

Look at the narrative viewpoint used in the text you are studying and make notes on what effect this has on the narrative.

9.5 Characters and their development

<table>
<tr><td>LEARNING SUMMARY</td><td>

After studying this section, you should be able to:

- recognise ways in which writers can create characters
- understand some of the functions of characters in a narrative
- understand some of the ways in which writers can reveal characters to their readers

</td></tr>
</table>

How characters are created and revealed to us

AQA A	U 2, 3, 4
AQA B	U 1, 3, 4
Edexcel	U 1, 3, 4
OCR	U 1, 2, 4
WJEC	U 1, 3
CCEA	AS U2, A2 U2

When reading a novel, much of the interest lies in the characters and their actions and interactions. The writer tries hard to create characters that are convincing. However, you must not forget, as students, that characters are creations of the writer. You need to be analytical in your approach to studying a novel – with the ability to see how language has been used to create and present characters, and to understand the role characters perform in the narrative.

> **KEY POINT**
>
> Writers can present and reveal their characters in various ways.

> **PROGRESS CHECK**
>
> Think about a novel that you have read. Write down the ways in which you learned things about the characters and formed your impressions of them.
>
> Characters are created and revealed to us through:
> 1. the description of them given by the narrator
> 2. the dialogue of the novel, in other words by what they say and what others say about them
> 3. the thoughts and feelings that they have
> 4. their behaviour and reaction to other characters
> 5. the writer's use of imagery and symbols.

Examples

Here are some introductory character sketches from Charles Dickens' *Hard Times*, D.H. Lawrence's *Sons and Lovers* and Jane Austen's *Pride and Prejudice*.

Read the extracts through carefully and make notes on the following:
- What do you learn about each character from the author's description?
- Are you just given factual information, or do you learn anything about the character's 'inner life'?
- What particular words or phrases strike you as effective in each description?
- Does the author seem to have a particular attitude towards the character?

Look at the extract on the next page. What impression is created of Bounderby through the author's description?

217

Why, Mr Bounderby was as near being Mr Gradgrind's bosom friend, as a man perfectly devoid of sentiment can approach that spiritual relationship towards another man perfectly devoid of sentiment. So near was Mr Bounderby – or, if the reader should prefer it, so far off.

He was a rich man: banker, merchant, manufacturer, and what not. A big, loud man, with a stare and a metallic laugh. A man made out of a coarse material, which seemed to have been stretched to make so much of him. A man with a great puffed head and forehead, swelled veins in his temples, and such a strained skin to his face that it seemed to hold his eyes open and lift his eyebrows up. A man with a pervading appearance on him of being inflated like a balloon, and ready to start. A man who could never sufficiently vaunt himself a self-made man. A man who was always proclaiming, through that brassy speaking-trumpet of a voice of his, his old ignorance and his old poverty. A man who was the Bully of humility.

A year or two younger than his eminently practical friend, Mr Bounderby looked older; his seven or eight and forty might have had the seven or eight added to it again, without surprising anybody. He had not much hair. One might have fancied he had talked it off; and that what was left, all standing up in disorder, was in that condition from being constantly blown about by his windy boastfulness.

Extract from Hard Times *by Charles Dickens*

In this character sketch, which members of the family does Lawrence link Paul with?

Paul would be built like his mother, slightly and rather small. His fair hair went reddish, and then dark brown; his eyes were grey. He was a pale, quiet child, with eyes that seemed to listen, and with a full, dropping underlip.

As a rule he seemed old for his years. He was so conscious of what other people felt, particularly his mother. When she fretted he understood, and could have no peace. His soul seemed always attentive to her.

As he grew older he became stronger. William was too far removed from him to accept him as a companion. So the smaller boy belonged at first almost entirely to Annie. She was a tom-boy and a 'flybie-skybie', as her mother called her. But she was intensely fond of her second brother. So Paul was towed round at the heels of Annie, sharing her game. She raced wildly at lerky with the other young wild-cats of the Bottoms. And always Paul flew beside her, living her share of the game, having as yet no part of his own. He was quiet and not noticeable. But his sister adored him. He always seemed to care for things if she wanted him to.

Extract from Sons and Lovers *by D.H. Lawrence*

What differences between Darcy and Bingley are highlighted in this extract?

Between him and Darcy there was a very steady friendship, in spite of a great opposition of character – Bingley was endeared to Darcy by the easiness, openness, ductility of his temper, though no disposition could offer a greater contrast to his own, and though with his own he never appeared dissatisfied. On the strength of Darcy's regard Bingley had the firmest reliance, and of his judgment the highest opinion. In understanding Darcy was the superior. Bingley was by no means deficient, but Darcy was clever. He was at the same time haughty, reserved, and fastidious, and his manners, though well bred, were not inviting. In that respect his friend had greatly the advantage. Bingley was sure of being liked wherever he appeared, Darcy was continually giving offence.

The manner in which they spoke of the Meryton assembly was sufficiently characteristic. Bingley had never met with pleasanter people or prettier girls in his life; everybody had been most kind and attentive to him, there had been no formality, no stiffness, he had soon felt acquainted with all the room; and as to Miss Bennet, he could not conceive an angel more beautiful. Darcy, on the contrary, had seen a collection of people in whom there was little beauty and no fashion, for none of whom he had felt the smallest interest, and from none received either attention or pleasure. Miss Bennet he acknowledged to be pretty, but she smiled too much.

Extract from Pride and Prejudice *by Jane Austen*

Here are some points you may have noted about the way the authors have created these characters:

1. In the first extract, Bounderby is very much defined by his physical appearance, although we are given other details about him too. For example, we are told that he is a man 'devoid of sentiment'. We are also told that he is rich. Dickens' description of him as being like a balloon gives the impression of someone far too full of his own importance, which is confirmed by reference to his 'brassy ... voice' and 'windy boastfulness'. It seems clear from the tone and content of Dickens' description that he is not presenting a character that he wants to appeal to his reader, rather one who represents values with which he himself has no sympathy.

2. In the second extract, it is clear that Paul is very much associated with his mother and with his older sister. The references to him being 'pale' and 'quiet' 'with eyes that seemed to listen' and having 'a full, dropping underlip' give the impression of a rather sad, thoughtful child. He is perhaps physically not very strong, and we are told 'he seemed old for his years'. He is very close to his sister, and he seems sensitive and caring about her.

3. In the third extract, Darcy is described as an intelligent man – more intelligent than Bingley, in fact – but unlike Bingley we are told that he was often 'haughty' and 'reserved'. Austen uses their very different reactions to the people they meet to highlight the differences between the two, often using very subtle hints of what is to come, such as Darcy's view of Miss Bennet, whom 'he acknowledged to be pretty, but she smiled too much'.

KEY POINT

We learn about characters in many different ways, and writers can create and present them in many different ways.

PROGRESS CHECK

Look at a text you are studying and make a list of the central characters. For each character, make brief notes on how the writer reveals details about them to the reader.

How characters are presented and interact with each other

AQA A U 2, 3, 4
AQA B U 1, 3, 4
Edexcel U 1, 3, 4
OCR   U 1, 2, 4
WJEC   U 1, 3
CCEA   AS U2, A2 U2

Now let's look at character in more detail. Very often in an exam question you are asked to look at the ways in which a character is presented, and how they relate to other characters, or change and develop throughout the course of the novel.

Example

Read the following extract carefully. It is from D.H. Lawrence's *Sons and Lovers*, and describes how the young Gertrude Coppard met the man she was to marry, Walter Morel.

As you read, think about the following points:
- Notice the vocabulary used to describe Morel – 'erect', 'vigorous', 'ruddy'.
- What is the significance of the laugh?
- How does the description of Gertrude contrast with the description of Morel?
- Notice that Morel uses dialect speech form, whereas Gertrude speaks in Standard English. Why does Lawrence do this?

When she was twenty-three years old, she met, at a Christmas party, a young man from the Erewash Valley. Morel was then twenty-seven years old. He was well set-up, erect, and very smart. He had wavy black hair that shone again, and a vigorous black beard that had never been shaved. His cheeks were ruddy, and his red, moist mouth was noticeable because he laughed so often. And so heartily. He had that rare thing, a rich ringing laugh. Gertrude Coppard had watched him, fascinated. He was so full of colour and animation, his voice ran so easily into comic grotesque, he was so ready and so pleasant with everybody. Her own father had a rich fund of humour, but it was satiric. This man's was different: soft, non-intellectual, warm, a kind of gambolling.

She herself was opposite. She had a curious, receptive mind, which found much pleasure and amusement in listening to other folk. She was clever in leading folk on to talk. She loved ideas and was considered very intellectual. What she liked most of all was an argument on religion or philosophy or politics with some educated man. This she did not often enjoy. So she always had people tell her about themselves, finding her pleasure so.

In her person she was rather small and delicate, with a large brow, and dropping bunches of brown silk curls. Her blue eyes were very straight, honest, and searching. She had the beautiful hands of the Coppards. Her dress was always subdued. She wore dark blue silk, with a peculiar silver chain of silver scallops. This, and a heavy brooch of twisted gold, was her only ornament. She was still perfectly intact, deeply religious, and full of beautiful candour.

Walter Morel seemed melted away before her. She was to the miner that thing of mystery and fascination, a lady. When she spoke to him, it was with a southern pronunciation and a purity of English which thrilled him to hear. She watched him. He danced well, as if it were natural and joyous in him to dance. His grandfather was a French refugee who had married an English barmaid – if it had been a marriage. Gertrude Coppard watched the young miner as he danced, a certain subtle exultation like glamour in his movement, and his face the flower of his body, ruddy, with tumbled black hair, and laughing alike whatever partner he bowed above. She thought him rather wonderful, never having met anyone like him. Her father was to her the type of all men. And George Coppard, proud in his bearing, handsome, and rather bitter; who preferred theology in reading, and who drew near in sympathy only to one man, the Apostle Paul; who was harsh in government, and in familiarity ironic; who ignored all sensuous pleasure; – he was very different from the miner. Gertrude herself was rather contemptuous of dancing; she had not the slightest inclination towards that accomplishment, and had never learned even a Roger de Coverley. She was a puritan, like her father, high-minded, and really stern. Therefore the dusky, golden softness of this man's sensuous flame of life, that flowed off his flesh like the flame from a candle, not baffled and gripped into incandescence by thought and spirit as her life was, seemed to her something wonderful, beyond her.

He came and bowed above her. A warmth radiated through her as if she had drunk wine.

'Now do come and have this one wi' me,' he said caressively. 'It's easy, you know. I'm pining to see you dance.'

She had told him before she could not dance. She glanced at his humility and smiled. Her smile was very beautiful. It moved the man so that he forgot everything.

'No, I won't dance,' she said softly. Her words came clean and ringing.

continued

Not knowing what he was doing – he often did the right thing by instinct – he sat beside her, inclining reverentially.

'But you mustn't miss your dance,' she reproved.

'Nay, I don't want to dancc that – it's not one as I care about.'

'Yet you invited me to it.'

He laughed very heartily at this.

'I never thought o' that. Tha'rt not long in taking the curl out of me.' It was her turn to laugh quickly.

'You don't look as if you'd come much uncurled,' she said.

'I'm like a pig's tail, I curl because I canna help it,' he laughed, rather boisterously.

'And you are a miner!' she exclaimed in surprise.

'Yes. I went down when I was ten.'

She looked at him in wondering dismay.

'When you were ten! And wasn't it very hard?' she asked.

'You soon get used to it. You live like th' mice, an' you pop out at night to see what's going on.'

'It makes me feel blind,' she frowned.

'Like a moudiwarp! he laughed. 'Yi, an' there's some chaps as does go round like moudiwarps.' He thrust his face forward in the blind, snout-like way of a mole, seeming to sniff and peer for direction.

Extract from Sons and Lovers *by D.H. Lawrence*

Now study the passage closely and answer the following questions:

1. How do you learn about the characters of Gertrude and Morel? What kind of imagery or ideas does Lawrence associate with each of the characters?
2. What is revealed about each of the characters through the dialogue?
3. What indications are there that they may not be a very well-matched couple?

COMMENTARY

Here are some ideas that you may have noted:

1. In this extract, Morel is described very much through his physical appearance – his 'vigorous' beard, his 'ruddy' cheeks and his 'red' mouth giving an impression of life and vitality and fire. His 'rich, ringing laugh' adds to the picture of a sensuous and attractive man. Lawrence tells us that Gertrude is the opposite of this man, and he describes her through her mind and intellect. Where he does use physical description, it is linked with Gertrude's character. For example, her 'blue eyes were very straight, honest, and searching' and 'her dress was always subdued'.

2. Lawrence accentuates the difference between the two characters through the dialogue. Morel speaks in the broad Nottinghamshire dialect of the miner, whereas Gertrude speaks in the Standard English of the educated lady. Nevertheless, she is drawn to him in the same way as opposites are said to attract. She has never encountered a man like him before, and she is fascinated by him.

3. There are signs that a relationship between them would be destined to failure – the attraction is very much based on the physical, but underneath they have quite different characters, and Lawrence very clearly highlights these differences.

> **KEY POINT**
>
> It is important to look at the ways in which characters are presented, and the ways in which they interact with each other. The author often uses these aspects to convey information to the audience.

> **PROGRESS CHECK**
>
> Now look at the characters in a text that you are studying. Choose **three** of these characters and examine the ways in which the writer presents them to the reader.

9.6 Setting and atmosphere

LEARNING SUMMARY

After studying this section, you should be able to:
- understand the importance of setting in a novel
- recognise some of the ways that writers can create settings and a sense of place
- see how the setting of a novel can be an important influence on other aspects of the narrative

The importance of setting and atmosphere in a novel

AQA A	**U 2, 3, 4**
AQA B	**U 1, 3, 4**
Edexcel	**U 1, 3, 4**
OCR	**U 1, 2, 4**
WJEC	**U 1, 3**
CCEA	**AS U2, A2 U2**

The **setting** can be an important element of a novel, and can be closely related to the development of the plot. Setting can be much more than a simple 'backdrop' against which the action takes place, and often can be closely bound up with the characters themselves. Often the setting is closely associated with the **atmosphere** created.

> **KEY POINT**
>
> The setting and atmosphere that a writer creates can be important elements in the novel.

Creating the setting and a sense of place – example

In the following extract from *Jane Eyre* by Charlotte Brontë, a young orphan, Jane, who is being looked after by her aunt, is locked in the red-room as a punishment for attacking her 14-year old cousin John, who has been tormenting her.

Read the extract carefully. As you do so, think about these questions:
1. What impression does Brontë's physical description of the room create?
2. What detail adds to the sense of atmosphere created?
3. How does Jane respond to being locked in the room?

The red-room was a square chamber, very seldom slept in, I might say never, indeed, unless when a chance influx of visitors at Gateshead Hall rendered it necessary to turn to account all the accommodation it contained: yet it was one of the largest and stateliest chambers in the mansion. A bed supported on massive pillars of mahogany, hung with curtains of deep red damask, stood out like a tabernacle in the centre; the two large windows, with their blinds always drawn down, were half shrouded in festoons and falls of similar drapery; the carpet was red; the table at the foot of the bed was covered with a crimson cloth; the walls were a soft fawn colour with a blush of pink in it; the wardrobe, the toilet-table, the chairs were of darkly polished old mahogany. Out of these deep surrounding shades rose high, and glared white, the piled-up mattresses and pillows of the bed, spread with a snowy Marseilles counterpane. Scarcely less prominent was an ample cushioned easy-chair near the head of the bed, also white, with a footstool before it; and looking, as I thought, like a pale throne.

This room was chill, because it seldom had a fire; it was silent, because remote from the nursery and kitchen; solemn, because it was known to be so seldom entered. The house-maid alone came here on Saturdays, to wipe from the mirrors and the furniture a week's quiet dust: and Mrs. Reed herself, at far intervals, visited it to review the contents of a certain secret drawer in the wardrobe, where were stored divers parchments, her jewel-casket, and a miniature of her deceased husband; and in those last words lies the secret of the red-room—the spell which kept it so lonely in spite of its grandeur. Mr. Reed had been dead nine years: it was in this chamber he breathed his last; here he lay in state; hence his coffin was borne by the undertaker's men; and, since that day, a sense of dreary consecration had guarded it from frequent intrusion.

My seat, to which Bessie and the bitter Miss Abbot had left me riveted, was a low ottoman near the marble chimney-piece; the bed rose before me; to my right hand there was the high, dark wardrobe, with subdued, broken reflections varying the gloss of its panels; to my left were the muffled windows; a great looking-glass between them repeated the vacant majesty of the bed and room. I was not quite sure whether they had locked the door; and when I dared move, I got up and went to see. Alas! yes: no jail was ever more secure. Returning, I had to cross before the looking-glass; my fascinated glance involuntarily explored the depth it revealed. All looked colder and darker in that visionary hollow than in reality: and the strange little figure there gazing at me, with a white face and arms specking the gloom, and glittering eyes of fear moving where all else was still, had the effect of a real spirit: I thought it like one of the tiny phantoms, half fairy, half imp, Bessie's evening stories represented as coming out of lone, ferny dells in moors, and appearing before the eyes of belated travellers. I returned to my stool.

COMMENTARY

Here are some responses you may have thought of:

1. The room appears dark and oppressive with the huge dark mahogany bed with dark red curtains, and the blinds that are always drawn down. The room is never used, and no one except the maid goes there, which gives the room a cold and lonely air.

2. The thought of Mr Reed having died in this room and being laid in state in his coffin here adds to the dark atmosphere created.

3. Jane is angry when she is locked in the room and does not seem afraid. However, when she sees her reflection in the mirror it brings to her mind stories of imps and fairies, and it is clear that all kinds of thoughts are going through her mind.

How the setting can be a key influence on other aspects of the narrative

AQA A	**U 2, 3, 4**
AQA B	**U 1, 3, 4**
Edexcel	**U 1, 3, 4**
OCR	**U 1, 2, 4**
WJEC	**U 1, 3**
CCEA	**AS U2, A2 U2**

In other novels the setting can play a much more significant role. In Hardy's *The Return of the Native*, for example, the story is set against the imposing background of Egdon Heath. The presence of this wild and untamed heath exerts such an influence on the action in terms of mood and atmosphere that some critics have described it as almost becoming a character in itself. Hardy gives a good deal of attention to creating a sense of the heath's wildness, as in the following description, with which the novel opens.

As you read the extract, think about the following questions:

1. What kind of vocabulary does Hardy use to describe the heath?
2. What imagery does he use, and what effects does it create?
3. What kind of mood and atmosphere are associated with the heath?

A Saturday afternoon in November was approaching the time of twilight, and the vast tract of unenclosed wild known as Egdon Heath embrowned itself moment by moment. Overhead the hollow stretch of whitish cloud shutting out the sky was as a tent which had the whole heath for its floor.

The heaven being spread with this pallid screen and the earth with the darkest vegetation, their meeting-line at the horizon was clearly marked. In such contrast the heath wore the appearance of an instalment of night which had taken up its place before its astronomical hour was come: darkness had to a great extent arrived hereon, while day stood distinct in the sky. Looking upwards, a furze-cutter would have been inclined to continue work; looking down, he would have decided to finish his faggot and go home. The distant rims of the world and of the firmament seemed to be a division in time no less than a division in matter. The face of the heath by its mere complexion added half an hour to evening; it could in like manner retard the dawn, sadden noon, anticipate the frowning of storms scarcely generated, and intensify the opacity of a moonless midnight to a cause of shaking and dread.

In fact, precisely at this transitional point of its nightly roll into darkness the great and particular glory of the Egdon waste began, and nobody could be said to understand the heath who had not been there at such a time. It could best be felt when it could not clearly be seen, its complete effect and explanation lying in this and the succeeding hours before the next dawn: then, and only then, did it tell its true tale. The spot was, indeed, a near relation of night, and when night showed itself an apparent tendency to gravitate together could be perceived in its shades and the scene. The sombre stretch of rounds and hollows seemed to rise and meet the evening gloom in pure sympathy, the heath exhaling darkness as rapidly as the heavens precipitated it. And so the obscurity in the air and the obscurity in the land closed together in a black fraternization towards which each advance half-way.

Extract from The Return of the Native *by Thomas Hardy*

COMMENTARY

Here are some of the points you may have thought of:

1. You might have noted the use of words such as 'vast', 'wild' and 'waste', which convey the essential sense of the heath. Hardy also uses 'darkest' and 'darkness' in his description of the heath, and notes how it looks dark even when the sky is still light. These three words – 'vast', 'wild' and 'dark' – quickly establish the character of the wasteland that is Egdon Heath.

2. Hardy uses personification to create the sense of the heath almost as a living thing – for example, 'The sombre stretch of rounds and hollows seemed to rise and meet the evening gloom in pure sympathy', and 'the heath exhaling darkness'.

3. The prevailing mood is a sombre one that captures the dark, vast wildness of the heath. It has such a presence that it is almost like a living entity that has an atmosphere of its own – one that needs to be experienced to be understood.

PROGRESS CHECK

Now look at a novel you are studying. Make notes on the setting or settings that the writer creates. What kind of atmosphere is created in the novel?

9.7 Studying short stories

LEARNING SUMMARY

After studying this section, you should be able to:

- think about ways in which you can approach the reading of short stories
- think about ways you can prepare yourself for writing about short stories
- consider some of the particular features of short stories

How to read – and write about – short stories

AQA A	**U 2, 3, 4**
AQA B	**U 1, 3, 4**
Edexcel	**U 1, 3, 4**
OCR	**U 1, 2, 4**
WJEC	**U 1, 3**
CCEA	**AS U2, A2 U2**

You may be studying a collection of short stories as one of your prose texts. If you are, then it is important to recognise that most of what has been dealt with so far in this chapter also applies to short stories.

However, it is also important to recognise that although the novel and the short story share the same prose medium, the short story has its own artistic methods, which can be quite different from those of the novel. The differences that exist between these two genres are very often in scale rather than in kind. If a novel can deal with the growth of a character, trace changes in thought, follow changes in fortune and so forth, a short story can too.

Features of short stories

Here are the main features of short stories:

- Very often a short story focuses on a single character in a single situation, rather than tracing a range of characters through a variety of situations and phases of development as novels often do.
- Often, the focus for a short story is the point at which the central character undergoes some event or experience that presents a significant moment in their personal development. It can be seen as a 'moment of truth' in which something or some perception, large or small, changes within the character.
- Not all short stories reach some kind of climax, though. Some stories may give a kind of 'snapshot' of a period of time or an experience, for example 'a day in the life of'.
- Some short stories end inconclusively, leaving the reader with feelings of uncertainty, while other kinds of story do not seem to have a discernible plot at all.
- Sometimes readers might feel completely baffled by what they have read, and might tentatively explore a range of possible interpretations in their heads. This may, of course, have been exactly the response that the writer intended.

Overall, then, because by their very nature short stories are 'short', they tend to focus on fewer characters than novels, because there is simply not the time or space to develop a large cast of characters. Again, because of the shortness, they often have a fairly short timescale.

> **KEY POINT**
>
> Short stories possess many of the features of the novel, but they are very much a separate genre. Be aware of the particular features and strengths of the short-story form.

> **PROGRESS CHECK**
>
> Look at the short-story collection you are studying. What kind of stories are they? How do they differ from novels that you have read?

9.8 Studying non-fiction

LEARNING SUMMARY

After studying this section, you should be able to:

- recognise different types of non-fiction prose texts
- consider the variety and aims of prose non-fiction
- think about where you might encounter non-fiction prose on your course

How non-fiction prose fits into your A-Level course

AQA A	**U 2, 3, 4**
AQA B	**U 1, 3, 4**
Edexcel	**U 1, 3, 4**
OCR	**U 1, 2, 4**
WJEC	**U 1, 3**
CCEA	**AS U2, A2 U2**

There are two possible ways in which you might encounter non-fiction prose texts on your A-Level course.

You might study a non-fiction text:

- as part of your wider reading, or for the purposes of contextual linking
- as part of your coursework assessment.

How to approach your study of non-fiction writing

Prose texts can take many different forms. Very often, many of the techniques of the novelist are also the techniques of the non-fiction writer, and so much of what has been discussed so far in this chapter is applicable to non-fiction writing too. For example, non-fiction writers often write about characters – although their characters really existed, they still need to re-create them in words. Similarly, they often describe scenes and settings, create moods and atmospheres, and their texts often contain themes, ideas or messages that the writer wants to convey to the reader. Some texts, of course, also combine factual information with ideas that come from the imagination of the writer.

When studying non-fiction prose texts, our approach is not necessarily any different from when we study novels, or even drama or poetry.

We still need to ask these key questions:
- What is this text about?
- How has the author chosen to write about it?
- What is the purpose in writing it?

Different types of non-fiction writing

AQA A	**U 2, 3, 4**
AQA B	**U 1, 3, 4**
Edexcel	**U 1, 3, 4**
OCR	**U 1, 2, 4**
WJEC	**U 1, 3**
CCEA	**AS U2, A2 U2**

Forms of non-fiction writing that you might encounter include:
- essays
- autobiographical or biographical writing
- diaries
- documentaries
- journalism.

Example – autobiography

Look at the extract on the next page. It is taken from *Testament of Youth*, the autobiography of Vera Brittain. Vera left Oxford University in 1916 and volunteered to go to France as a VAD (Voluntary Aid Detachment). In this extract she describes her arrival at a camp hospital at Etaples.

When you have looked at the piece carefully, think about the following questions:
1. What techniques does Brittain use to give the reader an impression of her surroundings?
2. Do her methods have anything in common with those of the novelist? Are there any differences?

Extract from *Testament of Youth*

A heavy shower had only just ceased as I arrived at Etaples with three other V.A.D.s ordered to the same hospital, and the roads were liquid with such mud as only wartime France could produce after a few days of rain.

Leaving our camp-kit to be picked up by an ambulance, we squelched through the littered, grimy square and along a narrow, straggling street where the sole repositories for household rubbish appeared to be the pavement and the gutter. We finally emerged into open country and the huge area of camps, in which, at one time or another, practically every soldier in the British Army was dumped to await further orders for a still less agreeable destination. The main railway line from Boulogne to Paris ran between the hospitals and the distant sea, and amongst the camps, and along the sides of the road to Camiers, the humped sandhills bristled with tufts of spiky grass.

The noise of the distant guns was a sense rather than a sound; sometimes a quiver shook the earth, a vibration trembled upon the wind, when I could actually hear nothing. But that sense made any feeling of complete peace impossible; in the atmosphere was always the tenseness, the restlessness, the slight rustling, that comes before an earthquake or with imminent thunder. The glamour of the place was even more compelling, though less delirious, than the enchantment of Malta's beauty; it could not be banished though one feared and resisted it, knowing that it had to be bought at the cost of loss and frustration. France was the scene of titanic, illimitable death, and for this very reason it had become the heart of the fiercest living ever known to any generation. Nothing was permanent; everyone and everything was always on the move; friendships were temporary, appointments were temporary, life itself was the most temporary of all. Never, in any time or place, had been so appropriate the lament of 'James Lee's Wife';

> To draw one beauty into our heart's core,
> And keep it changeless! Such our claim;
> So answered, - Never more!

Whenever I think of the War to-day, it is not as summer but always as winter; always as cold and darkness and discomfort, and an intermittent warmth of exhilarating excitement which made us irrationally exult in all three. Its permanent symbol, for me, is a candle stuck in the neck of a bottle, the tiny flame flickering in an ice-cold draught, yet creating a miniature illusion of light against an opaque infinity of blackness.

Vera Brittain

COMMENTARY

Here are some points that you may have thought of:

1. Brittain uses vivid and detailed description to give the reader an impression of her surroundings. Note how she brings in the various senses to strengthen the impression of the place – 'The noise of the distant guns was a sense rather than a sound; sometimes a quiver shook the earth, a vibration trembled upon the wind, when I could actually hear nothing'. Here, clearly, she is using the same techniques as a novelist would to set the scene and create a sense of atmosphere.

2. As far as this extract is concerned there are no differences between her writing and that of a novelist or short-story writer. We know that Brittain was writing from first-hand experience, but it could equally be a piece of prose written in the first person and created purely from the writer's imagination.

PROGRESS CHECK

If you are studying a non-fiction text, answer the following questions:

1. What kind of non-fiction text is it?
2. In what ways are the writing techniques used similar to those of the novelist?
3. In what ways are they different?

KEY POINT

The techniques of the non-fiction writer can have many things in common with those of the novelist or short-story writer.

9.9 Preparing yourself for the exam

LEARNING SUMMARY	After studying this section, you should be able to:
	• think of a range of ideas to help you prepare for exam questions on prose texts
	• plan your key areas of study effectively

How to prepare for exam questions on prose texts

AQA A	U 2, 3, 4
AQA B	U 1, 3, 4
Edexcel	U 1, 3, 4
OCR	U 1, 2, 4
WJEC	U 1, 3
CCEA	AS U2, A2 U2

There are a number of things you can do to prepare yourself for the exam questions on prose texts.

Here are some suggestions:

- Make notes on your impressions right from the first reading. You may change your mind later, but those initial impressions can be important.
- Make sure that you have read your text several times and know your way around it in detail – do not skimp that final read before the exam.
- If there is a film, DVD or video recording of your text, it is worth watching it. Remember, though, the storylines are often altered for film or television, so make sure you are aware of this. In the exam you should be writing about the text, not the film.

Planning your key areas of study effectively

Think about relationships between the various elements of the text and how together they present a 'whole'.

Here are some areas to think about and make notes on:

- **Characterisation** – look for information about how we learn about characters; indications of characters changing or developing; significant new information about a character; views on what the writer is trying to achieve in the presentation of character; look at key speeches, shifts in focus, and different ways of interpreting what characters do and say.
- **Themes** – look for various possible 'meanings' in the text; the development of any themes; introduction of new thematic elements; and moral problems or issues raised for the characters or the reader.
- **Narrative technique** – look at the ways in which the writer manipulates the narrative; the narrative voice and perspective, and narrative intrusion or comment; think about the pace and variety of the action.
- **Structure** – think about the overall shape and structure of the text, and the impact that this could have on the reader.
- **Tone** – is the tone familiar or formal, personal or impersonal? Who is being addressed?
- **Language use** – look at the vocabulary and syntax. Is imagery or symbolism used? If so, what is its effect?
- **Speech and dialogue** – what kind of speech is used – direct or indirect? Do characters speak for themselves, or does the narrator intrude or comment? Is the dialogue realistic? What function does speech and dialogue perform – development of character, plot, themes, or introduction of a dramatic element?
- **Setting and description** – what is significant about where the action takes place? How is the setting described?
- **Your own response** – think about your own reactions to the text. What are your initial impressions? Do these change after you have read the text several times?

PROGRESS CHECK

Produce a plan of approach for your study of your prose text, making sure that you cover all the key areas.

Sample question and model answer

Wuthering Heights – Emily Brontë

To what extent does the setting and atmosphere contribute to the Gothic effect of the novel?

QUESTION OVERVIEW

This question is in the style of a question from AQA B Unit 3.

> This is an effective introduction, with a focus on context and genre.

Gothic novels are often concerned with supernatural, unnatural or horrifying situations and events. Although not a truly Gothic novel in the sense that `Frankenstein´ by Mary Shelley or `The Castle of Otranto´ by Horace Walpole can be said to be, `Gothic´ `Wuthering Heights´ does have Gothic elements to it. Examples include the intense and unnatural passions that it presents, the portrayal of Heathcliff as the dark, mysterious hero with his unpredictable and sometimes violent nature, and the sense of the dead haunting the living established at the start of the novel. However, the setting and atmosphere that Brontë creates also contributes much to the Gothic effect of the novel.

> The candidate looks at three settings.

> The candidate makes the link that Wuthering Heights is linked to the appearance of a ghost.

The action of much of the novel is rooted in the two houses of Wuthering Heights and Thrushcross Grange, both of which are set within the isolation of wild moors, which in themselves contribute a dark and brooding atmosphere to the novel. Wuthering Heights is an old, bare house standing isolated in the moors. It has strong walls to withstand the fierce weather of the wild landscape, and has warm fires, much to Lockwood's relief when he has to take refuge there. It is here that - when he is cut off by a snow storm and has to stay the night - he has the terrifying experience of encountering the ghost of Catherine Linton, begging to be let in. The house as a setting is closely associated with Heathcliff and Catherine.

> The candidate explores the contrast between the two houses.

Thrushcross Grange presents a complete contrast to Wuthering Heights. Our first impression of the house comes from Heathcliff's description when he and Catherine had been across the moors to look through the windows and see how the Lintons spent their Sundays. He describes it as a beautiful place with a crimson carpet and crimson-covered chairs and tables, a `pure white ceiling´ with a `shower of glass-drops hanging in silver chains from the centre´.

> The candidate shows his understanding of the significance of the moors and houses as settings.

> The candidate focuses on the Gothic effect of the moors as a setting, and develops this idea.

> The candidate provides a range of examples to support his point.

It is clearly a civilised and comfortable house, which makes the contrast with Wuthering Heights all the more marked - one representing civilisation, a haven in a desolate landscape - and the other a wildness reflecting the spirited characters of Heathcliff and Catherine. The two houses are separated by the moors. Although little action takes place on the moors, their presence is always there and is significant in the atmosphere created. The moors can be desolate, wild and dangerous, and in that sense they create a backdrop to the events of the novel that have an element of the Gothic about them. We are reminded of the brooding and dangerous nature of the moors at various points in the novel. For example, Lockwood is in danger of getting lost and dying in the snow if he tries to cross back to Thrushcross Grange after his second visit there. When Catherine and Heathcliff cross the moors to Thrushcross Grange, Nelly fears that they have been hurt or are lost, and when Nelly and Cathy are held prisoner by Heathcliff while he forces Cathy to marry Linton, people from the Grange fear that they have been drowned in a bog. Throughout the novel people often come in from the moors soaking wet having been caught in a rain or snowstorm. The dangers of the moors mean that the houses are important as safe havens, but the moors also make the houses places of containment.

Sample question and model answer *(continued)*

The candidate comments on the wider significance of the moors and an alternative view of them.

The candidate shows a good use of illustration.

This is an effective conclusion.

However, the moors have another significance. They represent liberation for Heathcliff and Catherine - the pair roam the moors to escape into a world of their own. The moors change with the seasons, and they hold their own beauty for Catherine. In this setting she feels invigorated and enjoys the natural environment and the feeling of freedom they provide. When she is dying at the Grange she asks Nelly to open the window so she can feel the wind from the moors, and she longs to hear the sound of the wind in the fir trees near her window back at Wuthering Heights. At the end of the novel Lockwood visits the graves of Catherine, Edgar and Heathcliff. As he looks at the headstones he watches the moths fluttering amongst the harebells and listens to `the soft wind breathing through the grass'. He wonders how anyone could `ever imagine unquiet slumbers for the sleepers in that quiet earth'. Here, the atmosphere created by the setting of the moors is benign and peaceful as the three characters are united in death, and the heath and nature is claiming them.

`Wuthering Heights' is a dark and brooding novel. It is full of violence, cruelty and unnatural events and deeds, such as Catherine's ghost in Lockwood's dream, Heathcliff digging up Catherine's grave, the reports of Catherine and Heathcliff's ghosts being seen, and the repeated links of Heathcliff with the demonic. The book is concerned with destructive and powerful emotions - the setting of the moors, with their violent weather and dangers, contributes to the Gothic atmosphere created, but they have a wider significance too in a novel that goes beyond the purely Gothic.

SUMMATIVE COMMENT

The candidate shows a clear focus on the task, and a detailed understanding of the text. There is some detailed evaluation of the connections of the text to the idea of the gothic. He uses some sense of context, and a well-structured argument and good exploration of ideas. The essay tends to lack a more detailed exploration of aspects of language. The candidate uses clear and fluent expression.

Practice examination questions

AQA A Unit 1

Read the following extract carefully. It is taken from an article written by Charles Dickens for the weekly magazine he edited between 1850 and 1859 – *Household Words*. In this article, entitled 'A Walk in a Workhouse', Dickens describes his visit to a large London workhouse in 1850 and gives a sense of the conditions he found there.

(a) How does the writer present his thoughts and feelings about aspects of Victorian life?

(b) How far is the extract similar to and different from your wider reading in Victorian literature?

(c) You should consider the writer's choices of form, structure and language.

In a room opening from a squalid yard, where a number of listless women were lounging to and fro, trying to get warm in the ineffectual sunshine of the tardy May morning – in the 'Itch Ward,' not to compromise the truth – a woman such as HOGARTH has often drawn, was hurriedly getting on her gown before a dusty fire. She was the nurse, or wardswoman, of that insalubrious department – herself a pauper – flabby, raw-boned, untidy – unpromising and coarse of aspect as need be. But, on being spoken to about the patients whom she had in charge, she turned round, with her shabby gown half on, half off, and fell a crying with all her might. Not for show, not querulously, not in any mawkish sentiment, but in the deep grief and affliction of her heart; turning away her dishevelled head: sobbing most bitterly, wringing her hands, and letting fall abundance of great tears, that choked her utterance. What was the matter with the nurse of the itch-ward? Oh, 'the dropped child' was dead! Oh, the child that was found in the street, and she had brought up ever since, had died an hour ago, and see where the little creature lay, beneath this cloth! The dear, the pretty dear!

The dropped child seemed too small and poor a thing for Death to be in earnest with, but Death had taken it; and already its diminutive form was neatly washed, composed, and stretched as if in sleep upon a box. I thought I heard a voice from Heaven saying, It shall be well for thee, O nurse of the itch-ward, when some less gentle pauper does those offices to thy cold form, that such as the dropped child are the angels who behold my Father's face!

In another room, were several ugly old women crouching, witch-like, round a hearth, and chattering and nodding, after the manner of the monkeys. 'All well here? And enough to eat?' A general chattering and chuckling; at last an answer from a volunteer. 'Oh yes, gentleman! Bless you, gentleman! Lord bless the Parish of St. So-and-So! It feed the hungry, sir, and give drink to the thusty, and it warm them which is cold, so it do, and good luck to the parish of St. So-and-So, and thankee, gentleman!' Elsewhere, a party of pauper nurses were at dinner. 'How do YOU get on?' 'Oh pretty well, sir! We works hard, and we lives hard – like the sodgers!'

Practice examination questions *(continued)*

AQA B Unit 1

Great Expectations – **Charles Dickens**

(a) How does Dickens tell the story in Chapter 1?

(b) How does the past shape the future in *Great Expectations*?

AQA B Unit 3

Tess of the D'Urbervilles – **Thomas Hardy**

To what extent is the pastoral setting an important element in the overall effectiveness of the novel?

Edexcel Unit 1

Pride and Prejudice (Penguin Classics) and either *French Lieutenant's Woman* (Vintage) or *The Yellow Wallpaper* (Virago)

'*Pride and Prejudice* is essentially a novel about the individual asserting their right to be individual.'

(a) Explore the ways in which writers present the struggle for individuality in their novels.

In your response, you should focus on *Pride and Prejudice* to establish your argument and you should refer to the second text you have read to support and develop your line of argument.

OCR Unit 1

Thomas Hardy: *Tess of the D'Urbervilles*

Tess says, 'My life looks as if it had been wasted for want of chances!'

In the light of this remark, explore ways in which Hardy presents Tess's life as being 'wasted' in Tess of the D'Urbervilles.

CCEA Unit AS 2

Thomas Hardy: *The Mayor of Casterbridge*

Henchard's downfall is largely a result of his inability to embrace change.

With reference to appropriately selected parts of the novel, and **relevant external contextual information**, give your response to the above view.

10 Creative reading and writing

The following topics are covered in this chapter:

- **What examiners are looking for**
- **Transformational writing**
- **Reviews, pitches and talks**
- **Short stories, non-fiction prose and scripts**
- **Commentaries**

10.1 What examiners are looking for

LEARNING SUMMARY	**After studying this section, you should be able to:**
	- understand how creative reading and writing fits into your studies
	- understand what examiners want to see in your creative reading and writing

How does creative reading and writing fit into your course?

AQA A **U 2**
AQA B **U 2**
Edexcel **U 2, 4**
OCR   **U 2**
WJEC   **U 2**
CCEA   **AS U1**

Assessment Objective (AO) 1 asks that students 'articulate **creative**, informed and relevant responses to literary texts, using … coherent, accurate written expression'. The wording of this AO is interpreted in many ways by different exam boards. In normal usage, creative means imaginative or inventive. Most exam boards equate a 'creative' response to a text with one which is personal, and – to some degree – original. This kind of response is expected from a good student in the context of an AS or A-Level answer, so this part of the AO can be considered during the marking of any task.

However, all the exam boards take the meaning of creative a step further, and either require students to produce a piece of original creative writing, or give them the option of doing so. Such writing is often referred to as 're-creative', meaning that you are expected to take an existing text as a starting point for writing something of your own. In some specifications the existing text will be a set text. In others you are given a fairly free choice of texts, possibly within a given genre or period.

How closely you are required to tie your piece of writing to the original depends on the exam board. Some tasks ask for a piece of writing (for example, a review or scripted talk) specifically about the chosen text. Others might ask you to re-tell part of your text from the point of view of a particular character. There are also units where the original writing can be quite loosely related to the chosen text in terms of themes or style. Most, but not all, tasks ask for a commentary, in which you make explicit the connections between your writing and the stimulus text. Whether or not you write a commentary, the examiners and moderators want to see evidence that you have studied, understood and appreciated the stimulus text.

> **KEY POINT**
>
> A creative response is essentially a response that is imaginative and inventive. This kind of response can take many different forms.

What the examiners want to see in your creative reading and writing

AQA A **U 2**	
AQA B **U 2**	
Edexcel **U 2, 4**	
OCR **U 2**	
WJEC **U 2**	
CCEA **AS U1**	

All the creative reading and writing units are centre-assessed, and most of them form part of a folder of work that also includes a more conventional essay. However, there are many differences between the specifications, and you should make sure that you are familiar with the demands of your own specification before embarking on a creative response.

Below is a summary of the requirements of the units that include a creative response. (Chapter 12 also includes details of these units, within the framework of overall coursework requirements – see pages 283–285.)

AQA A

Unit 2 Creative Study

1. Optional.
2. Creative/transformational writing, for example writing in role as a character from the stimulus text.
3. One of two pieces in a folder.
4. There is no specific word count for the creative piece, but the total word count for the folder is 2000–2500 words.

AQA B

Unit 2 Dramatic Genres

1. Optional.
2. Either on a Shakespeare play or on an aspect of the dramatic/tragic genre.
3. Creative/transformational writing, for example writing in role as a character from the stimulus text.
4. One of two pieces of coursework.
5. Must include a commentary.
6. The word count for the creative piece is 1200–1500 words.

Edexcel

Unit 2 Explorations in Drama

1. Compulsory.
2. Based on a play by Shakespeare, or another play written between 1300 and 1800.
3. Writing about the chosen text in the form of a review, a pitch, a scripted talk, etc.
4. One of two tasks.
5. The approximate word count is 500 words.

Unit 4 Reflections in Literary Studies

1. Optional.
2. Based on one or more texts – poetry, prose or drama.
3. In the form of a script for a talk/review/pitch, etc.
4. Commentary included.
5. Total word count (including commentary) is 2500–3000 words.
6. Most of the marks are given for the commentary.

OCR

Unit 2 Literature post-1900

1. Optional.
2. Based on a selected passage of a chosen text (prose or poetry), which must be included with the work.
3. One of two tasks.
4. Must include a commentary.
5. The maximum word count for the folder is 3000 words.

WJEC

Unit 2 Prose Study and Creative Reading

1. Compulsory.
2. Response to wider reading of prose.
3. In a specific genre (short story, autobiography, life writing, drama script, collection of poems, travel writing).
4. One of two tasks.
5. Includes commentary.
6. The word count is 750 words for the original writing and 750 words for the commentary.

CCEA

Unit 1 The Study of Drama

1. Compulsory.
2. Response to the study of twentieth-century drama.
3. Must make connections between two playwrights from a list.
4. The word count is a maximum of 1500 words.

10.2 Transformational writing

LEARNING SUMMARY

After studying this section, you should be able to:

- understand how to write in an existing character's voice
- write diary entries or letters in a character's voice
- script conversations between two or more characters
- write obituaries or articles about a character

Writing in a character's voice

AQA A	**U 2**
AQA B	**U 2**
Edexcel	**U 4**
OCR	**U 2**
CCEA	**AS U1**

One of the most popular ways of 'transforming' an existing text is to write a version of events from the point of view of a chosen character (not, obviously, the existing narrator). Giving a voice to a character whose point of view is not often heard can be very effective, enabling you to show your understanding of the text, while offering an entertaining piece of original writing.

Sources of inspiration

You might choose to give a voice to a character who you feel is seen entirely from the protagonist's point of view and is not fully developed – perhaps one of Dickens' more delicate women, or a servant in a Shakespeare play. You could try writing a self-justifying monologue for a villain or other disreputable character, such as Iago in *Othello* or Wickham in *Pride and Prejudice*.

Quite a few successful novels and stories have been inspired by this idea. Perhaps the most famous is Jean Rhys' *The Wide Sargasso Sea*, which recreates the story of Bertha Rochester – the 'mad woman in the attic' in *Jane Eyre* – imagining her background in the Caribbean and her love affair with Rochester. Tom Stoppard created a comic version of *Hamlet* as seen through the eyes of two minor characters, in his play *Rosencrantz and Guildenstern Are Dead*. Reading either or both of these texts – and any other similarly inspired works you can find – will help your preparation for writing your own piece.

Monologues

The most straightforward and often most effective way of giving a voice to your character is in a **monologue**, where the character speaks directly to the reader or listener. You can approach a monologue in two ways. You can think of it as an 'interior monologue', imagining that you are inside the character's head, recording his or her thoughts. Or you can imagine that your character is speaking to someone, perhaps a friend or an interviewer, who does not interrupt. The latter tends to be the approach taken when a monologue is written to be performed.

Perhaps the best available examples of monologues are in Alan Bennett's collection, *Talking Heads*. A study of these short pieces, written originally for television, can be very helpful. Bennett creates a series of very distinct voices, using diction and speech patterns appropriate to the individual character's age, class and regional background. The characters talk informally, as though chatting to a friend. However, they are not always completely honest to us, or even to themselves. Nevertheless, as they tell their stories, they gradually and unwittingly tell us more about themselves than perhaps they intend to.

When planning your own monologue, you should ensure that you have a **thorough understanding of the character** that is portrayed in the original text. There may be very little to go on, so you will need to fill in some of the details about his or her background, tastes and opinions. A good way of doing this is to use 'hot seating'. Begin by making notes on what you think you know about your character. Then ask another student to 'interview' you in role, asking you a range of questions.

Here are some examples of the kinds of questions your 'interviewer' may want to ask you:
- How old are you?
- Where were you born?
- What was your childhood like?
- How did you meet x?
- What do you think of y?
- Why did you do what you did?
- How do you feel now that it's all over?

It might help if your 'interviewer' also asks you some less obvious, and apparently irrelevant, questions:
- Where do you do your shopping?
- Where did you last go on holiday?
- Do you think education should be compulsory?
- What sports do you like, and why?
- Who is your favourite judge on *The X Factor,* and why?

Answering these kinds of questions can help you to put flesh on the bones of your character. When you know his or her tastes, opinions and feelings, you will find it easier to speak in his/her voice.

Next, try to establish how the character would speak. Start by looking at any occasions in the original text when he or she is given a voice. Look at the character's diction – colloquialisms, slang, dialect, specialised vocabulary – even swear words and obscenities. Also consider whether he or she has unusual ways of putting words together, or habits such as the use of catch phrases, clichés, malapropisms, or linguistic tics such as 'um' and 'er'. Some characters might adjust their speech patterns according to their listener and situation. For example, a servant might be over-formal with his master, but slip into dialect when speaking to other servants. So, if your character is going to be talking to a particular person, you will need to establish the identity of that person.

Your question might specify that you should try to capture the style and tone of the original (this style of question is recommended by AQA), in which case you need to pay particular attention to the diction and speech mannerisms of the character in the original text. Other questions, however, will give you more freedom. It is unlikely, for instance, that you will be expected to reproduce the style of Shakespeare – an attempt at doing so may not be successful, unless you are aiming for a comic pastiche! In these cases you might be better giving your persona a modern voice, perhaps using the occasional quotation from the text, but focusing on how your persona might speak if he or she were alive today.

Even though there is only one voice heard, you should **consider other characters**. As we have mentioned above, if your character is talking directly to someone else, that person's identity will make a difference to both what the speaker says, and how he or she speaks. If your character is going to be talking to a complete stranger, you might feel the need to explain certain aspects of your story, as in this example.

> Well, you can imagine my surprise when it turned out that it was Hamlet who killed Polonius. Apparently there was no doubt about it. Gertrude told me. She was there.

On the other hand, if you were talking to Gertrude, she would already know about this, so you might say something like the following.

> It must have been a terrible shock for you. Your own son! But what's always puzzled me is what Polonius was doing behind the arras in the first place.

In both the examples, the same incident is referred to. The first assumes no prior knowledge, while the second implies a shared experience.

Your character's tone and speech patterns might also differ according to the audience. Think about the relative status of the speaker and the listener. Are you speaking with authority, or are you in awe of the listener? Are you trying to impress your listener, perhaps by using an over-formal register, or are you on very easy terms, in which case you are more likely to use colloquialisms and slang?

You will need to refer to other characters within your monologue. This is your chance to give a new, imaginative perspective on them, while revealing more about your speaker's attitudes and values. You could comment overtly on their actions and personalities, as in this example.

> Personally, I think Polonius deserved everything he got. Always interfering in other people's business and far too full of himself. After all, he was nothing more than a jumped-up secretary.

Here, the writer is giving what some people might consider a fair assessment of Polonius' character. At the same time, we might think that the speaker is heartless and perhaps jealous of Polonius. You could even quote from the text, adding your character's gloss on the original words.

> It's all very well going on about 'neither a lender nor a borrower be', but he never needed a loan, did he? He never knew what it was like to be an unemployed butler with no references. Well, there was no one left to give us references was there? They were all dead. And this Fortinbras chap just brought in his own people, as they always do. Norwegians! What do they know about silver service?

Time and place are also important considerations when planning a monologue. Think about exactly when your monologue is taking place – at a given point during the story, at several different points in the story, or some time (how long?) after the end of the story? The timing of the monologue will determine how much your character knows about the events and characters of the text. If it is a 'long view' from many years after the events, your character might know as much as – if not more than – we do. If it is a view from within the time-frame of the text, you will have to consider what has happened so far, and how much your character is likely to know.

Consider where the monologue is taking place (whether it is an interior monologue or a speech to a listener). Is the monologue going to happen in or near a place where some of the action of the original takes place, for example the butler's pantry at Elsinore? Or is it going to be in a variety of places (on the beach, in the great hall, in a cell)? Alternatively, is it going to be in an imagined place that might even be anachronistic (a newspaper office or a job centre)?

Diaries and letters

AQA A	**U 2**
AQA B	**U 2**
Edexcel	**U 4**
OCR	**U 2**
CCEA	**AS U1**

Examiners have commented recently on how disappointing many submissions in the form of diaries and letters have been. Their main concern is that there is a tendency to simply re-tell the story of the original text. However, you should not disregard these forms altogether. The personal, confessional nature of diary writing can bring to life events seen by the writer with great immediacy, and give an opportunity for the writer to reflect.

Sources of inspiration

Popular examples of the diary genre include real diaries published after the writer's death, such as *The Diary of Anne Frank*, and works of fiction, such as *The Diary of a Nobody* by George and Weedon Grossmith, and Sue Townsend's *The Diary of Adrian Mole*. Similarly, there have been many successful collections of real letters, such as Helen Hanff's *84 Charing Cross Road*, as well as eighteenth-century 'epistolary' novels like Richardson's *Clarissa*. Novelists have also made use of letters within other narrative forms to shed light on the actions and motives of various characters, and reveal information previously unknown to the narrator. Jane Austen's novels use letters particularly effectively.

How to write a successful creative response in diary form

The way to avoid examiners commenting that you are simply re-telling the story is to **focus on your persona's feelings and responses**. If you keep a diary, it is probably less an account of what happened to you during the day, and more a vehicle for explaining your reactions to those events, and your feelings about people and issues. By all means use the story of your stimulus text to provide a structure for your diary, but try to mention events which happen in the text very briefly, as a reference point. Here is an example.

> Last night I asked the doctor to stay up with me and observe the Queen sleep-walking. He was reluctant at first – I think he thought I was exaggerating – but after he saw what happened he had to admit I had cause for worry. He thinks that by constantly trying to wash imaginary blood from her hands she might be trying to wash away her sins. This got me thinking, and I've come to a conclusion which I am afraid even to write here.

This passage, from a diary entry by Lady Macbeth's gentlewoman, provides an interpretation of the 'sleep-walking' scene, and also an insight into how it might have affected the minor character who witnesses it. A less successful version might read something like this.

> Last night I asked the doctor to stay up with me and observe the Queen sleep-walking. She came downstairs in her nightdress and started washing her hands over and over again. We heard her say 'Out, damned spot!' He thinks she has a guilty conscience and was probably involved in Duncan's murder.

The second example adds little to our understanding of the themes or characters of the play, merely putting a part of the story into new words.

You should have noticed a difference in style between the first diary entry and the extracts from the monologue. Essentially, it is the difference between spoken and written language. The monologue is written as if the person were speaking spontaneously to us. Generally speaking, a diary entry is more considered and, therefore, more formal. However, this is not always the case. Some diaries, such as *The Diary of Adrian Mole*, are very informal and full of colloquialisms.

When embarking on writing diary entries, you need to consider the various ways in which different people make use of their diaries. Some use them to scribble down fairly random thoughts about their experiences. Others use them as a form of 'confession'. Some people, such as politicians, may write them with one eye on future publication. These factors will influence the tone and style of your diary entries. For example, if your persona is thinking about publication, the diary might well include a lot of self-justification and self-promotion. In a 'confessional' type diary, on the other hand, examiners would expect to see a more honest appraisal of the character's role.

How to write a successful creative response in letter form

If you decide to write letters as your creative response, there is another factor to consider – the **identity of the recipient**. You will by now be very familiar with 'purpose and audience', concepts that you probably met frequently at GCSE level.

The degree of formality of your letters and the kind of language you use depend on purpose and audience:

- In terms of your **audience**, are you writing to a friend, a relative, an acquaintance, or a complete stranger? In this context, it is likely that your audience is a character or characters from your stimulus text, so the nature of your persona's relationship with them will have been established in the text. However, you might decide to write to someone who is only mentioned briefly in the text, or even invent a new character of your own.
- In terms of your **purpose**, are you writing to inform the other person about something, to explain things, or perhaps to ask for something?
- In terms of **language** and **tone**, is this a formal letter – for example, a letter to a powerful person asking for a favour – or an informal one – maybe a love letter? The kind of language you use depends not only on the identity of your character, but also on the identity of the recipient, and the content of the letter.

It is unlikely that you will just write one letter, so think about whether you want your collection of letters to be a series of letters from one person to another, a collection of letters between two people (perhaps showing a developing relationship), a collection of letters sent by one person to a number of recipients, or a collection of letters from various correspondents to a single recipient. Each of these choices creates different challenges to overcome and different opportunities.

> **KEY POINT**
>
> When writing in the form of a diary or letter, think carefully about **FLAP** – Form, Language, Audience and Purpose.

> **PROGRESS CHECK**
>
> Read a published diary or collection of letters (fiction or non-fiction) that you have not previously read.

Scripted conversations

AQA A	U 2
AQA B	U 2
Edexcel	U 4
OCR	U 2
CCEA	AS U1

If you are interested in drama, and feel that you can write convincing and effective dialogue, it is worth thinking about writing a short script. This form has been recommended by CCEA and, although other exam boards have not had much to say about it, it can fulfil the requirements of their specifications.

Choosing the right characters

If you are planning to write a scripted conversation, the first thing to do is choose your characters carefully. For the purposes of CCEA Unit 1, it is recommended that you choose two characters – one character from each of two plays you have studied. You are advised to choose characters with contrasting views, attitudes and backgrounds, in order to give you potential for dramatic conflict. You should think about where, how and why these two people might meet. If the plays are set in similar times and places, your setting might plausibly fit into both of the plays. On the other hand, you might prefer to give them an unlikely – even incongruous – setting.

Giving your characters a 'voice'

One of the most important aspects of writing dialogue is giving your characters distinctive 'voices'. If you are using existing characters you need to study the original carefully, just as you would when writing a monologue, in order to capture their diction and speech patterns. A good test of whether you have done this successfully is to delete or cover up the character names in the script, give it to someone else to read, and ask the reader if he or she can tell which character is speaking just by reading the dialogue.

The focus of your scripted conversation

You will also need, of course, to decide what the characters will talk about.

If the two plays you are studying have similar themes, you could pick an issue for them to discuss, perhaps using incidents from each play to back up the points being made. Alternatively, you could 'import' a character from one play into the situation of another. For example, you could imagine that Abigail Williams from Arthur Miller's *The Crucible* had been invited to the dinner party in Caryl Churchill's *Top Girls*, and been challenged to justify her actions by Joan of Arc!

For exam boards other than CCEA, this kind of fantasy meeting of characters is not appropriate, as their creative reading and writing units are not based on the study of two plays. However, you might want to create a situation in which two characters from your text meet after the end of their story, for example, or in which a character from the text is being interviewed by a character of your own invention.

If you would like to write a script but are unsure about whether your exam board would welcome it, ask your teacher or lecturer to enquire on your behalf. Exam boards are happy to respond to queries like this.

> **KEY POINT**
>
> Scripts can provide opportunities for exploring similarities and differences between characters from existing texts.

Obituaries and other articles

AQA A	**U 2**
AQA B	**U 2**
Edexcel	**U 4**
OCR	**U 2**
CCEA	**AS U1**

You might decide not to write in your character's own voice. You may prefer to write a third person narrative – the sort of thing that might be found in an article about the character, or even an obituary (an article about someone who has recently died).

This form is clearly not suitable for questions that ask you to imitate the style of the original text, but it can show your understanding of themes, issues and characters from the text.

Factors to consider

Here are the main factors to think about if you are considering writing a third person narrative:

- Before you embark on your article, decide what **form** it will take. It could be an obituary, an article based on an interview with the subject, or a critical appraisal of the character's career to date, drawing on all available information.
- Decide what sort of publication your article is written for – for instance, a broadsheet newspaper, or a celebrity magazine. What is its **audience**?
- What is the **purpose** of the article? Is it meant to be a serious appraisal of a public figure, or is it the sort of article often found in magazines that seek to promote the career of a celebrity? If it is an obituary, is it meant to eulogise its subject, or offer a balanced view on his or her achievements?
- When you write your article or obituary, you will be adopting the persona of a journalist. Think about who you want to be – a young, ambitious political journalist, a gossip columnist, a campaigner with an axe to grind, a satirical writer, or a toadying sycophant?
- The **language** you use will depend on all the above.

When choosing your approach, you should consider the demands of the specification. You need to demonstrate 'coherent, accurate' written expression (see AO1 on page 235). Some forms, such as the celebrity magazine interview (with its short sentences and paragraphs, limited vocabulary, and reliance on direct speech) might be rather limiting. This problem could be overcome by writing two articles on the same subject for different publications, which will demonstrate your understanding of the forms and your own versatility as a writer.

> **KEY POINT**
>
> Transformational writing is not necessarily empathetic first person writing. It can take the form of an article written by an outsider.

> **PROGRESS CHECK**
>
> Try to find two articles about someone who is in the news – one from a broadsheet and the other from a tabloid – and compare the tone and style of the articles.

10.3 Reviews, pitches and talks

LEARNING SUMMARY

After studying this section, you should be able to:

- plan and write a theatre review
- plan and write a pitch, proposal or treatment
- plan and script a talk

An overview

Edexcel **U2, 4**
OCR **U2**
CCEA **AS U1**

Reviews, pitches and talks are examples of re-creative writing which have more in common with traditional analytical essays than the forms discussed in the previous section. They are recommended by Edexcel for Unit 2, and it may be possible to use them in other units. As with all coursework tasks, it is advisable for your teacher or lecturer to check with your exam board before you start work on these forms.

Reviews

Edexcel **U2,4**
OCR   **U2**
CCEA   **AS U1**

Reviews are particularly appropriate if you are studying a play and have seen a live production, although you could also review a film or television version of your text, or perhaps even a book. In this section we will focus on theatre reviews, though most of the discussion applies to all reviews.

Theatre reviews

Theatre reviews have several purposes:
- They inform readers about new productions.
- They try to persuade readers of a point of view.
- They entertain readers.

Theatre critics can be very influential. Readers look at their reviews to help them decide whether to buy tickets to see a show. A person may trust a particular critic, with whose views he or she usually concurs, or may read a variety of reviews and weigh them up before deciding whether to see a play.

As with other re-creative tasks, the main pitfall you must avoid in a theatre review is 'telling the story'. Some poor reviews do little more than this, perhaps adding one or two comments about actors' performances. A good review gives you a certain amount of information about the play – perhaps including a brief synopsis or partial synopsis of the plot – but goes on to evaluate the production in some detail.

Aspects of a production that a reviewer might comment on include:
- script
- direction
- acting
- design.

Reviews can be entirely positive, or entirely negative, or somewhere in between. However, a 'rave review' – which tells the reader how wonderful everything about the production is, using strings of superlatives, but lacking in analysis – might not be suitable for the purposes of A-Level coursework. Equally, a damning review that simply sneers at the production and seeks only to amuse the reader would probably not work. There is nothing wrong with having strong feelings, but, whatever your feelings are (and readers of reviews want to know what the critics really think), you should acknowledge both good and bad aspects, support all the points you make with evidence, and try to present a well-structured and convincing argument.

Before starting your review, you need to think about what kind of publication you are going to write it for. Do you want to write a review for a broadsheet, such as *The Times* or *The Guardian*, for a tabloid like *The Daily Mirror*, or for a more academic specialised publication, such as *New Theatre Quarterly*? Look at examples of all of these to help you decide. A single tabloid-style review would probably not enable you to fulfil the criteria for high marks, but you might want to write a tabloid and a broadsheet review for the same production. You might also consider writing two contrasting reviews.

Here is a theatre review by critic Charles Spencer, taken from *Telegraph.co.uk*.
Spencer is reviewing a theatre production of the Arthur Miller play, *All My Sons*.

Sometimes cavilling criticism must fall silent and this is one such occasion.

Over the years I have sometimes denigrated Arthur Miller, the self-proclaimed 'impatient moralist' who often delivers his message like a preacher in his pulpit.

After watching Howard Davies's magnificent revival of All My Sons (1947), however, such carping seems like a mouse squeaking at a mighty giant.

This is a play of extraordinary power and emotional depth, and when it is performed as wonderfully as it is here, Miller's theme of man's responsibility towards his fellow men feels genuinely noble rather than merely didactic.

It is also urgently topical. Watching this story of a manufacturer who condemned 21 young pilots to their deaths in the Second World War by knowingly supplying their planes with faulty cylinder heads, one can't help but be reminded of allegations that our Forces in Afghanistan have been inadequately equipped by the Government.

In the present climate of political optimism and honesty, one feels that David Cameron should insist that his entire Cabinet sees this play, and be reminded with such thrilling dramatic force that truth matters, and deceit has terrible consequences.

But I'm in danger of making the show sound worthy, when in fact it exerts the hypnotic force of a first-rate thriller as the noose of truth slowly tightens on its tragic hero, Joe Keller. There is the inevitability of Greek tragedy about All My Sons but it also elicits gasps of surprise from the audience as the truth slowly emerges.

It is also profoundly moving. Last night I even spotted a hardened fellow critic weeping.

Davies creates an atmosphere of ominous unease right from the start, with a thrilling storm scene on William Dudley's beautifully realised garden design, complete with real grass and great fronds of willows.

We are in the backyard of the Kellers, one of whose sons went missing in the Second World War and whose surviving boy, Chris, now wants to marry his brother's former sweetheart.

His mother is implacably opposed to the marriage, refusing to believe, three years on, that her beloved Larry is dead. If she admits that, she will have to admit a great deal more.

The superbly constructed plot progresses inexorably and the play is brilliantly persuasive on the way the human mind and heart can know a dark truth and yet still somehow deny it.

The great David Suchet has never been better than he is here as the initially jovial Joe Keller, who seems to shrink within his own body as the chickens come home to roost.

His gathering desperation and guilt is at times almost too painful to watch.

Zoë Wanamaker is also outstanding as his wife, clenched with grief and driven almost mad by the lie on which her life is based, and there is terrific support from Stephen Campbell Moore as the honourable surviving son and Jemima Roper as the girlfriend who delivers the coup de grace.

This is a stunning production of a modern classic and one that those who see it will never forget.

'All My Sons at the Apollo Theatre, review' by Charles Spencer, Telegraph.co.uk

COMMENTARY

This theatre review starts with a sentence designed to hook and intrigue the reader. The critic assumes a certain amount of knowledge on the reader's part – Arthur Miller is so well known that the critic can assume theatre goers know something about him. He uses rhetorical and literary devices for impact (alliteration and simile), and quotes from Miller himself. Most importantly, he claims not to be a fan of Miller's work before nailing his colours to the mast and declaring the play to be 'wonderful'. In this way he might persuade readers who also find Miller's work unsympathetic to read on, intrigued by the critic's conversion, and perhaps willing also to be converted.

By linking the play to current events, he tries to make the play relevant to his readers. They may feel that a play written about the Second World War is of no interest to them. They may also resist Miller's 'preaching'. The critic is writing for *The Telegraph*, a newspaper which consistently supports the Conservative party and whose readers might feel that the left-wing Miller has nothing to say to them. Although some might feel that the parallel to Afghanistan is disingenuous and does not stand up to scrutiny, that – and the flattering reference to Cameron – could be seen as 'softening up' the readers.

Spencer goes on to put the play in context in terms of genre, with his references to thrillers and Greek tragedy. He also considers potential audience response, showing an awareness that theatre has as much to do with emotions as with ideas.

He then goes on to discuss the contribution of individuals to the whole, starting by giving the director credit for creating an appropriate atmosphere, and continuing with a brief but relevant reference to the designer. This leads him to mention (briefly) how the plot is set up, praising the play's structure and focusing on one of its main themes.

The critic then considers the performances of four actors. They are all praised but to different degrees. Note that their performances are criticised in terms of their interpretation of the characters they play and the function of those characters. He does not simply tell us that Suchet's performance is 'great', but mentions his physical interpretation of the character ('… seems to shrink within his own body …'), and refers to the character's growing 'desperation and guilt'.

Spencer concludes with a resounding endorsement of the production, leaving us in no doubt that he would like us to see it, and that he has more than overcome his personal prejudice against Miller.

This is an excellent example of a real review of a production of a well-known play. For the purposes of coursework, you might want to develop your points in greater detail than Spencer does (your word limit is a lot greater than his will have been). You might also wish to quote directly from the play, analysing the actors' and the director's interpretations of key moments in the play, and perhaps even comparing the production you are reviewing to others you have seen.

Pitches, proposals and treatments

Edexcel **U2,4**
OCR   **U2**
CCEA   **AS U1**

When a writer has an idea for a radio, television or film script, he or she does not necessarily write a complete script before submitting it to a potential producer. In fact, established writers never write scripts 'on spec'. Instead, they try to sell their ideas to producers in order to gain commissions. Only when they have secured a deal, or at least some degree of interest, will they start work on a script.

Ideas are presented in various ways and these forms are given various names, among them pitch, proposal and treatment. Basically, these are short documents (although in the case of film, a 'treatment' can be quite lengthy and detailed) that outline the main features of the proposed programme or film, and attempt to sell the idea to the commissioner. They do tell the story, because a strong story is the most important thing to producers, but they do a lot more than that. Essentially, they are marketing tools.

How to put a pitch together

Pitches feature among the forms suggested by Edexcel for re-creative writing. You may be able to use the form for OCR or CCEA, but please check with the exam board before starting.

If you do decide to write a pitch, it will need to be related fairly closely to a text or texts you are studying for the unit. It might be a pitch for an adaptation of your text, possibly transferring it to another time or another culture. There have recently been successful television series of updated Shakespeare plays, and stories from Chaucer's *The Canterbury Tales*. There have also been a number of popular Hollywood films based on literary texts, such as *Clueless* (a version of Jane Austen's *Emma*) and *Ten Things I Hate About You* (adapted from Shakespeare's *The Taming of the Shrew*). Some of these are based loosely around themes and characters from the original texts, while others stick very closely to their sources.

There are a number of factors you should consider when putting your pitch together:
- **Title** – try to find a good snappy title, perhaps one that recalls the original in some way, or (as in the case of the films mentioned above) one that would appeal to the intended audience.
- **Audience** – think about your intended audience. Do you want to appeal to teenagers and young adults (who form the bulk of the film-going audience), older, educated people who might go to 'art house' films or listen to the radio, or a more general, mass audience, who might watch soaps and detective dramas on television?

- **Plot** – you should outline the main features of the plot, demonstrating a clear story structure (see Chapter 2 for more analysis of story structure), but do not go into too much detail. You might even leave out your climax and resolution to make the reader curious.
- **Characters** – focus on your protagonist, indicating the sort of person he or she is, and how he or she develops during the 'journey'. Mention other major characters. You might want to point out their relationship to characters in the 'original'.
- **Setting** – the reader needs to get a flavour of the setting. As well as explaining where and when it is set, try to convey the mood and atmosphere of the piece.
- **Genre/style** – it is important that you show that you know what kind of piece you want to write. If you can link it to a particular genre or genres (e.g. gothic, pastoral, thriller, fantasy), do so. It can also help to refer to existing programmes/films. The style, as well as the content, of your proposal should reflect the style of the proposed product (ironic, sombre, light-hearted, etc.).
- **Themes** – think about how your story relates to the original in terms of themes and issues. Does it have a 'twist'?

KEY POINT

A pitch, proposal or treatment is a piece of persuasive writing. Your style should reflect this.

PROGRESS CHECK

Using the bullet points above as a guide, make very brief notes on your proposal to check that you have covered all aspects of the idea.

Here is a possible answer, based on *King Lear*:

- **Title** – *Pelican Daughters*.
- **Audience** – young adults/teenagers.
- **Plot** – Ellie, a disabled teenager who has been brought up in children's homes, is trying to find her birth mother. She does not know that her mother has been left penniless and homeless by her wealthy husband, and humiliated by her two successful daughters. Ellie finds her on the brink of despair....
- **Characters** – the protagonist is innocent but gutsy. Her mother is over-privileged and, in her own way, just as naïve. They seem to have nothing in common.
- **Setting** – various locations, urban and rural, throughout Britain.
- **Genre/style** – naturalistic and gritty, but with a fantasy element. Dark humour.
- **Themes** – the focus is on the daughter (Ellie/Cordelia), and 'Lear' is a woman.

Talks

Edexcel **U2,4**
OCR **U2**
CCEA **AS U1**

Your re-creative task could take the form of the script for a talk about your text to a group of people. It could be a talk to other students about your personal views on the text, or a talk where you take on a role, for example of a director discussing a play with a group of actors.

This format is closer to the traditional discursive critical essay than either a review or a pitch, and will give you the opportunity to explore themes and issues, settings, characters, language and context in a fairly analytical way. Nevertheless, you should remember that this task is asking for a creative response and, therefore, should be distinguishable from an essay. To achieve this you should focus on your role, the situation and the audience. You also need to be aware that you are writing something to be spoken, not read.

Taking on a role for your talk

If you are taking on a role for your talk, such as a theatre director, think about why that person would be giving a talk about your text. If you are directing a play, you need to think about when the talk is being given. It would probably be at an early meeting with the actors. You would not know them, and you cannot assume that they will have any detailed knowledge or understanding of the text, although you would expect them to have read it. The actors need to know how you intend to approach the text.

Think about:
- what you consider to be the most important themes and issues in the text
- how you can explain these themes and issues to your cast, perhaps making connections and references that will help them to understand
- whether you are planning to do anything innovative, exciting or eccentric with the text, e.g. setting it in outer space, or having all the men play women and vice versa
- what mood and atmosphere you are seeking to create, and how you plan to do it
- any ideas you would have already discussed with your designer about the set, lighting and sound, and costumes (a real director might have a model of the set and designs to show the actors)
- how you would like the actors to approach their characters, and how you see those characters in relation to the play as a whole
- how you would like the audience to respond
- how you can inspire the actors to share your enthusiasm for the project and give of their best.

Talking to a group about your text

If you are giving a talk to other students or another group, e.g. a book club or an evening class, you should consider:
- how much prior knowledge of the text your audience has, i.e. whether you have all been studying the text together, or if your audience is being introduced to the text for the first time
- what strikes you as the most interesting aspects of the text, and what you think will appeal to them
- how you can make a connection between the concerns of the text, and the concerns of your audience
- how you responded to the text when you read or saw it – on an emotional as much as an intellectual level
- if applicable, how you can convince your audience that it is worth reading and studying.

Tips to help make your talk stand out

Whatever kind of talk you are giving, bear in mind some of the differences between spoken and written texts.

In your talk, you might:
- use colloquialisms, dialect forms and abbreviated forms if appropriate
- use shorter sentences, thinking about when you should pause for breath
- address the audience directly, involving them with the use of the second person pronoun
- use rhetorical devices, such as rhetorical questions, repetition and lists of three
- refer to common experiences and current issues
- try to be friendly, but not patronising
- entertain your audience – make them laugh!

KEY POINT

Talks should be entertaining as well as informative, and should include a strong personal response to your text.

PROGRESS CHECK

If you are planning to script a talk, make brief notes about the identity of your audience, what you think they already know, and what they want to know about the text.

10.4 Short stories, non-fiction prose and scripts

LEARNING SUMMARY

After studying this section, you should be able to:
- understand how to use your stimulus texts
- plan and write short stories or non-fiction prose linked to your wider reading
- plan and write scripts linked to your wider reading

Using your stimulus texts

OCR	U2
WJEC	U2
CCEA	AS U1

This section relates mainly to Unit 2 of the WJEC specification – where the re-creative writing task is linked to wider reading of twentieth-century prose, and the creative piece is marked only against the criteria for AO1. However, you may be able to use these forms for other specifications.

In order to demonstrate that your own creative writing is a response to wider reading, you need first to identify what your stimulus text is. You should choose a well regarded and influential writer and read as much of his or her work as you can. You will need to analyse the work, and identify aspects of style and genre, and the themes that are typical of your writer. You do not need to imitate every aspect of your writer's work – if you do you will end up with a parody rather than an original piece of your own work. Rather, you should think about which aspects of the work appeal to you and inspire you.

If you are reading Ernest Hemingway, for example, you might find that his 'spare' style appeals to you, and would work well in a story about a contemporary issue. F. Scott Fitzgerald, on the other hand, is known for rather lush descriptive passages. This might be more your style. Roddy Doyle's work is characterised by a strong sense of place, reinforced by extensive use of direct speech. You might want to use similar techniques to write about people from the area you are from, rather than Dublin. Angela Carter's adaptations of fairy stories might inspire you to try something similar, with or without the elements of 'magic realism'.

You might want to adapt aspects of your chosen writer's style to another form or genre. For example, you might write about your own life using a style similar to Doyle's *Paddy Clarke Ha Ha Ha*, or you could write an Angela Carter style fantasy in script form.

> **KEY POINT**
>
> You should not try to imitate all aspects of your writer's work. Use aspects of the work to inspire you.

Short stories and non-fiction prose

OCR	**U2**
WJEC	**U2**
CCEA	**AS U1**

Short stories

Short stories need a strong structure. To help you with structuring your work, look again at the discussions about structure in Chapter 2. Your story will, of necessity, be very short, so you should probably not overload it with turning points and crises. Simplicity often works best. You will find many successful short stories focus very clearly on one character and are concerned with an 'epiphany' – a single life changing event.

Before starting to write, think carefully about the following elements:
● What sort of narrator will you use? Will you have a first or third person narrator? Will he/she be omniscient or unreliable?
● If you have a first person narrator, is he or she looking back on events from much later on, or has the story just happened?
● Do you want to write using a distinctive – perhaps regional – voice, or would you prefer to stick to Standard English?
● Who is your protagonist? Make copious notes on him or her, perhaps using 'hot seating' (see page 238). Remember, though, that these notes will not all be used in your story – what you reveal to your reader is only the tip of the iceberg.
● Who or what is your antagonist?
● What does your protagonist want?
● What obstacles will you put in his or her way?
● What other characters do you want to introduce?
● Where and when is the story set?
● Do you intend to describe settings, people, etc. in detail, perhaps using striking and original imagery?
● How is your story ordered? Is it going to be in chronological order, or told in 'flashback'?
● Will you use past or present tense – or a mixture of both?
● Will you use direct speech? (It is usually better to use direct speech sparingly, if at all, but there are always exceptions.)

- Are you writing in a particular genre, such as thriller, romance or horror?
- Will you have a 'twist' at the end?
- Will your ending tie up loose ends neatly, or will it be ambiguous, making the reader think?

Notable short story writers whose work you could study include Katherine Mansfield, O. Henry, Ernest Hemingway, Muriel Spark and Frank O'Connor. There are many more, and also many collections of short stories by different writers. Read as many as you can.

> **KEY POINT**
>
> Successful short stories often centre on an 'epiphany'. Think about how and why your protagonist changes.

> **PROGRESS CHECK**
>
> Read a short story by a well-known writer and make brief notes on it using the short story bullet points for guidance.

Non-fiction prose

Among the other forms recommended by WJEC for its Creative Reading unit are biography, autobiography, journals and travel writing. Although these are all non-fiction, in practice there are not many significant differences between these forms and the short story. Many short stories are based very closely on their writers' personal experiences and are, therefore, barely distinguishable from autobiographical writing.

Whether you are writing about fictional characters, real people or yourself, you need to create a strong structure and interesting characters. If you are thinking about using real events and experiences as the basis for your writing, test your true story against the criteria in the short stories bullet points. It does not have to be an extraordinary story to make a good piece of writing. On the other hand, an exciting experience does not necessarily make a good read. Whether your story works or not is down to your skills as a writer.

Scripts

OCR	**U2**
WJEC	**U2**
CCEA	**AS U1**

If you decide to write a script, you should look for a moment of dramatic conflict that has a transforming effect on your characters. Given the length of the required piece, it is unlikely that you will have many characters – a duologue between a protagonist and an antagonist might be the most effective approach.

Remember that in a script, your ideas and concerns must be expressed primarily through dialogue. There is no opportunity for narrative comment or discussion. Any description of settings or people must be limited to stage directions – avoid the temptation to make these too detailed. Also avoid spending too long setting up your situation. In such a short piece there will be little time for small talk. Get straight to the point.

When planning structure, plot and character, you could ask some of the same questions that you did in relation to short stories and non-fiction prose. Clearly, some of the bullet points are not relevant to scripts. Look back briefly and decide which questions you need to ask before starting to write your script.

People often talk about writers having a 'good ear' for dialogue, as if it is something that comes naturally and cannot be taught. In reality, it is all a matter of listening. If you listen carefully to people who are talking to you – or eavesdrop on other people's conversations – you will start to notice their characteristic speech patterns and be able to reproduce them. A good exercise for scriptwriters is to collect 'overheard voices' – little bits of conversation that they find interesting, intriguing or amusing.

> **PROGRESS CHECK**
>
> Make a note of one or two snippets of overheard conversation a day – but try not to make it too obvious. It is usually better to wait until you get home to make notes, rather than getting a notebook out in front of the people on whom you are eavesdropping!

Here are the main elements that make good **dialogue**:

- Dialogue should be **appropriate** – i.e. it should fit the situation and the characters in terms of place, time, age, background, etc.
- Dialogue should be **natural** – it should sound like real speech. However, if you record real speech, you will often find that you cannot use it in a script, because of hesitations, repetitions, rambling or other things that would make a listener lose interest. So really it's a trick – it sounds as if it's real.
- Dialogue should be **necessary** – do not waste your own and your audience's time with a lot of scene-setting conversations, small talk, greetings, etc. Every word should be there for a reason, whether to advance the plot, tell you something about the character, or shed light on your themes and ideas.
- Dialogue should be **acceptable** – will your dialogue be acceptable to its intended audience? For example, there are certain words and phrases you would not be allowed to use on BBC Radio 4. For the purposes of your coursework, however, this is unlikely to be a consideration.
- Dialogue should be **speakable** – it is very easy to forget that you are writing words that someone has to speak. Beware of writing long and complicated sentences that look fine on the page, but cannot be spoken convincingly and naturally. It is essential to read your work out loud. If possible, ask a couple of friends to read it while you listen.

You could use the above points as a checklist after writing.

> **KEY POINT**
>
> When writing dialogue, remember ANNAS (Appropriate, Natural, Necessary, Acceptable, Speakable).

> **PROGRESS CHECK**
>
> Before starting your own piece, take a short section of your stimulus text and turn it into a script.

10.5 Commentaries

LEARNING SUMMARY

After studying this section, you should be able to:
- appreciate what examiners are looking for in a commentary
- plan and write a commentary more effectively

What examiners are looking for in a commentary

AQA B **U 2**
Edexcel **U 4**
OCR   **U 2**
WJEC   **U 2**

When you are asked to write a commentary to accompany your piece of creative writing, you are usually expected to explore two areas:
1. The creative process that led to the finished piece.
2. The links between your writing and your reading.

It can be quite difficult to explore both of these areas effectively in a short essay and it is important to understand what your exam board is looking for.

How the different specifications approach commentaries

The specifications that require commentaries all have slightly different approaches, and they mark according to different criteria.

AQA B considers all four AOs, giving them equal weight, but awards more marks for the commentary than for the creative writing.

In the commentary, the board wants you to:
- comment on aspects of form, structure and language (AO2)
- make reference to other texts (AO3)
- show awareness of literary and cultural contexts (AO4)
- show how the re-creative process highlights different interpretations of texts (AO3)
- use critical vocabulary effectively (AO1).

Edexcel uses only AO1 and AO4. The criteria for AO1 are used mainly for the creative piece, so for the commentary the emphasis is clearly on context.

To gain high marks, Edexcel requires you to:
- demonstrate confidence and skill in discussing and presenting ideas about texts in context (AO4)
- present an effective and thoughtful interpretation of texts in their contexts, with a clear awareness of how they are received (AO4).

OCR focuses on AO1 and AO2. AO1 provides the criteria for assessing the creative piece, but should not be ignored when writing the commentary.

You should:
- give a creative, informed and relevant response, using appropriate terminology and concepts, and coherent, accurate written expression (AO1)
- demonstrate detailed critical understanding in analysing the ways in which structure, form and language shape meanings in literary texts (AO2).

WJEC marks the commentary according to the criteria for AO2 and AO4.

To gain high marks, you should:
- give a sound analysis and evaluation of writers' techniques (AO2)
- show detailed critical understanding of texts, with increasingly confident handling of implicit meanings (AO2)
- make specific connections between texts and contexts (AO4)
- show sound, confident appreciation of the significance and influence of relevant contexts (AO4).

KEY POINT

Your commentary should complement your creative work, illuminating the work itself and its relationship with your stimulus text.

PROGRESS CHECK

Make sure that you are fully familiar with the mark scheme for the unit you are doing.

Planning and writing your commentary

AQA B	U 2
Edexcel	U 4
OCR	U 2
WJEC	U 2

Given the differences between the demands of the specifications, it is quite difficult to give general advice about writing a commentary. However, there are certain things you should try to do whatever specification you are studying.

Conveying a personal response

You should try to convey a personal response to your reading and show how it inspired your writing – what was it about the text that you found stimulating and made you want to write what you wrote? It could be a particular theme (for example, domestic violence in *The Woman Who Walked Into Doors*), a distinctive use of setting (as in *Trainspotting*) or language (*A Clockwork Orange*), or perhaps a character you wanted to explore (Julia in *1984*). It could be a combination of these elements, or none of them. What was it about the text that appealed to you personally?

How to approach similarities and differences

Show clearly what the links and similarities are between the stimulus and your piece. Have you perhaps used a similar setting in terms of place or time? *1984* could have inspired you to write about what life might be like in the future, or perhaps about life in the real 1984. You might, like Antony Burgess, have invented your own specialised vocabulary. Try to be precise in making links, referring in detail to form, structure and language.

You should also, of course, discuss the differences between the two texts, and the reasons for the differences. Often this will link to context. If you have decided to use the story of *King Lear*, say, but transfer it to a contemporary setting, many of the differences will flow from this decision. Clearly, your language will be updated, but you might decide to retain the use of verse. You might retain the relationships between the characters, but change their social status, their ages or their genders.

In an examiners' report, WJEC pointed out that many candidates struggle to discuss the context of their own work, perhaps because they have chosen to set their pieces in times and places they are unfamiliar with (usually America). Writers are often advised to 'write about what they know'. Following that advice could make the writing of your commentary a lot easier.

When making comparisons, be aware that you are expected to analyse your own work as well as the stimulus text. The main focus is on your work, so it is probably best to approach the commentary as a critique of your piece, with comparisons to the stimulus text being made in order to illuminate the reader's understanding of your work.

Using terminology effectively

Apply critical terminology to both texts, but remember that you need to explain how and why you have used particular techniques. For instance, it is not enough to say something like 'Like Fitzgerald, I used pathetic fallacy'. As the following example illustrates, you need to show that you understand both Fitzgerald's technique and how you have used it.

> While Fitzgerald uses pathetic fallacy to warn us of what is to come in Nicole and Dick's relationship – the storm in the mountains conveying something of its excitement as well as its destructiveness – the storm in my piece (this time over an urban landscape) reflects the state of mind of the protagonist – his anger, his isolation and his frustration.

This passage analyses both a key moment from *Tender is the Night*, and a key moment from the writer's own work, drawing attention to both similarities and differences.

A reminder of the purpose of a commentary

Above all, remember that your commentary gives you a chance to explore the process of writing your piece. It is about what you did, how you did it, and why you did it. Writing is a process of asking questions, developing ideas, making decisions and overcoming problems. The assessor will read your piece and want to know how it came into being.

KEY POINT

Your commentary describes a creative process. It should be honest, reflective and illuminating.

PROGRESS CHECK

When you have written a draft of your commentary, check that you have covered the points above.

Exemplar response to a creative reading and writing task (AQA B)

As detailed at the start of the chapter, creative reading and writing is always internally assessed, so we have not included a sample question and model answer, or practice examination questions for this chapter.

Instead, we have provided two extracts from a dramatic monologue that give a contemporary voice to Malcolm from *Macbeth*, and two extracts from the commentary. This is the type of task favoured by AQA specification B, and is assessed using all four AOs.

Extracts from the dramatic monologue

AO1: The vocabulary is appropriate to the character created. The candidate has re-imagined Malcolm as a modern politician. He speaks informally but uses rhetorical tricks – questions, repetition, clichéd images. There is a clear focus on the task. The content of the two extracts shows an understanding of Malcolm's role in the play.

I know it might have looked cowardly. But I can assure you it wasn't done out of panic or fear, although my brother might have thought so. The thing is, I made the decision. I didn't have time to go into all the reasons. I just told him to take himself off to Ireland, out of the way. I knew exactly what I was doing. Yes, I was worried that the thanes might have thought I was responsible; after all, my father had named me as his heir. And I knew that one of them must have committed the crime. Did I suspect Macbeth? Of course I did. Did I have any proof that he did it? Frankly, no. So any idea that I could have confronted him with his actions and wrested the crown from him is ludicrous. I knew he was the stronger at the time. I made a cool, logical and, as it turned out, correct decision to go to England. Not 'flee'. I've never 'flown' from anything in my life. I went to England because I had a plan ...

AO2: The text shows a detailed and quite sophisticated use of features of form and structure, including rhetorical devices and varied sentence structures, as well as a clear structure for the whole, which takes a number of key moments from the play and gives us Malcolm's version of them.

Shall I be brutally honest? It's a mess. The whole bloody country's a mess. It will take years to recover from the devastation caused by that butcher - I can't even bring myself to say his name - and his fiend-like wife. I realise I'm using strong language. I realise that some eyebrows might be raised at my lack of diplomacy but, to be frank, there are times when diplomacy goes out of the window. Standing here now, before my people, the people of the country I love, I could weep. But I will not weep. I will work. I will work tirelessly, day and night, to restore this country to prosperity and to greatness, to restore the Scotland of your fathers and of mine.

Exemplar response to a creative reading and writing task (AQA B) *(continued)*

AO2: Here, the writer → explores 'key aspects of form and structure' and how they shape meaning by discussing the structure of *Macbeth*, focusing on the end of the play and by relating his own use of modern rhetoric to Malcolm's speech in *Macbeth*.
AO3: The discussion of Malcolm's role in the play shows an appreciation of the conventions of Shakespearean tragedy. The candidate also shows awareness of other texts and possible ambiguity.
AO4: Both the literary context of *Macbeth* as a tragedy and the modern political context are explored.

Extracts from the commentary

I chose Malcolm as my `voice' initially because his final speech reminded me of the way modern politicians speak when they come to power, promising new hope and reconciliation. I was aware that Shakespeare's tragedies often include a figure like Malcolm who comes in at the end to take over the country - Fortinbras in `Hamlet' and Albany in `King Lear' are other examples - but these characters often seem little more than convenient dramatic devices. I felt that Malcolm was more interesting, especially because of the ambiguity surrounding his flight to England, and would reward exploration in this form ...

I have tried to make him sound friendly in a slightly false way, trying a little too hard to appear honest and trustworthy. The use of words and phrases like `frankly' and `brutally honest' suggest, paradoxically, that he is not entirely honest. His use of rhetorical questions, which he then answers, is reminiscent of the much-imitated style of Barack Obama. His lengthy justification of his flight to England smacks of being wise after the event. Why, if he acted coolly and logically at the time, would he feel the need to justify his actions to the audience?

11 Approaching unseen texts

The following topics are covered in this chapter:

- Preparing to write about unseen texts
- Question types involving unseen texts
- Writing about unseen poetry
- Writing about unseen prose and drama extracts

11.1 Preparing to write about unseen texts

LEARNING SUMMARY

After studying this section, you should be able to:

- recognise some things you can do to prepare yourself for handling unseen material
- identify techniques that you can use when writing about unseen and unprepared materials

How unseen texts fit into your A-Level course

AQA A	**U 1, 3**
Edexcel	**U 1, 3**
WJEC	**U 4**

Exactly where you will be tested on your ability to write about texts that you have not seen or studied before depends on the particular exam specification that you are studying.

The form that any unseen element of your exam takes can vary a good deal, depending on which specification you are studying. (Some specifications do not have an unseen element.) Unseen elements are not necessarily restricted to poetry, and some may contain a passage from a novel or play. Some specifications are clear to point out that a wide range of text types can be drawn upon, including poetry, prose, drama, extracts from literary criticism, journalism, essays and autobiography.

> Look carefully at the wording of the questions on past papers, and at what they require you to do.

Just as the material itself can vary, so can the kind of questions that you are asked, and it is important that you become very familiar with the particular format that is used on the specification you are studying. Looking at specimen or past papers is essential here.

Approaching questions about unseen texts

Here are some suggestions that may help when you are faced with a question about an unseen text:

- Begin by carefully looking at what the question asks you to do, and identify and highlight the key words and phrases.
- Read the piece through carefully at least twice.
- If you do not understand certain words or phrases or parts of the piece, concentrate on the rest of the text – do not get bogged down in individual words or phrases.

- Remember that whatever poem or passage you encounter, there will be many different aspects of it to comment on.
- Look for any useful information you are given about the piece, such as when it was written, who wrote it, etc.
- Do not concentrate all of your efforts on content. The examiner will be much more interested in your comments on how the piece is written, and the ways in which the writer has used language to create the intended effects.

> **KEY POINT**
>
> Adopt a structured approach to questions on unseen texts.

Tips for tackling unseen texts

Generally speaking, how can you prepare yourself for a question involving an unseen text?

Here are some of the particular features that you need to exhibit to do well in this element of your exam:

- Make sure that you have a solid level of **background reading** across a whole range of literature. This level of reading is not always explicit in students' answers because the questions are not necessarily devised to show background reading (it depends on the specific exam board and the particular way they are using unseen material). It often comes through implicitly, but clearly, when a student has read widely. Throughout your studies you will have been gaining invaluable experience of encountering literary texts of all kinds, and it should stand you in good stead. Those students who achieve higher grades are invariably those who have read well beyond the set texts prescribed by the specification.
- Have some familiarity with the techniques of **literary critical appreciation**. This does not mean learning by heart a whole battery of critical terms that you can try to work into your responses, or a rigid formula which can be applied to whatever text you encounter. Rather, it is the awareness that texts consist of language, and that writers have used this in a particular way to achieve particular effects. The ability to describe these – and the means by which they are created – is essential.
- Recognise that **every text is individual** and that there is not a 'correct' view of what a text is about, **but** that **subjective views alone are not valid**. Successful students show individual and fresh responses that are firmly rooted in the text and supported by clear and detailed textual reference.

> **KEY POINT**
>
> There is a range of things that you can do to help prepare for handling unseen and unprepared material.

> **PROGRESS CHECK**
>
> Look carefully at the specification you are studying and find out where you may encounter unseen texts in your studies.

11.2 Question types involving unseen texts

<table>
<tr><td>**LEARNING SUMMARY**</td><td>**After studying this section, you should be able to:**
• understand that different specifications have different approaches to unseen questions
• understand the requirements of the specification you are studying</td></tr>
</table>

Examples of question types used on exam papers

AQA A	**U 1, 3**
Edexcel	**U 1, 3**
WJEC	**U 4**

Here are some of the different question types involving an unseen element that are used on exam papers:

1. You are given an unseen extract related to the area of study you are covering (e.g. Victorian Literature, World War One Literature, or The Struggle for Identity in Modern Literature) and are asked to link the extract to your reading in the chosen area of literature. This reading covers both set texts and your wider reading. The unseen extract could be taken from a source such as a work of criticism, diary, letter, biography or cultural commentary (AQA A AS Unit 1).

2. You are presented with four unseen texts covering all three genres, based on a theme (e.g. 'Love Through the Ages'). The texts are from a mixture of genres and may consist of complete poems, extracts from longer poems, extracts from plays, extracts from novels or short stories. You need to answer two questions. One question asks you to compare two unseen texts of the same genre. The second question asks you to compare the two texts from the remaining two genres. Both of these questions will require close reading and analysis, as well as reference to your wider reading around the theme (AQA A A2 Unit 3).

3. You are presented with a question that gives you a choice of unseen poetry or unseen prose. Short questions require you to comment on the use of key features in the text you have chosen (Edexcel AS Unit 1).

4. You are asked to select either one unprepared prose passage or one unprepared poem, and explore, through close reference, how the writer's choice of structure, form and language shape meaning (Edexcel A2 Unit 3).

5. You are asked to answer a question that offers a particular view of poetry, discussing the view with reference to the set poetry text you have studied, and one of a choice of five poems you are given on the exam paper. Your response should include detailed analysis of your set text and close reference to your chosen unseen poem (WJEC A2 Unit 4).

> **PROGRESS CHECK**
>
> Check the specification you are studying and make sure you are familiar with the kind of question(s) involving an unseen element.

11.3 Writing about unseen poetry

After studying this section, you should be able to:

- plan how to approach writing about an unseen poem
- recognise ways of comparing unseen poems

Unseen poems – and how to tackle them

AQA A **U 1, 3**
Edexcel **U 1, 3**
WJEC **U 4**

This section comprises examples of unseen poems to help prepare you for writing about them in an exam.

Writing about one unseen poem – examples

Look at the following poem and write down your initial ideas about it. What is the writer criticising, and what techniques does he use?

> *Unknown Citizen*
>
> (To JS/07/M 378 This Marble Monument is Erected by the State)
>
> He was found by the Bureau of Statistics to be
> One against whom there was no official complaint,
> And all the reports on his conduct agree
> That, in the modern sense of an old-fashioned word, he was a saint,
> For in everything he did he served the Greater Community.
> Except for the War till the day he retired
> He worked in a factory and never got fired,
> But satisfied his employers, Fudge Motors Inc.
> Yet he wasn't a scab or odd in his views.
> For his Union reports that he paid his dues,
> (Our report on his Union shows it was sound)
> And our Social Psychology workers found
> That he was popular with his mates and liked a drink.
> The Press are convinced that he bought a paper every day
> And that his reactions to advertisements were normal in every way.
> Policies taken out in his name prove that he was fully insured,
> And his Health-card shows he was once in hospital but left it, cured
> Both Producers Research and High Grade Living declare
> He was fully sensible to the advantages of the Instalment Plan
> And had everything necessary to the Modern Man,
> A phonograph, a radio, a car and a frigidaire.
> Our researchers into Public Opinion are content
> That he held the proper opinions for the time of year;
> When there was peace, he was for peace: when there was war, he went.
> He was married and added five children to the population,
> Which our Eugenist says was the right number for a parent of his generation,
> And our teachers report that he never interfered with their education
> Was he free? Was he happy? The question is absurd:
> Had anything been wrong, we should certainly have heard.
>
> *W.H. Auden*

COMMENTARY

Here are some points you might have noted:

1 The significance of the title *The Unknown Citizen* is a direct reference to the idea of the Tomb of the Unknown Soldier. In various wars many soldiers have died without their remains being identified, and many nations have a Tomb of the Unknown Soldier in which the unidentified remains of a soldier are interred (in Britain, it is in Westminster Abbey). The identity of the soldier is not known – he stands for all soldiers – just as in this poem the unknown man does not refer to one man – he represents the millions of 'ordinary' people who make up society.

2 The word 'citizen' gives the sense of this man being a member of a society in which everyone is equal, and the poem appears to present the state praising this man for being a model citizen. Note the list of features that are given to support the idea that his behaviour and conduct was exactly what was expected in every respect – he was an exemplary citizen in every way.

3 The final two lines, however, reveal Auden's true purpose in the poem. His real intention is just the opposite – he is really attacking the state for the value it places on uniformity, and the conflict it sets up between individualism and state control. Auden presents a society in which the individual is reduced to a faceless number. Auden's approach is satirical, and the poem achieves much of its effect through the use of irony.

Read the poem on the next page: *First Love*, by John Clare. When you have looked at it carefully, answer this exam-style question on it.

1. There are a number of key features that we bear in mind when we consider poetry.

   (a) The poet's language choices are an extremely important feature in poetry. Discuss the use of language in conveying a sense of the dramatic nature of the poet's experience.
   (b) Poets often make use of imagery. Using **two** examples from the poem, explore the effect of imagery in the poem.
   (c) In poetry, themes and ideas are explored and presented in different ways Using your knowledge of poetry, discuss what overall views of love are presented and comment on the ways they are developed.

We have made some suggestions on page 266 about what you could include in your answer.

First Love

I ne'er was struck before that hour
With love so sudden and so sweet.
Her face it bloomed like a sweet flower
And stole my heart away complete.

My face turned pale, a deadly pale.
My legs refused to walk away,
And when she looked what could I ail
My life and all seemed turned to clay.

And then my blood rushed to my face
And took my eyesight quite away.
The trees and bushes round the place
Seemed midnight at noonday.

I could not see a single thing,
Words from my eyes did start.
They spoke as chords do from the string,
And blood burnt round my heart.

Are flowers the winter's choice
Is love's bed always snow
She seemed to hear my silent voice
Not love appeals to know.

I never saw so sweet a face
As that I stood before.
My heart has left its dwelling place
And can return no more.

John Clare

COMMENTARY

There are various details of language and style you might have commented on.

Here are some possible ideas for each part of the question.

(a) The word 'struck' in 'I ne'er was struck' creates a sense of the physical impact of being in love. The use of the word 'stole' to express how he has lost his heart to love creates a dramatic effect. The use of the image 'My face turned pale, a deadly pale' again reinforces the physical impact of falling in love, and adds to the sense of tension and drama. 'My legs refused to walk away' adds another detail of the physical effect love has on the speaker.

The overall effect is of the strong physical impact the sense of being in love has on him – love has changed him and he can never again be as he was:

> My heart has left its dwelling place
> And can return no more.

(b) In stanza one, the simile 'Her face it bloomed like a sweet flower' is used to suggest beauty and freshness in the face of his love. The image of the flower is used again in stanza five, but in a different way. Here it is used to suggest the different sides to love – perhaps the pleasure and the pain of it. Flowers have associations with the warmth and life of summer, but in stanza five this warmth is contrasted with the cold of winter.

The metaphor 'blood burnt round my heart' is used to convey a sense of the intensity of the speaker's passion and feelings of love. The word 'blood' is used earlier to describe the blood rushing to his face, which forms a contrast to his face turning 'deadly pale'.

(c) The poem creates an impression of the physical impact and manifestations of love. These leave the sufferer powerless to move, think or see as his emotions are thrown into turmoil. The idea is presented that emotions dominate the normal sense of reason and that the heart rules the head. The idea is developed that once love has struck, things can never return to quite the same state as before. Love is presented using the traditional image of it as a 'sickness' and, like a sickness, it has its physical symptoms and consequences. There is also the suggestion of both the physical pain associated with love and the intense pleasure of its sweetness – the paradoxical nature of love.

Comparing and contrasting unseen poems – an example

Now read the following two poems.

When you have looked at them both carefully, compare and contrast the two poems, highlighting their similarities and their differences.

Since there's no help, come let us kiss and part;
Nay, I have done, you get no more of me;
And I am glad, yea glad with all my heart
That thus so cleanly I myself can free;
Shake hands forever, cancel all our vows,
And when we meet at any time again,
Be it not seen in either of our brows
That we one jot of former love retain.
Now at the last gasp of love's latest breath,
When, his pulse failing, passion speechless lies,
When faith is kneeling by his bed of death,
And innocence is closing up his eyes;
Now if thou would'st, when all have given him over,
From death to life thou might'st him yet recover.

Michael Drayton, 1563–1631

Mark where the pressing wind shoots javelin-like,
Its skeleton shadow on the broad-backed wave!
Here is a fitting spot to dig Love's grave;
Here where the ponderous breakers plunge and strike,
And dart their hissing tongues high up the sand:
In hearing of the ocean, and in sight
Of those ribbed wind-streaks running into white.
If I the death of Love had deeply planned,
I never could have made it half so sure,
As by the unblest kisses which upbraid
The full-waked sense; or failing that, degrade!
'Tis morning; but no morning can restore
What we have forfeited. I see no sin:
The wrong is mixed. In tragic life, God wot,
No villain need be! Passions spin the plot:
We are betrayed by what is false within.

George Meredith, 1828–1909

COMMENTARY

Here are some points that you might have noted:

1. The two poems initially appear to have the same central image. Both poets depict the failure of a relationship.

2. The presentation of this image, however, is entirely different. While Drayton portrays the loss of a love as something simple but not irreversible, Meredith shows the failure of a relationship as something dramatic and inevitable.

3. It is the similarity between the subject of these two poems, however, that immediately strikes the reader. Both poets emphasise that the central theme in their poems is lost love. They achieve this through their use of imagery. In both pieces the concept of love is personified and described as dying. Drayton refers to 'the last gasp of love's latest breath'. Meredith describes 'the death of Love' and 'Love's grave'.

4. This conventional theme is reflected in both pieces by their conventional structure. Drayton's poem adheres to the form of an English sonnet. The rhythm of his writing is dictated by this.

5. The difference in the way that this conventional theme is presented, however, is also very striking. The reader is clearly shown that Drayton sees the loss of a love as something sad but common, while Meredith views the break-up of a relationship as something momentous.

6. This difference in the presentation of their common theme is also reflected in the poets' use of imagery. Drayton depicts the ending of his relationship as a clean break. Much of his imagery suggests he is breaking free from some kind of restriction – 'you get no more of me', 'I myself can free'. Drayton's use of language also illustrates that this is an amicable break. He repeats the word 'glad', giving it added impact – 'And I am glad, yea glad with all my heart'. Drayton also uses imagery of shaking hands and kissing, which symbolises the idea of a friendly parting.

These two poems, therefore, have very little similarity beyond their conventional theme. The poets attempt to show this subject in entirely different lights.

PROGRESS CHECK

Read the poem on the next page: *To Autumn*, by John Keats. In the poem Keats uses a number of stylistic techniques to achieve his effects. Make a list of these techniques, give an example of each one, and then write a short essay giving a more detailed analysis of the poem. There are some ideas for techniques, with examples, in the Progress Check box underneath the poem.

1.

Season of mists and mellow fruitfulness,
Close bosom friend of the maturing sun;
Conspiring with him how to load and bless
With fruit the vines that round the thatch-eves run;
To bend with apples the moss'd cottage-trees,
And fill all fruit with ripeness to the core;
To swell the gourd, and plump the hazel shells
With a sweet kernel; to set budding more,
And still more, later flowers for the bees,
Until they think warm days will never cease,
For Summer has o'er-brimm'd their clammy cells.

2.

Who hath not seen thee oft amid thy store?
Sometimes whoever seeks abroad may find
Thee sitting careless on a granary floor,
Thy hair soft-lifted by the winnowing wind;
Or on a half-reap'd furrow sound asleep,
Drows'd with the fume of poppies, while thy hook
Spares the next swath and all its twined flowers:
And sometimes like a gleaner thou dost keep
Steady thy laden head across a brook;
Or by a cyder-press, with patient look,
Thou watchest the last oozings hours by hours.

3.

Where are the songs of Spring? Ay, where are they?
Think not of them, thou hast thy music too,—
While barred clouds bloom the soft-dying day,
And touch the stubble plains with rosy hue;
Then in a wailful choir the small gnats mourn
Among the river sallows, borne aloft
Or sinking as the light wind lives or dies;
And full-grown lambs loud bleat from hilly bourn;
Hedge-crickets sing; and now with treble soft
The red-breast whistles from a garden-croft;
And gathering swallows twitter in the skies.

PROGRESS CHECK

Look back at the progress check on page 268. Below are some ideas
for techniques, with examples.

- Keats uses similes, for instance 'sometimes like a gleaner'.
- Metaphors are used to achieve Keats's effects, for instance 'songs of Spring'.
- Alliteration is used, for example 'winnowing wind'.
- Personification is one technique used – both Autumn and the sun are personified in the first four lines of the poem.

11.4 Writing about unseen prose and drama texts

LEARNING SUMMARY	**After studying this section, you should be able to:** • consider ways of approaching unseen prose and drama texts • understand features you can recognise and write about

How to approach unseen prose and drama texts

AQA A **U 1, 3**
Edexcel **U 1, 3**
WJEC **U 4**

Essentially, your approach to prose or drama texts is the same as the approach that you adopt when looking at poetry. At the heart of your analysis is how the writer has used language to create effects.

In prose texts your focus will be on the narrative techniques used and in drama the dramatic techniques used, always bearing in mind the different qualities of each of the genres.

Writing about an unseen prose text – example

Look at the extract on the next page, in which Dickens describes the changes that the coming of the railway has brought to an area known as Stagg's Gardens.

How does Dickens present a picture of the change that has occurred, and create a sense of place?

There was no such place as Staggs's Gardens. It had vanished from the earth. Where the old rotten summer-houses once had stood, palaces now reared their heads, and granite columns of gigantic girth opened a vista to the railway world beyond. The miserable waste ground, where the refuse-matter had been heaped of yore, was swallowed up and gone; and in its frowsy stead were tiers of warehouses, crammed with rich goods and costly merchandise. The old by-streets now swarmed with passengers and vehicles of every kind: the new streets that had stopped disheartened in the mud and waggon-ruts, formed towns within themselves, originating wholesome comforts and conveniences belonging to themselves, and never tried nor thought of until they sprung into existence. Bridges that had led to nothing, led to villas, gardens, churches, healthy public walks. The carcasses of houses, and beginnings of new thoroughfares, had started off upon the line at steam's own speed, and shot away into the country in a monster train.

As to the neighbourhood which had hesitated to acknowledge the railroad in its straggling days, that had grown wise and penitent, as any Christian might in such a case, and now boasted of its powerful and prosperous relation. There were railway patterns in its drapers' shops, and railway journals in the windows of its newsmen. There were railway hotels, office-houses, lodging-houses, boarding-houses; railway plans, maps, views, wrappers, bottles, sandwich-boxes, and time-tables; railway hackney-coach and stands; railway omnibuses, railway streets and buildings, railway hangers-on and parasites, and flatterers out of all calculation. There was even railway time observed in clocks, as if the sun itself had given in. Among the vanquished was the master chimney-sweeper, whilom incredulous at Staggs's Gardens, who now lived in a stuccoed house three stories high, and gave himself out, with golden flourishes upon a varnished board, as contractor for the cleansing of railway chimneys by machinery.

To and from the heart of this great change, all day and night, throbbing currents rushed and returned incessantly like its life's blood. Crowds of people and mountains of goods, departing and arriving scores upon scores of times in every four-and-twenty hours, produced a fermentation in the place that was always in action. The very houses seemed disposed to pack up and take trips. Wonderful Members of Parliament, who, little more than twenty years before, had made themselves merry with the wild railroad theories of engineers, and given them the liveliest rubs in cross-examination, went down into the north with their watches in their hands, and sent on messages before by the electric telegraph, to say that they were coming. Night and day the conquering engines rumbled at their distant work, or, advancing smoothly to their journey's end, and gliding like tame dragons into the allotted corners grooved out to the inch for their reception, stood bubbling and trembling there, making the walls quake, as if they were dilating with the secret knowledge of great powers yet unsuspected in them, and strong purposes not yet achieved.

But Staggs's Gardens had been cut up root and branch. Oh woe the day when 'not a rood of English ground' – laid out in Staggs's Gardens – is secure!

Extract from Dombey and Son *by Charles Dickens*

COMMENTARY

Here are some points that you might have noted:

1. The opening sentence of the extract immediately creates an impression of just how great a change has occurred: 'There was no such place as Stagg's Gardens. It had vanished from the earth.' The place has been completely obliterated.

2. To convey to the reader just what has vanished and how much the place has changed, Dickens describes the place as it was, what features had disappeared, and what they had been replaced with.

3. The vocabulary he uses creates a sense of contrast between what had been there and what is there now. Here is an example: 'The miserable waste ground, where the refuse-matter had been heaped of yore, was swallowed up and gone; and in its frowsy stead were tiers of warehouses, crammed with rich goods and costly merchandise.'

4. The bustle of the place is now emphasised and the streets 'swarmed with passengers'.

5. The repetition of 'railway' in the second paragraph emphasises the fact that everything centres around the railway, and its influence pervades everything.

6. Dickens uses a listing technique to emphasise the new features that have been created.

7. The final paragraph creates a strong sense of the life and bustle of the place through the use of imagery, for instance 'throbbing currents rushed and returned incessantly'.

8. Note the imagery Dickens uses to describe the engines, creating an impression of them as powerful living beasts with a secret and mysterious purpose, and suggesting something to be feared.

Writing about an unseen prose and drama text – example

Now read the following two extracts. The first is from *Far From the Madding Crowd* by Thomas Hardy; the second is an extract from William Shakespeare's *Much Ado About Nothing*.

Think about how the interactions between men and women are presented in these extracts, and then look at the commentary notes.

Never since the broadsword became the national weapon had there been more dexterity shown in its management than by the hands of Sergeant Troy, and never had he been in such splendid temper for the performance as now in the evening sunshine among the ferns with Bathsheba. It may safely be asserted with respect to the closeness of his cuts, that had it been possible for the edge of the sword to leave in the air a permanent substance wherever it flew past, the space left untouched would have been almost a mould of Bathsheba's figure.

Behind the luminous streams of this aurora militaris, she could see the hue of Troy's sword arm, spread in a scarlet haze over the space covered by its motions, like a twanged harpstring, and behind all Troy himself, mostly facing her; sometimes, to show the rear cuts, half turned away, his eye nevertheless always keenly measuring her breadth and outline, and his lips tightly closed in sustained effort. Next, his movements lapsed slower, and she could see them individually. The hissing of the sword had ceased, and he stopped entirely.

continued

"That outer loose lock of hair wants tidying," he said, before she had moved or spoken. "Wait: I'll do it for you."

An arc of silver shone on her right side: the sword had descended. The lock dropped to the ground.

"Bravely borne!" said Troy. "You didn't flinch a shade's thickness. Wonderful in a woman!"

"It was because I didn't expect it. O, you have spoilt my hair!"

"Only once more."

"No — no! I am afraid of you — indeed I am!" she cried.

"I won't touch you at all — not even your hair. I am only going to kill that caterpillar settling on you. Now: still!"

It appeared that a caterpillar had come from the fern and chosen the front of her bodice as his resting place. She saw the point glisten towards her bosom, and seemingly enter it. Bathsheba closed her eyes in the full persuasion that she was killed at last. However, feeling just as usual, she opened them again.

"There it is, look," said the sergeant, holding his sword before her eyes.

The caterpillar was spitted upon its point.

"Why, it is magic!" said Bathsheba, amazed.

"O no — dexterity. I merely gave point to your bosom where the caterpillar was, and instead of running you through checked the extension a thousandth of an inch short of your surface."

"But how could you chop off a curl of my hair with a sword that has no edge?"

"No edge! This sword will shave like a razor. Look here."

He touched the palm of his hand with the blade, and then, lifting it, showed her a thin shaving of scarf-skin dangling therefrom.

"But you said before beginning that it was blunt and couldn't cut me!"

"That was to get you to stand still, and so make sure of your safety. The risk of injuring you through your moving was too great not to force me to tell you a fib to escape it."

She shuddered. "I have been within an inch of my life, and didn't know it!"

"More precisely speaking, you have been within half an inch of being pared alive two hundred and ninety-five times."

"Cruel, cruel, 'tis of you!"

"You have been perfectly safe, nevertheless. My sword never errs." And Troy returned the weapon to the scabbard.

Bathsheba, overcome by a hundred tumultuous feelings resulting from the scene, abstractedly sat down on a tuft of heather.

"I must leave you now," said Troy, softly. "And I'll venture to take and keep this in remembrance of you."

She saw him stoop to the grass, pick up the winding lock which he had severed from her manifold tresses, twist it round his fingers, unfasten a button in the breast of his coat, and carefully put it inside. She felt powerless to withstand or deny him. He was altogether too much for her, and Bathsheba seemed as one who, facing a reviving wind, finds it blow so strongly that it stops the breath.

Extract from Far From the Madding Crowd *by Thomas Hardy*

Below is the extract from *Much Ado About Nothing*.

BEATRICE: I wonder that you will still be talking, Signior Benedick: nobody marks you.

BENEDICK: What, my dear Lady Disdain! are you yet living?

BEATRICE: Is it possible disdain should die while she hath such meet food to feed it as Signior Benedick? Courtesy itself must convert to disdain, if you come in her presence.

BENEDICK: Then is courtesy a turncoat. But it is certain I am loved of all ladies, only you excepted: and I would I could find in my heart that I had not a hard heart; for, truly, I love none.

BEATRICE: A dear happiness to women: they would else have been troubled with a pernicious suitor. I thank God and my cold blood, I am of your humour for that: I had rather hear my dog bark at a crow than a man swear he loves me.

BENEDICK: God keep your ladyship still in that mind! so some gentleman or other shall 'scape a predestinate scratched face.

BEATRICE: Scratching could not make it worse, an 'twere such a face as yours were.

BENEDICK: Well, you are a rare parrot-teacher.

BEATRICE: A bird of my tongue is better than a beast of yours.

BENEDICK: I would my horse had the speed of your tongue, and so good a continuer. But keep your way, i' God's name; I have done.

BEATRICE: You always end with a jade's trick: I know you of old.

(Act 1, Scene 1, lines 108–137)

COMMENTARY

Here are some possible ideas.

In the *Far From the Madding Crowd* extract, you may have noted:

1. the dashing nature of Troy's presentation, with Hardy using words like 'performance' – Troy is putting on a performance for Bathsheba to try to woo (or seduce) her
2. Hardy's description of Troy's swordplay, e.g. the 'scarlet haze' of his uniform as his arm flashes to and fro
3. the dramatic effect of Troy cutting a lock of Bathsheba's hair, further heightened by him piercing the caterpillar on her bosom – note the sexual tension Hardy generates here
4. Bathsheba's response to Troy and his skill with the sword, e.g. 'Why, it is magic!'
5. the impact created by her realisation of the true sharpness of the sword
6. Bathsheba's clear sense of being overwhelmed (perhaps infatuated) by Troy, created by the image of the final sentence – she is completely in his hands – he has taken her breath away.

You may have thought of the following points in relation to *Much Ado About Nothing*:

1. Beatrice and Benedick seem used to verbally sparring with each other, e.g. Beatrice's barbed remark to Benedick that nobody is listening to him and Benedick's response, calling her 'Lady Disdain'.
2. Beatrice immediately responds to Benedick, picking up on his reference to 'disdain'.
3. Their exchange seems to become more acrimonious when Benedick claims he is 'loved of all ladies', but that he loves none.
4. Beatrice replies with a comparison that makes her attitude clear: 'I had rather hear my dog bark at a crow than a man swear he loves me.'
5. Benedick tries to have the last word, but Beatrice's final comment suggests she knows Benedick's tricks, and creates the impression that this is not her first encounter with him.
6. Consider how playful or serious the exchange in this extract is meant to be, and what you think it reveals about the relationship between Beatrice and Benedick.

KEY POINT

If you are writing a comparison of two texts in an exam, make sure that you produce an integrated comparison rather than write about the two texts separately. You should make some clear comparative points.

PROGRESS CHECK

Write an essay comparing the ways that the writers present the interaction between their characters in these extracts. Make sure that you produce an integrated comparison, rather than writing about the texts separately.

Sample question and model answer

Read the following poem. It is a poem written by Thomas Hardy, first published in 1912. Comment on and analyse how the writer's choices of structure, form and language shape meaning.

The Voice

Woman much missed, how you call to me, call to me,
Saying that now you are not as you were
When you had changed from the one who was all to me,
But as at first, when our day was fair.

Can it be you that I hear? Let me view you, then,
Standing as when I drew near to the town
Where you would wait for me: yes, as I knew you then,
Even to the original air-blue gown!

Or is it only the breeze, in its listlessness
Travelling across the wet mead to me here,
You being ever dissolved to wan wistlessness,
Heard no more again far or near?

Thus I; faltering forward,
Leaves around me falling,
Wind oozing thin through the thorn from norward,
And the woman calling.

Thomas Hardy

The candidate shows focus and expresses her ideas about the poem.

This poem seems to be a lament by the poet for a woman he has lost. Although the poem does not actually state that she is dead, there is very much a sense that she is through the overall tone, and the bitter regret that the poet expresses.

Hardy's first wife, Emma, died in November 1912, and in response to her death he wrote a series of poems that expressed his grief at her death.

The first three stanzas are written in anapaestic metre, which gives the poem a flowing, lilting kind of rhythm, but is used here to capture a reflective tone as he remembers the woman as she had been in the past. This might seem an unusual form, bearing in mind the serious subject of the poem, but the tone it creates does give a sense of the poet's memories of the woman in his life, and the pain he feels now she is gone.

The candidate shows a clear understanding of effects created by rhythm pattern.

In the first stanza, the poet begins by imagining that he hears the voice of the woman he misses so much calling to him. The repetition of the lilting rhythm of `call to me, call to me´ gives a haunting quality to the opening line, as if he hears the voice calling on the wind. In the next two lines the imagined voice continues, and the poet imagines how she was in life, when she had meant so much - everything - to him. This suggests that in some ways, before he had lost her, their relationship had changed in some way from what it was `at first, when our day was fair´. The alternately rhymed lines reinforce this feeling, with `call to me´ and `all to me´ separated by `as you were´ and `when our day was fair´.

The candidate shows a good awareness of the effects of the rhythm and is sensitive to the suggestions inherent in the lines.

In the second stanza, the sound imagery is replaced with visual imagery. The poet imagines his lost love as she had been when he had arrived at the town (perhaps returning home from a trip) to be met by her waiting for him. This picture, in his mind's eye, is so vivid that he even remembers `the original air-blue gown´ that she used to wear. In this stanza, then, the poet has moved on from hearing the voice of his loved one to imagining that he actually

Sample question and model answer (continued)

Again, there Is good awareness of the effect of the poem and the way in which the poet moves on to the next stage.

The candidate is sensitive to changing moods – the sense of illusion – she makes good comments on vocabulary.

Some interesting ideas are explored here – the comments on 'wistlessness' show perception and understanding.

The candidate comments on the use of alliteration and gives textual support.

There is a detailed understanding of the way in which the rhyme and the rhythm patterns work together, and some perceptive comments made about the effects achieved.

This is a good ending to the piece, showing awareness of how the poet has used language to create effects and clear sensitivity to mood and tone.

sees her there, as she was in the days when they were close. Again, the sense of loss is accentuated through the rhyme scheme - the almost tangible memories of 'town' and 'gown' balanced against the sense of these being past memories in the repeated 'then' and 'then' of the fifth and seventh lines.

In the third stanza, though, the poet begins to realise that his loved one is not really there, that it is merely an illusion - perhaps the sound of the wind blowing across the wet meadow. In this stanza - as he realises that the presence of the one he once loved has been evoked through his memories and imagination - there is a sense that he finds himself alone and full of sadness. This mood is reinforced through the vocabulary. For example, 'wan' suggests a sense of paleness, of being exhausted, tired and worn, and this links with the earlier 'listlessness', suggesting that the death of his loved one has left him lacking in energy and enthusiasm in everything, including life itself. An interesting usage here is in the use of 'wistlessness'. Normally the word 'wistful' is used to mean someone who is yearningly expectant or wishful; it is also suggestive of a kind of hope. The poet turns the word around here to 'wistlessness', which accentuates the sense that he feels that there is no hope. Note also how the poet's use of alliteration adds emphasis to this feeling as he realises that she has gone forever, even though he addresses her directly:

> You being ever dissolved to wan wistlessness,
> Heard no more again far or near?

Up until this point the first three stanzas have created a regular rhythm pattern that works closely with the rhyme scheme, language and imagery to create the poet's effects. The repeated rhyme of 'call to me' and 'all to me' in the first stanza creates a link between the imagined caller and the poet, and emphasises how much he misses her now. In the second stanza the rhyming 'Let me view you, then' and 'as I knew you then' emphasises the contrast between the poet's present pain and the happiness the couple had enjoyed in years gone by. In the third stanza, the rhyme of 'in its listlessness' and 'wan wistlessness' captures the pervading mood, and increases the sense of pain and uncertainty leading into the final stanza.

The most striking and immediately noticeable feature of the final stanza is the way that it breaks from the rhythm and rhyme patterns established in the first three stanzas. The caesura of 'Thus I / faltering forward' creates a halting and stumbling feel and reflects the breakdown that the poet experiences as his grief overwhelms him. The leaves 'falling' create a sense of something at an end, and the sense of pain is graphically present in the image of 'Wind oozing thin through the thorn from norward'. As the final line trails off almost unfinished, we are left with the image created through the rhyme - 'falling/calling'. This encapsulates the poet's feelings here and leaves us with a sense of the despair, desolation and loneliness he feels, left only with the haunting sound of '...the woman calling'.

SUMMATIVE COMMENT

Overall, this is a very good response that shows a high level of sensitivity to structure, form and language, and is sensitive to the ways in which the writer's choices shape meaning. There is some perceptive analysis of the effects of rhyme and rhythm and the ways in which they contribute to the overall effect of the poem. There is a good sense of mood and tone. This is a well-structured and fluent response.

Practice examination questions

AQA A Unit 1

In your response to this section of the paper, you must refer to your wider reading across all three genres (prose, poetry and drama). You may also refer to your AS coursework texts.

1. Read the following extract carefully. It is taken from *Memoirs of an Infantry Officer*, the fictionalised autobiography of Siegfried Sassoon, who served as an army officer in France during the First World War.

How does the writer present his thoughts and feelings about World War One?

How far is the extract similar to and different from your wider reading of the literature of World War One? You should consider the writer's choices of form, structure and language.

The circumstances being what they were, I had no justification for feeling either shocked or astonished by the sudden extinction of Lance-Corporal Kendle. But after blank awareness that he was killed, all feelings tightened and contracted to a single intention – to "settle that sniper" on the other side of the valley. If I had stopped to think, I shouldn't have gone at all. As it was, I discarded my tin hat and equipment, slung a bag of bombs across my shoulder, abruptly informed Fernby that I was going to find out who was there, and set off at a downhill double. While I was running I pulled the safety-pin out of a Mills bomb; my right hand being loaded, I did the same for my left. I mention this because I was obliged to extract the second safety-pin with my teeth, and the grating sensation reminded me that I was half way across and not so reckless as I had been when I started. I was even a little out of breath as I trotted up the opposite slope. Just before I arrived at the top I slowed up and threw my two bombs. Then I rushed at the bank, vaguely expecting some sort of scuffle with my imagined enemy. I had lost my temper with the man who had shot Kendle; quite unexpectedly, I found myself looking down into a well-conducted trench with a great many Germans in it. Fortunately for me they were already retreating. It had not occurred to them that they were being attacked by a single foe; and Fernby, with presence of mind which probably saved me, had covered my advance by traversing the top of the trench with his Lewis gun. I slung a few more bombs, but they fell short of the clumsy field-grey figures, some of whom half turned to fire their rifles over the left shoulder as they ran across the open toward the wood, while a crowd of jostling helmets vanished along the trench. Idiotically elated, I stood there with my finger in my right ear and emitted a series of "view-holloas" (a gesture which ought to win the approval of people who still regard war as a form of outdoor sport). Having thus failed to commit suicide, I proceeded to occupy the trench – that is to say, I sat down on the fire-step, very much out of breath, and hoped the Germans wouldn't come back again.

Practice examination questions (continued)

AQA A Unit 3

Read the two poems (Extracts A and B) carefully. They were written at different times by different writers.

Basing your answer on the poems and, where appropriate, your wider reading of the poetry of love, compare the ways the two poets have used poetic form, structure and language to express their thoughts and ideas.

Extract A

Neutral Tones

We stood by a pond that winter day,
And the sun was white, as though chidden of God,
And a few leaves lay on the starving sod;
   – They had fallen from an ash, and were gray.

Your eyes on me were as eyes that rove
Over tedious riddles of years ago;
And some words played between us to and fro
   On which lost the more by our love.

The smile on your mouth was the deadest thing
Alive enough to have strength to die;
And a grin of bitterness swept thereby
   Like an ominous bird a-wing....

Since then, keen lessons that love deceives,
And wrings with wrong, have shaped to me
Your face, and the God curst sun, and a tree,
   And a pond edged with grayish leaves.

Thomas Hardy

Extract B

Sonnet 109

O, never say that I was false of heart,
Though absence seemed my flame to qualify.
As easy might I from my self depart
As from my soul which in thy breast doth lie.
That is my home of love; if I have ranged,
Like him that travels I return again,
Just to the time, not with the time exchanged,
So that myself bring water for my stain.
Never believe though in my nature reigned
All frailties that besiege all kinds of blood,
That it could so preposterously be stained
To leave for nothing all thy sum of good;
   For nothing this wide universe I call
   Save thou, my rose, in it thou art my all.

William Shakespeare

Practice examination questions *(continued)*

Edexcel Unit 1

Prose: Read Text B and answer the questions that follow.

Text B

The moon was full and broad in the dark blue starless sky, and the broken ground of the heath looked wild enough in the mysterious light to be hundreds of miles away from the great city that lay beneath it. The idea of descending any sooner than I could help into the heat and gloom of London repelled me. The prospect of going to bed in my airless chambers, and the prospect of gradual suffocation, seemed, in my present restless frame of mind and body, to be one and the same thing. I determined to stroll home in the purer air by the most roundabout way I could take; to follow the white winding paths across the lonely heath; and to approach London through its most open suburb by striking into the Finchley Road, and so getting back, in the cool of the new morning, by the western side of the Regent's Park.

I wound my way down slowly over the heath, enjoying the divine stillness of the scene, and admiring the soft alternations of light and shade as they followed each other over the broken ground on every side of me. So long as I was proceeding through this first and prettiest part of my night walk my mind remained passively open to the impressions produced by the view; and I thought but little on any subject—indeed, so far as my own sensations were concerned, I can hardly say that I thought at all.

But when I had left the heath and had turned into the by-road, where there was less to see, the ideas naturally engendered by the approaching change in my habits and occupations gradually drew more and more of my attention exclusively to themselves. By the time I had arrived at the end of the road I had become completely absorbed in my own fanciful visions of Limmeridge House, of Mr. Fairlie, and of the two ladies whose practice in the art of water-colour painting I was so soon to superintend.

I had now arrived at that particular point of my walk where four roads met—the road to Hampstead, along which I had returned, the road to Finchley, the road to West End, and the road back to London. I had mechanically turned in this latter direction, and was strolling along the lonely high-road—idly wondering, I remember, what the Cumberland young ladies would look like—when, in one moment, every drop of blood in my body was brought to a stop by the touch of a hand laid lightly and suddenly on my shoulder from behind me.

I turned on the instant, with my fingers tightening round the handle of my stick.

There, in the middle of the broad bright high-road—there, as if it had that moment sprung out of the earth or dropped from the heaven—stood the figure of a solitary Woman, dressed from head to foot in white garments, her face bent in grave inquiry on mine, her hand pointing to the dark cloud over London, as I faced her.

I was far too seriously startled by the suddenness with which this extraordinary apparition stood before me, in the dead of night and in that lonely place, to ask what she wanted. The strange woman spoke first.

From The Woman in White *by Wilkie Collins*

(a) Novelists use settings to create interest.

Comment on the ways in which Collins uses setting here.

(b) Novelists often use imagery to create particular effects.

Identify **two** examples of imagery that add to the effect of the description, and comment on their use.

(c) Novelists use narrative voice to create effects in their writing. Using your knowledge of narrative voice, discuss the ways in which Wilkie Collins uses it in this passage.

12 Approaches to coursework

The following topics are covered in this chapter:

- **Features of coursework assessment**
- **Tasks and assessment**
- **Titles and word counts**
- **Comparing texts**
- **Using secondary sources**
- **Potential pitfalls and tips for success**

12.1 Features of coursework assessment

LEARNING SUMMARY

After studying this section, you should be able to:

- understand the importance of coursework assessment
- understand the opportunities that coursework provides
- appreciate the ways that coursework can benefit other areas of your studies

The opportunities that coursework provides

AQA A	U 2, 4
AQA B	U 2, 4
Edexcel	U 2, 4
OCR	U 2, 4
WJEC	U 2, 3
CCEA	AS U1

All A-Level specifications include coursework units, and coursework forms a very important element in your assessment.

Coursework provides you with an opportunity to approach your work in a different way from when you are studying for an exam.

In particular, coursework can:

- give you an element of choice about the texts your task (or tasks) are going to be focused on
- give you some scope to develop your own task (or tasks), allowing you to focus on particular areas that interest you
- allow you to develop more independence in your reading and your learning
- allow you to produce work free of the constraints of exam conditions, so that you can present more carefully planned and considered responses and have a drafting process
- help you develop skills that will help you perform more effectively in the exams
- help you to gain experience in undertaking research and wider reading, in preparation for pursuing your studies further.

12.2 Tasks and assessment

<table>
<tr><td>LEARNING SUMMARY</td><td>

After studying this section, you should be able to:

- understand the significance of the assessment objectives to the coursework element of your course
- understand the coursework task for your specification
</td></tr>
</table>

The assessment objectives

AQA A	**U 2, 4**
AQA B	**U 2, 4**
Edexcel	**U 2, 4**
OCR	**U 2, 4**
WJEC	**U 2, 3**
CCEA	**AS U1**

The exact requirements of the coursework element of your course will depend on the particular specification you are studying, but the assessment objectives (AOs) on which your work will be judged are the same across all examination boards.

PROGRESS CHECK

Check your specification and make sure you are clear about the exact coursework requirements for your course.

Your coursework will be assessed on all four AOs. These are the same assessment objectives which are at the heart of the whole course, and which we have referred to throughout this book.

We have reproduced them below as a reminder.

AO1	Articulate creative, informed and relevant responses to literary texts, using appropriate terminology and concepts, and coherent, accurate written expression.
AO2	Demonstrate detailed critical understanding in analysing the ways in which structure, form and language shape meanings in literary texts.
AO3	Explore connections and comparisons between different literary texts, informed by interpretations of other readers.
AO4	Demonstrate understanding of the significance and influence of the contexts in which literary texts are written and received.

You need to look carefully at the particular specification you are studying, and how the AOs work in the specific coursework elements. Sometimes, although all the AOs feature, some AOs are dominant (in that they carry more marks than others). It is important that you focus on the key areas that you are going to be assessed on in your coursework.

Coursework tasks

AQA A	**U 2, 4**
AQA B	**U 2, 4**
Edexcel	**U 2, 4**
OCR	**U 2, 4**
WJEC	**U 2, 3**
CCEA	**AS U1**

The type of coursework task (or tasks) that you complete will depend on a number of factors. For instance, your whole group may study the same coursework text, or you may be given the opportunity to choose (through discussion with your teacher) the text or texts that you will focus on. Your tasks may be set by your teacher – for example, you may be able to select your question from a number of questions that you have been given. On the other hand, you may be able to negotiate an essay title with your teacher. If so, you will need to identify aspects of the text that you would like to write about. Your teacher will discuss these ideas with you and will help you to formulate an essay title that is both suitable and phrased in the right way.

How the exam boards structure coursework tasks

Here is how the different exam boards structure the coursework element in their specifications.

AQA A
Unit 2 Creative Study

Two pieces of writing are required, one on a prose text and one on a drama text selected for study from the lists provided by the exam board. These are grouped according to the particular thematic area you are studying (A. Victorian Literature; B. World War One Literature; C. The Struggle for Identity in Modern Literature).

The two pieces of work together should total between 2000–2500 words.

Each piece of work should be 1000–1250 words in length (excluding quotations).

Unit 4 Extended Essay and Shakespeare Study

One extended piece of comparative writing is required, based on three texts. The texts can be selected by the student (or teacher). One text must be a play by Shakespeare, the other two texts can be from any genre, and all three texts must reflect a shared theme. None of the texts should have been studied at AS level.

The extended essay should be about 3000 words in length.

AQA B
Unit 2 Dramatic Genres

At least two plays must be studied within the genre specified by the exam board (e.g. tragedy).

Two pieces of coursework are required:
(a) A study of an aspect of the dramatic genre with regard to a Shakespeare play. This piece should be about 1200–1500 words in length.
(b) A study of an aspect of the dramatic genre with regard to at least one other play. This piece should be about 1200–1500 words in length.

One of the two pieces can be in the form of a re-creative piece accompanied with a commentary.

Unit 4 Further and Independent Reading

At least three texts must be studied (one of the three based on a pre-release anthology of critical writing applied to a piece of literature).

Two pieces of work are required:
(a) A comparative study of an aspect of two texts chosen by the student. This piece should be 1500–2000 words.
(b) The application of critical ideas taken from the pre-released anthology to a text or texts of the student's own choice. This piece should be 1200–1500 words.

Edexcel

Unit 2 Explorations in Drama

Three texts are studied, including at least one play by Shakespeare. The centre or the student is free to choose their own texts.

Two pieces of work are required:

(a) An exploratory study.

(b) A creative response.

The total word length of the coursework folder is 2000–2500 words maximum (including quotations).

Word counts must be adhered to. Assessors and moderators stop marking once the required word count has been reached.

Unit 4 Reflections in Literary Studies

Students have a free choice of three texts, which could include works of literary criticism or cultural commentary. They should not be texts that have been studied elsewhere in the course.

The coursework folder should consist of **either**:

- one extended study referring to all text studied for the unit, **or**
- two shorter studies – if two studies are included each must refer to more than one text studied, **or**
- one creative response with a commentary.

The total word length for the coursework folder is 2500–3000 words maximum (including quotations).

OCR

Unit 2 Literature post-1900

At least two literary texts must be studied. One must have been first published or performed after 1990. One of the texts could be a text in translation and one may be a work of literary criticism or cultural commentary.

Two tasks are required:

(a) Either a close critical analysis of a section of a chosen text **or** a piece of re-creative writing based on a selected passage of a chosen text together with a commentary.

(b) An essay considering two texts exploring the contrasts and comparisons between them.

The two tasks together should be a maximum of 3000 words in length.

Unit 4 Texts in Time

Three texts must be studied, including one prose and one poetry text. The third text can be from any genre. One literary text may be a text in translation and one may be a work of literary criticism or cultural commentary. Texts that appear on the set text lists for other units, or texts that have been used for AS coursework must not be used.

One extended essay is required of a maximum of 3000 words, in which you compare all of the texts.

WJEC

Unit 2 Prose Study and Creative Reading

Students are required to complete a folder of **three** pieces of work, all of which require a response to wider reading of prose.

(a) **Prose Study** – a study based on **two** prose texts – one chosen for detailed study and the other for wider reading.

This piece of work should be approximately 1500 words in length.

(b) **Creative Reading** – two pieces of work of approximately 750 words each are required:

(i) A personal creative response written in a specific literary genre.

(ii) A commentary on the creative response.

Unit 3 Period and Genre Study

Students are required to produce a folder of about 3000 words based on a free choice of selected literary focus. **Three** texts must be explored, two of which must be a prose text and a poetry text of different periods and genres. The third text may be a drama text or another poetry or prose text. The emphasis in this unit is on independent reading and research.

CCEA

Unit 1 The Study of Drama

The coursework folder consists of two pieces of work:

(a) One piece is based on the chosen Shakespeare play, placing the play in context and focusing on aspects such as theme, structure, dramatic techniques, characterisation, etc.

This piece should be approximately 1500 words in length.

(b) The other piece focuses on a personal, creative response to the study of the work of a twentieth-century dramatist.

This piece should be approximately 1500 words in length.

Texts should be chosen from the lists provided by CCEA.

PROGRESS CHECK

Check the specification for the exam board you are studying, to make sure you thoroughly understand the coursework tasks that you need to undertake.

12.3 Titles and word counts

LEARNING SUMMARY	After studying this section, you should be able to:
	• understand what you need to consider when you are formulating a title for your coursework
	• understand the significance of word counts

Points to consider when thinking about a title for your coursework

AQA A	**U 2, 4**
AQA B	**U 2, 4**
Edexcel	**U 2, 4**
OCR	**U 2, 4**
WJEC	**U 2, 3**
CCEA	**AS U1**

Devising a suitable title for your coursework is essential.

Here are some points to bear in mind:
- Keep the title simple and straightforward – overly complex titles should be avoided.
- Make sure that the title gives you scope to analyse the language of the texts.
- Avoid titles that involve only description, or plot or character summary. Your title must allow for clear and thorough coverage of the AOs.
- Make sure that the title allows you to compare texts where required.

> **KEY POINT**
>
> Formulating an appropriate title for your coursework assignment is essential to success.

The importance of word counts

AQA A	**U 2, 4**
AQA B	**U 2, 4**
Edexcel	**U 2, 4**
OCR	**U 2, 4**
WJEC	**U 2, 3**
CCEA	**AS U1**

All exam boards give an indication of how long your pieces of coursework should be in terms of word length.

Some boards give the word count as an approximate number, for instance 'a piece of work of approximately **1500 words**'. If this is the instruction, then you should keep as closely as possible to the word guidance, although if you are a little over or under the 1500 words this is acceptable.

Other boards give approximate word lengths for individual pieces in a coursework folder, but also give a range for what the **total** word length of the whole folder should be, for example 'Coursework folder: 2500–3000 words maximum'. If a **maximum** word length is given it is very important that you do not exceed this maximum length. You will normally be told whether or not the word count includes quotations.

> **KEY POINT**
>
> Word counts are there for a purpose. Make sure that you stick to them. 'More' is not necessarily 'better'.

12.4 Comparing texts

LEARNING SUMMARY	**After studying this section, you should be able to:**
	• understand what you need to consider when you are undertaking a textual comparison
	• approach a textual comparison with confidence

How to approach a textual comparison task

AQA A   **U 2, 4**
AQA B   **U 2, 4**
Edexcel **U 2, 4**
OCR   **U 2, 4**
WJEC   **U 2, 3**
CCEA   **AS U1**

Some coursework tasks involve the comparison of texts – to 'explore connections and comparisons between different literary texts' (AO3). Writing comparatively about texts is obviously a more complex process than writing about a single text, and you will need to think carefully about your task and the ways in which you can approach it.

What to consider

Before you can really begin to think about the comparison of texts, you must study each of your texts carefully and be aware of the thematic and stylistic features of them. When you have developed a sound knowledge of the two texts, you will need to think carefully about their similarities and differences.

The key comparative areas that you might think about in relation to your texts include:
- how writers create and present characters
- the thematic areas and how the writers explore them
- the ways in which language is used to create effects
- stylistic or dramatic techniques
- historical, political, social and personal context
- interpretations by other readers.

It is essential to plan your approach to comparative coursework carefully if you are to produce a well-structured and balanced piece of work that fully addresses the assessment objectives.

> **KEY POINT**
>
> Writing a successful textual comparison piece needs careful planning.

A suggested outline

This is one way in which you could approach your comparative study:
- Identification of comparative areas and issues in the texts.
- Analysis and explanation, which comprises:
  - identification and exemplification of central features of the texts, using contextual and structural ideas
  - comparison of the key features of the text, e.g. exploration of ideas, themes, character, linguistic issues
  - consideration and comparison of meanings and effects created in each text, through close analysis.

Useful words and phrases

When writing your comparative essay, you will find it useful to use certain words and phrases that signal to the assessor that you are comparing features in the texts.

Examples of comparative phrases include:

- on the other hand
- contrastingly
- similarly
- comparatively
- correspondingly
- likewise
- conflictingly
- unlike
- in contrast to
- diversely
- however
- moreover
- but
- though
- differently
- whereas.

> **KEY POINT**
>
> Using comparative phrases will help you make points of comparison or contrast between the texts.

12.5 Using secondary sources

LEARNING SUMMARY	**After studying this section, you should be able to:** - understand the importance of using secondary sources in your coursework - produce a bibliography for your coursework

The importance of referencing

AQA A	**U 2, 4**
AQA B	**U 2, 4**
Edexcel	**U 2, 4**
OCR	**U 2, 4**
WJEC	**U 2, 3**
CCEA	**AS U1**

When you are undertaking coursework, the text or texts that are the focus of the question – the primary texts – will be central to your studies. However, it is also highly advisable to use secondary sources to help develop and expand your understanding of the texts and all of the issues surrounding them.

Secondary sources are any other materials that help you in your work, such as critical works or articles about the text, biographical, social or political material, or study aids, etc. They can help to broaden your view of the text and show you other ways of looking at it. It does not matter whether you agree or disagree with the views and interpretations you read, because they will all help you to arrive at what you think.

Remember that there are rarely right answers as far as literature is concerned – all texts are open to a variety of interpretations. Your view can be 'informed' by other sources, but never let other views substitute your own. Have confidence in your view, develop your own voice, and **never** plagiarise. Reading 'around the text' can be an important element in developing your own ideas, but it is crucial that if you use quotations or ideas that you have drawn from another source, you acknowledge this in your work. See page 84 for more information about plagiarism, and about the importance of acknowledging sources accurately.

Producing a bibliography

As we discussed in Chapter 4, you must include a bibliography at the end of your coursework. Even if you have read only part of a particular book or article, it should be included in your bibliography.

It is highly advisable to use secondary sources and list them in a bibliography, but if you have used only the text itself in your coursework you should still include a bibliography, simply consisting of relevant details about the edition used. This will clearly show the examiner that you have referred only to the primary text in your work, and it will also give information about the particular edition that you have used.

There are details about how to write and set out a bibliography in Chapter 4 (see pages 86–88).

12.6 Potential pitfalls and tips for success

<table>
<tr><td>**LEARNING SUMMARY**</td><td>**After studying this section, you should be able to:**
● understand the potential problem areas in your coursework
● identify ways to help you produce a good piece of coursework</td></tr>
</table>

Problem areas in coursework

AQA A   **U 2, 4**
AQA B   **U 2, 4**
Edexcel **U 2, 4**
OCR   **U 2, 4**
WJEC   **U 2, 3**
CCEA   **AS U1**

Overall, examiners report that students produce a high standard of coursework.

However, they have highlighted weaknesses and problem areas in some of the work they have assessed.

The weaknesses include:
● inappropriately framed or worded assignment titles
● tasks that focus on a general discussion of themes or 'character studies'
● titles that do not allow the candidate to pay close attention to texts and critical judgement
● responses that are limited to a personal response only, and lack analysis
● biographical, political, historical, social and contextual information that is given as 'add on paragraphs', rather than integrated into the textual analysis (AO4)
● lack of consideration of how literary texts might be informed by the 'interpretations of other readers' (AO3)
● narrative re-telling of the plot or events.

Tips for coursework success

AQA A   **U 2, 4**
AQA B   **U 2, 4**
Edexcel **U 2, 4**
OCR   **U 2, 4**
WJEC   **U 2, 3**
CCEA   **AS U1**

To produce a good piece of coursework:
● make notes before starting your assignment
● focus in detail on the analysis of language and effects
● use specific details from the texts to support the points you make
● make sure that your quotations are short and to the point – do not use over-long quotations
● make sure that you answer the question you have chosen and select an appropriate title
● write about the text and not the historical, biographical, political, social or contextual background to it
● use appropriate terminology
● write accurately and express your ideas clearly.

Sample question and model answer

This question is in the style of a question from AQA A AS Unit 2, Coursework Essay 1.

Strange Meeting by Susan Hill

Explore the ways in which Hill uses letters in her narrative to develop her presentation of the character of Barton.

This is the first of two assignments that make up the coursework folder.

The two pieces of work should be 2000–2500 words in total.

The introduction establishes context, with a focus on the function and importance of the letters as a device for developing character and presenting the soldier's perspective and reactions to circumstances and events. →

Hill uses the setting of the First World War as a backdrop to support the strength of the bond that is forged quickly between the two main characters, David Barton and John Hilliard. They meet when they share billets at a rest camp. Hill uses Barton's experiences - he is slightly younger and new to the company - to develop her multi-dimensional character. We see his personality evolve and witness his reactions to the extremes of situations he faces through his letters. Hill works Barton's character portrayal through his correspondence to his family around the relationships he forms. Hill progressively gives us the soldier's perspective on transforming the attitudes of those at home to the squalor of trench life and the horrors of battle.

The candidate shows how Barton is presented through letters and shows an understanding of voice, with supporting evidence given. He contextualises the relationship between characters. →

It is significant that we are introduced to Barton while he is reading a letter, as his letters are how Hill presents Barton's genuine warmth and depth of character. His developing relationship with Hilliard is central to the plot, and our understanding of him also develops as a result of letters. When Barton first met Hilliard and he cracked his head on the beam, Barton is able to laugh at himself: `I've been doing that for three days! You think you won't forget it another time but you generally do.´ He writes as he talks - generously, in a good humoured way, and easily. Hill uses an initial short dialogue between Barton and Hilliard to inform us of the content of his letters: `What do you find to say?´ `I tell them what we do all day; I describe this place, what I can see…. Oh, we have jokes and so forth.´ This knowledge sets into context the fast developing relationship.

The candidate focuses on Barton's letters and what they reveal about his character, with some supporting illustration. →

Hill tells us Barton is a great letter writer. He writes freely and fluidly, careful to include interest for his parents, brothers, sisters and their children: `Roly would enjoy seeing it all.´ Barton comments on family members' interests. He is friendly, sociable, full of life and open to the positive aspects of the other characters: `Perhaps that's the advantage of coming from a large family!´ These qualities have come as a result of his close family ties: `We are really quite happy here; it has been the greatest good luck, our meeting and coming together. It has meant my missing all of you has not been quite so bad - but somehow, having John about has taken the edge off it.´

There is further development of character through the letters, and lexical examples are given to support ideas. →

Hill covers Barton's past in more detail in the narrative, but we do know he had done some walking, so Barton's response to having to march to the next billet met with favour. The first letter we share supports Barton's positive character and is full of encouraging vocabulary, such as `lucky´, `perfectly happy´, `amazing´, and he says: `The splendid thing about marching is, you just have to go´ - he is referring to marching up to the support line. He is keen to share his new environment with his family and is embracing of the whole Army experience.

The candidate highlights the importance of the letters in conveying a sense of setting and mood, linked to Barton's changing mood, again with supporting evidence. →

The various settings used by Hill are central to the evolving mood of David Barton. Hill tells us of his love for the natural world and he often comments on the destruction of the landscape: `I feel we shall have this on our consciences every bit as much as the deaths of men. What right do we have to do such damage to the earth?´ The weather has always reflected the mood of Barton: `… draw my map that terrible day´. As soon as he had his map-drawing mission, the weather is described as heavy-bellied clouds, which goes to highlight his changing frame of mind.

This dimension to his character is echoed by his seeking enlightenment by reading Sir Thomas Browne, who portrays identical traits. Sir Thomas Browne has a mind that loves going a little

Sample question and model answer *(continued)*

There is a focus on the ways that his letters reveal his philosophical development, causing him to ask fundamental questions about himself.

There is a further focus on Hill's shaping of character through Barton's changing language and its structure.

There is a further sense of Barton's changing character, with examples given. There is an awareness of the shaping of effects.

This again shows a sense of Hill shaping character through the letters, as well as giving the soldier's perspective on situation and events. It also acknowledges Barton's increased criticism of his superior.

This completes the sense of change as presented through the letters, with supporting lexical examples.

The conclusion effectively sums up ideas.

beyond common sense and reason. He is one of those people who can find something of interest in just about anything. Barton also displays tolerance and good humour, rare qualities in a situation of conflict and changing moral values. It is Sir Thomas Browne's theorising divine order in the world that causes Barton to question his role in the war.

Hill's choice of language develops Barton's character further with his next experience. Barton is now much darker in this letter when he expresses his dismay at arriving at the scene in Feuvry `broke, bloodstained and appalling'. There is less additional punctuation, depicting loss of enthusiasm for life and his adventure. Hill builds up the tension felt by Barton as he describes the town - `I do not think there is a building left intact' - and his feeling of anxiety -`hopeless'. Hill uses this letter to show us an end to his innocence at `seeing more ugliness and mess'.

Barton's changing character speaks of `putting off' writing to a dead soldier's parents. We are able to empathise with his reluctance because of the way Hill has opened up his thoughts to the reader through his letters: `I've a pretty good idea about what is coming'; `I have learned a great deal about deceit, since coming to this war.' He is ashamed at becoming `thoroughly hardened so quickly'. Hill uses this letter to express Barton's profound impression and realisation of the bleak realities he had to face. He does not spare his family's ignorance at the truth: `I am sorry to pile on these agonies but I need to tell you.' Barton uses his letter writing to unburden his mind of thoughts: `Now - I seem to have written myself out of the awful depression.'

Hill uses powerful description to portray how Barton's senses are heightened by the horrors of war: `I tell them what I can see; I hadn't realised how much noise the guns make; tastes of the stuff they use to sterilise it: everything smells so much worse and my hair feels dusty and sticky'; `A mess. That's all.' Here, Hill very effectively gets over the theme of the story, using Barton to express the soldiers' perspective. She conveys the waste of life and outdated tactics: `bloody useless and pointless the whole thing is'. In his last letter home Barton is critical of his superior's lack of value for human life - men who make decisions and yet are never victim to them: `We had a pep talk for the Brigadier, and last week, a pep letter came round - entirely unmoving.'

In the last part of this three-part story, Hill makes the most dramatic change to Barton's character. He is in `very low spirits and physically exhausted'. Hill uses the weather again to support his depressive mood, and he complains `it has rained solidly for a fortnight'. This is in contrast to the Barton his family knows and he admits to being `continually upset'; `I am feeling very resentful altogether now - I have seen enough'. Hill shows us that Barton has been deeply affected by his experiences and he has lost the naïvety and enthusiasm expressed in his earlier letters.

The situations he has encountered have opened up the limits of his character - Hill presents a fast maturing young man pushed to the boundaries of his morality within a short space of time. Hill has shown us how Barton responds to his environment, the weather, his pleasures, his relationships and the war through personal comments to his family through his letters, and it is clear that Hill's use of letters in her novel is central to the structure and design of her narrative.

BIBLIOGRAPHY Hill, S. (1971) `Strange Meeting'. Penguin Books.
Lawrance, W. (2005) `Strange Meeting'. Great War Literature.

SUMMATIVE COMMENT

Overall, the response shows a good understanding of the text, keeps the focus of the essay – the use of letters – in view throughout, and presents relevant and informed responses. There is some exploration of how the writer uses letters to shape meaning and the candidate uses specific references to illustrate and support ideas. The piece is well structured and communicates ideas fluently and accurately.

Example coursework assignments

The following examples should give you an idea of some of the question types that are used in coursework assignments.

It is important that you look carefully at the specification you are studying before finalising your coursework. You need to check with your teacher that a coursework title is appropriate for you before you start to work on it.

AQA A AS
Unit 2

Explore the ways in which the effects of war on the individual are presented in *Journey's End*.

Then compare the ways in which Sherriff presents the effects of war on the individual with the ways in which Hill shows the impact of war on characters in *Strange Meeting*.

AQA A A2
Unit 4

Compare the ways in which attitudes to women are revealed in *Othello*, *The Yellow Wallpaper* and *The Color Purple*.

AQA B AS
Unit 2

Aristotle's definition of tragedy is of 'the imitation of an action that is serious and also, as having magnitude, complete in itself'. It incorporates 'incidents arousing pity and fear, wherewith to accomplish the catharsis of such emotions'. How relevant is this definition to an understanding of *Hamlet*?

AQA B A2
Unit 4

Focusing on Brontë's *Wuthering Heights* and Fowles' *The French Lieutenant's Woman* as starting points – but ranging more widely if you wish – compare some of the ways authors present ideas about social class.

Edexcel AS
Unit 2

Explorative Study: Study Shakespeare's *Measure for Measure* as a central text and Webster's *The Duchess of Malfi* as a supporting text in order to explore the ways writers approach issues of corruption.

Edexcel A2
Unit 4

The presentation of women in drama: *King Lear* and *Much Ado About Nothing* are read and the assignment explores Shakespeare's presentation of women in these plays.

A range of critical comment is read to enable you to choose more precisely where to focus your coursework response.

Example coursework assignments (continued)

OCR AS

Unit 2

Compare and contrast ways in which two of your chosen writers present ideas about love.

OCR A2

Unit 4

Romantic writing

'Poetry lifts the veil from the hidden beauty of the world, and makes familiar objects be as if they were not familiar.' Compare and contrast your three chosen texts in the light of this comment.

WJEC AS

Unit 2

Compare the ways in which Brontë and Collins use narrative voice through detailed discussion of *Wuthering Heights* and wider reference to *The Woman in White*.

WJEC A2

Unit 3

Explore the presentation of love in *The Franklin's Tale* and *Jane Eyre*. In the course of your writing show how your ideas have been illuminated by your response to *The Rivals* and other readings of both core texts.

CCEA AS

Unit 1

With reference to Shakespeare's dramatic methods and use of language in *Henry IV*, Part 1, how central to the effect of the play is the presentation of Prince Henry, and how would the audience of the time have responded to the character?

Practice examination answers

The bullet points provided give an indication of some of the ideas that you might explore in a response to each question. They are not meant to be prescriptive or exhaustive.

Chapter 5

AS

AQA B Unit 1

Samuel Taylor Coleridge: *The Rime of the Ancient Mariner*

Here are some of the key areas you should bear in mind:
- Part A of this question is assessed against AO2 only. Therefore, the focus should be on form, structure and language.
- Consider the significance of this part within the poem as a whole – a turning point when the mariner prays and the albatross falls from him.
- The significance of the wedding guest, reintroduced at the beginning of Part IV, and the effect of distancing the experience.
- The significance of Coleridge's use of ballad form.
- The significance of Coleridge's 'commentary' on the poem.
- His use of imagery.
- Part B is assessed on AO1, 2 and 4.
- Consider the poem's relationship to Romantic ideas about poetry.
- The importance of sensations and emotions.
- Is the imagery used in a 'sensationalist' way?
- Question what is meant by 'revelatory'.
- What, if anything, is the wider significance of the mariner's visions?

Edexcel Unit 1

Jane Austen: *Pride and Prejudice*

Here are some of the key areas you should bear in mind:
- Consider the female characters presented in the novel – not just Elizabeth, but also Jane, Lydia, Charlotte, Mrs Bennet and Lady Catherine de Burgh.
- They have differing views on marriage – is there a 'norm'?
- Is there a difference between wealth and social status – which is more important to whom?
- Look at the social and economic context – the importance of marriage for middle-class women, given their dependence on men and the restrictions of law and custom.
- There are extremes shown in the sensible marriage of Charlotte and the elopement of Lydia.
- Jane's and Elizabeth's lack of money and status is a handicap to them, but that is because of the attitude of the men. Unlike their mothers, they are not actively pursuing wealth.
- However, the happy ending is all the happier because the girls marry wealthy men.

WJEC Unit 1

Arthur Miller: *Broken Glass*

Here are some of the key areas you should bear in mind:
- The dominant AO here is AO4, but AO1 and AO2 are also considered.
- It is important to get the balance right between commenting on this scene and discussing the play as a whole. As you analyse the scene, refer backwards and forwards, making connections.
- Sylvia's developing relationship with Hyman is important, as is her relationship with her husband. Hyman seems to understand her and she reacts quite differently to him from how she reacts to Gellburg. She can seem cruel and unfeeling to Gellburg.
- Her mysterious handicap is central in this scene and throughout the play.
- The reasons for it are never fully explained – it is connected with the Nazis, but also with her marriage and her position as a woman.
- In terms of context, look at the economics of the time and gender issues, as well as events in Germany and American reactions to them.
- Remember that the text was written in the 1990s – the context of that time is as important as the context of the 1930s.

CCEA Unit 2

Elizabeth Gaskell: *North and South*

Here are some of the key areas you should bear in mind:
- Consider carefully what the question means. What is meant by 'oppression'? How could women and the working classes be said to be oppressed in the novel and at the time it was written?
- Look at the character of Margaret Hale – middle-class, intelligent, vigorous – is she oppressed? Does she feel oppressed?
- Are other female characters oppressed because they are female, rather than because they are poor?
- Is she associated with/sympathetic to the workers because she is a woman?
- In the context of Victorian literature, Margaret is not unusual in being a strong-minded woman. How does she fit into Victorian ideas about women? You might think about other writers such as Charlotte Brontë, George Eliot and Charles Dickens.
- Some would say that in comparison with the reality of starving in the slums, the lot of middle-class women was of little significance. Gaskell was, like Dickens, a campaigner for the poor. Can she also be seen as a feminist?
- Are these two forms of oppression linked, or is there a tension between them?

A2

AQA Unit 3

Here are some of the key areas you should bear in mind:
- Analyse both poems in detail using correct terminology.

- In terms of structure, form and language, think about, for example, the effect of shorter lines and rhyme schemes, as well as imagery and diction.
- Look at the effect of language and structure on the contrasting tone and mood of the poems.
- Both poems are addressed to loved ones, but with quite different objects.
- The Jonson poem is sexual and can be compared to poems such as Marvell's *To His Coy Mistress*.
- The Rossetti poem, in contrast, is rather sexless and mournful. It could be connected to Barrett Browning's *How Do I Love Thee…*
- What difference do the contexts of sixteenth and nineteenth centuries make? Does the gender of the poets make a difference?

AQA B Unit 3

Elements of the Gothic

John Webster: *The White Devil*

Here are some of the key areas you should bear in mind:
- Should the stated view be challenged?
- Look at the violence in the play. How much is there and what kind of violence is it? Is this telling us something about the society it is set in?
- Look at examples of corruption in church and state.
- Are violence and corruption connected in the play?
- Is the violence that is depicted sensationalist – designed to excite and shock?
- Is there any sense of a moral norm and, if so, where does it come from?
- Look at the relationship between morality and religion.
- How important is the religious context of the time to an understanding of the play?
- Make connections with the idea of 'gothic' in your wider reading.

Edexcel Unit 3

Shakespeare: *Twelfth Night*

Here are some of the key areas you should bear in mind:
- The question would seem to be about an understanding of the nature of a Shakespearean comedy.
- What is meant by a 'happy ending'?
- All the lovers seem happy enough and the twins are reunited.
- Does Malvolio's final scene spoil the ending and disturb the audience?
- There is a sense of melancholy in Feste's song.
- Perhaps the conventional ending, with its marriages and reconciliations, can be seen as simply that – a convention, but with no deeper significance.
- *Twelfth Night* is about a night of anarchy and disorder, but also of freedom and equality. The restoration of order is not necessarily a 'happy ending'.

Chapter 6

AS

WJEC Unit 1

Diane Samuels: *Kindertransport*

Here are some of the key areas you should bear in mind:
- Flashbacks are not separate from the present – the past crosses with the present.
- Eva has a desire to erase past experience.
- Her name change is an attempt to distance herself from the past.
- Helga's search for her daughter.
- The appearances of The Ratcatcher.
- Subconscious linking of Ratcatcher with mother.
- Eva hides her feelings for her own daughter.

A2

AQA B Unit 3

Christopher Marlowe: *Doctor Faustus*

Here are some of the key areas you should bear in mind:
- The 'sympathetic devil'.
- Some have seen him as a distortion of Christianity.
- His mixed motives – the agent of Faustus' damnation and he himself is damned.
- He warns Faustus against making a bargain with Lucifer.
- Part of Mephistophilis sees himself in Faustus – his regret at losing God and heaven.
- He wants Faustus' soul, but he also wants to save him from making the same mistake as he did.

John Webster: *The White Devil*

Here are some of the key areas you should bear in mind:
- From the first scene, Webster presents a society run by absolute and corrupt leaders.
- Both church and state are corrupt.
- No justice, rule of law, or spiritual guidance.
- Both Broccacio and Francisco act out of self-interest.
- Isabella and Camillo are murdered for lust.
- Cardinal Monticelso is concerned only with wealth and family honour – note his part in the corrupt trial of Vittoria.
- Corruption spreads through the whole of society.

OCR Unit 3

The responses to these questions depend very much on the texts chosen for study, and so it is not possible to give specific guidance.

Generally speaking, you must make sure that your response:
- responds to the focus provided by the quotation
- is analytical and exploratory
- compares both texts.

Practice examination answers

The responses to these questions will be determined by the view you take of the proposition offered.

Generally speaking, you must make sure that your response:
- focuses on the key issue raised by the proposition
- presents your argument clearly
- analyses each writer's dramatic methods
- takes account of contextual factors
- compares and contrasts the texts.

Chapter 7

AQA B Unit 3

1. Here are some of the key areas you should bear in mind:
   - Macbeth's initial reaction to the witches' prophecy.
   - Lady Macbeth's response to Macbeth's letter and what it reveals about her relationship with her husband.
   - The pressure she exerts on Macbeth.
   - The dramatic impact of the murder scene, and the ways she is the driving force behind Macbeth.
   - The effect of the changing balance in their relationship.
   - Her death, Macbeth's response, and the dramatic impact on the play.

2. Here are some of the key areas you should bear in mind:
   - Presents the contrast between town and country life.
   - Urban life, for instance as governed by Duke Frederick, and the way that Oliver is presented. Note the injustices highlighted here.
   - The Forest of Arden provides an escape from oppression for various characters. This provides the environment for the development of a more caring and just society.
   - The use of comedy within the pastoral tradition framework.

OCR Unit 3

1. Here are some of the key areas you should bear in mind:
   - Iago's explanation of his motives. He gives a variety of reasons – how do you respond to them?
   - Look at the contradictions he presents – and assess the relevance of the term 'motiveless' applied to him.
   - Examine what he reveals in his soliloquies – does this present a 'motiveless malignity'?
   - His 'malign' actions in the play.
   - Give your own assessment of the truth in the statement.

2. Here are some of the key areas you should bear in mind:
   - Look at Prince Henry's soliloquies and what they tell you about his character.
   - Explore your ideas about the presentation of Falstaff – does he hold a symbolic significance?
   - Explore the nature of the Prince's relationship with Falstaff. What are the different ways of looking at this? How do you respond to them?
   - Assess your views in relations to the proposition.

WJEC Unit 4

1. There are many ways you could approach this question, but clearly the idea of 'revenge' needs to be at the heart of your answer and it is likely that Hamlet and Vindice, as the revenging protagonists, will be key. However, there are other areas linked to the idea of revenge in both plays that you might explore. You need to focus closely on Shakespeare's presentation of revenge and show how your study of *The Revenger's Tragedy* has informed your reading of this aspect of the play.

2. There are various ways in which you could approach this question, but it is likely that one key focus will be on Isabella and the Duchess, and the treatment that they receive at the hands of men and society. However, there are other areas you could explore in relation to the status of women. You need to make sure that your response focuses closely on the status of women in *Measure for Measure*, and on how your appreciation and understanding of this aspect of the play has been informed by your reading of *The Duchess of Malfi*.

CCEA Unit A2 1

In answering this question, you need to focus closely on the proposition offered and assess it in the light of your understanding of both plays. There are a range of ideas you could explore, centred around the parallels between Cordelia and Antigone and Lear and Creon. It is essential that you compare and contrast the texts in your response and that you focus your ideas closely on the question.

Chapter 8

AS

AQA A Unit 1

Thomas Hardy: *Selected Poems*

Here are some of the key areas you should bear in mind:
- This question is not assessed for AO4, so there is no need to relate the poems to their contexts, although clearly some understanding of the context in which Hardy wrote will have informed your views. Equal weighting is given to the other three AOs.
- Carefully select the poems that you are going to analyse. Make sure that they offer enough scope to answer the question fully.
- Look at natural imagery and think about its effect.
- What does nature mean to Hardy in terms of his philosophy?
- What do you think is meant by the supernatural? Think about attitudes to death in the poems.
- Consider whether you can make a meaningful distinction between natural and supernatural. Perhaps they are one and the same thing?
- Make sure that you address AO2 and AO3 by giving a detailed comparison of the poems in terms of structure, form and language.

OCR Unit 1

William Wordsworth

Here are some of the key areas you should bear in mind:
- Read the poem carefully, making notes about structure, form and language, and connections to other poems.
- AO2 is the dominant objective here, so you should present a detailed analysis of the form, structure and language of the given poem.
- Focus on the presentation of childhood and what it means to Wordsworth.
- Make relevant connections with other Wordsworth poems during the course of your essay. AO3 is not assessed here, so the examiners are not looking for a conventional 'comparison' essay.

WJEC U1

Plath and Hughes

Here are some of the key areas you should bear in mind:
- This question is marked with reference to AO1, 2 and 3, so there is no need to consider context, although your understanding of the contexts in which the poets wrote will have informed your study.
- However, you should not write an account of the poets' own relationship.
- Remember that Plath is the main text and Hughes the 'partner'. Therefore, you are expected to devote roughly 75 percent of your essay to Plath and 25 percent to Hughes.

- Carefully choose two or three Plath poems that, in your view, give the most scope for exploring the question.
- Consider the nature of the relationships explored, referring to any similarities to – and differences from – Hughes that spring to mind.
- Look at the kind of imagery used and its effect, again considering connections with Hughes.
- Focus on your chosen poems, but refer briefly to others as appropriate.
- Keep your focus on imagery, but discuss other aspects of form, structure and language in detail.
- Remember that your references to Hughes should 'illuminate' the points you make about Plath.

A2

AQA B Unit 3

Elements of the Pastoral

William Blake: *Songs of Innocence and Experience*

Here are some of the key areas you should bear in mind:
- Think about what is meant by 'attractive' and 'desirable'.
- Look critically at the point of view – it is unusual and controversial. Look at evidence for and against.
- Choose your poems carefully to give you scope for exploring the issue.
- Look at both 'Innocence' and 'Experience'.
- Is there a tension between the surface of the poems and their deeper meaning?
- Analyse a few poems in detail, looking at form, structure and language, and how these elements shape meaning.
- Think about the contexts in which the songs were written – ideas about religion and philosophy current at the time, Blake's own attitudes to religion and morality, and his place in literary tradition.
- This question could inspire a strong personal response.

CCEA Unit 3

Here are some of the key areas you should bear in mind:
- Choose a poem which provides plenty of opportunities for comparison, and which you can write about confidently.
- Consider the concerns of metaphysical poetry and the attitudes of the poet to love and desire.
- How do these particular poems relate to your wider study of metaphysical poetry?
- Analyse form, structure and language in detail, making apposite comparisons.
- Think about the tone of the poems – clever, serious and playful.

Practice examination answers

Chapter 9

AQA A Unit 1

Your initial focus should be on how Dickens presents his ideas on aspects of Victorian life, but then you need to think about the extract and how far it is similar to – and different from – other texts that you have read during your study of Victorian literature. Rather than writing in general terms, be specific about the points you make, and focus on writers' choices of form, structure and language.

AQA B Unit 1

Here are some of the key areas you should bear in mind:
- The first person narrative voice of Pip is established.
- Dickens presents various information to set the plot.
- A sense of Pip's youthful innocence is created.
- The opening scene is important in shaping Pip's future, in terms of his actions here in helping Magwitch.
- Examples of the past shaping the future – for instance, Estella's relationship with Pip; the meeting with Miss Havisham.

AQA B Unit 3

Here are some of the key areas you should bear in mind:
- The pastoral setting and nature provides more than just a setting – it is an integral part of the narrative.
- Character and setting often mirror each other. For example, happiness is found in a green, fertile environment, whilst harsh barren country forms the environment for Tess's pain and suffering.
- The pastoral environment provides a pattern to life and existence – for example, the natural seasons and rural calendar.
- The pastoral setting provides a sense of timelessness – the activities and traditions had remained unchanged for centuries.
- It provides links with the past – a sense of history.

Edexcel Unit 1

In your response, you should focus closely on the proposition and its application to *Pride and Prejudice*. However, your exploration of the proposition should be developed through a consideration of your second text to support the ideas you have made and develop these further. You should make sure that you keep focused on the main point of the question throughout your answer.

OCR Unit 1

Here are some of the key areas you should bear in mind:
- Tess's life is 'wasted' in the sense that she loses all chance of happiness, and in the end loses her liberty and her life.
- Hardy presents this 'waste' as being a result of the various circumstances that 'Fate' inflicts on her, and does not think that she deserves the misfortunes she encounters.

- Tess lives in her own small world, and her ability to influence events is very limited.
- She tries to rectify her mistakes and is willing to sacrifice for others.
- Hardy presents her as a victim whose chances for happiness in life are snatched away from her through no real fault of her own.

CCEA Unit AS 2

Here are some of the key areas you should bear in mind:
- At the beginning of the novel, Casterbridge is untouched by progressive or modern influences.
- Tradition is at the heart of the way things run.
- Farfrae brings with him new ideas for modernising the way things operate, but Henchard is reluctant to embrace change.
- In one sense, Henchard represents tradition and Farfrae change.
- Contextual ideas on the Agricultural Revolution should be integrated into your response to illustrate and develop ideas.

Chapter 11

AQA A Unit 1

Your initial focus should be on how the writer presents his ideas about World War One, but then you need to think about the extract and how far it is similar to – and different from – other texts you have read during your study of World War One. Rather than writing in general terms, be specific about the points you make, and focus on writers' choices of form, structure and language.

AQA A Unit 3

Here are some of the key areas you should bear in mind:
- A comparison of how the poets use tone – e.g. the bitter tone of Neutral Tones, and the assured, assertive tone of Sonnet 109.
- The use of imagery, e.g. the use of metaphor in both poems.
- The use of form, e.g. Hardy's four stanza form, and Shakespeare's use of the sonnet form.
- The language choices of the poets, with detailed focus on specific details of language and effects.
- You should incorporate aspects of your wider reading on the theme of 'love', where appropriate, to develop your ideas.

Edexcel Unit 1

(a) You might comment on aspects such as:
- the impression of the dark and starless night
- the still, quiet, isolated sense that is created
- the sense of the oppressive heat of London, contrasted with the openness and coolness of the narrator's night walk.

(b) There are a number of images you could use here, for example:
- 'the heath looked wild enough in the mysterious light to be hundreds of miles away from the great city that lay beneath it'
- '... the prospect of gradual suffocation...'
- '... admiring the soft alternations of light and shade as they followed each other over the broken ground on every side of me'
- '... in one moment, every drop of blood in my body was brought to a stop by the touch of a hand... '.

(c) Here are some of the key areas you could include:
- The first person narration gives a sense of the narrator's feelings.
- His thoughts are revealed as he walks in the darkness.
- The shock effect of his description of the sight of the woman in white who appears out of the darkness.

Notes

Index

Index

Acknowledgements

Page 66 and 214 Extract from: '*The Remains of the Day*' by Kazuo Ishiguro. Published by Faber and Faber

Pages 119–120 Extract from: '*Translations*' by Brian Friel, published by Faber and Faber

Page 125 Extract from '*A Streetcar named Desire*' by Tennessee Williams. Copyright © 1947 by the University of The South. Reprinted by permission of Georges Borchardt Inc. for the Estate of Tennessee Williams. All Rights Reserved

Pages 136–137 Extract from: '*Murmuring Judges*' by David Hare, published by Faber and Faber

Page 182 Extract from: '*Naturally the Foundation Will Bear Your Expenses*' from The '*Whitsun Weddings*' by Philip Larkin. Published by Faber and Faber

Page 190 Prayer: *Some days, although we cannot pray, a prayer*, by Carol Ann Duffy

Page 192 Extract from the poem: '*Engineers Corner*' taken from, "Making Cocoa for Kingsley Amis" by Wendy Cope published by Faber and Faber is reprinted by permission of United Agents on behalf of: Wendy Cope

Page 209 Extract from: '*The Woman in Black*' by Susan Hill. Published by Penguin

Page 228 The excerpt from Vera Brittain's '*Testament of Youth*' (1933) is reproduced by permission of Mark Bostridge and T.J. Brittain-Catlin, Literary Executors for the Estate of Vera Brittain 1970

Page 246 Review of '*All my sons at the Apollo Theatre*' by Charles Spencer, 28 May 2010. Copyright © Telegraph Media Group Limited 2010. Reproduced by permission of the Telegraph Media Group Limited

Page 263 *The Unknown Citizen*' from Another Time by W.H. Auden. Copyright © 1976, 1991, used by permission of The Estate of W.H. Auden

Bibliography

Chapter 2.3 *Literary terminology* – Chris Baldick (ed). The Concise Oxford Dictionary of Literary Terms, Oxford Reference (1990)

Chapter 4.3 *Referring to Critics* MHRA Style Book, London MHRA (1996).

Chapter 12 Hills. (1971) *Strange Meeting* Penguin Books.